Can You Hear Me Now?

Can You Hear Me Now?

How I Found My Voice and
Learned to Live with Passion and Purpose

Celina Caesar-Chavannes

RANDOM HOUSE CANADA

PUBLISHED BY RANDOM HOUSE CANADA

Library and Archives Canada Cataloguing in Publication

Title: Can you hear me now? : how I found my voice and learned to live with passion
    and purpose / Celina Caesar-Chavannes.
Names: Caesar-Chavannes, Celina, 1974- author.
Identifiers: Canadiana (print) 20200252399 | Canadiana (ebook) 20200252534 |
    ISBN 9780735279599 (hardcover) | ISBN 9780735279605 (EPUB)
Subjects: LCSH: Caesar-Chavannes, Celina, 1974- | LCSH: Businesspeople—Canada—
    Biography. | LCSH: Politicians—Canada—Biography. | LCSH: Leadership. |
    LCGFT: Autobiographies.
Classification: LCC HC112.5.C24 A3 2021 | DDC 338.092—dc23

Text design: Leah Springate
Jacket design: Leah Springate
Jacket photo and concept: Candice Rayne Chavannes

Printed and bound in Canada

10 9 8 7 6 5 4 3 2 1

Penguin
Random House
RANDOM HOUSE CANADA

To my mother, O'Dessa Caesar.
The iron that sharpened me

To my children, Desiray, Candice and Vidal John.
The inspiration and hope in my voice

To my husband, Vidal Alexander Chavannes.
The rock that steadies my disruption

CONTENTS

INTRODUCTION

EVERY TIME I WAKE up on my own, and not to the annoying sound of my alarm, I am amazed. I am not a morning person. Pre-noon daylight has an irritating hue I cannot stand, especially during the winter, when the sun shines sharpest and brightest on the coldest days.

On the morning of Thursday, March 21, 2019, I opened my eyes to that aggravating light shining through the window of my twenty-sixth-floor condo in Ottawa, and wondered if I'd slept through the alarm. I could have checked the time on my phone, but that required energy I did not have. I blinked, and tiny black particles of day-old mascara fell into my eyes. I rubbed them, which only made the situation worse. I sighed. Here I was, conscious before I had to be, dealing with 24-hour mascara dust and the same incredible headache I'd gone to bed with the night before.

The headache was from the stress generated the previous day over revealing my new-found freedom from the Canadian political party system. The day—the first in my career as an Independent member of Parliament and not as a part of the Liberal caucus—had been long and hard. I felt like an empty tube of toothpaste someone had tried to squeeze one last time.

And then my cell phone began to buzz, message after message reminding me of the previous day's events and promising a difficult time ahead. I ignored them, rolled out of bed and went over to look out the window. The neighbouring rooftops had no signs of snow and neither did the streets. That was a good thing: any hint of white on the rooftops or the roadways completely threw off my shoe game, forcing me to wear an oversized pair of Sorels I'd inherited from my eldest daughter, who no longer wanted to be seen in them. Today, I could wear a pair of heeled boots. My moment of fashion satisfaction was interrupted by more buzzing from the phone. For heaven's sake! It didn't stop. Remember the days when in order to communicate with someone, you had to find a piece of paper, locate a pen or pencil, write the letter, find an envelope, figure out the address, paste on a stamp and walk to the mailbox? I longed for those days.

But there was no getting away from it: everyone I knew—and lots of people I didn't—had strong opinions about my decision to leave the Liberals after several tense weeks of confrontation with Prime Minister Justin Trudeau. And with social media and my public presence as an MP, all of them knew how to reach me to express those opinions directly. What they didn't know was that it wasn't just my issues with the prime minister that had brought me to this point.

I'd been swept out of my quiet life—running a business and raising my family in Whitby, Ontario—by the tornado of an election, and dropped in Ottawa. An Oz, for sure, but in shades of grey. Unlike many of my colleagues, I had never dreamed about being a politician, had never even taken a political science course or been interested in more than the headlines, and had never done the school trip to our nation's capital. The first time I entered the House of Commons was when I started my job as a member of Parliament. I thought business and research were my things, and that philanthropy was the way I'd give back to society. I had zero political aspirations.

But then Jim Flaherty, the finance minister in Stephen Harper's Conservative government, died suddenly on April 10, 2014, just after he had stepped down to spend more time with his family. A by-election was called in his riding, which was my riding. I found myself running (more on how that came about later). I lost that contest to the former mayor of Whitby: not surprising given that the mayor had name recognition in the community and I did not; that I was a Black woman running in a constituency that was 70 percent white and had never voted in a Black candidate; and that hardly anyone could remember the last time Whitby had voted Liberal.

But I didn't lose by much, and I really don't like to lose—a powerful motivator. When the next general election came around, in 2015, I ran again. This time I found even more support on the doorsteps of my riding. People—and not only Liberals—were looking for a fresh perspective on politics and found it in me: not only a Black woman from an immigrant background who had built her own company from scratch and had the business acumen Conservative voters believed they could trust, but also a person who embodied the values of diversity and inclusion that the times demanded, and that Trudeau's Liberal Party was featuring in its campaign.

This time I won. A fairy tale, right?

So why walk away from the party only four years after that victory to sit as an Independent? That was what all the people buzzing my phone wanted to know: my constituents, who liked the way I'd been representing the riding, and were disappointed that I wasn't a Liberal anymore; Black leaders, who thought now that I had a seat at the table I should learn how to compromise in order to keep it, and that I was letting the community down by not playing the game; other politicians who didn't want to lose an ally; and party functionaries who wanted to berate me for what they saw as me piling on against a leader who was already in hot water over the SNC-Lavalin affair and the way he had treated two female ministers who stood up to him. The feminist PM with a female problem.

I had my own point to make and different battles to fight. Something unexpected had happened to me in Ottawa. I would say that I had arrived on Parliament Hill ready to play for the Liberal team. I had encountered many cynical voters who predicted that as soon as I faced my first challenge as an MP, I would become just another politician. I promised them that I would not. I'd spoken with others who believed in me, but who thought that the old elite ways were so entrenched I had no hope of changing anything. I'd also met voters who wanted me to live up to our campaign promise that we would do politics differently, who hoped I would remain the authentic Celina they'd voted for, who wanted me to challenge the old ways in which our country was run. I promised them that I would strive to bend the status quo, that I would bring change. There were a lot of promises to keep, and I'd intended to keep every one.

During my first months as a politician I was so fresh to it all it was like I was up at 30,000 feet staring down at the whole strange landscape, at the same time as I was struggling to take a few steps on the ground towards the aims I felt I was elected to achieve. It seemed to me that most of the people here were not interested in doing politics differently; they just said they were. Was I naïve? Perhaps. But I could also see what wasn't working in Ottawa even on the human resources level: we MPs were like a bunch of CEOs suddenly being ordered around by junior staffers empowered by the PMO and the ministers' offices to manage us. In effect, that layer of staff—Keith Beardsley, an advisor to Stephen Harper, had nicknamed them the "boys in short pants" (though some of them were women)—were bossing around members of Parliament and making profound decisions about policy that affected our country with no regard to what MPs could actually contribute. Some prime ministers are brilliant caucus leaders, building consensus on the issues where they want to make change; others lead by fear. Our leader always said that he wanted to engage with all caucus members, but even in the last year of his first term, there were some that had never met with him. In my opinion he was hiding behind the impenetrable shield of his principal secretaries, each of them smart people, but none of them responsible to a constituency themselves. To some degree, he was engaging more with international media than he was with his own caucus on critical issues.

But this isn't about the failings of one prime minister. This is about how going into politics made me understand the true meaning of the phrase "we have to do politics differently." Before I got to Ottawa I was well aware of the colour of my skin, and my gender, and the obstacles both raised, but I treated it all like a set of problems I could solve by basically outsmarting or outplaying those around me. Mostly I'd found that I could cut my cloth to whatever the circumstances required; witness my success in business and the fact that I was elected in the first place.

But I'd been running so hard for my whole life, I'd never taken time to truly reflect on what I was put on earth for. I was a wife, a mother of three, a successful business owner, but the first time I had ever lived alone, with time to think, was after I moved to Ottawa. This twenty-sixth-floor condo was the first place where I could close the door and be beholden only to myself. And what that led to, combined with what I was encountering in my work as an MP—having taken on responsibility for changing our public life so that it would apply to and represent everyone—was an awakening that was as powerful as it was painful.

It's not just politics we have to do differently, I realized. We have to do everything differently. If people like me keep trying to fit into spaces like the House of Commons, which run according to a narrative of power and privilege designed to exclude us, how can we expect those spaces to change? We need politics to be different, but the powers-that-be keep fiddling round the edges, not attacking the structure itself, which was designed to reinforce the status quo. We want our communities to be friendly and welcoming to all, but fear causes us to put up bigger fences. We want diversity, but we don't want inclusion, which requires us to move out of our comfort zones towards equity. We want to check the right boxes, but we're scared to do the work that would mean that change becomes real.

In Ottawa, I stood out so starkly I started to crack. Still, I had every opportunity to play it safe—I had the respect of most of my Liberal colleagues, and even of members across the aisle, one of whom told me early on that I should enjoy my freedom while I could because it wouldn't be long before I became a minister. Yet I chose to speak up about mental health, including my own, and about racism and equity. Paradoxically, rather than losing myself, I found my voice, my authentic self, in the House of Commons and in the give and take of serving my riding as an MP. So when I realized that the party I belonged to said they valued my unique voice and perspective, but did not want to actually listen to me, what was I supposed to do? What's the point of finding your voice, if it is muzzled because the simple truth of your message makes others uncomfortable?

Most importantly, I realized that my political journey did not start in 2014, when I first decided to put my name on a ballot. It started when a skinny little two-year-old girl from the island of Grenada in the Caribbean ended up in Canada. Although this journey felt like a roller coaster, electoral politics was only a small part of it—a scary part, sure, but I had been through scarier stuff and survived.

In Ottawa, I found the courage to stand up for myself and others, and, because of what I'd learned in the years before I got there, I realized that it was desperately important to maintain that integrity and my authentic self—so hard to do in a place that was not designed for me. It became clear to me that it was absolutely imperative that I resist the temptation to settle down and shut up, and abandon my new-found sense of purpose. In those four years in Ottawa, I found parts of me I thought were permanently lost or buried too deep to ever see the light again. I used my time in Ottawa to speak up for people who were not often heard in the House of Commons, which was a good thing, but I could not see how my efforts inside that place would lead to the kind of change we need.

Yes, I'd spent a whole day crying over my decision to walk away—I hate to let people down, and I knew that so many I respected would believe I had done just that. But I could not see how to reconcile the demands of party politics with the awakening I'd undergone. I had to leave. Sometimes the most powerful action you can take is to refuse to remain a part of the machine that is keeping you down. For a bold Black woman to keep hammering away on the political machine from the inside only enabled the people running it to say, "Yes, we can hear you hammering! Don't worry, we'll take all your concerns into account in the fullness of time."

That did not sit well with me. After all, we were supposed to be doing government differently. That is what I signed up for—to be bold, transformative and deliberate. We are running out of time to make important and necessary changes, not only in politics, but in every aspect of ourselves as human beings. I didn't know that before I got to Ottawa. But I know it now.

one

BOLD AT BIRTH

BEING BORN A GIRL, in any part of the world, has its challenges. Being born a girl of colour or a Black girl comes with an extra set of obstacles. Whether it is lack of access to education, sexualization, subjugation, trauma and violence, we face barriers no young person needs to face. I was no exception.

I was born on Monday, June 24, 1974, in the little island nation of Grenada in the Caribbean.

My first heartbreak came at six months old, when my parents and older brother, Roger, left me behind when they emigrated to Canada. I would not see them again until I was almost two years old.

It was not uncommon for Caribbean children to be left "back home" while their parents travelled abroad in search of a better life. My mom and dad didn't intend to leave me, but their visas, along with the one for my brother, came through first, and they couldn't wait for me. I was only a baby, after all, and surely I wouldn't miss them all that much—I probably wouldn't even remember. But I can't help thinking about how my relationship with my parents would have been different if I'd been on the plane with them. I think about my own children, and what it would have been like if I hadn't been there to see their first steps, soothe their cries or change their diapers.

The pain of such a rift would not fall only on the child or the parents, but on them all.

Something was lost in my relationship with my parents during those first couple of years and I have felt that loss for most of my life. But I had the blessing of staying with my paternal grandparents and my aunt Bernadette; that they loved me was a fact I never doubted. I would later come to model myself after Veronica Caesar, my grandmother. I didn't call her by any sweet name like Nana or even the more formal Grandmother—terms that should be reserved for women who smile at the whimsical things their grandchildren do, give them extra-squishy hugs or sneak them candy before dinner, because spoiling a child is more important than spoiling her dinner. I called my grandmother Mrs. Caesar. And Mrs. Caesar did not do any of those things. She was a fierce and formidable woman who was a pillar in her community and in her family. If she loved you, you knew it. If she didn't, you did not want to know it.

The Caesars were farmers, growing nutmeg, fruit and vegetables, and raising pigs and chickens, not only to feed their family of twelve children but to make a living. My father tells stories of Mrs. Caesar negotiating with the owners of the new resort hotels that were being built in Grenada in the sixties to guarantee they bought their local produce from her and paid her top dollar for it too. My father's job as a young man was to drive her around and to deliver the produce. It was a job he loved. He had the use of the truck and his mother paid him in cash, which meant he could take my mom, a country girl from farther up in the hills, on dates.

Mrs. Caesar was an entrepreneur you did not want to mess around with; the size of her success was reflected in the home the family built. The Caesar compound was surrounded by a pink concrete wall that contained a two-storey house with multiple bedrooms, a main living room, dining room and sitting area. To the side of it was a separate building that housed the kitchen with an eat-in breakfast area, all very modern for the Grenada of the period. The walled yard was big enough to hold a chicken coop and a pigpen, and enough territory to make for epic games of hide-and-seek. Mrs. Caesar was unapologetic and unafraid; a wife, mother, grandmother, business-woman, community leader and friend. She was everything I wanted to be when I grew up.

When it was time for me to leave for Toronto, where my parents had settled, my grandfather travelled with me to New York City, where my aunt was getting married. He handed me over to my parents, who met us at the wedding; I can only imagine how strange that whole situation must have been. There was no way I would have remembered them.

According to my Canadian immigration identification record, they brought me into Canada via Lewiston, New York, on January 4, 1976. I stare at that word "January" and wonder what my toddler self made of a grey Toronto winter, having lived for all my days in a tropical paradise surrounded by a pink wall.

My first Canadian home was an apartment on Martin Grove Road in Rexdale, an area just north of the city of Toronto. I have vague memories of using a plastic place mat from our dining room table as a makeshift toboggan and sliding down the snow-covered hills nearby. So I must have found some excitement in the snow.

Most of the people in the building were immigrants, but I didn't really register that at the time. I just remember the place felt dim, dark and small after the bright world I was used to. My initial portal into the big country of Canada was underwhelming and unfriendly. Surely I didn't belong here. It strikes me now that when I first walked into the Parliament buildings almost forty years later, I felt the same sense of dislocation as I had as a little child in Rexdale—a grey unbelonging.

My parents, who were working long and hard at their jobs, soon had enough money to move us to a townhouse complex on Silverstone Drive, still in Rexdale, but with a courtyard where the neighbourhood children played. It was there I learned that a Caribbean family's unwritten rules were very different from the rules for the other families around us. First, we rarely ate out, despite having a KFC around the corner. Second, other than a few good friends and family, we had few visitors. If the doorbell rang, my brother and I were told never to answer it. Third, we were to call every person old enough to be our parents Mr. or Mrs. So-and-So; close family friends were "Aunty" or "Uncle." You were never to address an elder by their first name. Ever. It was forbidden. I am still afraid to do it as an adult. Fourth, family parties usually lasted all night, and sometimes got messy. Finally, our house was not governed by Canadian laws. Which meant that inside our walls corporal punishment was completely acceptable and handed out on a regular basis. In my opinion, I got my unfair share.

All these rules felt even more stark since I had been taken from the only people I knew and delivered to a foreign place where I was under the thumb of a stern mother, who expected me to behave like a proper little Caribbean girl.

I wanted to please her, but I also wanted to fit into the complex's courtyard culture. A neighbour boy named Robert and my brother, Roger, were the cool kids, though Robert was the troublemaker of the two. Whether it was swinging a bat in a courtyard baseball game and knocking the catcher, Roger, out cold, or kissing me during a game of kissing tag (my father witnessed the whole thing from our kitchen window and my butt paid for that kiss later), Robert was the guy whom trouble followed. I wanted to be just like him.

When my brother was teasing me one day, I responded by telling him that he "sucked the bag"—yep, a Robert phrase. Roger never swore, and he could not tell on me to my parents fast enough. My backside paid the price. Yet a simple beating could not stop me. The rule about ladies needing to act like ladies was so stuffy and boring. I loved swearing. Saying bad words gave me power over those around me. Nobody in my house swore as well as I did; by the time I started kindergarten I knew all the words. I'd seen how Robert's cursing and wayward ways made him stand out. He was never the catcher, standing behind someone else in the game. He was always the centre of attention. I had gone from being the centre of attention with my aunt and grandparents in Grenada, to being the little sister, the one who had been left behind, an afterthought, and that was not cool. Swearing, kissing the boys and acting out was a way to get my parents' attention, and it seemed like I did not care whether that attention came in the form of a whipping.

A precocious child, I would often be caught standing at the top of the stairs, fully naked, belting out a Rod Stewart song: "If you want my body and you think I'm sexy, come on sugar let me know." Let me tell you, if that is your theme song at four or five years old, it is going to get worse before it gets better. It did not matter the situation, I felt the gravitational pull of standing out and being different, which never suited my parents' vision of me as a young girl, who was to be seen, just enough, and heard, just a little. That just wasn't me. It wasn't bold enough.

"Who left this toy on the floor in the middle of the basement hall?"

My mother was asking the question, and I was certain the perpetrator was me, but I could not think fast enough to ward off trouble. I kept my distance, hoping a clever response would come to me. It didn't. My mother pulled me towards her, and as she did I slipped on the mess made by the leak from the now-warm Snoopy Sno-cone Machine, which had spread over the floor. Face planted onto the floor, I noticed that the red liquid leaving my body was mixing with the water from the icemaker, and I did not like it.

I felt myself being lifted. The large hand that covered the path by which the liquid was escaping from my forehead partially covered my eyes too, so I was only able to see some of the red drops adding colour to the linoleum tile. I was carried towards the sink and a tap whooshed on, and more red, mixed with even more water, swirled down the drain.

Darkness.

I woke to cold air hitting my skin and the night sky pierced by street lights flashing by. I was going somewhere. Where?

Darkness.

"It's okay, little girl, we are going to fix you up in no time," someone said as he spread a white sheet over my face, leaving a gap for my forehead. I did not recognize the voice or see who the person was before my face was covered. My eyes darted up to try to see through the small opening. The room was very bright, and I was very scared.

"That fall down the stairs left you with a nasty gash," the voice said.

What? I did not fall down the stairs. Who was this person and what was he talking about? I was about to come up with an elaborate story about why the Snoopy toy had been left lying around, but it seems someone else had told a story about why I had leaked red all over the floor and down the drain. I knew better than to speak up and correct this person, who sounded like an adult, so I stayed quiet.

"I am going to put a needle into your forehead to freeze the area and then we are going to stitch it up. You won't feel a thing."

I saw the needle descend towards my face, felt the point enter my forehead and started screaming and I did not stop until it was dark again.

The scar on my forehead, in the shape of a backwards seven, never went away. Neither did my questions about the story of the stairs.

Why didn't anyone ask *me* what happened? Clearly, I was there. But no one ever did ask and the story that I had fallen down the stairs stuck. Eventually I did not even try to correct it. The lie was the truth, and there was no point in challenging it. Still, I was smart enough to note that it was not true to myself, at least every time the subject came up. I was also smart enough to learn how lies could rewrite bad stuff, and that was all I needed to know.

If stories were to be told, it seemed to me, then Black people were the best at doing it. The good, bad and ugly of our history have been captured and transformed by the griots of generations past and the great orators of our present. As an observant child, I watched and listened to everything. I paid attention to words, even ones that I did not understand, especially ones I knew were not true. I studied how bodies moved and hands swayed. I felt like I spent most of my childhood silently watching the story of the lives around me unfold. And although I knew the stories I over-heard were not intended for my eyes or ears, I could make myself invisible so as not to miss anything. If stories were being told, and more importantly changed, I wanted to know why.

It took me a long time to understand the story about who was rich and who was poor and what was meant by those terms in this new country. For me, coming from Grenada to Canada had meant more of an adjustment to temperature and the loss of a carefree life than anything measured in dollars and cents. I did not know if my parents had much money, but I did know that they did not like how they were earning it.

I remember my father sitting at the small kitchen table of our Silverstone townhouse with his head in his hands. It was almost as if I was watching from the ceiling, because I never would have got close enough to overhear that particular "adult" conversation. But

I remember the terrible strain on my father's face one night after he got home. Whatever had happened at work that day was so unsettling to him it had followed him home like a haunt. I was scared, but I did not know what about the situation made me feel that way. I understood that he did not like the job he was doing and that the way someone had spoken to him, the words they used, had bothered him terribly and made him look grey and emaciated.

I did not want whatever was happening to him to happen to me. I did not want someone else to use words that made me feel small or inferior. It would be years before I understood that the "haunt" around my dad was racism, and that it was a part of the Canadian experience for Black people. Was racism one of the reasons why the story about my fall was changed at the hospital? What would have happened if the truth were told? Would the haunt have taken me away?

That evening after my dad came home looking so grim, I watched my parents come up with a plan to start a trucking company so that they did not have to work where the haunt was. It was as if the spirit of Mrs. Caesar had been transported to my new life in Canada, and I was happy for it. The haunt did not destroy us; we changed the story to make it better. That is the complexity of the immigrant experience. Some of the stories that need to come to light in order to save us stay hidden. Others are revealed. I kept track of them all, for a long time unsure as to which was which.

When one day, in kindergarten, I decided to walk home from school by myself, I am sure my parents felt that they should have left me in Grenada forever. When they asked me later why I did it, I told them that I had studied the bus route and decided that the bus driver should be dropping me at home first, instead of leaving me for last. I hated being last. I figured it would be much faster if I walked home from school straight along John Garland Boulevard. I remember being surprised when I got to Finch Avenue West, because I did not recall Finch being so busy and wide. Still, I managed to make it safely across.

As I came up the path to the townhouse complex, I was shocked to see a crowd gathered outside my door. Sure, the walk had taken a lot longer than I imagined, and yes, taking the bus was probably faster, but what was all the commotion? My butt was praying louder than I was, hoping that the fuss was not related to me. The glares of my parents eliminated that hope. My backside needed to learn to pray better or find another person to be attached to.

To my parents, I may have been trouble, but at least I was smart. Definitely smarter than Roger, who avoided swearing or any form of real rebellion, but could not bring home the grades his little sister could. This sounds mean to my ears now, but at the time I felt I was in a struggle for survival and if I could do something that Roger couldn't, that was my competitive advantage. He wouldn't swear so I would; he didn't do well in school so I would always be at the top of my class. Also, every time I showed off my smartness, my mother (who, I understood much later, had had big academic dreams for herself) would shower me with praise.

In elementary school, I was top of my class in every subject. By third grade, we had moved to a semi-detached five-split house on Abell Drive in Brampton. My dad's trucking company must have been doing well. I loved that house, so much so that I live in a five-split now. The neighbourhood was full of children, and my best friend, Beverly, lived right across the road. There were afternoon dodgeball games, bike rides and walks to Bruce Beer Park, which was right behind our house.

My maternal grandmother, Ena Ella Wilson, who we called Gramsie, had come from Grenada to live with us and help take care of my little brother, Ryan. Although she was stern, she seemed to have a special soft spot for each of her grandchildren; when I got in trouble and suffered the consequences, she would tend to my wounds with all sorts of homemade remedies and special concoctions. Every one of her bush teas and healing creams worked; I wish now that I'd been clever enough to write down the recipes for some of them. As a child I dismissed a lot of her knowledge because she had no formal education. But she was our griot and her stories recalled our history. I wish that I hadn't taken her wisdom for granted.

The walk to school was terrible in the winters. I truly hated the cold (and have never gotten used to it). But the challenge of the cold did not compare with the challenge of my first true academic nemesis, a boy named Alex, who briefly ascended to the apex of our teacher's Pyramid of Champions when he beat me in the speed round of times tables. When I saw that I'd been bumped to the spot below his, right beside the third-place person, I went home bawling as if I had lost my favourite toy. Although I cannot fully remember what my mother said after I explained the situation, I am sure it was something like, "Well, if you want Alex to beat you, you will let him beat you." I truly hated that passive-aggressive shit. Why couldn't she say something like, "It's okay, dear. You will come first next time for sure." Or, "That boy has nothing on you." A hug would have been acceptable too.

But no, I got one of my mother's first lessons in independence. Only you can control what happens to you. If Alex came first, only you made that happen. Alex beating me was an opportunity to do things differently—to fight for what I wanted. She never said those last words out loud, and at the time I'm sure I didn't understand what she was trying to teach me. But by third grade my tough mother had given me enough life lessons to hand Alex's ass to him at least twice before lunch recess.

She was hard on me. And I feared her, while she feared for me. I believe now that she treated me the way she thought the world would eventually treat me, in order to prepare me for it. In her mind, maybe she was trying to protect me. In that moment, though, I was furious. I was tired of her beatings and life lessons, and mocked her in my head: "Well, if you want AAAAllleeexxx to beat you . . ." I knew better than to mock my mother out loud or to cry or stomp away in a huff. Any or all of those reactions would have had me swiftly at the tail end of a belt, and I was more interested in beating Alex than getting a beating from my mother.

For the rest of the term, I redoubled my studies of the times tables, and every other subject, in order to be better and faster than the other children. There was no way that Alex (or anyone else, including my brothers) would ever beat me again. And for all of grade school no one ever did. I am not sure that I was ever obsessed with learning for its own sake, but I was obsessed with placing first in my classes. If academic excellence was the only thing that made my parents proud of me, I was going to do what I had to do to achieve it.

But I also couldn't stop getting into trouble. I was constantly rebellious, though I only acted on it when I was out of earshot of my mother and I was truly frightened when I was caught. I was obviously still pissed that I had been left behind, and I also thought it was unfair that I was held to different standards of behaviour than my brothers, not only by my parents, but by society. Boys got to play by different rules. I did not really know why I was the way I was, and my parents weren't bringing me to any therapy sessions so I could find out. All I know is, I had as much of an affinity for times tables as I had for time outs, and I explored both with vigour.

In sixth grade, my friend Heather and I came up with a plan to go to the Becker's convenience store across the road from our school and steal some candy. I do not understand why I thought this was a good idea. I was the dumbest smart kid I knew. It did not take long for me to get caught with candy in my pocket and no money to pay for it. The owner called the school and the administration called my parents. I knew a beating was coming when my parents got home.

To my surprise, they walked in carrying bags of candy bars. They only bought us candy on the rarest of occasions, so I thought this was great. Maybe they had finally caught on to the Canadian way of disciplining children.

Soon they called me to the dining room where they had placed the bags of candy on the table. My mother asked me if I thought we could not afford candy and if I thought stealing it was okay. I responded no, clearly and audibly, to both questions because I knew she hated it when I mumbled. There was no belt in sight, and I was not going to risk aggravating her so that she got it out.

Next she asked me if I liked candy. Still clueless to her intentions, I eagerly answered yes.

All right, she said, you go ahead and eat every single candy bar on the table. For clarification, she and my father had brought home as many as ten bags of Halloween-sized Snickers bars. Twenty to thirty candy bars times ten bags equals a lot of candy. Suddenly, I wanted a beating instead. Were these people crazy? If this was Canadian discipline, I did not want it.

I ate candy until I almost threw up. My mother sat and watched, making sure I swallowed. When I tried to pretend a bag was empty, scrunching it so it looked like all the bars were gone, she reached out and carefully flattened the bag. Eff! How did she know? Then she ever so graciously picked out the one or two bars I'd left in the bag and placed them in front of me. "You forgot some," she said in the kindest of voices. I am sure the Devil's mother was not so terrible. I have never eaten a Snickers bar since. My children have never eaten a Snickers bar either. There are some lessons you only need to learn once.

Then there are the lessons you wish you never had to learn.

I was in Grade 6 at the time. I won't say his name, but he was much older of course.

When I felt him press his body against me from behind, I was scared. What was going to happen? His arms reached around to the front of my pants, he undid them and they fell to my feet, followed by my underwear. I was scared to turn around or to say anything. He had told me to meet him, and I had come, so it was my fault that this was happening. I had never seen a penis, but when that hard, warm thing pressed against my backside, I knew what it was. I waited for something more to happen, but he just stood there with his warmth against my body, until he heard a noise and hurried away. I did the same. When he told me to meet him again, I did. I was trapped by my fear that by agreeing to meet him the first time I was just as guilty as he was. When I went back the second time, he did the same thing. Again, and again, for months. I told no one, and only escaped when we moved away.

By the time I started Grade 7, we were living in our second home in Brampton, a fully detached house with a two-car garage in the newly developing N section of the city (don't ask me why it was "N"— something about it being a planned community, rather than one that grew organically). I had my own room, plenty of backyard space, and a library full of volumes of the *Encyclopaedia Britannica*. The winding staircase made the entrance hall appear majestic and although the wall of mirrors that followed its curve from the first to the second floor seems tacky to me now, it felt unique in the late 1980s.

Materially we were going up in the world, as my parents' transportation company thrived. I remember my father coming home with what he said was the "first cellular phone ever made." I believed it because I had never seen one before. He could make a phone call from his car! How revolutionary! The case was the size of a small briefcase, but so what. Our family was rich enough to afford phones you could drive around with and that was all that mattered.

The neighbourhood children here were not like the old gang on Silverstone Drive. No one ran around playing kissing tag or baseball in the middle of the street. Every now and again, back on Silverstone, a neighbour's house would be roped off with yellow police tape and blood would be seen on the door or walkway. I doubted that would happen here in the N section. We were a long way from Abell Drive, too, where the neighbourhood children played hide-and-seek until dusk because all Black kids in my neighbourhood had the same rule—our parents wanted us indoors before the street lights came on. No children "played" on our new street. We were either too grown for such childish things or too well off to bother.

In any case, I was all for it. The N section was awesome, as far as I was concerned, and before long I made friends with other children, hanging out in their rooms, playing Nintendo or watching music videos. I was also relieved to see other students of colour in my split seventh and eighth grade class at St. Marguerite Bourgeoys, especially a good-looking boy named Garvin. Nobody had been able to eclipse the appeal of Robert, the rebel of Silverstone Drive, but Garvin came close. He wore Polo and Ralph Lauren and every now and again a Club Monaco ensemble. Even though we could afford it, my parents were not about to buy me brand-name clothing when they could get the same thing for a quarter of the cost at BiWay or Bargain Harold's.

I was nowhere as cool as Garvin. I was physically awkward, and wore frosted lipstick, which was completely inappropriate for my dark skin. Also my mother made me clothing she couldn't find at the bargain outlets, tending to frills, puffy sleeves and polka dots in red, yellow and green, which made me stand out more than my dark skin did. It did not matter. I decided I would be brave enough to approach Garvin in a sophisticated manner. Since clearly he was not the "run up to him and kiss him in the middle of the court" kind of guy, I decided to write him a letter to express my feelings and solicit a favourable response. "Dear Abby," I wrote. Not sure why I started a love letter to a boy that way. "Dear Abby, I am in love with Garvin"—I forget the rest.

Much to my chagrin, not only did the letter fall into the wrong hands, it got passed around the class (including the Grade 8 side). I was mocked mercilessly for months afterward. As far as I was concerned, all "couth" had disappeared from the N section of Brampton—these juveniles couldn't even appreciate a well-written love letter to Abby. Worse, Garvin was one of the children mocking me. I could not let him get away with it, but I did not want our chance at friendship to be ruined by my stupid letter or the resulting cruel middle-school antics. One night I decided I had to call Garvin to straighten out the matter. Clearly, he did not mean to mock me. It was just that since he was a cool kid, he had to follow the unwritten protocol of his rank. If I could get him to talk to me, one on one, it could all be sorted, and we could begin our courtship.

The phone rang and rang. I was patient and let it. Garvin would certainly answer. He had to know it was me who was calling.

His mother picked up. "Hello," I said. "How are you? Is Garvin there?" Garvin's mother said yes he was, and she didn't know why he hadn't answered the phone. My heart sank. I did. My true love was not any form of love at all. I proceeded to tell his mother the whole story. I took responsibility for my own actions, but said that I thought that Garvin had acted inappropriately as well.

When I spoke to Garvin about this years later, he told me that the conversation he had with his mother after I hung up was one he would never forget. She reprimanded him sternly: "This young lady comes from a good family," she said, and "your behaviour reflects on our whole household and how you were raised." She told him he not only had to apologize to me, but to fix the whole situation.

Her attitude is not unfamiliar to me. Most immigrant families, and especially those who came from the Caribbean, did not want their business in the streets, and they regarded their children as a reflection of that business. If you behaved badly it cast a shadow on your entire household and upbringing. The gamble they had taken to leave everything behind for a chance to make their lives and those of their families better was not about to be undermined by children acting the fool. Garvin was not the only one acting the fool, of course. But there are things you understand as a child and things you don't. With my hot temper and tendency to cuss people out when I felt attacked, I've needed to learn the lesson of reconciliation again and again, along with the lesson of accepting my share of the responsibility for the breakdown of an important relationship. And those lessons all began in the mess around a childhood crush.

Going home to Grenada every summer was an oasis in my life. It was security and steadiness. There I was still the centre of attention. It was sunny and lush and I was a beloved treasure to my grandparents. My parents would come for a little while, but work would never let them stay, and I admit I loved being away from my mother and hated going home, as much as I had become a Canadian girl and liked being petted by my relatives for my nice clothes and northern sophistication.

I've said how much I admired my grandmother Mrs. Caesar, but my grandfather Doril was the person who loved me the most. When we got to my grandparents' home on summer break, Mrs. Caesar remained stoic, standing in the yard, giving my brothers and me dignified hellos. But my grandfather clapped and laughed with delight as the car filled with his grandchildren and their suitcases pulled up. He always wore the same knee-length denim shorts, tan-coloured shirt and cap, and as he clapped, he would also wave us to come close for a hug. We always knew what came next. When we got near, he would plant his unshaven face right into our necks and give us tickles. We squealed with joy.

I always felt like he gave me extra tickles and the tightest of hugs. When we walked with him to the shop up the road, he purchased any treat we asked for. By that time, the Caesar farm operation had been reduced to picking and selling nutmeg and mace. Although I rarely went with him to the lands they owned in the mountains to pick the nutmeg, I loved sitting with him under the front veranda to peel the mace from the nutmeg and put it out in the sun to dry. We would spend hours chatting as we worked, or staying quiet—it didn't matter. It was our time to be together. I loved him in a way that I loved nobody else, not even my parents. I always promised him that I would return to Grenada one day when I was grown up to take care of him.

I particularly loved summers on the island because I was effortlessly with my own. In grade school I stood out not only for my smarts—despite all my shenanigans I maintained a straight-A average—but also because of the colour of my skin. I was one of only a few Black kids in my Catholic grade schools, and so I was exceptional in a way that was an unspoken burden. I didn't know how much of a burden I was carrying until I could feel myself relax, sitting with my grandpa helping him husk nutmeg. I didn't know it could be any different, until I hit high school, and met a peer group that was Black like me, and proud of it.

two

BOLD OR BAD—OR BOTH

WHEN I ENTERED THE CAFETERIA on my first day of high school at St. Thomas Aquinas, I recognized the usual cliques I had known in elementary school: the jocks and the cool kids, the popular girls and the nerds. But I also noticed a large new group: Black teenagers, all sitting together in the front four rows of tables on the right side of the room. These kids were not huddled in the back as if they were afraid to be there. Not at all. They were right up front, laughing loud and speaking in a fake/not-so-fake Jamaican patois. Though most of them were older than me, I went right up to them, taking the chance to establish my dominance in new territory. It felt like I was coming home. With these friends I laughed loud, just like they did, wore my hair in the latest styles I saw in Black women's magazines, and out-swore them all, finally able to show off a little of my identity as a young Black woman in the world.

I was smart enough not to talk about any of my new crowd at home, but my parents must have felt the excitement radiating out of me, because they quickly established high-school ground rules: I had to be home by 4:30 p.m. every afternoon without fail or there would be trouble. The school was in the section of town where the streets started with G and, with my house in N, it took an hour and two buses to get home. To make it by 4:30 I had to leave immediately after the bell rang. I had to ask permission for each extracurricular activity I wanted to do weeks in advance, which gave my parents lots of time to use the threat of revoking their permission if I misbehaved. My patience for my parents' control was wearing thin, especially now that I could be hanging out with these cool older kids.

In Grade 9, I obeyed the rules. By Grade 10, though, I was dying to gain a little freedom. I'd also grown even more resentful that my brothers had no such rules to follow, and that even if they had, neither of my parents would have come down on them as hard as they did on me if they broke them. I decided that while I would keep up my grades, I'd have a little fun while doing it. If I missed my 4:30 curfew it would have led to physical punishment, and I did not want that. So I started to skip class instead, first heading to the local mall and, eventually, to hang-outs in neighbouring towns where I wouldn't be spotted by gossipy Brampton housewives who might tattle on me to my mother. If I could not beat my parents, I would deceive them.

There was one more thing I had to counter if I wanted to pull off my bid for freedom: the school calling my parents to tell them I had skipped class. I learned how to craft well-written excuse letters asking for permission to leave school over my father's forged signature. (I did not dare forge my mother's.) No one in the office suspected that the nice, honour-roll student would be so deceptive, and so I got away with it.

I found myself also starting to push back against authority at school, maybe because I could not do it openly at home. I wasn't always so smart about it. Maybe even insufferable. For instance, when I received 99 percent in my religion class, I went to my teacher to protest the single missing percentage point. He was the sweetest man ever, the personification of a nice Catholic school religion teacher; he could have played Jesus in a made-for-television movie. I marched up the steps to his portable and knocked on the door, glancing through the wire-reinforced window. When my teacher waved me in, I swung open the door and immediately started demanding an explanation for the docked point, shaking my report card at him defiantly. I wanted to see every test and assignment, I insisted, so I could show him where he'd made his mistake.

My teacher looked me up and down and quietly told me to leave his classroom or he would dock me 10 percent for my insolence. Yikes! That did not go as expected.

On my way back out the door, I begged him not to tell my parents. His natural sweetness returned and he told me not to worry, he wouldn't tell.

It was a rare setback for the new incarnation of me as a "bad gyal" with a growing rep for speaking up to teachers and skipping school. I mostly loved the new me. I'm not being big-headed when I say I was one of the prettiest and smartest girls in school; I had more than enough friends and male admirers to confirm that for me. I had also discovered that the mouthier I grew the more people wanted to hang around me; the more belligerent I was, the larger the crowd.

So, when on Halloween Day in Grade 10, some Black girls found "Ni**ers Get Out" written in one of the stalls in the girls' washroom, they came to me to deal with the situation. As I marched into the washroom to see the graffiti for myself, a crowd of girls and boys followed. When I saw those words, I got so angry it didn't seem to matter anymore which white girl had written them—somebody was going to pay.

Because it was Halloween, I was not in my school uniform, but wearing a black turtleneck and a pair of wide-legged jeans that one of the school artists had painted designs on, along with my red, gold and green necklace and earrings. The school administration tried to ban us from wearing such colours, arguing that expressing pride in our Black heritage this way caused as much grief as the skinheads expressing their nihilism and white pride by wearing Doc Martens. Give me a break. I wore those colours proudly in tribute to my heroes in history (and to gain popularity with my friends).

I don't know who found the suspected culprit, but soon a white girl wearing a football player costume was brought to the bathroom to stand impromptu trial. After very little questioning, we all concluded she really had written the horrible message. We dropped her to the floor, kicking and punching her. After the punishment was delivered, I threatened her: if she told anyone what had happened, we would beat her up some more.

As I headed for homeroom—all of this had happened before first period—my followers patted me on the back, giving me props for my handling of the incident. My satisfaction lasted about ten minutes—until I heard a PA announcement, asking me to come to the office. I headed out of my classroom, turned right down the first hallway and left towards the office, my stomach sinking with every step. This could not be good.

It wasn't. My victim was lying on a stretcher in the hall, surrounded by ambulance attendants and police officers. I ducked past them and into the office, where the principal told me that the girl had a suspected punctured lung and that the police wanted to speak to me about what had happened. I was terrified. The whole situation had gotten way out of control and I had allowed it to happen. I was not even sure that the girl was actually the culprit, but when the herd around me started to chant for justice, I complied. When the police came in, they asked me if I wanted my parents present. NO, I said firmly. If I had the option of keeping them out of the situation, I was going to take it.

Some of the other Black girls had been called down too, and after the cops talked to me they asked me to wait, and began interviewing them, one by one. While I was sitting there wondering what would happen next, my father walked in carrying the cane he had been using because of a recent knee injury. The other Black girls looked at me as if to ask, "Is your father going to beat you with that thing? Is he going to beat us?"

Holy shit, I thought. My mother had sent my father. He rarely attended school meetings or functions; for him to show up meant that I was in more trouble than a whipping would fix. He paid no attention to me or the line-up of delinquent girls sitting with me, but headed straight for the principal and the police officers, furious that they thought they had the right to speak to a minor without parental consent. Go, Dad!

At last, the officers asked me to go down to the police station to make a statement. My father immediately found me a lawyer: no way was he going to leave me undefended. On the drive to the station, he didn't speak to me. I did not mind. I was not afraid of him and preferred the silence to a lecture.

It turned out that the girl had not suffered broken ribs or a punctured lung, but I still was charged with assault and went to court at least ten times before the case against me was dismissed. My mother took the opportunity to repeat the words Garvin's mother had told him, but with more fury, along with a few slaps, every time we left for another hearing. She did not leave Grenada to sit in a courthouse with a daughter who was too dumb to be smart about her actions.

I was mentally slapping myself too. What was wrong with me? It seemed to me like suddenly I was breaking all the rules at once, as if to determine which would land me in serious trouble, regular trouble or not-so-serious trouble.

When I thought about what had happened, it made me feel sick. I had been out of control and it was only luck that the girl hadn't been seriously hurt. I had no desire to hurt anyone. Why would I want to do that when I knew how bad it felt to be hurt? But I was oscillating between being the good girl who maintained good grades and the bad girl who stood out in the crowd in increasingly dangerous ways, all because she wanted to defy her mother. If leadership was a lesson I was to learn, I was going about it ass-backwards. The bad girl side was starting to dominate and I needed to reverse the trend before it was too late. But maybe it was already too late, given how intoxicating I found the feeling of freedom and power my alter ego possessed. It was like being drawn to fire. I knew it would eventually burn me, but I wanted to feel the heat.

Trying to find a path forward, I pushed hard academically. I took courses in the summer to fast-track through high school and complete five years of credits in four. Maybe in the back of my head I was also thinking that the sooner I could finish high school, the sooner I could escape my parents' house and go to university. On some level, I still felt I had to pay attention to my parents' guidance: I had bought into my mother's dream that I would be a doctor. Around Grade 11, she gave me a copy of Ben Carson's memoir, *Gifted Hands*, describing how he had risen from nothing to become a renowned paediatric neurosurgeon. I read that book cover to cover and told my mother that I was going to be a paediatric neurosurgeon just like him. If Ben Carson was the first to separate twins joined at the head, then I would be the first to separate conjoined twins wherever they had not been separated before. I still loved the attention my mother paid me when I came first in everything, and she loved the fact that I was now aiming so high.

As part of the accelerated plan, in Grade 11 I took Grade 11 math in the first semester and Grade 12 calculus in the second semester. If I wanted to be a neurosurgeon, I reasoned, I needed to be prepared with all three math courses—calculus, trigonometry and algebra—as well as chemistry, physics and biology. I could have looked into the university requirements for getting into medical school, and figured out I didn't have to push on all those fronts, but it didn't even occur to me. Since I was the first person in my family to think about going to university, I did not know what I did not know, and investigating the requirements was something I did not think to do.

Also, my mother forbade me to consult a school guidance counsellor after one of them tried to stream my older brother into basic-level courses, telling him that a job in the trades was a "good fit" for him. My mother was furious, insisting that Roger was perfectly capable of taking general or even some advanced-level courses and applying to college (which he eventually did). Back then, it was not uncommon for some counsellors to encourage Black students into taking courses that offered them few options upon graduation. My mother was not having it, and so I talked about my options with no one but her.

Back to Grade 11 math. It was known in those days as one of the hardest subjects in high school, but it was a breeze for me. I aced it. As a result, I was under the impression that my Grade 12 calculus course would be a total walk in the park. Though I was the only Grade 11 student in my calculus class, which might have given me pause for thought, I started skipping class.

I was deeply into exploring the new-found world of boyfriends. Secret boyfriends, because my mother would have killed me if she'd found out her supposedly innocent, devoutly Catholic, sixteen-year-old was being loose, exploring her sexuality and losing her virginity. I had to watch it because she was often a step ahead of me.

One time I'd gotten permission to go to the movies with girlfriends, not letting on that the plan was to meet my boyfriend at the time, who was going as well. My mother showed up at the theatre, bought a ticket and sat in the back row. I found out that night that one actually could not die from embarrassment, but it sure felt like it.

But this time I outsmarted myself. I thought I'd gone to enough classes that I had a handle on the material, but my final mark was 69 percent. I had never had a mark that low. For the first time in my life, I opened my report card and knew exactly how Roger felt when he would make me hide my report card until after the weekend, so he wouldn't get grounded after he showed his. My stomach turned. I was certainly going to get the pulp beaten out of me when my mother saw that mark.

This time it was me asking my brother not to show our parents his report card until after the weekend, while I tried to figure out what to do. Wow, how the mighty had fallen. Roger may have wanted to rat me out, but he knew full well that he needed the insulation of the weekend too. He spent Friday night and Saturday with friends, going to the clubs, while I took the time to figure out how to doctor my report card so that the "6" looked like an "8" and my 69 percent turned into an 89 percent. I showed it to my parents on Monday after school, when Roger was not around, and I lived to breathe another day.

I could lie to my mother, but lying to myself was unacceptable. I took the course again the following year and scored above 80 percent.

That calculus mark, and resorting to subterfuge to hide it, was not the first clue that my personal spotlight had started to dim. By the time I reached Grade 12, maintaining good grades—with the promise of the different life they provided—seemed like the only escape from the beatings I still got if I stayed out past curfew, was caught skipping class or committing some other nonsense my parents thought I could or should do better. It was also an escape from the pain that I had been carrying from a very young age. Fear of my mother caused me to cheat and change my marks, but there were many other hurts that also silenced me.

I had both witnessed and been subject to many atrocities—ones many young Caribbean girls and women experience—and the only way I felt able to survive was to file each painful moment away in my brain and promise that my adult self would take corrective action.

Many sleepless nights I would look out of the window at the stars and talk to the universe. I longed to become an adult who people respected and who could not be hit or taken advantage of. I vowed that my adult self would be strong and confident and would never beat or hurt a child. Actually, I amended that vow, figuring that having children was too much to risk. I could not hit my children if I did not have them, and I never wanted another child to know how it felt when dried plasma tore away from a wound as she got out of her clothes to have a shower after a beating, or the excruciating pain from the spray of water hitting the newly reopened wound.

Not having children would also spare them the sickening feeling I'd had when I was sexually assaulted and was too afraid to tell. If I'd told, I might have been blamed, and I couldn't risk being victimized twice. Scared silent.

I needed to have a back-up plan in case I did have children, though, so I promised myself that corporal punishment would never be a part of my home. I would make sure that my children felt safe and comfortable enough with me to tell me anything.

Things weren't only happening to me. I remember eavesdropping on an adult conversation at a large gathering and hearing that a young girl I knew was being sexually assaulted. I was afraid for her, but I said nothing. I did not know how to get her out of trouble without getting myself in trouble for meddling in adult affairs. I promised myself that when I was grown up, I would find her and apologize for not being able to help her. In 2017, I called her and did just that. We spent hours crying together. While the culprit continued to live as if nothing had happened, she was sent away, and I had missed her tremendously.

Once someone caught me and another girl kissing—I might have been eleven or twelve—and threatened to tell. Not only did I feel ashamed, but the thought of others finding out that I was "weird" was too much to bear. Better not to have the feelings. I resolved to stay as straight as a pin, but I made myself another promise: if I did have children, I would never make them feel ashamed of who they were or who they loved.

The pressure in my soul was daunting. I couldn't be the young woman I was becoming—no longer innocent, desperately trying to carve out a space for herself—while being contained in the box my parents had built for me where the walls seemed to close tighter every year.

Did they think that a 4:30 curfew would prevent me from having sex? Did they think that taking the bus home right after school kept me from voyaging into the dark and troubled places they were trying to protect me from? Did they think that their only girl, the first in the family aiming to go to university, would be protected from the dangers of the world because they put some arbitrary rules in place? I was beginning to think my parents were more naïve than I was. And sometime in early Grade 12 I decided I did not care how often or how hard I was beaten. I was no longer going to abide by the rules.

But how would I find real freedom? I lived at home, dependent on them for every article of clothing, every bit of food, the car they let me drive on the occasions I was allowed to go out. If I was going to make some kind of break for it, I needed a way to support myself.

I decided to approach a guy a couple of years older than me, who was a known drug dealer, and pitch him the idea of getting me involved in selling. I needed money and I could see how much those people made. I figured for sure that he would take me on. Everyone in his crew liked me, and I knew I had the smarts to turn his petty drug ring into something big. I felt I had to decide whether I was going to use my powers for good or for evil; I was so pissed off and distressed with everything, I was finding the goody two shoes bit completely unamusing and unadventurous.

To my surprise, the guy said no. He told me, "This is not for you. You are one of the smartest girls—never mind that—the smartest *people* in school. You need to do something better. I heard you are applying to university. Do that. You are not allowed to do this."

At the time it felt like another door closing. Now I thank him. He knew me better than I knew myself.

Here I am going to pause for a moment to admit, before my story disappears totally into wounds and recriminations, that there is no simple way to describe my relationship with my mother. I still wanted to please her. I still wanted her to think the best of me even as I was vowing to rebel.

She didn't just give me misery, and I gave her as much lip as she gave me licks. I never saw her take crap from anyone, and now, all grown up, I don't take any crap either. I got that from her.

She punished me in ways that I would never punish a child, but she was also the first to teach me who I was as a Black person. She gave me not only Ben Carson's book, but other books about Black history and identity. She was the one who forced me to participate in spelling bees, and other community programs. I was a competitive swimmer and involved with the Grenada Association. She was proud of me when I stood up for the Black community in smart ways (as opposed to taking out my anger on the white girl in the football costume). She taught me how to stand up for my community, and to be unafraid and unapologetic about my place (and space) in the world.

On April 29, 1992, the verdict at the Rodney King trial came down in Los Angeles. As I watched the news, I was both shaken by the violence of the riots that followed the verdict, and inspired by the actions of the community to collectively oppose the acquittal of the four white police officers who had viciously beaten a Black man.

On Monday, May 4, 1992, I got to school early in order to meet with the principal to ask if I could host a demonstration at the school that day. He was new to the school, but I had heard rumours that he had been arrested himself in the past for peacefully demonstrating; I figured he could not say no, and I was correct.

But in order for me to miss school for the day, he needed my parent's consent.

Well, there goes that plan! I thought as he made the call. There was only a slim chance that my mother would say yes, given that in her eyes, my one job was to go to school and do well.

"Good luck with the protest!" the principal said as he hung up the phone, giving me the thumbs up.

"She said yes?" I was shocked.

He nodded.

I didn't wait. I prepared my Bristol board posters in the front foyer of the school, writing "No Justice No Peace" and "Honk for Justice" in great big letters, and headed out the front doors to start my one-person protest. That is correct. For most of the day, I was the only person holding up one sign and then the other, as a handful of gracious passers-by honked in support. The crowds of Black youth that followed me when I was acting the fool were scarce when it came to doing something productive.

When students and parents did stop to ask me what my protest was all about, I took the time to explain what had happened to Rodney King. When they objected that the incident had happened in the United States, and that things were not that bad in Canada, I reminded them that a twenty-two-year-old man named Raymond Lawrence had been recently killed in the west end of Toronto by a white undercover police officer. I also reminded them that here in Brampton, earlier in the year, two police officers had been acquitted by an all-white jury of the 1988 shooting and killing of a seventeen-year-old Black youth, Michael Wade Lawson.

I stood there for most of the day, until I heard that Dudley Laws, a Black lawyer who was an icon in the community, and the Black Action Defence Committee were calling for people to come to a protest in downtown Toronto that night. I phoned my mother and asked if I could go. To my surprise, again she said yes. Her only warning was that if I saw that anything violent was about to happen, I should get out of there fast. She had been watching the riots in Los Angeles unfold and did not want me to get caught in any similar melee. Of all the days for her to be in a giving mood, this was the one that I would most appreciate.

I caught the bus to Toronto. By the time I got there the demonstrators had already left the US consulate, where they had gathered in support of justice for Rodney King and all Black people suffering and dying at the hands of police, and moved on to Nathan Phillips Square at Toronto City Hall. I moved through the crowd until I got close enough to lay eyes on Dudley Laws. I felt proud to be a part of something bigger than myself, something that could mean change for Black communities in Canada. As the crowd headed away from the square and up Yonge Street, I followed, exhilarated to be chanting "No Justice, No Peace" in solidarity with all these people in the street.

Then I heard the sound of smashing glass and frantically looked around. People were breaking the windows of the stores beside me, and up ahead was a line of police. My mother's warning sounded in my head and I bolted down the stairs of the first subway entrance I saw and pulled on the doors. They were locked. I banged, and a transit officer came and explained they were locked because of the protest. I started to cry, pleading with the man to open the doors and let me through—that my mother would kill me if I didn't get out of there right away. I'd never heard as sweet a sound as that latch clicking and the door opening. I thanked the officer profusely. My heart did not stop beating hard all the way home.

Just as I was finishing Grade 12, my grandfather Doril passed away at the age of eighty. It was devastating. Until that moment, on May 25, 1992, I didn't believe my grandparents would ever die.

Miracles happened every day, I told myself, and as we flew to Grenada, I was sure that I would find him alive. But when all the family members who had travelled from Canada and the United States arrived at the La Qua Brothers funeral home, the attendant pulled a gurney carrying my grandfather's body, covered by a white sheet, into the main room. When he pulled the sheet back, I felt such pain it was like every bone in my body had broken. As I softly touched his face, I noticed how discoloured it was; he had died of a massive heart attack. My knees went weak as I bent over to kiss his forehead. He was the one person I knew who loved me without a doubt and now he was gone.

On the day of the funeral, as the casket was being lowered into the ground, I sobbed like I never had before. I would never be able to keep my promise to return home to take care of him. If I had already become a doctor, I could have saved him from the heart attack that killed him. The day he died, he'd complained about a stomach ache, thinking he had gas pains. Still, in the evening, he had walked up the road to the shop for his rum, as usual. When he came home, he lay down and never woke up.

As I stood at the graveside, I saw the funeral directors passing shovels so the family members could drop scoops of soil on top of the casket. As the first shovelful of dirt fell into the six-foot hole and landed, it made such a terrible noise. I screamed. That terrible noise meant that his death was final. My tears would not stop coming and the noise did not stop until everything went dark.

When I came to, I was in my grandfather's room, lying on the bed he'd died in. I was comfortable there. I had no fear and I felt his love. Still, I promised myself that I would never allow anyone's death to affect me the way my grandfather's had. The pain was too much to bear.

The goalpost I kept in front of me as we flew home to Canada after my grandfather's funeral was that soon I'd be graduating from high school, and moving away from home to go to university. My marks were such that I could be accepted by McGill, Queen's and McMaster University, universities that had good medical programs, and were far enough away from home that I'd have to live in residence.

Then my mother put her foot down. Even though we could easily afford it, there was no way she was going to allow her unmarried daughter to sleep away from home. Yes, I would be going to university as planned, but to one that was commuting distance from Brampton; all the rules that governed my existence would still apply.

WTF (I yelled in my head). *What did she know about university? Why did she have the final say?*

I hated everything about the prospect of going to the University of Toronto or York University—the only options acceptable to my mother. York didn't even have a medical program and the University of Toronto wasn't far enough away! I needed to escape. University was supposed to be my chance to get away from my parents' rules and my mother's heavy hand, maybe even to find out who I really was.

But I didn't have the internal strength to win this fight. Not yet. So I applied to U of T, McMaster and Queen's and got accepted into all three. Even though it felt like swallowing a poison pill—and not the kind used to prevent a hostile takeover, but a literal one that would end my life—I agreed that I would go to the University of Toronto. My mother's demand that I live at home was the final straw. I was furious and may have even started to hate her. The beatings I endured bruised and tore my skin, but her decision not to allow me to go away to school broke my heart. If my grandfather's death foreshadowed the darkness to come, this decision pushed me into it.

three

LIES, ALL LIES

I ENTERED THE UNIVERSITY of Toronto in September 1992, in search of a bachelor of science, my first step, I thought, on the way to medical school. However, finding that bachelor would turn out to be one of the most challenging things I've ever done.

My first class was Biology 150, held in Convocation Hall. I got to the university early that morning so I could find my classroom and get comfortable. It was a beautiful fall day, the air warm enough to make me feel confident, but crisp enough to make me question why my mother made me come to this intimidating university. I studied the campus map, which showed me that Convocation Hall was a large building on the southwest end of King's College Circle, at the centre of the grand campus. So not that hard to find.

I pulled the large door open, walked inside the spacious entrance-way and looked for the classrooms. They were nowhere to be found. I went outside, reviewed the map, went inside and looked around again. No luck. I went outside again and finally a passer-by noticed I looked lost and asked if I needed help. When I told her I was looking for Convocation Hall, she smirked and pointed: I was, indeed, standing right in front of it.

By the time I got myself sorted, the only seat I could find was in the large theatre's third balcony. Why was my course being held here and not in a classroom? I could barely see what was happening on the stage. And why so many people?

The professor's voice came loud and clear over the sound system. "Look to the person on your left. Now look to the person on your right," he demanded. We all did as we were told. I graciously said hello and shook hands with my fellow first years. This was good, I thought. We would likely be study partners or, even, friends.

The uneasy feeling in my stomach was starting to go away when the professor delivered the punchline: "Two out of three of you will be gone by the end of the year." I felt light-headed. The people on either side of me looked as if they were here to stay. I was the one who seemed out of place, the darkest person out of the three of us. Someone should have stuck a fork in me, because I instantly figured that I was done. I had gone from being the centre of attention in a high school full of Black students, to sitting out of sight at the back of the class, a smart girl in a sea of equally smart people. Nobody would care about my African-coloured necklaces or hoop earrings here. This was a race to academic dominance and I was literally starting at the back of the pack.

I had been able to ace my grades in high school, but here I just felt lost. I had to be home in Brampton at night, so I couldn't go to any of the campus social events or hang out in residence, making friends, which would have made the place more welcoming. The U of T campus in the early nineties felt largely white and Asian to me; I only saw a few Black students, and it was not like I could just go up to them and say, "Hey, I'm here too." I didn't have the confidence to do that. I knew I was smart, but my brain kept telling me I didn't belong here. When I was between classes, I wandered the campus aimlessly. I did not even want to be here.

I wanted to be at McMaster or Queen's. I wanted to be anywhere but Toronto.

My insecurity and distraction made me do dumb things. For instance, during my first chemistry lab, we were supposed to make a powdered detergent like Tide. When I read the instructions the night before, I couldn't quite grasp them, even though they were written in plain English. Still I went to the dingy old basement lab in the chemistry building on campus at the right time and started to prepare the ingredients as instructed. I weighed, heated, measured and poured perfectly. I made exactly what I was supposed to make . . . until I didn't. I looked at the white substance I'd created and it still did not click that I was making a powdered soap. I was convinced it was supposed to be a liquid. So I added water to the mixture and handed it to the teaching assistant.

"Did you add water to this?" he asked with a very perplexed look on his face. I did not need to respond to know that I was going to fail the lab.

It was a large, cold campus with old, dirty spaces that made me feel isolated and afraid. But no matter how much I didn't like the place, I couldn't quit. The only thing I had to aim at in life was a medical degree. I didn't know any other path. I didn't even consider becoming a lawyer, an engineer, a pharmacist, a history major. I didn't realize those options existed. I'm astonished now to think back on how narrow my tunnel vision was. As far as I was concerned, sticking with it was my only shot at becoming the only thing I had ever dreamed about—a neurosurgeon. For a girl who got straight As, I was dumb about the world.

Every day I longed to go back to high school, to my friends and the comfort of knowing who I was. Here my smart girl identity was a faded memory of someone I once knew. The person who took her place was deeply confused and lost.

Soon, instead of going to class, I was spending my days with one troubled boyfriend or another. The badder the better. Not going to school, earning an illegal income and not really caring about me seemed to be my prerequisites. I did not care if they cheated on me, because I was cheating on them. During the evenings and weekends I would lie to my parents in order to get out of the house. I drank too much and partied too hard. I often woke up the next morning wondering how I survived the night. When I had to write an exam, I had to cram. I took amphetamines so I could stay up and read the entire textbook the night before. Of course the inevitable happened. I barely passed first year, and was put on academic probation. This time, I did not worry about my parents' reaction. I simply doctored my transcript, changing my bad grades to good ones, and showed my parents the forgery.

To say it all made me feel bad is an understatement. I felt pretty much like I was dying every day. Over the summers, I recuperated with trips to see relatives in Grenada, which always restored me. I also had a steady job at a pharmacy in a Brampton grocery store, where I was relied upon and liked by everyone. My colleagues there were like a second family; among them I could pretend that all was well with the world. No matter how bad my day was, walking into that pharmacy made me feel better.

At the beginning of second year, I vowed to do things differently, but I was on a downward spiral, hunting for anything and anyone who could help me escape reality, even if only temporarily. I spent even more time with boyfriends than in class. By the end of the second year, my marks were so bad I was kicked out of the university. I was also pregnant.

That particular boyfriend and I had been dating on and off since high school; he was the one constant that reminded me of the girl I once was. I knew the relationship was toxic and that I should focus on school, but still I turned to him. He was my new version of fire, and though I got burned again and again, I kept coming back. However, as familiar as he was, I knew I did not want a family with him. And, while I could forge my marks to fool my parents and plead with the university to let me back in, I could not hide a pregnancy. I made the decision to have an abortion.

Even though I sat in the clinic waiting room for the same reason that everyone else was there, I felt ashamed to be there. I was part of a Catholic family who went to church every Sunday and always sat near the front. My parents gave generously to the church and we volunteered regularly. My father and I were called upon to read scripture at Sunday mass; he also sang in the choir. I was not only ashamed, I was damned.

The only thing I wanted more desperately than to leave that clinic was to have my mother with me. It was weird, but I needed to have her there. I wanted to tell her that I was in really big trouble. That I was in over my head and drowning. But I was a coward who was afraid to own my mistakes. Though I felt she was the only one who could help me out of the situation, there was too much pain and fear between us. I just couldn't tell her the truth. I kept my head bowed the entire time, so nobody would see me or, even worse, recognize me. I wished desperately for the kind of mother who would speak to me honestly and show me the options. A mother who would tell me to go on birth control to prevent this sort of mess from happening in the first place. But that was not my mother, and I would not risk giving her the chance to be there for me for fear that she wouldn't be. The only people who knew about the abortion were my boyfriend and my best friend.

The next time I was asked to sign up for a church rally for life, I ducked out of it. Lightning was bound to strike me as a hypocrite and sinner, and might kill the people on either side of me too.

—

You'd think I wouldn't have doubted my abilities so much, when it turned out that once again I was able to persuade the university to let me back in. But I was not really thinking. The proof? I just couldn't crawl out of the same bad habits that had led to academic disaster.

Towards the end of the second semester that year, I received a message from the Registrar's Office that I needed to meet with a counsellor named Sally Walker. I remember every detail of that walk through the curved corridors of New College on my way to the appointment. I was fucking up big time, and hoped desperately that this person would be able to tell me how to fix everything.

Sally, a slim woman with big curly red hair, met me in reception. She smiled at me and led me to her office, chatting all the way. I slouched in her chair as she told me, quite kindly, that I was going to be placed on academic probation again. I stared at her. She seemed so gentle and I loved the way she moved her hands as she spoke. Her office was a warm place, full of books, plants, ornaments and pictures. I longed to move into this tiny space and stay forever—the first time I'd felt at home at the university. Where had this woman and this mystical room been three years ago? Why was she just finding me now?

I can't explain why she had such an effect on me, except to say that she genuinely wanted to help me. She saw me clearly: not a Black girl, a smart girl, a dumb girl, or a bad girl, just a lost girl needing guidance. I had rarely encountered anyone who expected nothing from me except perhaps for me to reach out my hand and accept her help.

The more Sally spoke the more relaxed I became, until she asked, "Do you understand?" and I realized that I had not taken in one word she had said. I felt sick. I wanted to confess, *No, I don't understand, because I was not listening. You made me feel welcome and accepted for the first time in this terrifying place. You put me under a spell.*

How the fuck do you expect me to understand while I am under your nicest-person-in-the-world spell?

I swallowed the saliva filling my mouth and sighed. (Ever since I'd gotten pregnant, my mouth would fill with saliva every time my stomach was upset. It was my scarlet letter, the burden I bore for my sins.) I decided it did not matter if I understood Sally or not. I was doomed. I would never be a neurosurgeon and my parents would kill me once they found out about all my lies. I pressed my lips together to fight away the tears and nodded. Yes, I understand.

I understood nothing. I got up and left. It turned out (I learned from Sally later—I stayed in touch and we still meet on occasion) that she had recommended I cut the number of courses I was taking so I could get my average up and graduate with a three-year degree. Maybe I didn't hear her because that was never the plan: I had to graduate with honours.

Instead of reducing my load, I signed up for six fourth-year courses. I ended up skipping even more days and taking more amphetamines in order to cram for tests and papers; as a result, my GPA dropped below the graduation cut-off point of 1.56. At the end of that year, most people who had entered university with me graduated and I was left behind. I'd come from the top of my class in high school to not graduating with my class in university.

What I wanted to do was drop out, but it was too late. My parents had invested too much money and I had told too many lies. And with this fourth-year disaster, I had more lies to tell.

First, I had to forge my marks again. Second, I had to figure out how to explain why I would not be crossing the stage at Convocation Hall to receive my degree.

When I'm in the right mood, I can laugh about the level of ingenuity I brought to bear on this. Forging the marks was no issue: I was a pro at that. I'd saved the transcript template on the computer and a little bit of keyboard work and a short trip to the print shop took care of everything. But explaining why neither I nor my parents could go to the graduation ceremony for the first person in the family to go to university was harder.

The solution: after I presented them with my fake transcripts, I followed up with a fake letter announcing that I'd been accepted into medical school. Then I invented an incident of vandalism that had shut down Convocation Hall so that the whole graduation ceremony had to be cancelled. I even wrote a letter from the administration that sounded as official as a heart attack, requesting that students with any information about the suspected vandalism call a number that looked exactly like a U of T campus number. There were big holes in this story, but having shown my parents the shiny object of my acceptance into medical school, they were so happy they didn't think things through.

Bloody fucking hell. If there was a God, He needed to show up fast and rescue me from this tangled web I was weaving. Or punish me for the liar that I was. I was both shocked and relieved when He eventually did show up in the form of my best friend.

I kept on running my personal Ponzi scheme, believing that if I danced fast enough, I could make reality eventually match the lies I was telling. I wanted to get a real honours bachelor of science degree, so back I went to the university.

Towards the end of second semester of my fifth year—which, as far as my parents were concerned, was the end of my first year of medical school—my best friend, Jessica, and I decided to go to a new club that was opening in downtown Toronto. I was secretly dating one of the owners, behind my steady Brampton boyfriend's back, and he let Jessica and me, along with another friend of ours, in for free.

About an hour into the night, Jessica and the other girl disappeared. I wandered the crowded dance floors for what seemed like hours, but could not spot them. At the end of the night I headed outside, wondering how I was going to get home, and found them both laughing away with a group of people in the parking lot. I lost it, yelling, "Who the fuck do you think you are? Leaving me all fucking night after I got you into the club for free."

Jessica pleaded with me to calm down and just get in the car with her to go home.

"Go fuck yourself!"

I saw right away that I had hurt her badly. I don't know why I was so mad. We had been friends since high school and she had always looked out for me. She had covered for me many times with my parents. I wanted to take the words back, but it was too late.

The next morning, a Saturday, I went to work at the pharmacy. I did not let myself think of the situation with Jessica all day, but when I got home that night and found my mother sitting by the front door, I immediately knew that my behaviour had come home to roost. Any time I found my mother waiting for me like that, I knew trouble was coming my way.

It turned out that in the aftermath of me cussing her out, Jessica had gone straight to my parents and told them everything: the lies, the drugs, the boyfriends, and even the abortion.

The next few weeks were hell on earth in my house. The constant slaps and questioning of my actions over the past five years had my head and every other part of me sore. I explained and re-explained the convoluted mess I'd got myself in, told and re-told the story of how I did not graduate and answered question upon question about my drug use and boyfriends. The truth had finally caught up to me. But instead of being angry with my friend, I was relieved. I should have thanked her (and maybe if she reads this book, I finally can). She did me a favour by telling them everything I did not have the courage to say. My family was devastated, but the truth finally set me free.

In as much as the five-year spiral had been dark and devastating, and my parents' suspicion and disappointment was hard to live through, I was acutely aware that somewhere inside of me a little spark now shone. My best friend's betrayal of my secrets had offered me hope again. For years now, the dominant feeling in my life had been guilt. I was finally able to move forward, still ashamed, but at least in truth.

When I think about the millions of human interactions and experiences that have brought me to where I am today, I end up wondering whether every single one of them, right or wrong, had a specific purpose. Whether we realize it or not, we are shaped by every interaction we have. The good and the bad. The joyful and the hurtful. The mistakes and the triumphs. All of them make us the person we are.

No one is perfect. But I know now what I didn't know then: our failures, mistakes, imperfections and shortcomings define us. In fact, sometimes they help us see the best parts of ourselves. We make such painstaking efforts to hide our faults and failings from ourselves and others. But being vulnerable and open, and owning our flaws, gives us strength; when we share our failures with others, we all learn and grow.

I used to hate mistakes. I used to hate them so badly, I thought of them as a person I wanted to avoid at all costs: Ms. Take. Every time she showed up, disaster followed. This woman comes in unannounced, makes sure you mess up, does not apologize for how badly she makes you feel and just walks away, leaving you to deal with the mess.

Ms. Take has been in my life at some of the lowest, darkest, most incredibly embarrassing moments. She may be sitting beside me right now. Her visits are awful, and the aftermath is worse. She leaves gifts of hurt, guilt, anger, resentment, pity, anxiety, regret, disappointment, insecurity and other feelings that last for a very long time, if not forever.

But Ms. Take is survivable, I've learned. I have come to realize that she is actually one of the smartest women I know. She understands that there are only two things to do with mistakes: make them and learn from them. When she comes around, someone will usually tell you, "Get back up on that horse right away, or else you will never ride again." In my opinion, we shouldn't get right back on the horse. We should take the time to figure out the lesson Ms. Take is trying to teach us.

It is okay to rest, down on the ground, for a little while. I am not saying you need to stay flat on your face. You can turn over, put your hands behind your head and breathe, as you figure out what you did to get yourself into that mess. Don't blame your friends, teachers, parents or coworkers. You need to own your mistakes and understand how you came to make them. If you do not do this, you will continue to blame others—like I used to blame everything on my mother—and the fear, insecurity, anger and resentment will stay with you forever. I know this now, but I had a lot of ground to cover until I learned the lessons my mistakes at university had to teach me.

After the truth was exposed, I was relieved I didn't have to build up any more layers of guilt or spin any more lies, but I was ashamed of myself. The other really hard thing was that, after living dishonestly for years, I was finally finished with the business of only pretending to live my life. Now I had to do it for real.

But I was still stuck at home with my parents. The tension was so thick I thought it would choke me. I also didn't have a best friend anymore, which was awkward, too, because Jessica's parents and mine were still friends.

That first summer, I decided I had to get out of Brampton for a while. The fact that my parents were too proud to have told anyone in the family about my disgrace worked in my favour. My cousin Debbie wanted me to come with her to Grenada for a week to visit Mrs. Caesar. That seemed like a good idea to me: I could celebrate my twenty-second birthday with people who were unaware of all of the drama, so I would be free to breathe. My parents couldn't find a reason to say no that wouldn't blow our cover, so in the end I set off with Debbie and Lisa, another cousin, as well as my brother's girlfriend (now my sister-in-law) for a week in the sun.

My grandmother was glad to have us, and used my birthday as a reason to invite every person in the village of Pomme Rose, St. David's, Grenada, to a party. She baked a five-tier cake and about a hundred of the little loaves she called "pencil bread," killed a goat and cooked a feast.

After the birthday party, we young ladies took the island by storm. We were invited to beach parties and downtown hot spots by the local boys who loved the idea of Canadian girls giving them attention. After hanging around downtown one day, we decided that we would sleep over at a cousin's house closer to the city instead of travelling back to Pomme Rose. Even under my parents' rules, we would be allowed to sleep over at our cousin's house. But in Mrs. Caesar's world, this was absolutely forbidden. Not only would we be sleeping away from home, rumour had made it back to Pomme Rose that her granddaughters were "carrying on" in the streets of St. George's. She was not about to have it and called my cousin demanding that her granddaughters be sent back home.

He told her over the phone that she had nothing to worry about and that we would be just fine sleeping at his place. Whatever Mrs. Caesar said in reply removed the confident expression on his face. "Okay, Mrs. Caesar," he said, "I will let them know."

I started putting my shoes on as he was hanging up the phone. Remember earlier when I said that Mrs. Caesar was unapologetic and unafraid? She absolutely was, and if we did not get ourselves back to her house, I did not know what stunt she would pull.

"Your grandmother wants you home. She also said that you can't take a clean sheet to cover a dirty mattress," my cousin reported. I don't know quite what she meant, but every time I remember this story, I laugh. She was the ultimate family matriarch. All of us regarded her with unconditional love . . . and, possibly, fear. Her number one rule was that family members were required to sleep at home. She wouldn't even allow Debbie, the eldest of us on the trip, to sleep at her paternal Grenadian grandmother's house. She was so strict, it was hilarious; after all, we were adults.

So back we went, and we all joined her on her Saturday morning trip to the market in Grenville. As we walked hand in hand, she negotiated prices for the vegetables she wanted and purchased the treats she thought we needed, totally in her element. The sun was shining brightly on her that day. Her prodigal granddaughters had returned.

When our week was up, and we had packed to go to the airport, my grandmother told each of us that the next time she saw us, she would be dead. It was her version of hugs and kisses, a way of telling us that we had given her the week of a lifetime and she was sad to see us go.

After saying our goodbyes to Mrs. Caesar, we set off with a big caravan of family and friends who wanted to wish us bon voyage. But as we approached the airport, we realized that there were no passengers but us in sight. We found an airline attendant at the check-in desk, though, who took one look at us and said, "If you were not having so much fun at the local restaurant the night before, you would not have missed your plane." We checked our tickets. Our flight had taken off the night before.

The entire caravan drove back home to our grandmother's estate. When she saw us pulling up, the old lady had never looked so happy. Mrs. Caesar laughed and stomped her feet and clapped, as if she had taken lessons from her late husband, Doril. Her grand-daughters had returned home and she was ecstatic.

"Well," I said, trying not to laugh, "you certainly are happy for a dead lady."

That look on her face when she saw us return was well worth the penalty fee the airline charged to book a new flight.

The next time I saw Mrs. Caesar, she was indeed in a casket at her funeral. I would give anything to have another moment or two with her.

four

WIFE? MOTHER? REALLY?

I CAME BACK TO Canada prepared to start my sixth year at university by taking the advice my counsellor, Sally, had given me at the end of third year. I reduced my course load. It was a humbling experience because I was also forced to take a couple of second- and third-year courses to boost my GPA. That semester I received my first B while at the university, which boosted my cumulative GPA to 1.58. Finally, I would be able to graduate. Getting that news was one of the happiest and scariest moments of my life. Partly because I did not know what to do with a degree that would not get me into medical school and partly because I had lost myself in all of the scheming. I was better known for who I was dating than who I was. I had a chance at a fresh start and I did not want to blow it.

The morning of my graduation ceremony, I heard my mother getting dressed and wondered where she was going. I was certain that the shame and anger of the past few months meant she would not want to be seen with me.

Then she knocked on my door and told me that she was taking me to graduation. She said that she was proud that I had graduated and that I should not feel ashamed. I was getting the piece of paper, and that was everything. I wanted to cry, but I didn't. In that moment, I think we both got a glimpse of how much we loved each other.

That June day in 1998, as I walked across the lawn at King's College Circle, I thought a lot about Sally Walker and the advice that had taken me two years to understand. All I had to do was reduce the load to finish my degree and I had finally done it. I also thought about how important it is to ask questions, even ones that shame you. If I had just asked her to repeat herself, and taken the time to understand what she was saying, I could have spared myself years of torment.

As I got closer to Convocation Hall, I remembered how lost I'd been as I'd entered the building the first time, and laughed about the fact that I had finally found myself going in the right direction. And as I crossed the stage, shook the hand of the chancellor and got my degree, I think I might have smirked. I checked and that piece of paper did not have my GPA on it anywhere. I had the bachelor and nothing Ms. Take could do now would take him away from me.

I did not know what I was going to do next, but I figured if I could make it through this, the sky was the limit. Maybe if a challenge scares you so much you want to vomit, it is more than likely worth doing. I had spent the last six years just trying to survive. It was time for me to grow up. The vomity feeling in my stomach—butterflies, maybe, or maybe little cheerleaders shaking their pom-poms, rooting for me—were telling me "It is my time."

As luck would have it, my time alone to forge a path into the future was shorter than the preceding paragraph. Three weeks before graduation, on the May 24 long weekend in 1998, I ran into Vidal Chavannes at a club. You might wonder how I was even out at a club since my parents had grounded me for as long as I was under their roof. But that Saturday night I'd mustered up the courage to ask them to lend me the car so I could go to the night-club, and, strangely, they said yes.

I put on a mini jean dress and matching denim heels, the perfect outfit, I thought, to kick off the summer. As I walked into the club I saw Vidal on the dance floor surrounded by his friends; he had dated a friend of mine and it hadn't ended well, but he had stuck in my mind. I tapped him on the shoulder. When he turned, I asked him if he remembered me. He smiled and said, "I never forgot you." There was something wonderful about the way he took me in. He looked different, too, as if since the last time I had seen him he had filled out to match his oversized hands. He did not need to ask me to dance because I stayed close to him for most of the night.

At some point I wandered off to meet up with other friends and head home. As we were leaving, I saw Vidal chatting with someone. I didn't want to disturb him, so I kept walking. He grabbed my hand as I went past and twirled me around, bringing me close enough to whisper my phone number in my ear. He wanted to make sure that he'd got it correct. I nodded, and then he leaned in close and kissed me. I did not pull away. I wanted him to kiss me, and the longer he did, the better it was. He held me in that moment like I had never been held before and I did not want him to let me go.

For years, I had kept a list of characteristics I wanted in a partner: tall, dark, handsome, Catholic, doesn't have children, bathes with a washcloth or loofah (in my world you need more than your hands to scrub yourself clean), the potential to make a six-figure income. . . . The list went on and on. On those nights when I gazed out the window at the stars searching for the adult version of me, I prayed for my "list person" to come and rescue me. I knew they were out there, I just needed to find them.

A few weeks before I ran into Vidal, I'd added another item to the list. My coworkers at the pharmacy had heard all about my list.

With every person I dumped, they tried to guess which box the last victim hadn't checked. Were they too short? Did they bite their nails? No loofah?

On that particular day, Mike, the pharmacist, was laughing at an article he was reading in the paper and suggested that I take a look. The story was about a billionaire who was searching the world for a bride. The man had two post-secondary degrees, the article noted. Mike asked if he should contact the man in the article on my behalf. He was only half joking. Mike cared about me and wanted me to find someone really great.

"Of course not," I replied. "But I am adding another item to my list! My soul mate needs to have two post-secondary degrees." I lifted the index and middle fingers of my right hand to the ceiling. "Two degrees!" I decreed. "My life partner will have two degrees!" Mike rolled his eyes. He was almost certain that I would never find true love if I kept adding such items to my list.

As Vidal kissed me, I found myself hoping that he was my "list person." I didn't know that much about him, but I knew he was respectable enough to win over my ultra-strict, controlling parents. He was certainly tall, dark and handsome. Did he have two degrees? Did he meet all the other criteria? I pulled away slightly to look into his eyes. I hoped so, and I let him kiss me again.

The next day I was at Ontario Place with my niece when Vidal called. He was reassured that I had not given him a fake number and I was reassured that he called. There was something about him that made me feel secure, a feeling I am not sure I had ever known.

During that first phone call, Vidal calmly said, "You know you'll be my wife."

I was busy balancing the phone on my ear, holding my niece with one hand and scaling an angled rock-climbing structure at the time, and responded, "Sure you will, buddy. Remember I know who you are. Do you recall that time when your old girlfriend returned all of your gifts? Well, she was at my house an hour before that, begging me to go with her. I happened to look at some of the stuff you bought for her. That bracelet was horrible. But I did ask for that big white stuffed gorilla you won for her at the CNE, and she gave it to me. I have it in my room. All I am saying is that you cannot afford for me to be your wife. I won't accept your shit."

He laughed. "We'll see."

I could not believe this man was speaking to me about marriage. No one had ever done that before. If I could blush, I would have. My niece was demanding to go to another part of the park and so I said I had to get off the phone. "Can I take you out?" he asked before I could hang up. He really did not need to ask.

As the evening of our first date drew closer, my pharmacy gang peppered me with questions. Vidal was driving from where he and his family lived in Pickering to Brampton to pick me up after work. It was a one-hour drive across the top of Toronto on a good traffic day, and a lot longer during rush hour. I had never brought a date around, and they were wildly curious. "Is this one the list guy?" they all wanted to know.

When Vidal walked in near the end of my shift, everyone behind the counter froze. "Is that him?" my colleague Fran asked. "Holy shit," said Judi. Even Mike the pharmacist seemed mesmerized.

This is corny as hell, but I felt as if everything was happening in slow motion. Our eyes locked as soon as Vidal walked in. He was smiling as he strode towards me, wearing his usual button-down shirt tucked neatly into his pants. Not even a trace of bad boy in this man.

I smiled back and somehow managed to finish whatever I was doing without losing eye contact. Then I opened the release on the gate to let him behind the counter. "Vidal, these are my coworkers—Fran, her daughter Andrea, Judi and Mike. Everyone, this is Vidal." They acted like I was introducing royalty.

I had a few minutes left of my shift, and Vidal spent the time chatting easily with my coworkers. It pleased me that they were getting along. When I was done, we hopped into his light blue Dodge Caravan and headed to the movies. We had some time before the show, so he suggested we go to Chapters for a while. *Chapters?* I thought. He was actually a nerd. I loved it.

As we strolled through the aisles of books he pointed out the ones he'd read, giving me the Coles Notes summaries. I rolled my eyes at his cockiness. Could he be more arrogant? Did he think I did not read? I graciously let him continue.

He rattled on, book after book. I was intrigued by how well read he was, but goodness gracious, he loved the boring sections: American History, Canadian History, English Literature and every book written by a prominent Black thought leader. I'd read some of those too, but don't think I had appreciated them in the way that he seemed to appreciate them. I looked at my watch. Thank goodness the movie was starting.

It is interesting that Vidal and I can both remember what happened before and after the movie, but to this day, we cannot remember what movie we saw. When it ended, we headed back to Brampton with plenty of time to spare before my curfew. I suggested that we "park" at Chinguacousy Park for a while. I wanted him to kiss me again, and this kiss was better than the previous ones and it started to get steamy . . . until it didn't. Vidal wanted the moment to be right and he did not want us to get hot and heavy in the back of a Dodge Caravan.

Something about him made me quiet in a good way. Not silenced, but peaceful.

We got out of the van and took a stroll through the park instead. We chatted about everything, and I started to ask questions related to "the list." And when he answered every single one perfectly, I started to believe that the marriage thing could be real.

Shortly after our first date, my parents threw one of our big family parties. Big family parties were not out of the ordinary. Our family members tended to drop in on each other and "stay a while"— basically until there was enough food cooked and music playing to call it a party. However, this time, my female cousins were all inviting their boyfriends—a first. I figured there would be no better opportunity to introduce Vidal to the Caesar clan. I had never introduced anyone that I was remotely serious about to my parents. But there was something different about Vidal.

And sure enough, all went smoothly. He hit it off with my parents. We laughed, danced and ate our way long into the night. I was falling and falling fast.

By the time my twenty-fourth birthday came around on June 24, Vidal and I were an item. He planned the perfect celebration and came to pick me up in the van. I was wearing a black velvet mini halter dress, and had my hair styled in a bob. We took a couple of pictures of us looking good and then headed for Toronto. First we saw *The Phantom of the Opera*. I'd told him that I really wanted to see that show and I was excited to see it with him. When it was over, we walked over to the Top o' the Senator restaurant where he had booked us a table. I did wonder how he was paying for everything. He had a teaching job starting in September, but his summer job was doing the photocopying for a law firm, and that didn't pay a lot.

The host showed us to a cute little table for two in a little nook of the restaurant. I was beaming as I looked at Vidal. Nobody I had dated had ever done anything this special for me. Vidal, however, was looking pale. "Is everything okay?" I asked. He nodded as he looked over the menu.

The host came back to the table. "Can I get you anything to drink?"

"Water," Vidal said promptly. "We will just stick to water."

"Everything okay?" I asked Vidal again. He was even paler and admitted that he really could not afford the restaurant. I didn't mind. We were a team, and we came up with a plan. We would drink water and order one plate of rosemary chicken to split between the two of us.

When the host came back, we ordered and even had the audacity to ask him to take our picture. He knew we were children playing in the adult world, but we didn't care.

The closer Vidal and I grew, the more he wanted me to meet his parents too. No matter what I've just written, at the time, I was still under the impression that Vidal and I would date for the summer, and then call it quits in October. As a way to finally get out from under my parents' roof, I had planned an exchange trip to Australia. I'd even partially paid for it. Still how could I say no to this request?

We were chatting on the driveway in front of Vidal's Pickering home when his father, John, pulled up, having driven back from a job in northern Ontario. A tall, handsome fair-skinned man, he got out of his car and greeted me warmly after Vidal introduced us. Then he started to tell Vidal about his trip. I was instantly drawn to the relationship they had. Their ease with each other was foreign to me. It was as if I had never learned the correct way of communicating with my own parents. They were two men, who respected and loved each other, talking on the driveway as if they were old friends. I loved to see it.

I felt drawn to their conversation, not to be a part of it, but to be part of their world. I could have watched the interaction forever, but my trance was broken when Big John (as everyone affection-ately calls him) suddenly switched into patois when Vidal told him about his new job; we could have been on the street in Kingston, Jamaica. I burst out laughing.

"So wha," Big John said. "Yuh laughin' a meh accent?"

I shook my head no, but I couldn't stop laughing.

That was the start of an amazing friendship with my father-in-law, one I cherish to this day. When I eventually told Big John about my disappointment with my years at university, he gave me a piece of advice that I will never forget, and that I have repeated often. He said I shouldn't be too hard on myself. I could live my entire life all over again, start from scratch, and not be as old as he was.

I was so ashamed of my past mistakes I had never taken the time to realize that I could start fresh. If I wanted to, I could start over again at kindergarten, or more realistically, go back to school. I had no control over the past, and couldn't change it. But I could go forward.

Fat chance. By the end of the summer, I was pregnant. Given that they knew Vidal, and he was ecstatic, we had to tell my parents, whose glares of disapproval could have etched a scarlet letter in my forehead. As if my university performance and shenanigans were not disappointing enough, now I was pregnant out of wedlock.

I could not catch a break. I needed to find a direction for myself, and here I was breaking a major vow I'd made to not have children. A baby. Could I protect her? Given what I'd seen in my life, what chance did I have to be a good mother? What if I hit her?

The tension at home was stifling, and my own self-loathing did not help, so I left home to stay with Vidal for a few days. He was living at a friend's house, but they were away for a week, so we would have a little privacy.

I sat on his bed and cried. I was not ready to take care of a baby. I could hardly take care of myself. Vidal stroked my head, and then my belly. He begged for me to stop crying: "You are going to make yourself sick, and that's not good for the baby." His concern made me cry even more. How did I get so lucky? I found the perfect guy. The list guy. The scrub with a loofah guy (yes, I asked). The man who said all the right things, at exactly the right time. As I sat on the edge of the bed, I heard Vidal open the closet and rummage through some stuff. When he came back to me, he knelt holding a little red box. "I was waiting to give this to you at the perfect moment," he said, "but I want you to have it now. I will take care of you and this baby too. Please be my wife."

Then he opened the box to reveal the engagement ring I had designed in jest shortly after Vidal told me he was going to marry me. I did not like rings with the claw grip on the diamond and had drawn one that looked like an upside down omega, with the diamond cradled in its centre. He must have ordered the ring just after we started dating.

I stared at the box, and then at Vidal, who was wearing a white T-shirt and boxer briefs. (We would laugh about that outfit later. *So romantic.*) I'd been so unsure about everything in my life for so long, the moment seemed surreal. He had said from day one that I was going to be his wife and he had prepared for this moment.

I knew he loved me, and I loved him, but I was terrified. I thought we'd been playing when it came to getting married. I had so many unresolved issues it seemed unrealistic to get married. I had barely processed the bullshit of the previous six years. When was I going to have time to deal with my issues with a husband and a baby on the way? When was the adult version of me going to show up?

I was shaking and Vidal's big brown eyes, filled with tears, drew me in with the promise of protection, love and happiness. I couldn't hurt him by saying no, but I felt like I did not deserve him, so I couldn't say yes. So I said nothing and just nodded. We were getting married.

Still, I could not shake the unsettling feeling that everything was moving too fast. On top of that, I had morning sickness that lasted most of the day, every single day. My parents were not completely on board with the shotgun wedding—we wanted to get married as soon as we could—and I could not bear the thought of disappointing them again or letting Vidal down.

One night, during all this turmoil, I had a dream that I was in a house that my grandfather Doril had built in heaven. It was a beautiful, golden, shimmering building with many rooms. In the centre courtyard was a large pool. My cousins were all gathered around it, including my cousin Donna, who was pregnant (in real life too). I waded into the pool and somehow fell asleep. I dreamed that when I woke I was lying beside the pool in front of something that resembled a narrow altar. I looked up, and there was Vidal, leaning over the altar, looking down at me. What appeared to be an angel stood behind him and gently placed a white cloak over Vidal's shoulders. Then Vidal said to me, "Your grandfather has sent me to take care of you."

After that dream, I relaxed a little. And everyone else seemed to lose their reservations, too, and got into planning the upcoming nuptials. My dad's older sisters, Aunt Liz and Aunt Louisa—inseparable, highly opinionated and influential in the family (if they shun you, you are done)—were surprisingly excited about the wedding, and put everyone to work making invitations and wedding decorations. My mother got into the spirit in a big way: she sewed my wedding dress, complete with a little extra room around the belly, and the bridesmaids' dresses too. It was like my grandfather was making miracles of harmony happen from beyond the grave.

Then my body decided it would throw another little wrinkle into the works, just in case I was tempted to fully relax. About a month before the wedding date, in early December, I started to dilate prematurely due to an incompetent cervix (yes, that is the medical term); the medical team thought it best to have me on full bed rest. This meant no standing, let alone dancing at my wedding.

Our day, January 2, 1999, was memorable to say the least: it was the day of a blizzard that was the first of two major storms that caused the mayor of Toronto at the time, Mel Lastman, to call in the army to help deal with the snow. The large snowflakes made our wedding pictures really beautiful, but the storm turned the drive home after the wedding into an eight-hour ordeal for our guests from Pickering. During the reception the snow had buried the cars in the parking lot and made the exit out of the northwest Brampton reception hall impassable.

At the end of the night Vidal changed into my father's work boots and joined a group who were shovelling out the driveway of the hall. I was helped out of my dress and into track pants, then four people carried me out to our car. Since there was no way, in my condition, we could attempt the drive across the city to our newly rented basement apartment in Scarborough, we spent our honeymoon night in my childhood bedroom. Even if my incompetent cervix hadn't ruled it out, we were not having sex in my parents' house. It was a couple of days before the roads cleared up enough for us to go home.

Telling lies to others, like I had to my parents for all those years, was bad. Not telling Vidal how I truly felt about getting married and having a baby before I was ready was worse. But the potentially fatal lies are the ones we tell ourselves. We are not good enough. Not smart enough. Not pretty enough. Not worth love. I had been telling myself these lies for years.

Though Vidal was so willing, I did not need my list guy to rescue me. I needed to get out of my own way and learn to stand in my own truth, flaws and all. I needed to form a perfect union with me. I needed to rescue me. The blizzard of our wedding day foreshadowed more life storms ahead.

five

YES, REALLY. A WIFE AND A MOTHER

VIDAL HAD SPENT NIGHTS and weekends before we got married fixing up the basement apartment in Scarborough. He painted Desiray's nursery lilac and added a Winnie-the-Pooh wallpaper border, painted the master bedroom blue and the rest of the apartment a light pink. Not sure what we were thinking with the colours, but thankfully we eventually refined our colour palette.

I was anxious about moving into our new place, and the wedding-day storm had delayed us from spending the first couple of days there. Though I was almost twenty-five, this was the first time I would be living away from home. As much as I wanted to leave my parents' house, it had offered me a protection from the outside world that I hadn't appreciated until now. I'd never thought about bills or buying furniture or taking care of another person's needs. And although my parents were strict with me, I never had to worry about anything material. Our house had all the bells and whistles and all the new gadgets. We had more volumes of the *Encyclopaedia Britannica* than the local library and my bedroom had matching designer furniture. In our basement apartment I would be starting from scratch.

But once the snow had been cleared off the highways, I couldn't put it off any longer.

Since I was still supposed to be taking it easy in order to hang on to my pregnancy, Vidal really had no idea that there were some more surprises in store for him when it came to how I saw myself as a wife. At that point, I actually couldn't do all that much around the house, but there were a couple of things I never intended to do: ironing and cooking.

My mother had taught me to iron, and I often did so without fuss. But when she still lived with us, Gramsie told me one day that I wasn't ironing a shirt correctly. She took over, pulling the sleeve over the slender end of the ironing board and folding it such that the pleat along its length was perfect. She made sure that even the spots between the buttons were smoothed flat. She spent so much time on that one shirt, I thought we would be ironing it for days. When she was done, she looked at her masterpiece and said to me, "When you grow up, this is how you should iron your husband's shirts."

As-fucking-if! That was not my picture of how I was going to live my life. That day I swore I would never iron for a man. Ever! And I have kept that promise. To this day, I do not own an ironing board. Well, actually I do. Once, when my father-in-law was visiting, he asked one of the children to get him the iron and they fetched him the iron tablets I take for my anemia. Out of embarrassment, I purchased a small ironing board, but I keep it in storage except when he's staying with us.

Then there was the idea that a woman's place was in the kitchen. When I visited Grenada, my aunts would cook the most amazing meals—combinations of fried or stewed chicken, rice, macaroni pie, and greens. For Sunday dinner, it seemed like they cooked everything there was to cook. One day, as my aunt and I were waiting for my uncle to come home, I watched her prepare his plate. She actually took the time to place steamed rice in a small bowl and turn it over on the plate so that it formed a nice round dome. It was amazing. My dad would be lucky if my mother slapped the rice on the plate.

My aunt then added the best pieces of chicken, some greens and a mound of yams and other ground provisions. I salivated. At the time, I did not realize she was taking such care for someone who was not even home, and rushed forward to grab the plate.

She held up a warning hand. "That's not for you, dear. That is for Uncle."

I looked at the chicken pieces left for the rest of us—the dark meat and a few pieces of chicken back. What in the actual fuck was chicken back?

My uncle returned home after I'd gone to sleep, but I woke up when I heard them arguing about something. I got out of bed, crouched down and peeked around the door. I saw my uncle stumble over to the table, pick up the plate and smash it on the floor. I froze. How disrespectful! If this was the way things could go, there was no way that I was ever going to consider it my duty to feed my husband, and the day that husband demanded I cook for him would be the last time I ever did.

Those weren't the only rules of engagement I'd decided on. I did not want to start our marriage in the same way that I started my life—being left behind. Undoubtedly, this is no way to begin a marriage, but no one had given me the rule book where it said, "Do not start your marriage with threats." So I proceeded to give Vidal some instructions. In addition to no ironing and no expectations of hot meals when he came home from work, I told him that if he ever stopped loving me or was no longer interested in being with me, he could and should leave. That may sound like the opposite of not wanting to be left behind, but it wasn't. If he did not want to stay with me, I wanted him gone. I loved him enough to know that sticking around in order to stick around was no way to live, but

I was not going to make it easy for him to want to stay. To be honest, I think I was trying to push Vidal away from the moment he said, "I do."

For instance, I would still drive to my parents' place in Brampton when they asked for help with the simplest of tasks, like I was under a spell. I am sure it was confusing for him. The woman he loved did not fall under spells or acquiesce to the demands of others. She was fierce, unapologetic and bold, and didn't suffer fools. Now he was seeing the side of me that had always been under her parents' control. The more I went to Brampton, the more strain it put on our marriage. When Vidal asked me to think about not going so much—he wanted to see me on nights and weekends, after all—I was hard on him for not understanding. How could I say no to my parents?

In those early months of our marriage, waiting for our daughter to be born, I knew what I didn't want to be as a wife—or at least thought I did. I also knew what I did want to be as a mother. The problem was I didn't know what to expect when the child was actually on her way.

Nobody had ever talked to me about pregnancy or the pains of childbirth; I was in the dark. I needed the extended version of the story of the birds and the bees, the one that included the woes of pregnancy, because I was having a tough one.

I was nauseous for the entire nine months (something that happened every other time too), so nauseous that saliva constantly accumulated in my mouth. When I finally went into labour at the end of April, I could not make sense of the degree of pain. In TV dramas, women sweat and scream for a bit, the baby comes out and, suddenly, they are smiling. I was not smiling. The labour was so long and painful I did not want to hold my baby after she was born. The disconnect I felt as I watched the attendants clean Desiray and weigh her was so strange. When a nurse at last handed her to me, I held her as if she was a small pumpkin, and I wanted nothing more than to give her back.

In the following months, I waded through a fog of postpartum depression (which may be a natural reaction to having your vagina stretched in such unthinkable ways). I had lots of fears about becoming a mother, but high hopes too. This was not what I'd imagined. I'd gone through six years of relentless failures and lies, and now I felt like I was failing again.

I went back to work within weeks of Desiray's birth. At least work was a break from feeling badly about feeling badly about my daughter. Because we had moved to the east end of Toronto, I'd had to quit my job at the pharmacy. Yet when my parents told me I shouldn't be sitting around and should go to work in their warehouse as a forklift operator and part-time receptionist, I said yes. So as well as visiting them on weekends, I started driving to Etobicoke, where the warehouse was, every workday. It was not as far as Brampton, but during morning and evening rush hour, it may as well have been.

To say Vidal was confused by my choices was an understatement. The upside was that I could bring Desiray to work with me, so we didn't have to pay for childcare. The downside was that I was working for my parents and in their grip. Again. I'd had low points in my life, but this was one of the lowest points. Vidal, who was teaching high school in Pickering, a job he loved, saw how miserable I was and didn't understand why I didn't quit, especially since the pay wasn't all that great. "Why are you doing it?" he'd ask. I had no answer.

Every morning as I drove to work, I'd dream about getting out of that warehouse, which I knew was no place for my baby and me. I'd think about the fact that U of T had given me the piece of paper. I did graduate. Though maybe they only gave the degree to me to get me out of there because my abysmal performance was causing their international rankings to drop. I desperately needed to find that fierce and confident child who sang naked at the top of the stairs. I now had a family and a daughter who looked up to me. I couldn't just wish for a better world for her, I had to be a part of the team creating it.

I'd remind myself that my GPA was not printed on the degree. Nobody would know what my score was except me. But that was the problem—I knew that score, and the whole shameful performance that led to it.

After a couple of years of feeling completely stuck, barely hanging on from day to day, I finally decided that the first move I needed to make in reclaiming myself was to go back to U of T. I was acutely aware that I was deliberately choosing to go back to the same university that chewed me up and spat me out. But this time, I was going back on my terms, and in an entirely different situation. I needed to prove to myself that I was capable of succeeding in university and that my past was not going to get the best of me.

One night after the baby was asleep I went on the university website and looked through all the courses offered to mature students. As I sat in front of the screen, tears streamed down my face—the imposter rearing her ugly head. I could not believe I was married with a child and looking through undergraduate research programs like I had in high school.

I searched and searched, continuing to beat myself up, until I finally clicked on the Department of Nutritional Sciences. Although I cannot accurately describe why I reacted this way, I stopped crying immediately, feeling a wave of comfort coming from the screen. I wrote down the name and number of the course director, Dr. Thomas Wolever, and called him the next day. He picked up the phone! I told him I wanted to come back to school to take a fourth-year research course. He responded that two professors in the department were accepting research students. I could go with Dr. X, he said, but "that guy is a bear—you do not want to go with him." He was right—no way could I deal with a bear in my state. I opted for his second suggestion, Dr. Carol Greenwood. I called her later that day and she told me to come in for an interview the following Tuesday. Huh? Just like that?

And so, the following Tuesday, I walked into Dr. Greenwood's narrow office at the Rotman Research Institute, on the grounds of Baycrest Centre for Geriatric Care in Toronto. She had no receptionist, just a desk and a couple of chairs in a space crowded with books. I cannot remember if she looked up at me when I arrived at her door, but before I could say much of anything she told me that it was a bad time and we needed to reschedule. I wanted to protest, but I was too scared and crushed. I just put my tail between my legs and left. By the time I reached the lobby, though, I'd gathered my resolve and called to make another appointment.

At our next meeting, Dr. Greenwood simply asked me when I could start.

"Now!"

Although I was a research student, the position paid minimum wage. Bonus! Not only would I get to continue my education, I would be getting paid. We enrolled Desiray in a French daycare, not far from our basement apartment. She was a bright child right out of the womb. Leaving her at a French daycare meant that if they taught her nothing else all day, at least she might pick up a second language (which she did).

My shifts were eight hours a day, five days a week, supporting the research of a doctoral student named Karen Young who was completing her thesis on nutrition and cognitive impairment in the elderly. I was required to serve weighed portions of food to the residents of Baycrest's Alzheimer's disease unit at breakfast, lunch, dinner and snack. Once they were finished their meal, I had to weigh the portion they didn't eat then calculate the difference between that, and the whole offering, to evaluate their individual caloric intake. These leftovers included anything remaining—the chewed-up bits the residents threw against the wall or wrapped in a napkin or tucked into a drawer. Wherever it was, I had to find it, weigh it and perform the appropriate calculations.

Learning about the different fridges and separate services for dairy and meat dishes necessary to keep kosher for the Jewish patients was fascinating—my life to that point had not brought me in contact with Jewish traditions—but not as fascinating as learning about each of the residents. During my breaks, I would sit with them. They might not remember what happened half an hour earlier, but most of them had their long-term memories intact, and they would tell me stories of the Second World War—harrowing tales of the concentration camps, but also of survival and love, and the triumph of the human spirit. I would often hear them screaming in their sleep, their dreams interrupted with nightmares, maybe of the camps. I grew to love and appreciate their gentle spirits and mourn the forgetfulness of their minds.

Every day, after I worked my full shift, I would stay on to complete the data entry and learn the appropriate statistical analysis. I picked Karen's brain and talked to other PhD students in the building about how best to interpret and present the data. Student after student gave generously of their time as I learned my way around the statistical software. One student spent an entire evening teaching me Excel, showing me how to graph the outcomes, how to account for outliers, how to change variables and other functions.

Those unpaid hours I put in not only gave me the experience I needed to get the next job, they were appreciated by those around me, especially Dr. Greenwood. She soon made me responsible for a small component of the project and told me that she wanted me to present the results at an international nutrition and ageing conference in Albuquerque, New Mexico. I blinked at her when she announced this and tilted my head—was she really speaking to me?

Dr. Greenwood did not take back what she said, she did not ask again, and she certainly was not waiting for my response. I was going to take the assignment and go to New Mexico to present it.

I got to work. I prepared a case study on one of the residents to determine the best time of day to offer a nutrient-dense snack, such as an energy bar, to ensure they would eat it. It was often difficult to get residents with dementia to eat extra calories. They would either insist they'd just eaten and didn't need a snack or preferred candies or cookies to the more nourishing option. Dr. Greenwood supervised from a distance as I completed the research and prepared my findings. She never hovered or made me feel like I did not know what I was doing. She allowed me to fully appreciate the research process, including making mistakes. When my analysis went awry, I asked questions, got answers and course-corrected. When I was ready to prepare the poster for the conference to display my finding that a mid-morning intervention provided the best result, she was beside me to help. I had never had anyone willing to put so much energy into simply helping me.

The experience of New Mexico was fantastic. I listened to other presenters share their research, visited some tourist areas, ate some great food and had wonderful laughs. When my poster was placed in the main conference hallway, I stood beside it hoping no one would come over and ask questions at the same time as hoping everyone would come over and ask questions. I was a nervous wreck. Karen and another student stayed with me, standing at a distance and reminding me to breathe. Soon, there was one person in front of me staring at the board. I remember letting them stare, as if they were browsing a rack at a clothing store. Then another came over, then another. I glanced at Karen, who gently waved her hand, indicating that I should talk to them. As simple as the case study was, people were genuinely interested in the results and congratulated me on my findings. For the first time, since high school, I felt at home.

Dr. Greenwood became one of my greatest sponsors. More than just a mentor, she invested time and resources in my development and was not afraid to push me beyond my limits. As eager as I was to learn, I am sure she recognized how the shame and guilt of my past mistakes weighed on me. In telling me to present my research myself, she nudged me to the edge of the deep end and ever so delicately pushed me in. She knew full well that I could swim on my own, but that I had temporarily forgotten how. And she stayed at the edge of the pool, patiently waiting for me to remember that I was actually good at it.

I finished that year with the only A grade on my University of Toronto undergraduate transcript. And on top of the boost that gave to my damaged self-esteem, that year I encountered someone else who lifted my spirits and made me think differently about my future. One day I had to go on an errand—I forget what—to the top floor of the Rotman Institute and walked past an office that was so bright and beautifully decorated I stopped to peer in. It was a huge corner office decorated with pottery and plants of every kind. There was art and photographs and . . . hold up . . . there were Black people in the photographs. Whose office was this?

As I poked my head farther in, I saw her. A beautiful, dark-skinned woman whose natural curly hair was accentuated with the most brilliant grey. I looked at the nameplate on the door: *Jean Lazarus, Director of Research Operations.* Director of Research Operations? I did not realize a job like that was possible. That first time, I did not dare to interrupt her, but I made a point from then on of walking through the top floor every chance I got, hoping she'd notice me. When we finally were introduced, I was ecstatic. My conversations with Jean were the bonus on top of an already life-changing experience. She became the big research sister I never knew I needed. Knowing that a Black woman was in charge meant everything to me. She sat at the table with the other directors, and I felt like she represented me at that table. I wanted to make her proud of everything I did, and I worked my tail off so that I would not embarrass her and could show others that all Black women were as amazing as Jean was.

Representation matters. But Jean taught me that access to representation is even more important. Not only did she allow me to watch her in the position, she allowed me to ask questions and make decisions about a career in research. During my time in politics years later, I would insist on such access for everyone, but especially Black women and girls. Not only did I want them to see me in that public sphere, but I would invite them to Parliament, to my riding office and to my home. I made myself, and the position I held, accessible to them, just as Jean had done for me. I knew that the impact of seeing me interact and be a regular human being in politics would last them a lifetime—giving them permission to be their authentic selves, too, wherever they ended up.

Jean's example made me want to dream bigger. So when I saw a job posting for a research assistant, I decided to apply. Such opportunities were rare and, when one became available, every student pounced on it. The posting called for someone with a background in psychology and statistics. I had neither. I'd never studied psychology and the after-work guidance I'd received from the other students did not make me a statistician. But I needed the job. I was falling in love with research and wanted to pursue it as a career, and you cannot become a research coordinator without having been a research assistant, and you cannot become a research manager or director without having been a research coordinator.

When I showed up for my interview with Dr. Donald Stuss, the head of the Rotman Research Institute, and his own rescarch assistant, he asked me off the top to tell him a little bit about myself. I immediately blurted out that I did not have any training in psychology or statistics experience. He and his colleague looked perplexed. They must have been thinking, *Can she even read? Did she not see what the posting said?* But I was in survivor mode—everyone wanted the job but I needed it—and before they could show my unqualified self out the door, I said, "Look. I may not have any psych, and I certainly do not have enough stats, but I have passion and drive and am a quick learner, and you can't teach that. You can teach me stats, and you can teach me psych, and I will learn it. Fast. But you cannot teach passion and drive, and I have that in abundance."

I got the job. The only way I can explain why Dr. Stuss took such a chance on me is that he was not a manager or a boss, he was a leader, and as such he wasn't afraid to trust his own judgement no matter my lack of credentials.

It was a real turning point. The next week I went to work for Dr. Stuss as a critical part of his cognitive neurorehabilitation research team, funded by a million-dollar grant. The work involved testing participants with mild cognitive impairments or traumatic brain injuries to determine if training could improve their executive function and short-term memory. We take for granted how things such as writing lists, self-talk and putting our keys in the same spot when returning home keep us on track. But for a PhD who couldn't remember how to make a sandwich because he hit his head when he fell off a ladder putting up holiday lights or a senior who was worried about their partner's inability to remember simple tasks, such little lessons and tactics helped make their lives better. (Understanding how a seemingly innocuous bump on the head could damage the brain has made bike helmets mandatory in our household.)

Dr. Stuss paid keen interest to what his team members wanted out of their work, how we wanted to develop as researchers and in our careers. Like Dr. Greenwood, he took the time to ask questions and get to know everyone on the team. Every time he called me in for a meeting, I would get to his spacious office early. I loved looking at the trinkets and books he'd collected over the years related to the brain and found myself smiling at the serendipity of ending up studying the brain, even though I wasn't, and would never be, a neurosurgeon. It was as if the universe was giving me a hint that I was on the right track by keeping the brain in my life and I was so grateful for it.

The research was challenging, and when the study was complete and the manuscripts prepared, there was my name, listed along with the lead researchers and other team members, on publications in several medical journals. My hard work had been recognized and credited. Figuring that all signs were pointing to me staying in the brain lane, I went to see Dr. Stuss, hoping he would write a reference letter recommending me for a master of science degree program, so I could continue working with him. I sat on the chair across the desk from him and pleaded my case for the endorsement, confident he would write a stellar letter. Dr. Stuss agreed to write me a letter, but not to the science program. The thing about true mentors is that they see something in you that you often don't see in yourself. Based on my performance and what he'd observed during the time I worked with him, he said, he believed that my skills were suited best to business.

I felt like I had been transported back to Sally Walker's office. Words were coming out of his mouth and I was not hearing anything. I was crushed—but only for a minute. The person sitting in front of Don Stuss was not the same girl who'd flamed out in undergrad.

"Why are you saying this?" I asked.

It turned out that Dr. Stuss could not envision me sitting in a lab running cognitive tests on willing participants for the next few years. He saw someone who was analytical and strategic, someone who had helped to make his whole project a success. Like Dr. Greenwood, he cared enough about my future to steer me towards challenge and away from complacency.

I swallowed hard. Could I study business? The thought was completely foreign to anything I had ever imagined for myself. What if he was right? What if he was wrong? Usually, Kenny Rogers' voice pops into my head when I have a tough decision to make: "You gotta know when to hold 'em, know when to fold 'em, know when to walk away and know when to run." But Kenny wasn't helping. I did not want to do any of those things. I wanted to follow Dr. Stuss's advice. He'd taken a chance on me when he knew nothing about me and I knew nothing about the project he was running. He knew me now, and I knew that he would not steer me wrong. So I took the offered reference letter and applied for a master's in business administration at the University of Phoenix, a program that was all online, meaning that I could keep working while I was doing it.

When Don Stuss died in September 2019, it hit me almost as hard as when my grandfather Caesar passed. He taught me so much about my own capabilities, I will be forever grateful. He showed me that mentors don't have to look like you, or come from where you come from, to be able to see you clearly. He showed me once again, just as Sally Walker and Carol Greenwood had, that people can be selfless.

six

BECAUSE NOTHING EVER RUNS IN A STRAIGHT LINE

I HAD A ROAD map now. I'd ticked off the research assistant box, had my application for my MBA in, and now I landed a job as a research coordinator with the University of Toronto, working on an Alzheimer's registry, tracking generations of families with the disease to see what patterns could be discerned. I was also seconded to work with two physicians at Toronto Western Hospital's Memory Clinic, a hospital role that gave me my first opportunity to see the pharmaceutical side of memory research. When we couldn't recruit enough participants for the study at the hospital, the lead researchers asked me to visit Ontario Shores Centre for Mental Health Sciences in Whitby to recruit more. During one of the early visits to the Whitby site, my blood pressure dropped suddenly and I fainted. It turned out I was pregnant with baby number two and, due to complications similar to the ones I experienced with Desiray, I was immediately put on bed rest. My stint as a research coordinator was over.

No good could come from me being on a second bout of bed rest. I was restless and agitated, and since I couldn't take care of Desiray in this state, she stayed on at daycare and I was alone all day, going stir crazy in our basement apartment. To pass the time, I spent hours on the internet.

One day Vidal called home from work, completely confused about a phone call he'd just received. "Babe, I just got a call from a high school in England," he said. "The person told me they were glad to receive my application and thought I would be perfect for the job. They want me to interview for a teaching position there. What is going on?"

The words couldn't come out of my mouth fast enough. "Did you say yes? Please tell me you said yes." While I was noodling around on the web, passing the time, the recruiting pitch for the position had caught my eye. It had been easy to fill out the application and send in a résumé on Vidal's behalf. I would be off for a year on maternity leave after our baby was born. This was our chance to see the world.

"Baaaabbbbbe-uh!"

Whenever Vidal made the word "babe" sound like it had more than one syllable, I knew I was in trouble. I didn't care. Trouble was my middle name and at least here I felt like I was using my talent for deception for good, not evil. Though, when I reflect on this now, I see how much I took it for granted that Vidal was mine to control, that he would always follow my lead. Our marriage would suffer for it down the road. But Vidal, as always, was kind.

"Babe," he said again, more softly. "You are seven months pregnant. This job starts in September. What are we going to do, have the baby, pack up Desiray and all our stuff and move halfway around the world for me to teach English to the English?"

"Absolutely," I said.

And that is exactly what we did.

Two months after our second daughter, Candice, was born, Vidal arranged a leave from his job at the Pickering high school where he taught, and there we were, landing at Manchester Airport with way more suitcases than four human beings should carry. All the new teachers had arrived at the same time and the school had sent a bus to pick us up.

The one thing neither of us wanted to do was leave a basement in Scarborough to live in another basement flat. Vidal and I had spent time on the internet to find what we thought would be a comfortable home. One by one, the other families were being dropped off in front of places that looked small and cramped with nonexistent yards. When the bus finally stopped at our new address on Brooke Drive in the little town of Astley, we both breathed a sigh of relief. It was a cute, fully furnished, two-bedroom, semi-detached house with a small front yard and more than enough space in the back yard. The landlord renting us the place welcomed us with some freshly baked bread and a pot of soup; we were hungry and tired and grateful for the thoughtful gesture. Already the place felt like home. Before I knew it, the children and I were all asleep.

I woke up to the sounds of laughter and loud talking coming from outside. Too timid to go out and investigate, I peeked out the bedroom window. There was Vidal and a crowd of new neighbours in the middle of the street with a good dozen empty beer bottles at their feet. Desiray was riding around on some other kid's bike and little girls and boys were squealing as they chased her. I sighed and tried to step back out of sight, but Vidal saw me and waved for me to come meet our new friends.

I hate that sort of thing; even now, I find meeting a new crowd of people all at once totally overwhelming. Besides, what did my hair look like? I'd just spent seven hours on a plane and had fallen asleep without wrapping it in my headscarf. But if I didn't go out there, Vidal would come to get me or, worse, invite all the neighbours in.

I quickly went to the washroom, smoothed out my wild mane as best I could and rinsed my mouth. There were bags of toiletries and house supplies everywhere. Where did we get all the stuff? I changed the baby, then carried her outside in the crook of my arm, waving hello to everybody and nervously patting my head to try to tame my hair further. I shot a wide-eyed glare at the empties and then at Vidal, trying to will him to tidy them up. "I see you have made yourself right at home," I said, but Vidal ignored my hints and calmly introduced me to the Brooke Drive crew, including our immediate neighbour who had taken him to the shopping centre to get all the bags of stuff in the house, as well as the beer. It seemed that Astley was abuzz about the new Canadians who had come to stay.

For the rest of 2004 and the first part of 2005, Vidal taught at Moorside High School in Swinton, a town in greater Manchester. The kids and I would wake up early to watch him walk to the bus stop in the morning. Then I'd take Desiray, now five, to school, and spend the rest of my day going on outings with Candice, having tea with neighbours, and, when the baby was napping, completing my MBA online.

It was just the break Vidal and I needed—an opportunity to shape our little family away from the competing influences of family and friends. In the evenings, I'd put the baby down for the night, and Desiray and I would amuse ourselves by giving Vidal facials or waxing the hair on his arms. He put up with it all, even the pain of hair removal; his students went crazy over what their new teacher was getting up to. The news that "Chavannes waxed his arms" went viral before going viral was a thing.

We watched television at night after the kids were both in bed until the cable man came around to collect the television tax. A tax for watching TV? I wanted to get rid of the set, but Vidal convinced me to keep it, so we could invite the other Canadian teachers over to watch the Super Bowl.

We could not afford a car, so we explored our new world on foot or by bus. We bought our produce from the farm at the end of our street, purchased meat from the butcher down the road and got the Tesco supermarket to deliver everything else.

And it was intoxicating that Europe was so close. I'd never been anywhere but the United States and the Caribbean. So, in addition to travelling around England during school breaks, we spent the holidays travelling through Venice, Milan and Rome. We had Christmas dinner at a Venetian Burger King. And when we fell prey to a telephone credit card scam that charged us $30 a minute to call home on Christmas, maxing out our credit, Vidal's parents paid for tickets on Alitalia to fly us back to the UK.

We loved the freedom we'd found, but even Vidal, who had a lot of patience when it came to tough kids, had a hard time handling the job. When foreign schools come looking to recruit Canadian teachers, we now know the glossier the brochure, the rougher the school. One of the new hires had gone on stress leave almost immediately; one by one, as the months passed, the others started to return to Canada. Although most of his students liked Vidal, when they set his classroom on fire after throwing fireworks through the window, we knew it was time to go back home too.

Vidal could pick up his old teaching job where he'd left off, but we'd given up our apartment and re-entry was rough. The four of us stayed with family and friends until we found a ground-floor apartment to rent in Ajax, Ontario, which was close to Vidal's school in Pickering.

I'd finished my MBA, and I needed a job too. I started looking for work as a research manager, the next step up the ladder I'd imagined for myself. Yet every time I sent out a résumé, I would feel my spirit pulling me in another direction. It was easy to put out résumé after résumé. It was the comfortable thing to do. But my capstone project for my degree had been putting together a business plan for a start-up and I couldn't stop thinking about what it would be like to actually follow through on all that planning and try to pull it off. It was unfamiliar and scary territory for sure, but it sparked the same feeling I'd had crossing the stage at Convocation Hall. The cheerleaders/butterflies were back, and I could not get rid of them.

I had enough contacts in the research world to start the business I'd mapped out—taking on the management of clinical trials for pharmaceutical companies or big academic research projects. But I told myself I was dreaming and kept sending out my résumé—in the end, 732 times. When all that effort resulted in four interviews, two second interviews and zero jobs—I was told that I had no managerial experience and now that I had my MBA I was over-qualified—I realized that no matter how hard you try to go in another direction, nothing meant for you can ever pass you by. I pulled out my plan and got down to the business of being an entrepreneur.

I incorporated ReSolve Research Solutions in 2005, and just as I'd planned, it was a healthcare-focused research management firm. The first year was a grind. Vidal, who believed in me and in the idea (he was the one who came up with the name for the company), started teaching night school, too, and on the weekends got a job in the paint department of a local hardware store. We worked hard and prayed even harder, but still had a difficult time making ends meet with two kids to support as well as the new business.

We'd sold most of our furniture before we moved to England; the only two items we had brought with us to our new apartment was a mattress, which Vidal, Candice and I shared, and a bed for Desiray. Friends gave us some small items, but every Monday evening (garbage night in Ajax) we would go for a walk around the neighbourhood

looking for treasures people had thrown away. If we spotted something great, I would guard it while Vidal went to get the car. We
would struggle to load the item and then Vidal would drive it home
while I walked back with the girls.

One such evening, a little boy watched from the window as we
stood in front of his home considering whether we could use
something his family had discarded. I don't remember what it was,
but from the way he was staring at us, it must have been something he didn't want to part with. When Desiray asked me why we
were taking that little boy's stuff, my eyes welled up. I hate that
I am such a crier. I cry over everything. But this was not the time
to cry. I put on my game face. We needed the item, and one day
Desiray would understand.

Still, I was frustrated and tired of living in an apartment furnished with other people's shit. As with every other time when
I was in trouble or needed help, I asked for help. If you don't ask,
you don't get. Even the Bible says "seek, and ye shall find, knock
and the door shall be open." I was not sure that my faith was strong
enough to believe that a miracle would happen, but my faith was
strong enough to know that I deserved to ask.

"Lord," I said, as I leaned dejectedly on the kitchen counter one
afternoon, looking around our place. "I need a miracle. I need a miracle now. Not the burning bush kind where I have to work to figure
out what you're trying to tell me. I just need a good, old-fashioned,
clearly articulated miracle. I need a house. I need a real home for my
family." I cannot remember if I said please at the end, but I did drop
to my knees and let all the tears out.

When I got up from the floor, I called our accountant, who was
a family friend. I wondered why I hadn't thought to consult him
before. I explained the situation. He said, "No problem. Call Rita.
She's a mortgage broker and I'm sure she can help." So I did. After

speaking to Rita, Vidal and I gathered the documents we needed to fill out a mortgage application, and within a couple of days, we pre-qualified for a $200,000 mortgage. This time I cried tears of joy. We were movin' on up like the Jeffersons. But nothing worth getting is easy—we still needed to figure out how to put together a down payment.

I started hustling harder with ReSolve. I worked dawn to dusk, never taking a break, and sent thousands of faxes to every pharmaceutical company in North America describing the services I offered. Not a lot of companies at the time were operating in the field I'd chosen for ReSolve, and I was confident that someone, somewhere would soon see the advantage in hiring me.

At last, I received a call from a major pharmaceutical company that was looking for a company based in Canada to manage a paediatric epilepsy clinical study. The woman at the other end of the line asked if we were interested in being the management site in Toronto for the research. "Of course," I replied. She then asked if we had experience with epilepsy clinical research and access to a local network of paediatric neuropsychologists. "Of course!" I replied again.

I lied. What and what? I did not have that experience and I did not have that specific network, but I needed the money. And of course I had passion and drive.

I worked even harder after that call, sometimes eighteen to twenty hours a day. Desiray was at school, but I still had Candice at home. She seemed to understand the pressure I was under and did not cry at all—until the phone rang. She also timed her demands for cookies or juice precisely. Stuffing her with cookies so I could to start a research study was all right by me. Changing diapers, laundry, bottle prep, marketing, advertising, client engagement and reception—no job was too big or too small. Although I had worked as a research coordinator, this was an entirely different beast.

I needed to learn everything I could about running a clinical research project with multiple sites. I needed to prepare a contract and a budget so the physicians I hired got paid, and I got paid as well. I needed to submit regulatory documents to the FDA and Health Canada, as well as make submissions to ethics boards to get the study approved. Crucially, I needed to recruit the doctors. I quickly realized that finding a paediatric neuropsychologist in Toronto who had experience with clinical research was like finding a needle in a haystack. I could not have asked for a harder first client.

The challenge was daunting, but there I was emailing and faxing and calling and driving around to visit physicians and asking questions and preparing budgets and submitting regulatory documents and getting ethics approvals and, and, and . . . successfully running the research study. I was doing it. I was levelling up. In May 2006, a week before the closing date on our first home, I opened the mail to find the first major cheque addressed to ReSolve Research Solutions, Inc. It covered the entire down payment.

When it came time to move, we had started to load our furniture into the truck when Vidal came running into the apartment and announced that he'd found something in the building's garbage room for our new home. I could not believe it. We were moving on up, and he was bringing in another dumpster-dive item. Those days were supposed to be behind us. I stopped packing to watch him manoeuvre a beautiful, wood-framed mirror through the door. It was exquisite. That mirror has moved with us from house to house. It is a permanent reminder that we should never forget where we come from, and that humility is the best way to stay grounded.

The first ReSolve cheque drove me to want bigger and better for the company. But bigger and better is expensive, and we did not have that kind of money to reinvest in the company. I needed to be smarter about gaining the competitive advantage I needed to keep it growing.

I knew I was one of very few site management organizations helping pharmaceutical researchers run clinical studies in Canada. Early on, I decided that I did not want anyone to be distracted by my gender or race, so I chose to exclude any images of me on the promotional material. Instead, I used a logo I designed myself, customer testimonials and their pictures.

Since I couldn't afford an advertising budget, I signed up to receive all the free industry periodicals and read them from cover to cover. Then I would write letters to the editor explaining why I agreed or disagreed with an article, making sure to include my company name and coordinates after my signature. Bit by bit, through such efforts, I started to be viewed as an expert in clinical research management. However, I didn't want to be just an expert. I wanted to be the go-to voice on issues related to research management. So I decided to conduct a small study on the inclusion of marginalized people, especially people of colour, in research studies. Very few people were in this territory at the time, and very few, if any, Black women were speaking about it.

The work was a hit. I was invited to speak at the top conferences across Canada and in the US. I was turning nothing into something spectacular. I kept my focus on getting clients, as I believed that grants and loans would enable the business, but clients allowed it to grow.

To save on overhead, I ran the company out of the front room in our home. We all know that room—the one that our parents never let us enter, where the vacuum lines stayed perfect from Saturday to Saturday and the plastic stayed on the furniture for eternity. I was working with some of the best physicians in Toronto. When we needed to, we could host meetings with pharmaceutical representatives in their fancy boardrooms. Nobody needed to know I didn't have one. And I did not allow my ego to pressure me into renting an office and putting "ReSolve Research Solutions, Inc." on some fancy sign.

Coming up with creative ways to make the company appear larger than life at the same time as saving every cent I could and never hiring the help I needed for the work, came with a cost. I spent most of my time on the job. I decided that seeking out contracts from big pharma wasn't enough, and I started doing secondments with various charitable neurological organizations. When we went on vacation, my phone, computer and all other necessary notes and supplies came with me. I felt I couldn't miss a call, text, fax or beep. If (and when) I did, I would melt down in a panic. One missed call was one missed call too many.

It put a strain on everything, especially my marriage. No amount of zeros on the cheque could buffer that. I was making a success of my business, but I had so much left to learn about how to live my life.

seven

THERE'S NO SUCH THING AS BALANCE

THERE ARE PAINFUL EXPERIENCES that happen to each of us that no one else will ever know if we don't tell. Sometimes it's shame that causes us, wrongly, to keep what happened a secret, but sometimes we push things down in an attempt to avoid reliving the pain. No matter how hard we try to ignore it, though, such pain will eat away slowly at our reserves of love and kindness. That's what pain does: it shuts you down and closes you off. The challenge is to acknowledge it and let the pain go. From my own experience, some of the most painful stories many women never tell are the stories of miscarriages. I had two between the births of Candice and our third and last child, Johnny.

On the morning I had my first miscarriage, Vidal and I had had a terrible fight. I was still yelling at him as I left the house and I stayed mad as I drove to Toronto for a meeting. In the car, I felt a heaviness in my stomach and chest. I knew I needed to calm down, but in the moment staying mad was a more important priority.

ReSolve Research Solutions was taking off and I was in the middle of that first major contract, running the paediatric epilepsy clinical trial. I arrived at the site still enraged, though to be honest, I had forgotten what we had been fighting about. I was there to meet with a young research participant and his mother to review some of the study protocol and do some preliminary tests. As I was in the examination room with them, I felt something strange pass through me, as if I was on my period. I froze. If I ran out of the room, I could jeopardize the care of the child, the research results and the reputation of my company. I remember thinking, "If what I felt is what I think I felt, then there is nothing I can do about it."

I finished the examination. I took the time to enter the data and complete the patient chart, and only then did I allow terror to take over. I walked to the washroom, sat on the toilet and did the kind of crying that many women are familiar with—the kind where the tears are falling, your mouth opens wide as if to scream, but no sound comes out. I did that again and again, screaming so nobody could hear me, as the blood fell into the bowl.

When I calmed down a little, I called my cousin Debbie, who worked at the high-risk pregnancy unit of the hospital where Desiray and Candice were born. She tried to tell me that nothing was wrong, but that I should come in for a pelvic examination.

"I am having a miscarriage, aren't I? Don't lie to me, please."

"I can't tell if that is the case over the phone. You need to come in. Don't worry. Spotting during pregnancy is normal."

"This is not spotting, these are clots."

"Just come to the hospital and let's check it out."

I cleaned myself up as best I could, and drove towards the hospital. On the way, I called Vidal. I did not want to call him, because I absolutely felt like the miscarriage was my fault. I was such a hothead (still am) and was always looking for a fight with him (still am), and now it had cost me our pregnancy. He didn't have to say a word, though—I knew immediately that he understood how I felt. We both stayed silently on the phone until I arrived at the hospital. Too many unnecessary and hurtful words had been expressed that morning. Any more words, even pleasant ones, wouldn't help much.

I waited in the entrance for Vidal to arrive. I didn't want to go up to the unit until he was there. I knew that he would need me during this experience as much as I needed him. We had both been looking forward to growing our family. There was a five-year gap between Desiray and Candice, and we'd wanted our next child to be closer in age.

It did not take long to confirm what I already knew. The obstetrician gave me a couple of options. I could either be checked in to have a D&C to complete the miscarriage, or go home and take a drug called misoprostol that would allow me to pass the remaining tissue. The mere thought of a D&C awakened the old ghosts, so I opted for the drug.

When we got home, I used the medication as instructed and waited. What happened next felt worse than childbirth. The pain of the contractions caused me to contemplate suicide for the first time in my life. I was a wreck. We were a wreck. There was no consoling me and the physical and emotional toll was unbearable. I was not sure which hurt more, the contractions or the heartache.

I miscarried for the second time only a year later. During the second one, I faced my fears and opted for the D&C. Physically, I handled it much better. Emotionally? Not so much.

I felt terrible for months after each miscarriage. The medical staff told me that they were not my fault, and that there was nothing I could have done to prevent them from happening. But their reassurances did not matter to me. I was certain that my temper had something to do with them, or that I was being punished for past mistakes.

While I was still in the grip of despair after the second one, I ran into a friend who asked why she had not seen me for a while. I had not talked about what I was going through with anyone, but found myself telling her not only what had happened but how sad and guilty I was feeling.

"I felt that way after my miscarriage, too. You know it is not your fault, right?" she said.

I felt a weight lift off my shoulders. "Really? You had a miscarriage? When? Where?" I reached to touch her leg as if I was about to examine her southern region. I am not sure what I was thinking! I was just so relieved to share the experience with someone who had been through it before herself and could empathize. Of all the people who spoke to me about the miscarriages and told me how I should be feeling, she was the only one who admitted to going through the experience herself.

That one story gave me what I needed to no longer feel alone and ashamed. Stories are sticky, which is why we need to tell them. True, sharing our experiences helps others feel like they are not alone in a given circumstance. But I also believe that the vulnerability we show in telling our stories gives other people hope. It was in that moment that I realized the power of using our most vulnerable moments to build strength and resilience in other people, as well as ourselves. To empower others and create the sense of humanity that is so often lacking in our society because we are too busy trying to show off to our neighbours instead of trying to show up for them.

When Johnny was born in 2008, our family was complete. Unlike most mothers I've talked to, I do not think that the best days of my life were the days my children came into the world. The pain, the sadness, the losses, the morning sickness, the horrible labours: they always say that mothers forget all about them. I haven't forgotten any of it.

But my children are my touchstones, my energy source—they drive my determination and willingness to do whatever it takes to be successful. My greatest honour and joy is being a mother to these extraordinary children; the Lord knows that I need them as much as they need me. They kept me pushing forward and striving for better then, and they still do. I did not want them see me the way I often saw myself, as a failure and a fraud. I wanted to be the strong Black woman that they could model themselves on and be proud to call Mom.

Just as I'd vowed as a teenager, corporal punishment is not part of our home—I had received enough beatings to last my own and a hundred more lifetimes. And after they were born, I added one more vow: I would keep nothing from them. I was going to tell them everything. They were not going to be surprised by anything life dished out or ever wonder why their mother had kept an important insight from them.

And when I say everything, I mean everything. Whereas Vidal always stuck to the script about the birds and the bees, I gave the children all the gritty details. For instance, while taking a drive one spring a couple years ago, I overheard Desiray whispering to Candice.

"What are you saying about tampons?" I asked.

I had a captive audience in the car, so it pleased me to enunciate every letter in the word "tampons" to the point where it sounded like I was speaking in slow motion. Vidal gripped the steering wheel harder and I could see Johnny perk up in the rear seat. He loved these awkward conversations. Desiray shot Candice a look—they knew what was coming.

I reiterated for them that my mother gave me the basics, but she certainly never taught me how to use tampons. I used one for the first time late in my teenage years, I said, and my cousin Vanessa had to teach me how.

Well, to be clear, she did not actually "teach" me anything. I had gotten my period while visiting family in New York, and had asked her if she had any pads. She went away and came back holding a stick wrapped in paper. "Here," she said, handing the thing to me.

She knew very well that I had no idea what it was, but I didn't give her the satisfaction of asking any questions. Vanessa was loud and larger than life. She would have laughed uproariously while telling the entire household and everyone on all of East 82nd Street, where she lived, that her dumb Canadian cousin did not know what a tampon was.

I had already started to stain my underwear and I needed to fix the situation before it got worse. In the bathroom I opened the package and looked at the strange device. What was I supposed to do with this? I cringed at the thought of touching myself down there, but I found the right location and pushed the device in. I think I bruised most of my insides trying to complete the task and I walked around for the rest of the day as if I had ridden a horse.

At this point, one of my girls interrupted. "We can learn this on Google or YouTube. We don't need the whole lesson."

Learn from Google or YouTube? Hardly! I was their internet and encyclopaedia, and was not deterred by the comment from the back seat. I pressed on, explaining how to insert the tampon by holding on to the ribbed portion of the head, inserting it fully and then (and only then) placing your other hand on the stick and pushing upward.

Candice squealed, "OMG, Lady! That sounds like it hurts!" (Candice always calls me Lady.)

I pressed on to explain that one should purchase tampons with the pearled rounded top. But even those can pinch a little, so it might be necessary to rub the top portion of the tampon on your clitoris to help provide some extra lubrication in your vagina.

At that Vidal swerved the vehicle. Everyone but Johnny, who seemed pleased with the educational content, was screaming! "Babe!" (from Vidal), "Mom!" (from Desiray), "TMI, Lady!" (from Candice).

Since when did such practical advice equal too much information? I knew that one day, the little vice grips on the top of a tampon would catch their delicate flesh and I wanted them to be able to avoid that pain.

"Johnny certainly does not need to hear any more of this," Vidal warned.

"Why?" I demanded, "What if he has daughters? We have had discussions about his balls dropping and he told all of us about the length of the hair on his scrotum." A few weeks before this particular conversation, Johnny had announced that he had found three-centimetre hairs growing on his self-named "sack of toys." We investigated, and found no such hairs. At the dinner table that night, Johnny explained that his three-centimetre announcement was a "hyperbowl."

I looked at Desiray and Desiray looked at me. A hyperbowl? During those split seconds I tried to remember if the term described any part of the male genitalia. Johnny is a gifted child, so most of what he says makes me question my own intelligence. He often speaks about issues I have never heard of.

"Do you mean hyperbole—hy-pur-bow-lee?" Desiray finally blurted. The girls have no patience for Johnny's gifted brain and both of them welcome any opportunity to bring him down a few pegs. Everyone burst out laughing. A three-centimetre hyperbole was something we could all understand.

In addition to talking openly with my children about any subject, I was also the mother who followed the recommendations of all the reports that said that we, in the Black community in particular, need to show up and be present for our children at school. Vidal or I or both of us went to every parent-teacher meeting, school event and concert, volunteered for trips and the occasional drop-in to the classroom.

Even though the teachers, administration and support staff knew who we were because of all the showing up we did, our children still faced barriers in the system. I cannot imagine what it is like for children who do not have a parent present to defend them or advocate on their behalf. Sometimes, when I went into the school office and saw other Black children there, I would ask them why they were in the office. If they were in trouble, I would pretend that I knew their parents and say (loud enough for the administration to hear me) that I was going to call their mothers later and let them know I saw them in the office. The children usually looked at me as if I was crazy. I didn't care. The point was to make sure that everyone in authority at the school knew a parent was paying attention to what was going on. If it takes a village to raise a child, sometimes the village simply needs to show up unannounced.

Rarely were my children in the office without us knowing about it. In our house, the rule was, "Tell us the whole truth immediately and there will be no consequences. If we hear the story from someone else, there will be consequences." Our children would come home and tell us everything, even if it was inappropriate and/or had nothing to do with them. Once Desiray was on a school trip and called me to say that she had been pulled aside by a teacher who wanted to talk to her about entering a restricted area. She told me that she had not entered the area herself, but had seen one of the other girls doing it and told the teacher. "So why did the teacher pull you aside?" I asked. Desiray explained that the other girl had implicated her in the situation. When Desiray got home, I asked her twice if there was anything she wanted to add or change about her story, but she reassured me that she was telling the truth.

"Get your shoes on," I told her.

"Where are we going, Mom?" I shot her the look that all Black parents give when their children are told to do something and they talk back.

She put her shoes on and followed me out the door. I made a right turn, then a left and stopped in front of a familiar house.

"Mom! What are you doing?" Desiray was in full panic.

"I am going to ask this young lady why she did not tell the teacher that you were not in the area. That's all." I tilted my head at her, smiled and rang the doorbell. When the young woman's father answered the door, I greeted him with the necessary pleasantries, then proceeded to tell him the story. When I was done, I asked if I could talk to his daughter so she could explain why she lied to the teacher about Desiray.

He looked at me in shock, then said his daughter was tired after the trip and had fallen asleep. However, when she woke up, he would come over to discuss what happened. I wanted to say, "Wake her ass up," but agreed to the terms.

On that doorstep, Desiray had gone from Black to pale white. On the walk back home she was a grey colour. "Seriously, Mom. Why did you do that?"

Silence.

By the time we got home, she was a post-mortem green. "Mom! Why are you doing this?" Even after the girl and her father had come over and the girl apologized for trying to get Desiray in trouble, my smart daughter still didn't know why I had behaved the way I had, and asked, again, "Mom! Why did you do that?"

I took a breath to calm myself; to her it probably looked like I had blown a minor incident way out of proportion, but I didn't see it that way and I still don't. "Desiray," I said, "one day you will have a daughter, or a son, and you will want them to know what I want you to know now. I have your back. Even when you think you do not need me, I will be there for you. I will protect you. It was important for the truth to come out and it was important that your name was completely cleared. I did not want this incident to be on your record or to prevent you from achieving your goals." I hugged her then, extra tight. As usual, I wanted to cry. I'd seen myself in the girl who had just left my house, who had been trying to protect her own image so she didn't disappoint her parents. I also saw myself in Desiray and worried about her. She was on track to be the class valedictorian, and was working hard for the honour, yet she was oblivious to the fact that if the situation hadn't been cleared up, it might have derailed her. At that moment, I was transported back to my high-school graduation, where I did not receive any academic awards despite having been on the honour roll for four years and getting accepted to all the universities I'd applied to. Instead, other students, who were way less qualified, received award after award. I was angry at the time, but it didn't occur to me that I was being overlooked because of my identity, even after all my reading and protesting against police violence and inequality. I knew better now. I had taught Desiray that, like most Black girls in school, she needed to be twice as good and twice as smart. Now I had to teach her to be strategic and look twenty steps ahead of herself too.

When Candice found herself in similar situations, I responded just as protectively, though with my second daughter, it was usually the teachers giving her a hard time, not the other kids. Take a minute to imagine Candice, a tiny girl with glasses—the sweetest little thing you have ever seen. In kindergarten, she was reading at a fourth-grade level. At one point, she was fascinated with the solar system. As my little five-year-old was exiting the library with a book on Saturn, the school librarian stopped her and asked her why she was taking out such a book. Candice told the woman, quite proudly, that she could read and explained that she was studying the solar system by reading books about each planet, one by one, in order of their relationship to the sun. The librarian proceeded to remove the book from Candice's hands, saying, "I am sure you can read, but not that well." Candice was crushed. When she came home and told me what had happened, I confronted the librarian, who denied it. That didn't wash with me and I told the woman so. I always believed my child.

By the time Johnny got to kindergarten, I was more than fed up with the school. And soon he was too. In second grade he came home day after day frustrated with his teacher. One time he complained, "She is not letting me do my presentation on the difference between DNA and RNA. She said the class is not there yet." Why wouldn't she just let him do the presentation? Whether the other kids got it or not, he was not teaching them anything dangerous, just a simple introduction to genetics.

We decided to get him tested to see if he was "gifted." The tests confirmed what we already knew, that Johnny was an extremely smart boy. To his delight, he was able to transfer schools to enrol in a gifted program, where he excelled in math and science.

However, he also soon learned that he was not the Black boy everyone assumed him to be. When someone asked, as they almost always did, what sports he liked, he would respond that he didn't like sports. He was interested in math and science and was a competitive dancer in ballet, jazz and contemporary. He understood why they were almost always surprised by his answer and he spoke to us often about how it felt not to conform to the standard image of what a Black boy was like. He wore his sneakers with pink laces, because he believed that there should be no such thing as boy and girl colours. At ten, he was invited to join the #aboycantoo photo series campaign that dispelled gender stereotypes about boys, and was an invited speaker on the subject at the Vanier Institute's Families in Canada Conference.

Yet even with all of Johnny's strength of mind and smarts, and his resisting all the stereotypes, Vidal and I still made sure to teach him what a Black boy needs to know when dealing with authority and, more particularly, when dealing with police. We continuously reinforce the fact that during those first few seconds or minutes of an interaction with police, nobody will care that Johnny is a gifted boy or that his mother was a member of Parliament or that his father is a civilian who works with the local police services. They will just see a Black boy, who they will often perceive as bigger than he is, and more threatening, guilty or criminal. We taught our children about the criminalization of Black bodies in a way that a child should never have to understand, but needs to understand in order to survive an interaction with the police or with racists—physically, mentally and emotionally. I hate these conversations, because they rob them of the innocence that is necessary for children to be children and teleport him into the space of adulthood. A necessary evil in a world of growing populism, racism and the continuing destruction of Black bodies.

Such difficult conversations are hard to have because they expose a piece of me that I would much rather hide, forget or ignore. I never want my children to know the sting of racism, but racism exists. I cannot ignore it and leave them open to being blindsided by its ever-reaching tentacles.

When Desiray was in grade school her teacher asked the class to write the questions for a mock interview with a celebrity and then research the answers. My daughter chose to do this project on me. When the teacher dismissed the idea, telling her that her mother was not a celebrity, Desiray went over to the classroom computer, opened up Google and typed in my name. Hundreds of entries came up related to my business awards, speeches and research. She pointed to the 2007 Black Business and Professional Association's Harry Jerome Award in the "Young Entrepreneur of the Year" category, and then to my role as speaker and session chair at the Drug Information Association's annual conference, one of the biggest pharmaceutical industry events in the world. "Is this celebrity enough for you?" she asked. Her teacher shrugged, gave the thumbs up and Desiray was on her way.

But she annoyed me with her first question: How did I create work/life balance?

"First of all," I said, "I do not think you would ask your father that question, so why are you asking me? Is it because I am a woman? In any event, I'll give you an honest response. When you create a balance, how much does each side get?"

I held my palms up like scales, for dramatic effect.

Desiray responded that both sides get 50 percent each.

"Exactly!" I said. "Fifty percent on each side. Would you like me to give you only 50 percent of my attention when I am with you?"

She shook her head. No, definitely not.

"Right! When I am with you, you want 100 percent of me. So, I put my phone away and we have dinner as a family, we do homework, watch movies and go out together. Most of the time, I make a conscious effort to not have my phone out or do any work. When I am with our family, I want to give us 100 percent. Similarly, when I am at work, I need to give my clients all my attention. That is why I cannot have you calling me when I'm working. My clients are paying me good money to do a job, and they need to know that they have my undivided attention. At work I do not think of you, your sister or your brother. I know that you are at school or being taken care of."

My mind drifted as I recalled scolding Johnny for calling me after school to ask where the bread was. I needed to be emphatic and make sure that what I said stuck with him. "Only call me if something is severed from your body. Okay?"

"What is 'severed,' Mommy?"

"'Severed' means that your arm or leg or another part of you is now on the floor and there is blood everywhere. Only call me if that happens. If not, talk to Ms. Michelle." Michelle was our nanny—a lifesaver—whom we hired when the business started to take off. Johnny looked afraid, but appreciated the gory example.

"So, Desiray," I said. "There is no such thing as work/life balance. There is work and there is life and there are the priorities you place on each. When I am with you, you are my priority. When I am at work, my clients are my priority. Balance would be unfair."

I was expressing the guiding principle I was trying to live by, but was it the truth? I did think that work/life balance for women is a ridiculous, unattainable idea, but if I was honest, I had to admit that the amount of attention I was putting towards my clients was increasingly disproportionate in their favour and not my family's. Before I started ReSolve and in the early years of building the company, Vidal and the kids and I spent a lot of time travelling during the summers and holidays. We scraped together whatever cash we had, and sometimes even blew the rent money, to make sure we had a nice vacation. Some of my favourite moments of giving 100 percent to family came on vacations. Life experiences were so important to us that my children got their passports right after they received their birth certificates.

Travelling was our passion. We started a tradition of not purchasing Christmas gifts, but instead using what we might have spent to donate to another family. Our gift to each other was to travel together to amazing destinations. Europe, the Caribbean, Costa Rica. The warmer, the better. When work took me somewhere new, I'd bring the whole family too.

Vidal and I rarely travelled without the kids, but one of my favourite trips was just the two of us, to a less than exotic location—New Jersey. In December 2010 we flew there to see my favourite artist of all time, Prince, in the opening show of his Welcome 2 America tour. When Vidal decided that he would buy $36 tickets in the nosebleeds, I made him return them and put out the cash to buy VIP tickets.

The move worked. Midway through the concert, Prince called all the "sexy people" on stage, so I jumped over the barrier separating the VIP section from the more expensive "Purple Circle" seats and headed straight for him. Standing in front of my idol as he strummed his guitar, I told him how much I loved his music and how I had waited my whole life to meet him. As I reached out to touch him, the woman playing tambourine in his band looked at me like, "Honey, don't be stupid." I quickly retreated, even as Prince gave me a slight, seductive smile. At that moment I realized that I had abandoned Vidal without telling him where I was going and I ran along the edge of the stage, waving my arms so he could spot me. A woman named Michelle from Dallas (we are Facebook friends to this day), who was sitting next to him, tapped Vidal on the shoulder and said, "Isn't that your wife?" To Vidal's shock, there I was— his crazy wife on stage dancing in the purple rain!

Vidal ended up buying us premium "Purple Circle" tickets for the tour's stop at the Air Canada Centre in Toronto. As we drove towards the city for the show, I told Vidal that this time I was going to shake Prince's hand. For sure. He looked at me sideways. I said if anything untoward happened I would run really fast and meet up with him at the intersection of Front and Bay, a block from the venue. Hey! Let's Go Crazy, right?

We took our Purple Circle seats right beside the stage, and as he'd done at the New Jersey show, partway through the night Prince called all the sexy people to the stage. I bolted. Ran straight towards the little man, calling, "Hey, Prince. Do you remember me? I saw you in New Jersey!"

This time the tambourine lady looked at me with pity, no doubt thinking, "Chile, please! This little man doesn't remember yo ass." But I didn't care. I reached out a hand for him to take. Now he was the one looking at me, no doubt thinking, "Lady, please, I don't know where your hands have been." I looked deeper into his eyes, extended my hand farther and said, "Please, Prince, please."

Well, my idol took pity on me and shook my hand. I got an instant massive headache. I screamed, jumped back from him and started shimmying across the stage. The moment was epic. I could not ask for anything more.

Vidal and I would laugh about that moment for years, but we both knew that moments of joy between us were happening less and less.

I loved him a lot, but I admired him even more. I often say that while I have three children, Vidal has hundreds. Every one of his students loved him, and especially the Black kids. He would be there for them at recitals, athletic competitions or their first gig as a DJ. He would show up for them when they were in trouble. He would go with them to court. He was involved with their parents and would often act as a liaison between the school administration and a Black parent not sure how to navigate the system. He spent countless hours tutoring, mentoring and trying to raise a generation of children to take pride in who they are and the rich history they come from.

In the summers, Vidal would organize leadership camps for youth, lining up sponsors so parents would not have to pay too much. In 2006, he organized the Black Family Summit in Toronto, to get the community politically engaged and looking for solutions to some of the problems that plagued us. In 2010 he outlined some of his thoughts about those problems in a book he called *Detox*. Many of these initiatives came out of Vidal's heartfelt response to what people called Toronto's "Bloody Sunday"—October 27, 2002—when four young Black men were killed in separate incidents before the sun came up. This work was a natural extension of the way he advocated for Black students. Ultimately, Vidal decided to pursue a doctorate in higher education leadership, focusing his thesis on the factors that influenced Black students who chose to go to university. He wanted to see more students succeed. He was all in when it came to helping the Black community.

Then there was me. Although I helped Vidal with the organization and promotion of the events he was interested in, I was not that involved. I helped through donation. I also insisted that we donate to programs that assisted students, like the Imani Academic Mentorship Program at the University of Toronto. We made additional donations to the Aroni Awards and to support Congress of Black Women scholarships and to the Royal Ontario Museum.

ReSolve Research Solutions was doing well. While nobody knew who I was when the contracts were signed, I wanted to ensure that people knew who I was when thousands of dollars in donations were being made. Call it ego, I could not care less. I was building a brand, and philanthropy helps in that effort. But more importantly, I wanted people to see a Black couple making investments in our community and in organizations outside of the traditional spheres. I wanted people to see a married Black couple show up at events and galas and know that we were more than stereotypes. We were lovers, and contributors, and an important demographic in our society.

Except we weren't really such great lovers anymore. The truth was that there were a couple of things in my life I really needed to prioritize but didn't—my marriage and myself. I was running too hard. I was cracked and bruised. Some parts were clearly broken and were being held together with duct tape. Other parts had dropped off and were rolling down the road, even as the surface of me was staying nice and composed. I could deal with my children and my business, but the rest of me was taking a hell of a beating. And Vidal was drifting away. Even brilliant gestures, like gifting me with

Prince tickets, weren't enough, and if I'm honest, he was the only one making them.

I'd been engaged in contract work for Parkinson Society Canada off and on for a number of years, and in the summer of 2011 they asked if I would consult on a national epidemiology study related to neurological conditions, which the society was leading in partnership with several other organizations under the umbrella of a national group called Neurological Health Charities Canada (NHCC). I would work alongside the NHCC's director, Shannon Pugh-MacDonald, to study the impact of various diseases, their scope throughout Canada, risk factors and the health services available to people living with neurological conditions like Alzheimer's, Parkinson's, MS, ALS and epilepsy.

Over the months of working together, we had gotten close. Shannon is a tall, blonde, stunning woman. When she walked into a room, you noticed her. I am an average height, gorgeous, chocolate woman. When I walk into a room, people notice me. Together, we were invincible, and we worked together seamlessly and effortlessly. It felt like there was nothing we could not accomplish.

Soon it felt natural for us to tell each other secrets most people would keep to themselves. It was as if I could suspend the Black girl code, where we talk only with each other about things like our hair (or purchasing our hair), our attitude or mood, love life and family life. When it came to Shannon, she understood me, and I understood her.

When Shannon left to join another organization that October, she asked me to take over for her and I was named the co-chair of Canada's first national epidemiology study of neurological conditions. It was the first national research study I had managed, and the work was exhilarating. I was meeting new people, flying across the country, and building on my successes.

At the same time, however, I finally really noticed something strange going on with Vidal. When I asked him what was the matter, he would usually say nothing or brush me off. At one point I remember asking him if he was still passionate about me. (Remember my newlywed rules?) He was, he said, but not like he used to be. As it turned out, if I was honest, I felt the same way. For months we kept on growing further and further apart. Communicating less, rarely being intimate. Vidal finally moved into the basement, which he made into the perfect man cave. With that move, it was as if he left me, and it didn't me take long after this to meet someone and have an affair.

I felt horrible. But I told myself the attention I was getting made up for Vidal's lack of passion. By June 2012, I'd had enough. I could not continue with the affair and I could not stand that Vidal and I were falling apart. I packed a bag and left for a downtown Toronto hotel with the intention of making the separation permanent.

Did I really want to leave Vidal? Of course not. Being actually alone would be more painful than being with someone who made you feel alone. I decided to call Shannon. We met in the lobby of the hotel, which was just minutes from her home. When I finished telling her what was going on, she said, "Give your head a shake. Vidal needs to own his mistakes in the marriage, but you need to own yours too. You are constantly trying to make Vidal take centre stage with you in your world. From what I have seen, he doesn't want that. He doesn't mind supporting you and loving you from behind the scenes. You do your thing and take your hand off his wheel. Let him drive his own life and you drive yours. He just wants you. And you want him."

Her voice softened. "And I know you want to go home." She hugged me then, and said goodbye. I knew what Shannon was saying was right. I had been ignoring Vidal, and when I wasn't ignoring him, I was pushing him away, not deliberately, but doing it all the same. We had loved each other so much, though, wasn't it worth fighting to try to get that love back? Falling in love is easy. The hard part is the landing. You fall fast and hard through a distance that is uncertain. And then you land. Vidal and I were at that landing. But, instead of holding onto each other as we braced for impact, we'd let each other go.

Long gone were the children, sitting in a restaurant, playing in an adult world; we were adults with children who needed us both. So, after several days, I went home, and talked to Vidal, and he and I put a plan in place, the first requirement of which was a commitment to stay together. And while some may ask why we would do that, I ask, why not? Vidal and I were good together, but we had lost our way and we needed to give each other a chance to forgive ourselves and each other. It had nothing to do with the children, or our families. It was just about us. A marriage does not break down by itself and it needed both of us to be accountable, to figure out how we got here, how each of us contributed to the mess we were in.

The second step, we decided, was to go away on vacation; sometimes running away from reality is better than staying and fighting with each other in it. We flew to the Caribbean and rented a hotel with two adjoining rooms, one for the children and one for us. A separate bedroom would give us enough privacy to reconnect and be intimate, while having the children on the trip with us protected us from fighting like a couple of crazy people.

Admittedly, I'd been missing Vidal. So those few days of intense love on our vacation turned out to be easy. The hard part began when we returned home and started counselling. Telling our secrets to each other in front of the counsellor was sobering. I felt ashamed, but I was determined to tell Vidal everything. I dug into my past and told him stories I had buried, many of which are not contained in these pages. He dug deep, too, revealing his own fears and wounds. When he found he could not talk about something in counselling, he wrote to me instead.

As we did the homework required to build our relationship again, I finally understood how big a role unresolved issues from my past were playing in our present. I had been pushing Vidal away exactly because I was worried he would leave me, and wanted to feel like I was in control of things.

The magic was that after several counselling sessions, working hard on our lessons and completing the homework assignments, Vidal and I stopped trying to fall in love again and we started just being in love. Somehow we had managed to plant a seed of a healthy relationship that we would nurture together, growing in sync rather than growing apart. We needed to take care of each other and we committed to not hurting each other any more. If this sounds like it was simple, it was not.

eight

GET OFF THE DAMN BUS AND OUT OF YOUR OWN WAY

AS I REFLECTED ON THE events that led me to this point in my life—the work, the kids, the ups and downs of marriage—I imagined myself on a bus. Not a school bus, but the kind with the comfy, reclining seats and the washroom in the back. Everything I needed in life was with me, familiar and comfortable. I was fed, clothed, and the temperature was perfect. I had no need to leave my seat, let alone get off the bus. The windows were tinted so the sun didn't glare in on me and the hiss of the tires on the road was soothing.

I imagined myself wriggling my butt, rotating my shoulders and neck, adjusting my position as I sat back and contemplated life. The ride had mostly been good so far. Some bumps along the way, but mostly good. Right? Wrong. My company was a growing success, but I was stuck in a rut and had been stuck for a while.

The breakdown of my marriage, as painful as it was, showed me it was time to stop pretending that my life was the way I wanted it to be. I imagined myself anxiously walking to the front of the bus. As I cautiously stepped down and onto the shoulder, eyes adjusting to the brightness outside, I noticed a few things. The most obvious? The windows of my bus were not tinted, they were grimed over with detritus from my past. All the lies, the grief and mistakes I thought I'd moved on from were still hanging on like old baggage. I needed to clean that bus. But it was impossible to do that all by myself. There was too much stuff. Counselling had helped me see that I had survived the difficult stuff in my life. Now it was time to tackle the hurts one by one, release the pain, and strip away the barriers to my future.

When I saw it clearly, the whole bus was in rough shape. It needed a complete engine overhaul. The sound I thought was road hiss was the air leaving the tires. All of them were flat and looked like they had been that way for a while. All this time, all this effort, and I hadn't even been moving. Worse, there were other buses passing me by—opportunities I'd been ignoring while I was stuck in my rut of pride and pain, hanging on to my dirty baggage. I had been so comfortable on my dilapidated bus, sitting idly, thinking that I was moving along. I was not living with passion or purpose. I was existing to land the next client, collect the next cheque and go on another family vacation that I did not enjoy because I remained so plugged into work. I needed help not only to deal with my past, but to figure out how to be more present, stop merely existing and start living my life.

This exact point was driven home one day by Shannon, who out of the blue asked me what I did for fun. She probably knew I had no answer—I didn't do anything for fun. I told her I had a business to grow. It certainly was not going to grow itself.

Shannon understood where I was coming from, but said that if I did not have time for fun, I should at least try to create wider circles of influence, get to know people outside of the research space and put my skills to use in other areas. I'd learn stuff that would be useful to me and I'd meet more people who would inspire me. She then handed me a copy of the University of Toronto alumni magazine and pointed to an ad calling for people to apply to become members of the university's Governing Council. I blinked at her. She was one of the few people I'd told that I graduated from U of T with a 1.58 cumulative GPA. Did she not remember? The A on my research course looked like an outlier. Surely the Governing Council was reserved for professors or people who had achieved great success. That was not me.

Shannon took one look at my expression and said, "I bet they will take you."

With many reservations, I decided to take the bet. This was Shannon telling me, after all, and so far she'd always been right. I asked her to write me a reference letter and submitted my application.

I got an interview!

When I walked in, I found that I would be talking with fifty existing members of the council in the same room where I'd written one of my disastrous undergrad exams. My anxiety went into overdrive; maybe they only called me in because they had studied my transcripts and wanted to taunt me. I was embarrassed and uncertain, but took my place and proceeded to respond to question after question under the steady gaze of a hundred eyeballs.

An older gentleman sitting on the left side of the room asked the final question. He wore a tweed jacket and looked as if he smoked cigars, or possibly a pipe. As soon as he opened his mouth, I felt my throat knot.

"When you look back over your life, do you have any regrets?" he asked.

I was perplexed. What kind of question was that? This dude had clearly read my transcript.

When I opened my mouth to respond, the knot in my throat tightened and my eyes started to water. When I say I am a crier, I really mean it. There is nothing easier for me to do. I cry at everything. I do not care who sees me doing it. I just cry. However, this time I wasn't shedding tears because I was sad or embarrassed. I was crying because for the first time in my life I was able to speak the truth about how I felt about the mistakes I had made.

"No," I said as tears trickled down my face. It was so powerful. I was the owner of my mistakes, and I was telling the room that the mistakes didn't own me. The tears turned from trickles to full-blown streams. Speaking the truth in the same room in which I'd had my ass kicked in an exam was almost exhilarating.

I flashed back to taking amphetamines the night before I'd been here the last time. Every time I faced an exam, I promised myself that this would be the last time I'd resort to drugs. Then I would swallow my pills at about nine in the evening and fall asleep. A few hours later, I would wake up to the thundering beat of my own heart, which felt like it would burst from my chest. I would retrieve my textbook and try to consume all the information it contained. I was always able to cram enough to pass, but never enough to do well.

"No," I said again, shaking my head for emphasis, "I do not regret anything I have done in my life."

When I paused, a woman asked me if I would like to take a break. I shook my head again. "Everything I have done in my life has brought me here," I said. "Every mistake, every success, every failure, has brought me to this point. I think I am doing okay, so no, I have no regrets."

I got up, thanked them all and walked out of the room, down the stairs and out the door, crying every step of the way.

When I got in my car, I called Vidal and told him what had happened.

"You cried?" he said at one point. "But wait, you seriously cried?"

I could tell that he was trying not to laugh. He was right. It was really a moment. There was no way that a crying woman was going to become a governor at the University of Toronto. The university had no time for such foolishness.

Late that night, the phone rang. The woman on the other end told me that I was being invited to sit as an alumni member of the Governing Council. I asked her if she was joking, and she insisted that she was not. Still, Vidal and I couldn't help but laugh. Congratulations, Madame Governor, and welcome back to the University of Toronto.

Does any of this sound familiar? There you sit, thinking you are perfectly happy in a situation that seems comfortable. But some part of you knows it's not right for you. Afraid to try something new, you stay put, knowing full well that if you're not moving, you're not growing.

Shannon gave me the kick I needed to fix my bus. It was not good enough to sit back—I needed to be driving. I needed to pay attention when I was running out of gas or when something was about to break, and learn how to ask for help to fix me. Just as I had finally been delegating responsibilities at ReSolve Research, I needed to delegate some of my issues to others and accept that it was okay to let someone else come up with answers that I clearly did not have.

Branching out into other areas of life is as necessary as it is unnerving. Conversing with a new group of people, asking questions and sharing your own story and experiences, enriches not only yourself, but others around you as well. As far as I'm concerned, there was no getting away from occasional flare-ups of the imposter syndrome that tell you that you don't belong in these new places you're exploring. If you venture out of your comfort zone, sometimes you will be the only one who looks like you. The only woman, the only person of colour, the only one with a disability, the only one of a different sexual orientation or the only one wearing religious symbols. It can be scary and lonely, but the world needs us to show up and build relationships.

After the Governing Council, I continued to climb onto other buses. I joined an advisory board at the Canadian Institutes of Health Research—the Institute of Neurosciences, Mental Health and Addiction—at the encouragement of Joyce Gordon, who was then the CEO of Parkinson Society Canada. I also applied for, and won, the Toronto Board of Trade Entrepreneur of the Year Award in 2012. I was urged to go for it by Jenny Gumbs, the past consul general of Grenada in Toronto. I found that saying the first "yes" was often the hardest part. Learning and growing from the experience was the easiest.

I love this quote from Anaïs Nin: "And the day came when the risk to remain tight in a bud was more painful than the risk it took to blossom." You need to gather up your courage in order to get out of your head and out of your own way. It is the only way that you can blossom into your true self. Even so, you need the right conditions to ensure that the delicate petals open fully. And the process doesn't stop with your own flowering. It is important to teach others what you have learned. To reach back as you climb up. Plant other seeds and nurture them too.

On my best days, my past no longer owned me, but it was a critical part of how I'd come to understand my world. I'd had all of these experiences for a reason, and it was time to put the lessons to good use. The first opportunity to do so came when I was asked by the University of Toronto to adjudicate the John H. Moss Scholarship, a competition for students with strong academics and outstanding extracurricular achievements. During the 2013 competition, I received a package with the required documents from each of the student applicants. All of them were impressive, but one, from Samra Zafar, stood out to me. A young Muslim woman, she had had a troubled life and was the victim of a forced marriage and abuse. Now, she wanted something better for herself and her daughters. Her story resonated with me.

The committee members spent the evening of the adjudication interviewing the students. By the end of the night, we agreed that Samra and another student were our top contenders for finalist. Both were equally qualified and could represent the university and the integrity of the award easily, but I felt that Samra's story was so compelling I had to fight for her. She needed someone to be her Carol Greenwood or Don Stuss. While I was waiting for the final discussion, I reread the history of the scholarship and why it was established in 1920: "During the years of the War, no one strove more earnestly or unselfishly than Jack Moss for the success of the cause dear to us all. After the close of active hostilities, he took up with vigour and enthusiasm the equally important task of repairing the ravages of war and securing the fruits of a lasting peace . . . helping our soldier students to regain their place in civil life."

When I made my final plea, I argued that Samra was a true contemporary representation of what the award was meant to do. She took all the pain and hurt in her life, and through her charity work she made a better life for herself, her daughters, and her community. My pleas worked. The committee picked Samra as the 2013 John H. Moss Scholarship award winner. I was so overjoyed, it was as if I had won the award. Even better, the Chair of the selection committee asked me to be the one to call Samra to give her the good news. I do not remember my exact words, but when I talked to her, years later, she did. Apparently I said, "You struggled so much, it was time that you got some recognition. You deserve this more than anyone." She said the words, as much as the award, changed her life.

Samra changed my life too. She taught me that the empathy I had gained because of my own past hurts was a powerful tool to make change for others. All I had to do was use them.

—

These years were a confusing blend of big steps and equally big setbacks on the project of becoming myself. The transformation from a bud (keeping myself and my secrets safely furled inside) to a blossom on full display for the world to see, to praise or criticize, is never easy. One of the biggest and most unnerving steps I took was renaming myself. And my beloved Gramsie was the inspiration. After living with us for quite a few years when I was a child, my mother's mother decided to return home to Grenada. I missed her after she was gone; she had witnessed some of my biggest traumas and hardships, and taught me about the sweetness of humility, the power of gentleness and the boundless possibilities available to you when you have faith. A different personality from Mrs. Caesar, she was not shy about sharing her opinions, but she did it with a kind, loyal and loving determination.

In her early nineties, she became ill, and the circulation in her legs grew limited. I decided to bring her back to Canada to ensure that she received the appropriate medical attention. Within days of hearing the news, I was on a plane from Toronto to Puerto Rico, Puerto Rico to Grenada and back, with Gramsie in tow, all in one weekend. She stayed with us for about a year as I accompanied her to medical appointments and to various tests.

A deliberate, devoted, Seventh-day Adventist, she constantly pressured us to convert so that Vidal and I and the children could be "saved." Every time she tried, I always responded by saying, "I think I am good with God, Gramsie." But she was relentless. According to her, finding Jesus was my only hope of making it into heaven. What made her think that I had not already found Jesus? Was it the constant cussing and my love of alcohol? Each Saturday, Vidal drove her all the way from Whitby to the Malton Seventh-day Adventist Church, near Pearson International Airport—an hour-long trip each way. Vidal thought about joining, and even spoke to me about it a couple of times. When we all accompanied Gramsie to special services, he said that he felt the energy of the church fill him. He loved Gramsie and she, in turn, loved him, but she couldn't get him permanently inside the church either.

One Saturday, Gramsie had to forego her usual service so she and I could attend my cousin's wedding. As we were driving from the church to the reception, she once more told me the story of my birth. Her own mother, Celina Wilson, known as Ma SouSou, had died eight days before I was born. Before her death, Ma SouSou had told my mother that she was having a baby girl and asked that she name her daughter after her. My mother agreed to the letter of the request, but not the spirit, listing Celina as my third name on the birth certificate. After we had parked in the lot of the reception hall, Gramsie was slow to get out of the car. Turning to me, she asked if I would consider taking Celina as my first name. I said yes without even a moment's hesitation. And I went the distance, too, not just casually starting to go by Celina, but, in 2013, legally changing my name to Celina Rayonne Caesar-Chavannes. Rayonne is the bud that will always remain a part of me, but taking Celina as my first name signalled that I was ready to flower.

Maybe Ma SouSou knew my mother was stubborn enough not to let anyone else dictate what to call me and trusted that her daughter would give the name to me when I really needed it. My rebirth as Celina (Caelina, in Latin meaning "heaven or sky") Rayonne (from the French verb *rayonner*, meaning "to shine or glow") was the perfect signal of the energy I wished to radiate, the shining self I wished to be.

Gramsie went back to Grenada not longer after that. Her health problems were worsening, and she decided that she did not want the doctors wasting Canadian tax dollars on an old lady like her. There was no persuading her otherwise. Shortly after returning to Grenada,

Gramsie's condition deteriorated to the point where one of her legs had to be amputated. Vidal flew down to see her in her final days, but I chose not to. I wanted to remember her exactly the way I had loved her over the years; I also couldn't bear to see her confined to a wheelchair and in pain. I knew Vidal would be better at that than me: able to encourage her to drink her energy drinks and slip her some sweets if she wanted them.

On her ninety-seventh birthday, August 9, 2016, I called her and told her I loved her. When I hung up, I told Vidal I thought she was going to die later that day, or maybe the next—she loved her birthdays and wouldn't want to ruin one by dying. She died on August 10, 2016. I also chose not to attend her funeral. If I was going to remember Gramsie, I wanted to remember and cherish her as she was in life. I promised myself again that I would remember her lessons, I would live true to her mother's name and I would make Celina epic.

I had my new name, and I had my renewed resolve not to be brought down by my old griefs and trauma. But I have come to realize that no matter all the bold moves you are making to take the wheel, there are times when the universe decides you are no longer in charge.

I had suffered with the blues after Desiray was born, and after each miscarriage, and now I realized that I was slowly going into a darkness I could not explain and seemingly for no reason. I had worked in the area of neuroscience long enough and administered enough depression scales to know that I would fail one.

At church one Sunday morning, I knelt down and asked the Creator why I felt so out of sorts. As I stayed kneeling, my face in my palms and my eyes closed, I saw a vision of the Creator cradling a stranger who looked old and tired. As I drew closer, I realized that the person was me. It was startling. When I asked what was wrong with her (as if it wasn't me), I heard, "She needs to rest." Nothing more. Nothing less. She needs rest.

I was confused. I did not need rest, my mind insisted. I needed to be needed. I needed to "do" something. What that something was, was unclear, but I was sure that I should be doing something more productive than resting. Still I cried for her. That poor, wrecked, vulnerable version of myself. I felt sorry for her, and maybe a little angry too. How could Celina be epic if she was asleep?

As I type these words now, I wish I had loved her more. I wish I had loved her vulnerability, and her need to take time for herself. To rest, knowing that everything would be okay once she took that time to rest. I wish I saw that she needed to remain in the bud a little longer, instead of trying to force her to blossom. The image of this "resting" Celina plagued my thoughts. Who was she? Why did she need rest? What was happening in her life that rest was required? Yes, my marriage had been shaky, but Vidal and I were working on it. My business was doing very well—I could not bear the thought of slowing down. How could I get to the future I planned if I was sleeping?

But the more I resisted that need for rest, the worse my depression got. In retrospect, I should have given the resting Celina a break instead of fighting her. To be honest, I was ashamed of her. How can you be twice as good as everyone else if you are sleeping?

For months the image haunted me. But instead of heeding the warning and taking the time I needed, I would rouse her from her slumber. Each time, she was reluctant. Each time her Creator would say, "She needs to rest." I was not listening. She did not *want* to rest. She did not *wish* to rest. She *needed* to rest. I ignored it all. I was too busy criticizing myself. I wanted to see myself in the spotlight, taking centre stage in my life.

Why can't we see brilliance in our quietness? Why do we think we're less deserving if we stop every now and then to take time for ourselves? If we take off the superhero cape, will the world stop spinning? It would take me a few more years to appreciate that resting and healing is okay. In fact, it's necessary. But at the time, I was too busy forging my way forward to notice.

nine

"BUT YOU HATE POLITICS!"

FOR ME, FORGING FORWARD meant continuously making upwardly mobile moves. When people notice that I have not one, but two, MBAs—the first in business administration related to healthcare management and the second an executive MBA—they often seem impressed. Me? I feel disappointed. Why does anyone need two MBAs?

In my case, as my company was approaching its tenth anniversary and I was worrying about how to make it even more successful, I convinced myself that taking an executive MBA would be worth it, giving me the opportunity to refresh the knowledge I had gained in my first one. As I type these words, I call bullshit. The only reason I thought of an executive MBA program in the first place was because I had dropped out of the online PhD program in business administration at the University of Liverpool that I'd entered in 2012.

Adding the PhD to the other credentials at the end of my name was supposed to give me the extra leverage I needed to take my company to the next level. Those letters mean that you are an authority; as a Black woman in the male-dominated research world, I still felt I needed all the help I could get. When I started the company, I took steps to make sure my early clients did not know I was a Black woman until the contract was signed and we had started working together. Things were different now. I had strategically raised the profile of my company and hiding was no longer an option. I convinced myself that a PhD would make up for my melanin and the fact that I had boobs. Men rarely seem to have this issue of worrying about their legitimacy. We live in a world where a high-school drama teacher can confidently become prime minister and a reality television star can become president. I could not operate in the blind spot that privilege affords, so I tried to stay one step ahead of the pack.

But within days of starting the PhD program I started doubting myself. I blanked on the simplest concepts. I could not remember the difference between a balance sheet and "What was the other one called again?" I even fumbled over my words, and I am a talker. A few weeks in, and a few thousand dollars spent, I gave up and dropped out of the program. The PhD was supposed to help me find clarity and direction, but it left me feeling confused and lost. Again.

However, I couldn't just sit around brooding on that failure. So, in September 2013, I enrolled in the executive MBA program at the Rotman School of Management at the University of Toronto, which offered me the opportunity to take the one-year course on weekends. Unlike the online PhD program, I couldn't hide behind a screen when my brain, paralyzed by fear, wouldn't cough up the answers to simple questions. I was forced to sit in a classroom and to work on teams with peers who knew who I was and where I lived and expected me to study hard with them and tap my own experience to come up with solutions to the business problems we were set.

And that was the bonus: working with other human beings who weren't my employees or my family. At that point in my life, except for Shannon, I didn't really have friends. Since the betrayal/rescue by my best friend in my early twenties, I had cut off opportunities for real friendships. Sure, I had acquaintances; some of you reading this book may have regarded me as a friend. But what did you truly know about me? My past, my dreams, my failures? I am still particular when I use the word "friend" and I do not use it with just anyone.

At Rotman, I met one person who ended up becoming dear to me: Kyle Holmes. I could tell that most of the other people in our class couldn't understand why I gravitated towards him. He was blunt. He didn't have a filter. Once when he was answering a question from a professor, he called a child a "dud," causing waves of shock to ripple around the room. When I introduced myself to him, I said, "You are an asshole, but I like you." He appreciated hearing the truth about himself, as much as I appreciated saying it. I did not have to pretend with Kyle. We could laugh at silly jokes, and I could reprimand him when he took it too far without him feeling offended. In short, I could tell him to fuck right off without sparking the residual fear that my parents would get the memo.

In December of that year, while teaching the politics component of the program, the professor highlighted the pros and cons of political capital in advancing the objectives of business by helping business leaders push for policy reform, funding opportunities and other supports.

Political capital? It had never occurred to me that it was a thing. I did not know anyone in politics. In my youth, I had volunteered with my family on campaigns for Jean Augustine, the first Black female member of Parliament in Canada, who was also from Grenada. We would head to her riding of Etobicoke-Lakeshore and knock on doors to encourage people to go out and vote. But Ms. Augustine had left politics a while back, and even if she had still been in office, I would never have had the nerve to call her up for a business favour.

As an adult, I didn't follow politics for the simple reason that, though I always voted, the existing political establishment in

Canada left me feeling disenfranchised. The little I saw of politics on television made me resent the divisiveness of the party system. The theatre of the House of Commons frustrated me. What I thought should be a space for respectful dialogue, especially during Question Period, always dissolved into an opportunity for politicians to get clips for their websites and social media feeds. That said, I loved working to develop policy. I had seen the impact good policy has on people while working on the national epidemiology study. At the end of the project, I co-authored the final report, *Mapping Connections*, which detailed the research results and was a roadmap for the various ways government could provide caregivers support to continue to look after their loved ones living with neurological conditions. But I'd never put it together in my head that politics led to being in government and being in government meant the ability to enact public policy.

The professor continued to speak, and the more he did, the more intrigued I became. I had been acting as if I was only a spectator in our democracy, as if the only way I could participate was through voting. I had stood on the sidelines not paying much attention when the opportunity to get more involved was mine for the taking. As a naturally competitive individual, soon I was asking the next question: "How do I get some political capital real fast?"

I had no clue where to begin. My daughters were more politically savvy than I was. Candice, who had been named an Earth Rangers Ambassador after she had raised $1,000 for the Oregon spotted frog, was constantly telling me about the changes the government of the day was implementing to weaken our environmental protections. Desiray came home most days from high school talking about her role in the Model United Nations and Mock Parliament clubs. She talked about world leaders as if they were related to her, effortlessly recalling details about their home countries and the challenges they were facing. Vidal was always following the latest political events, not only in Canada but around the world, and particularly on the continent of Africa. I admired how much they knew, and I realized that I needed to get involved in political life somehow.

Throughout my research career I heard many stories of the lengths people had to go to survive after their own or a partner's diagnosis with a particular neurological disorder or disease. Due to the cost of medication, some people had to move out of their home province to get their drugs covered, since medications not paid for under one provincial formulary might be covered elsewhere. Other couples even filed for divorce so it would be easier for their partner to access services. I'd found the stories heartbreaking, and been frustrated by the lack of direct actions I could take. For years I had been gathering research data related to a host of issues and handing it over to a government relations specialist to figure out the policy implications. If I chose to get involved in politics, I could bring those stories, along with the data to support good policy decisions, to Parliament.

I decided to test the idea with the women in my EMBA course. There were nineteen of them, all highly intelligent, accomplished individuals who seemed to fear nothing. At our end-of-year holiday dinner, in the quaint upstairs dining room of a quiet Toronto restaurant, I broached the subject of possibly getting involved in politics. To be honest, I didn't know what I meant when I said "involved." Maybe I would attend some meetings, or political rallies, or find a way to join an association and provide my insights on policy to my local MP. This is not what my peers thought I meant—the room erupted over the idea of me running for office. One woman, who belonged to the NDP, said that she would gladly help with my campaign and donate; a Conservative Party member said that she would provide advice. Others offered to introduce me to friends who knew the ropes.

Until that point, I had not thought about the political affiliations of any of my classmates, or seriously about my own. I had always voted Liberal, out of blind dedication to what my parents described as Pierre Elliott Trudeau's "invitation to come to Canada." I never went so far as to say I was a Liberal. These women were talking to me as if it was a done deal, as if I knew what the heck I was talking about. They not only thought I should run, they thought I could win.

I then spoke to Kyle, who hated politics as much as I did; if he thought it was a bad idea, he wouldn't hesitate to tell me. But Kyle said he was in—if I was going into politics, he would support me all the way. Next came Shannon, who I'd seen beam like it was Christmas morning every time federal or provincial Budget Day arrived. "Oh my goodness, you would be great at it," she yelled, and then, just as emphatically, said, "but you hate politics!"

"I know," I responded, not realizing that I was foreshadowing my own story.

I spent the rest of the 2013 holiday season googling everything I could about the political parties, how to join them and how to be an active participant. Given my voting record, and from the policy positions I could find online, it seemed to me that the Liberals were the closest political fit, and so I joined the federal party in February 2014.

As soon as I paid my ten bucks and clicked on the box to join, the solicitation emails started to arrive. Lots of them. I did not mind because the solicitations gave me insight into upcoming events and party messaging. Since I had no understanding of how to run for office, I thought I would start by spending some months observing what it was all about. However, on March 8, 2014, International Women's Day, the Liberal Party of Canada started a new campaign designed to get more women to run for politics. Everything in my life changed when I received an email with the subject line "Invite Her to Run." The email went on to ask if I knew a woman who was talented, smart, interested in serving her community, and could contribute to the future of Canada as a political leader.

I pointed to myself, and said, "YES! I know the person. ME!" Then I replied to the email. "Hello Justin," I wrote. "I am interested. Sign me up!" (Yes, I was naïve enough to think that such emails actually went to the leader of the Liberal Party, Justin Trudeau.)

The incumbent MP in Whitby was Jim Flaherty, the minister of finance in Stephen Harper's government. He had represented the riding either provincially or federally since 1995 and he had been Canada's finance minister since 2006. I didn't think I had a chance against him, but I thought if I could win the nomination and run a good campaign, I could bring up some really important issues and gain some political capital. If I lost, which I was sure to do—not only did Flaherty seem unassailable, the riding I lived in was mostly white, conservative, and had never elected a Black person—I would be satisfied that I'd given it a shot and could go on with my life, having at least made some new connections.

I looked up the candidacy requirements and started working to fulfill them. I called the head of the riding association to ask for lists of local Liberals so I could begin canvassing for support. That was my first indication that this might be an even harder slog than I thought. Even though nobody else had expressed interest in running and the association hadn't been terribly active during the Conservative years in power, I sensed some resistance to giving me the list. Don't get me wrong—a handful of local Liberals were eager to help me out. But others felt some trepidation. Most people I approached looked at me like I was a lamb being led to the slaughter. Why would anyone want to run against Jim Flaherty? They had a point.

Then, on March 18, 2014, Flaherty resigned as minister of finance. Tragically, on April 10, before he could move back home, he had a heart attack in his Ottawa apartment and died. The news slammed against my brain so hard it made me dizzy. I actually felt guilty because I thought now I might have a shot at winning the riding.

I asked several people what they thought of me continuing to seek the nomination when the situation had changed so drastically, first among them Vidal and his dad. Both of them said, "Someone is going to have to run, Celina. Would you rather that it was some-one without passion, heart and compassion, or would you rather it be you?"

Maybe part of me was looking for an out, since declaring that I would seek the nomination to be the Liberal candidate in the Conservative riding of Whitby had already come at a high personal cost. The national neurological study I was co-chairing was funded to the tune of $15 million by the Harper government—not known to be a generous backer of scientific research. My clients did not want to risk the funding being pulled because of my new partisan affiliation just as we were finalizing the research and asked me to leave the role. Losing this contract was financially devastating. In order to be able to focus on the campaign, I'd also decided I shouldn't take on any new clients. By the time the by-election to fill Flaherty's seat was called, I was already deep into seeking the nomination, and I decided this was no time to let my financial woes stop me.

I pressed forward. When I finally got the list of active members from the association, I visited them one by one to introduce myself and present my case for becoming their elected member of Parliament. I was a political neophyte, perhaps the last person who Liberals so dedicated they'd joined a riding association would vote for. To have a shot at gaining their support, I needed to show them who I was.

One of the more memorable of these visits was to the home of Barb and Wayne, who invited me over early in the morning to sit with them at their kitchen table looking out at their garden, which was just coming into bloom. Barb did her best to make me feel welcome, but Wayne was silent. *This is going to be harder than I thought*, I said to myself. Still, I felt comfortable with them somehow. The expression in Wayne's eyes was kind, and if I was reading him right, he seemed as impressed by my gumption as by my business credentials. Each time I explained my background and experience to the next prospective signatory to my nomination, the more comfortable I felt with my decision to run. After I finished the requirements in my power, I underwent the telephone interview with the Liberal Party of Canada in which my background was probed to make sure I did not have any skeletons in my closet. Even after Flaherty's death, no other person came forward to vie for the chance to run as a Liberal in the by-election, so in June 2014, I was green-lighted to be the federal Liberal candidate for the Town of Whitby.

Although I was acclaimed, there was still a formal nomination meeting and I could not think of a better person to nominate me than Desiray. As she walked to the podium, speech in hand, I was beaming with pride. Friends and family filled the room and Vidal was by my side. I could not believe how many people had shown up. As I got up to speak, I saw the people there who'd signed my nomination papers—Mr. and Mrs. O, and Barb and Wayne. When Mr. O came to the campaign office later to volunteer, I told him that he'd looked so grumpy on nomination night, I'd adapted my entire speech to ensuring he was smiling by the end. He had not been grumpy, he said, he had been a fan from day one! Since the morning I'd sat at Wayne and Barb's breakfast table to make my pitch, I had developed such a great friendship with Wayne that I told him it reminded me of the one between the title characters in the movie

The Intern: he was Robert De Niro and I was Anne Hathaway. We have been calling each other Bob and Anne ever since.

Even though we had to wait for the by-election to be called, from the nomination meeting on, I campaigned non-stop. My Conservative opponent was Pat Perkins. She'd served as the mayor of Whitby for eight years, and before that had been a town councillor for nine. On top of her name recognition, she was campaigning as the heir appar- ent to Jim Flaherty stressing constantly that she would keep Whitby "Conservative blue."

My learning curve was steep, and I often felt at sea in this new world of politics; everything about me was on display and being tested. I did not mind. My campaign manager wanted to ensure that we won. He had me prepped and ready to take any question I received at the door. He looked for endless ways for me to meet constituents at barbecues, community events and church bazaars. But then he challenged my name, arguing that I needed to get rid of one of my last names because it was too long to fit on a sign. "Choose either Caesar or Chavannes, but not both," he said. I was firm. I told him that all the names stay or I do not run. Out of that argument, someone (it may have been him!) came up with the bril- liant idea to use long, skinny, rectangular campaign signs with my first name written vertically, which we ended up calling "Celina sticks." We lined the boulevards with those, while placing the tra- ditional signs, with my first name in big, bold, white letters across the entire width of the placard and my extra long last name in smaller letters underneath, proudly at the intersections and on the lawns of supporters.

We also had help from the top. From the time I was declared the candidate until the election on November 17, 2014, Justin Trudeau came to the riding four times to help rally the vote. Again, because I was new to politics, I thought this was par for the course. But

Trudeau, as the Liberals' new leader, was playing a larger game, going hard in all four ridings in which there were upcoming by-elections in order to test the waters to see just how weary Canadians were of the Harper government. The answer was yes, Canadians were ready for a change, and yes the Liberals, who'd been brought so low in the election that Michael Ignatieff lost to Harper, were making a comeback. The party won three of the four contests.

But not mine. I had learned a lot and we had built an amazing team of volunteers, donors, friends and family from across the Greater Toronto Area. Each person would be in my corner from that moment forward, even in the craziest of political towns— Ottawa. But I was not going there yet. I lost on election night, in more ways than one.

Remember the resting Celina? I would learn to appreciate the message she was sending me at this point, more than ever before.

When all the ballots were counted, with 280 of the 280 polls reporting, Pat Perkins had received 17,033 votes and I had received 14,082—49 percent versus 41 percent. I'd invited Trudeau to come to my house to watch the election results with me and my family, and he'd graciously agreed. Everybody around me, even Trudeau, seemed happy I had done so well; it boded well for my chances in the general election.

But I was crushed. I shouldn't have been. In the previous election in 2011, Jim Flaherty received 37,525 votes (59 percent); the NDP candidate came second, with 14,305 votes; and the Liberal candidate came third, with only 9,066 votes (14 percent). As an unknown, I had taken on an opponent with a significant profile in the community, the former mayor no less, and increased the Liberal share of the vote by almost 30 percent. And I'd done it in the face of the significant fact that the riding had never elected a person of colour. Even in defeat, I had shown that I would be a force to be reckoned with in the upcoming general election in October 2015.

I could rationally concede that the results were way better than anyone had expected, but my mind was clouded with embarrassment and a sense of failure. I felt as if the whole country had seen me lose and that everyone was laughing at the lamb who actually did get slaughtered.

For the first couple of months of 2015, I retreated to my bed. I refused to get out. I rarely showered, washed my hair, brushed my teeth or left the house. My bedroom turned into a battleground, as everything Vidal said to me was wrong or irritated me to no end. If I was not crying, I was sleeping. I ate very little, and when I did, nothing had any flavour. I knew something was deeply wrong but I refused to get the help I needed. I lay in bed, chastising myself for not being able to get up, but I still stayed put.

One day Vidal came into the bedroom. "Babe," he said, "you are going to have to get up at some point." His voice was as gentle as his eyes and I saw that he was hurting as much as I was.

"Do you want to run in the general election, my baby?" he asked.

I nodded.

"Do you want to win the next election?"

I nodded again. As badly as I felt in that moment, I knew I wanted to run and I would be damned if I lost to Pat Perkins again.

Vidal smiled. "Okay, my love. Do you think you can get up?"

I shook my head. I did not have the strength.

Vidal smiled again and kissed me. "Okay, this is what is going to happen. I will help you. I will leave my job, and go canvass for you. We have to start right now. We cannot afford to lose any more canvassing days. So you need to get up. You need to get some help. Okay?"

Tears were streaming down my face and Vidal was holding back some of his own. I could not believe what he had just offered to sacrifice for me and at the same time I did believe it. That is how we operated. When Vidal needed me, I stepped up. When I needed Vidal, he stepped up. By then, he was the vice president academic at a private college and the loss of his income on top of the financial setbacks to my company would put us in a deep hole. But we calculated that we had enough saved in our pensions, RRSPs and the children's education fund to live for a few months. We could figure out how to get the money back later. Right now, we needed to risk it all on the chance to win.

"Don't cry anymore, my baby," Vidal pleaded. "You just need to get up and get some help." When he crawled into the bed with me, all fear disappeared. He was my human weighted blanket, holding me securely, right there for me in the moment I needed him more than ever. We were going into a general election and we were going to do it together.

I found that getting help was the hardest part of the challenges that now faced me. Mental illness clouds the mind so that every thought turns negative. First, I dreaded making the phone call to the doctor. Then my mind raced ahead to dreading the thought of the doctor even finding out about my depression. I imagined the doctor calling friends, and the friends calling friends, until the whole country knew that I was depressed. And then, of course, I would lose the general election. I was so panicked about people finding out about my depression it was difficult to take action.

I eventually reached out to Dr. Jane Philpott, a physician practising in Markham-Stouffville, which was not far from Whitby; she also would be running as a Liberal in the upcoming election. Jane calmed me down and was able to confirm for me that I was in fact suffering depression. She then wrote a prescription and referred me to a psychiatrist in her team. I have always believed that if you do not ask, you do not get. But there was something close to impossible about asking for help when your mind would much rather stay sick. The only thing that got me to the doctor was my promise to Vidal and the fact that we were sacrificing so much.

In the weeks that followed, I got treatment and took my medication. When the cloudiness of my brain lifted, I needed to figure out how to win the upcoming election. The whole campaigning thing was turning into a Pyramid of Champions, with my opponent, Pat Perkins, as the new version of my childhood rival, Alex. But before I could figure out what I needed to do to beat her, I had to stop and have a talk with my old adversary, Ms. Take. I needed to figure out how "I" lost the election—not what other people did, or how circumstances played out, but what role I played in the loss. It sounds a little masochistic, but I sat and reflected and wrote down every wrong turn I made in order to figure out what I could have done better.

That's probably the most important thing to consider when facing adversity or when looking deep into the spiral of your own misfortune. What could I have done differently? I was the only person I could control (at least most of the time). I was the only person who could change the future outcome.

I discovered that the most salient memories for me to replay were the occasions Justin Trudeau came to Whitby to help campaign. During each visit, he took the time to speak with media. I saw myself, each time, standing at his side, subliminally pleading with the reporters not to ask me any questions. I was petrified at the thought of getting an answer wrong, even though I should have been confident in my own ability to intelligently counter any query. For some reason, all four times I was in this situation, I forgot that I was not a complete idiot. I stood beside him, completely mute, and that angered me. Why had I done that? Why was I afraid to answer questions? Why did I let him talk for me?

With a clear head, it did not take me long to realize that I'd tried to run the entire by-election campaign as if I was someone who knew about politics. Talk about imposter syndrome. My ignorance was immense. Desiray, who had been taking Grade 10 civics during the summer of 2014 to get ahead in high school, would come home with her notes and we would study them together. Then she would quiz me on things like the different areas of the House of Commons.

"Mom, now where does the prime minister sit?" she'd ask, showing me the layout.

I would point timidly to a section of the page.

"No, Mom. No. That is the opposition side. The PM sits on the government side."

Candice was charged with helping me remember the names of past prime ministers. She was ruthless. Every mistake I made she had me writing out lines of Canadian political history. (I was never that hard on my children when they did their homework. Where did they learn such behaviour?)

I tried, in vain, to consume as much Canadian politics as possible, like I was back in university cramming for an exam. The more I tried to learn, the more I didn't learn. It also did not help that I had been completing my final assignments for my EMBA, and the last one was due on November 13, four days before the by-election.

I had tried to run my campaign as a seasoned politician, when I should have been running it as the business woman I was. This time I had to show up as myself. I needed to remember who Celina was and gently nudge her to the edge of the deep end, where I would be the one pushing her in, not Dr. Greenwood. I could swim in political waters, but not if I kept pretending to be someone I wasn't. The Celina who could win was the woman who was more than capable of managing complex problems and coming up with creative solutions for her clients. The one who looked up at the night sky and did not see stars, but connected the little bright dots and saw the constellations. If that Celina did not show up and give it her all, the results would be the same.

The next time I was supposed to head to my campaign office before I went out to knock on doors, I put on a long, red, summer dress with a red and white design on the bodice. I made sure my make-up was done properly. When I pushed open the door and made my entrance, the entire room stopped and stared. Clearly, I was not wearing my canvassing clothes.

"Hey, Celina. What's going on?" someone called.

"You look great," another blurted. That comment tickled me. Had I looked like shit when I'd gone canvassing before?

I announced to my volunteers that we were suspending the campaign for the rest of the day, because going forward we needed to do things a little differently. I confessed my fears around politics and told them that for us to have any chance of winning—and for the victory to mean anything if I eventually did win—I needed to run the campaign my way. I was totally on board with the main Liberal message, which was that to have a better, more equitable, more diverse public life, we needed to do politics differently. That suited me. "In order to do politics differently, *we* need to do it differently," I said, "by being ourselves. I know that I can do this, but I need to change the shape of this campaign."

I went to the board and circled the date of the election on the calendar. "October nineteenth. Election Day! What do we have to do to get a win on Election Day?" To make it work in terms I understood and with tactics I'd employed successfully for my clients, we worked backwards from October 19, writing down all of the necessary steps to win.

Next, I changed the usual political titles. I would not act as the candidate but as CEO of the campaign. The Chief Financial Officer would be responsible for fundraising and understanding how much money we needed to raise to achieve our goals, purchase signs and print other materials. The Human Resources Manager would recruit volunteers, learn their skill sets and assign them accordingly. Everyone who came to volunteer would be given a job, even the children. I loved the child volunteers. One of them, Alex, was bilingual, so his job became to tutor me for half an hour every day in French. I decided that fifth graders Evan and Hazel, another couple of kids who knew more about politics than I did, were more than capable of canvassing door to door by themselves. Their parents may have thought I was crazy, but I put them in charge of canvassing their own polls. The Marketing and Communications teams were responsible for deciding which communication materials went to which parts of the riding, once we had divided it up into appropriate sections depending on the demographics. They also decided where to put signs, and which signs to use.

After I was done assigning duties to the core team, I told them that I was confident in the ability of each of them to execute their part of the overall strategy and recruit the right volunteers to help them. I was not going to micromanage, because my job was to be the face of the brand and to go out "selling the product" by knocking on doors. Finally, I vowed that, having made these changes and committed the team to campaign in the best way I knew how, "If we wake up on the morning of October 20 and the results are not what we expected, I will be okay. I will know that we did our best, with what we knew best, and that will be good enough for me."

There were still some dark moments going forward, but none of them were about the campaign. I even took one of them as a kind of compliment: ReSolve Research Solutions, Inc., got audited three times between the by-election and the general election. I had been audited before, of course, but never three times in under a year. Was the Conservative government so threatened by the gains I was making as a candidate in a riding they'd viewed as secure that someone had a word with someone? Who knows? But the last audit happened on October 19, 2015—Election Day.

That night, friends and family piled into the kitchen and living room of our Whitby home to watch the results, as they had done during the by-election. But there was something different about the election results this time around, and not only the fact that Justin Trudeau was not there. During the by-election, as the polls were counted, the results oscillated back and forth between Pat Perkins and me until she was finally declared the winner. This time around, my numbers were ahead of hers in each and every poll. At around ten, I retreated to a private room in the house with Vidal and his dad for the final stretch. As we watched the screen, the lead between me and my opponents began to widen.

"I think we are going to win this," I said. They both looked at me and nodded, though Vidal still looked cautious. He had been through a year of hell, and he certainly did not want to get ahead of himself. Neither did I. I was nervous, too, but at that point my nerves were not about losing. The reality of the situation was setting in. If I was elected as the member of Parliament for Whitby, the real work was about to begin, and I had no idea what that meant. I had campaigned to be the voice of the riding in Ottawa and to advocate for my constituents, but I really had no idea what the job was all about.

And then, there it was, a little after eleven that night—a check mark beside my name on the television screen, declaring that I had been elected. We cheered and we hugged, and then we headed out to celebrate my victory with all the people who had helped make it happen.

—

What was to come over the next few months and years would test who I am. It would require me to tap all the lessons I had learned to that point in my life. I not only entered a world that was foreign to me, it was a world that was not designed for me to be there at all—a place purposefully built by and for white men. To be honest, in that moment, I didn't fully grasp how bumpy the ride was going to get. And I didn't own a seat belt.

I didn't even clue in to the reality of my new circumstance on November 14, 2015, the day of my swearing-in ceremony. I deliberately did not choose to wear a simple modest dress or jacket and skirt combination. I knew that our official pictures would be taken that day and I was not about to blend in with the rest of the class of the 42nd Parliament. I couldn't anyway. I was the only dark chocolate female member of Parliament in the group of 338 people.

I went to the Rideau Centre mall in Ottawa, just east of Parliament Hill, searching for an outfit that would serve notice that I came to slay, not play. In the end, I purchased a black leather Karl Lagerfeld dress, a faux fur black gilet and black leather BCBG ankle-height stiletto boots. I figured that if people were going to talk about me anyway, I might as well give them something to talk about.

The ceremony was held in the Railway Committee Room of Centre Block, the large room where the Official Opposition gathered for weekly caucus meetings. As I placed my hand on the Bible, the Clerk mentioned that every member of Parliament who had preceded me had entered history by taking this oath and then signing their name into the record. As I proceeded to do this, my family members could not help but notice the enormous painting of the Fathers of Confederation hanging above my head. As I stood beaming in front of my guests, who had travelled from Whitby, Toronto and Grenada to be present, I was oblivious to the imagery. But as months turned to years on Parliament Hill, every now and then I thought back to the audacity of that Black woman standing boldly below the Fathers. The confident, defiant person in that leather dress was about to clash with the history of colonialism, institutional sexism, racist immigration policy and present-day structural violence. I would need every ounce of strength, and all the lessons I'd learned from my past, to survive.

ten

GO BIG OR GO HOME

EVERYTHING I DO—EVEN ENTERING POLITICS, where I really had no reason to think I'd shine—comes from the larger-than-life expectation I put on myself that my next move will be bigger and better than my last one. Sometimes I succeed in ways I never imagined possible. Sometimes I don't. But I'm not so much focused on the outcome—although winning the election was important—as on enjoying each step along the way. If each step feels dreadful, how can the destination be amazing? Success itself is not the prize. Enjoying the moments that allow you to express your passion and purpose along the way is the real goal.

I recently heard a speech by Dr. Ndifanji Namacha, a medical doctor and researcher from Blantyre, Malawi, who said that we should not reach for the stars, we should reach beyond them into the heavens. She's been doing that herself from a young age, striving to eradicate malaria in her home country. I could not agree more. You can see the stars. They are right there in front of you. Reaching for the stars is achievable. However, reaching for the heavens is something you have to do with faith. That next step that you enjoy, even when you cannot see where you are headed, is the "go big" approach that allows you to reach beyond your fingertips and into your wildest dreams.

Since becoming a member of Parliament had never been one of my wildest dreams, I was confident that the position, in and of itself, was not my destination, but a station in the journey to finding my true purpose. Still, how I used the position—to make a difference, to ensure that those who had previously felt marginalized by the political process could see themselves in it—would matter. Keeping the promise I made to my constituents to stay authentic as I fought for them in Ottawa would matter. Ensuring that I did not become just another name attached to a meaningless title in the history books, occupying space but not standing for anything, would matter. If I could achieve these things that mattered, I hoped that maybe the door to my true destination would open.

The day after the election, I called the Whitby mayor to schedule some meetings. I wanted to get a handle on the needs of the town so I could figure out how I could help the municipality meet them. I also got together with any constituents who messaged me. Since the role of MP came with no job description, in those early days I made it up as I went along, doing what I thought was required. Yes, I wanted to be bold and be noticed (although, given I was the only Black female face in the House of Commons, being noticed was not all that hard), but I also wanted to do an excellent job. I'd promised, based on the Liberal Party's platform and my own convictions, to be open and transparent, and to do politics differently, but I didn't have a roadmap. In the end I decided the best way to go was to hold regular town halls in the riding—I must have held hundreds of them during my four-year mandate—and publish a running tally of the days I was in the House and the days I was away for meetings, who I saw in those meetings and how I voted on every bill. If someone in my riding had a problem—even a problem with me—I wanted to know about it. I wanted to check the box marked "accountability" firmly: as long as I was their MP, my constituents would always know where I was and what I stood for.

I admit I felt some relief when I got the call inviting me for training provided by the House of Commons—although I felt like I was drinking out of a fire hose, at least someone was teaching me about House procedures, administrative duties and everything else a rookie politician needed to know. I also needed to staff an office on the Hill and another in my constituency; since I didn't understand the environment I was now operating in, I needed to find people who were smarter than I was about federal politics. I also felt it important to recruit people from racialized and LGBTQ2+ communities, women and those with visible and invisible disabilities. In Ottawa, I soon hired Alex Howell, who used to work for MP and minister Carolyn Bennett. She definitely knew what I did not know. Christel Ilunga and Kyle Larkin became my go-to team in Whitby. If I had questions, they helped me get the answers. If they had questions, they weren't afraid to ask for answers.

As the day approached when the prime minister would announce his Cabinet, I wasn't exactly daydreaming about becoming a minister. That position was the star most politicians reached for, I knew, but I was too busy learning the ropes. Then I noticed how often my name came up when pundits discussed potential picks; some of them had taken note of how involved the PM had been in the Whitby by-election and had apparently heard me mentioned as being in the running to become minister of Something. They planted a seed. The more I thought about it, the more excited I became. I turned my ringer volume to high and kept it constantly plugged in so I would not miss "the call."

Then, the day before the presentation of Cabinet, I read a newspaper column that joked that some rookie MPs were probably still waiting by their phones, though everyone else knew that the final decisions had been made weeks before. I was that rookie MP. I kept waiting by my phone until the moment I saw the new ministers walking along the driveway of Rideau Hall on the morning of November 5, poppies on their left lapels, smiling and waving as they headed for their swearing-in. Admittedly, I was gutted, even though I shouldn't have expected anything. And when the Liberal Party declared that this new Cabinet "looked like Canada," I was truly disappointed, publicly pointing out that it didn't look like Canada to me. There were a number of communities missing from it, including anyone from the Black community. That was the authentic Celina speaking, for sure; I didn't know that a first-time MP didn't usually launch her career in Ottawa by criticizing her party.

No matter my outspokenness, I soon received a call from Katie Telford, who, along with Gerald Butts, was one of Justin's key PMO staffers, to tell me that the prime minister had selected me as his parliamentary secretary. She explained that he was flying back from COP 21, his first United Nations Climate Change Conference, held in Paris that year, or he would have made the call himself. I was happy he'd chosen me, and I immediately began thinking about what the role would entail and how I could add value. I wanted to make some things clear, though, and decided that I'd speak to them at my first meeting with the prime minister after the election, in December 2015.

When we sat down together in his office in Centre Block, the prime minister and Katie Telford greeted me with some small talk about the recent election and plans for my appointment as his parliamentary secretary. It was a nice way to break the ice. I was nervous, conscious that I was maybe the only MP who hadn't spent time touring the nation's capital, and yet here I was sitting and chatting with the prime minister as his chosen parliamentary secretary.

But I could not let my purpose be lost to my general giddiness. I needed to let him know that I was not about to be a token in government. "Let me tell you something," I said, when I finally had the nerve to cut through the pleasantries. "If I have been appointed as your parliamentary secretary to fill some gender or racial gap you have in your government, I do not want the job. I am perfectly happy being the member of Parliament for Whitby."

Trudeau insisted that obviously this was not the case. I was there on merit. Besides, we'd formed such a great relationship during the by-election that I was the natural choice. We chatted a little more, and then he asked me if I "trusted his judgement."

Why would he ask me that? I had been married to Vidal for almost twenty years, and had moments when I didn't trust *his* judgement. Why would I trust someone I didn't really know? I was not at all surprised when the Black girl in me popped up and said, "Nuh-o."

I don't think the prime minister was prepared for that answer, and I certainly was unprepared for the level of tension in the room when I responded just as bluntly when he asked me why I felt that way: "Because you rewarded your friends and people who helped with your leadership campaign with ministerial positions." I thought, as the first parliamentary secretary to this PM, he needed me to tell him the truth, to be his eyes and ears when things were going awry, and this was something I had heard other Liberals say. I got the distinct impression from the look on their faces that neither he nor Katie Telford wanted such plain talk from me, but it turned out I did not care. I was not going to nod my head and just go along. Telling the whole truth might not work in my favour, but my lies had landed me in enough trouble in the past that I was most definitely always going to tell the truth here. Parliament was no place for a Black woman to be caught lying.

Somehow we got past that moment and I had achieved my aim, which was to deliver the message that I would not settle for being a token. At the end of our discussion, the prime minister asked me if there was anything I wanted. I was mad at myself for not coming prepared with a list of priorities. That hadn't even occurred to me. Half-joking I told him I had two items on my bucket list. I said I'd crossed off the first—shaking Prince's hand. The other item was to meet President Obama. As soon as I said this, the prime minister slapped his hand on the table in front of us and said, "Done!"

Done? Umm, what did he mean? What kind of done? Was the meeting done? Was I going to get to meet Obama?

I couldn't ask what he meant because he'd already left the room.

Now that I'd told my boss that I wasn't about to be a token, I was determined that no one else assumed I was only in the role for my beautiful Black face. There was work to be done. Once again, I looked around to see if there was a list of duties a PM's parliamentary secretary was expected to fulfill tucked away somewhere. No such luck. Off the top, I decided to take meetings with any and all groups who came to Ottawa asking to meet with me as a parliamentary secretary or MP, and attend every event I was invited to. I operated on the principle that I was supposed to help the people coming in to see me, from the International Association of Fire Fighters to the Canadian Nuclear Safety Commission. Politics done differently, right? I later found out that many veteran MPs rarely went to events. While I sometimes attended six or seven an evening, others would attend six or seven a year.

I prepared for meetings by reading copious amounts of notes and briefings in my rented Ottawa condo—did I mention that this was the first time I'd ever lived on my own and I secretly loved it? Although I am not a morning person, I got up early to read news from left- and right-leaning papers, pundits' columns and social media feeds. If I got called upon in Question Period or by the media to respond to issues on behalf of the prime minister, I did not want to be caught off guard, and I also wanted insights into what our opposition was thinking. To fulfill my role with a bilingual prime minister in a bilingual capital, I worked on my French with a tutor three times a week, and in between sessions, I practised using apps and reading briefings in French and listening to as much French as possible.

I had to keep on my toes because I wasn't the only parliamentary secretary to the prime minister. He'd appointed Adam Vaughan, a progressive MP from Toronto, as his parliamentary secretary on intergovernmental affairs. And because the PM was also the youth minister, he had a parliamentary secretary on that file, too—Peter Schiefke from Quebec. Remember my competition with Alex, back in grade school? Here, too, I felt compelled to work extra hard to ensure that I was better able to answer questions on behalf of the prime minister than my two male counterparts. Not, as it turned out, that I ever answered any questions. My liaison in the PMO soon made it plain that it wasn't part of my job—even during Friday sittings of the House, when very few members were there and other parliamentary secretaries answered on behalf of their ministers, who at the end of the week were often headed off to their ridings or attending to other duties. I wasn't sure what to think about this, or that fact that Peter sometimes answered a question on the youth brief for the PM. Other parliamentary secretaries were coming to me to ask how to do their jobs, upset about the variance in job descriptions and responsibilities from department to department. They must have figured that I was in a position to tell them. What did I know?

I was uneasy about it all, but I told myself the PM, and members of his team, were busy and just hadn't had the time yet to bring me up to speed. I'd observed that very few ministers had the close relationship the finance minister, Bill Morneau, had with his parliamentary secretary; I'd seen them dining together through the window of the ground floor bar at the Château Laurier hotel, and Morneau had also invited him to his home. But Morneau was a straight shooter who knew how to organize and delegate. He might have been a first-time politician, but he came from a business milieu, as I did, and he treated his parliamentary secretary the way he would have treated a trusted business colleague.

Though I wasn't allowed to speak in Question Period, I was still required to attend the mandatory one-hour pre–Question Period prep every week. That started to play on my mind. Why the charade?

On January 29, 2016, while sitting in the Cabinet room for one of these prep sessions, I started to feel faint and put my head down on the table to catch my breath. When I lifted my head, I saw stars floating around the room. I remember thinking about the cartoons I'd watched as a child, when Bugs Bunny would hit Daffy Duck over the head and stars would appear. I lifted my hand to touch one of the stars, when the reality of what I was about to do hit me.

I did not bother to excuse myself. I simply moved my chair back, stood up, and headed straight to the nurse's office. Soon an ambulance was called to the back entrance of Parliament, which took me to the emergency department at an Ottawa hospital. That's when I began to feel both guilty and embarrassed for missing the session. Why was I sitting on a hospital gurney when I should be in my assigned seat in the House of Commons? Here was resting Celina back again, making excuses for not being able to do her job. How was I going to prove that I was a competent politician, maybe even a future Cabinet minister, when I could not handle the first few months? I felt myself spinning and all I wanted was to go home to Vidal.

I checked myself out of emergency and got on a train back to Whitby. I spent the entire train ride sobbing, with my make-up streaming down my face and my head turned towards the window so no one would see me, wiping the snot and the tears on my sleeve. At some point, I pulled out my computer and typed an email to Katie Telford and Gerald Butts resigning as Trudeau's parliamentary secretary. I appreciated the job, I wrote, but I couldn't ignore any longer the nagging feeling that I was, indeed, only a token. I called Vidal *after* I clicked send so he wouldn't talk me out of it, but hung up before he answered. I couldn't bear the weariness and panic I knew I would hear in his voice: he'd sacrificed so much to help me get to Ottawa. Instead, I called my father-in-law and then my best friend, Kyle, from business school. I was certain that they would understand why I had to resign. Both were equally concerned and both of them told me that, in the state I was in, I should not have sent the note to the PMO.

The panic kept heightening. This felt a lot worse than my most recent episode of depression. Vidal picked me up at the Oshawa Via station and wanted to take me straight to the emergency, but the thought of spending hours in a sea of sick people in the feigned sterility of a hospital ward made my panic intensify. Seeing the state I was in, he agreed to take me home so I could get some sleep. We'd assess how I was feeling in the morning.

But there was nothing encouraging to assess. I remembered a conversation I had with Don Stuss, shortly after I had been elected. We met for lunch in Whitby to catch up on old times, and update each other on current happenings. When I told him about my depression, he wrote his cell number on a piece of paper and told me to call him if I was ever in trouble. At the time, I wondered what kind of trouble I would be in that would require me to call Don Stuss instead of my husband. But on January 30, I knew exactly what kind of trouble he meant and I called him. He told me not to worry, that he would handle it and ensure that I received the best treatment. Within the hour, I was at Sunnybrook Hospital in Toronto, under an alias, waiting in the emergency room for six hours beside a man who needed more help than I did and a woman who needed more help than he did. When I finally saw a doctor, there were no beds available, though the doctor told me I needed in-patient care.

After several hours of examination and treatment, I went back home. I was crumbling in front of my family, crying uncontrollably and completely inconsolable. My children and Vidal looked at me with pity. Everybody did. I looked at myself that way. How could this be happening? I was stronger than this.

Where was the savvy business woman? Where was the mom who raised three children, ensuring that they all could read before the age of five? Where was the woman who was asked to join the Governing Council at the University of Toronto, despite her undergraduate 1.58 GPA? Where was the fearless leader who spoke at national and international conferences about the inclusion of marginalized populations in clinical research? Where had she gone? Who was this crying, blubbering person? Everything I knew about me was lost in a sea of despair and darkness. It was like I was being sucked into a dark hole, fast and furiously swallowed up. My mind wandered to my childhood and the beatings I'd endured. I recalled the disconnection, the sadness and frustration I felt after Desiray's birth, the periods of darkness that followed the two miscarriages and the loss of the by-election. It seemed like I re-experienced every bit of pain and hurt in my entire life in that single moment. I felt as if I'd made so many mistakes and this was my penance. It was Judgement Day and I did not have the strength to plead my case. I stayed in that state of guilt and despair for four solid days, even as I drove back and forth between Whitby and Toronto for psychiatric treatment.

After those crisis days passed and I was able to function again, I entered a see-saw period in which my doctors tried medications for mood, motivation and to help with sleeping. Some made me gain weight, others made me nauseous, others simply did not work. There was no panacea to be found, and I was still feeling extremely guilty about how January had ended, so I picked up the pace again and, by mid-February, was working twice as hard, twice as fast and twice as long. I likely should have taken it easy, given that my erratic behaviour persisted. I fought constantly with Vidal, sent angry emails to colleagues and had to leave social gatherings early.

I had never received a reply to my resignation email, and the parliamentary secretary role was becoming even more challenging—not only because of my distress. I asked for and finally got a meeting with Gerry Butts to express my concerns. I told him that I was troubled by the lack of coordination between my office and the PMO. I never knew what the prime minister was doing, and therefore had no idea what gaps I should be filling. When I complained about this to my veteran staff they reassured me that the disconnect was the result of the newness of the administration. We had upwards of 180 members in our majority government, and we had hit the ground running. It sounded reasonable, but I did not believe it to be true. Sooner or later, either the PMO or the PM had to allow me to do the job properly. When I expressed these frustrations to Gerry, he seemed to understand.

After the meeting, I sent an email thanking him. I said that the last thing I wanted to do was add to anyone's burdens, acknowledging the sheer volume of work that the team in the PMO had been faced with over the first couple of months of governing. I reiterated that I wanted to be respected as Trudeau's parliamentary secretary not to soothe my ego, but because I believed I could contribute in a meaningful way. I liked Gerry, and being able to discuss the situation with him had given me a little boost.

Even so, I knew that a list of duties would not be coming, and might never exist, and I went ahead and prepared a framework outlining the responsibilities I believed fit the role. I included specific tasks with full descriptions, objectives and timelines. It seemed to me that a big missing piece I could handle was to act as a caucus liaison with backbench members who were feeling excluded. I had witnessed more tensions brewing among caucus members, who'd felt spurned by the Cabinet selection process and/or who felt alienated from the PMO. I also thought that I could act as a liaison with the other parliamentary secretaries, holding meetings with them to understand their needs and to ensure that they had adequate support. Most importantly, I suggested that it would be useful, too, for me to engage in community outreach to ensure that the needs of various community organizations and cultural groups were being adequately addressed. I had seen too many politicians show up at cultural events, profess their solidarity and then disappear, only to show up again at the same event the following year and do the same thing all over again. I found this kind of performative allyship nauseating. If our government was to be different, we needed to engage differently, and that meant going to celebrations, yes, but also listening to and acting on community concerns. How else were we to integrate diverse cultural perspectives into new policy and ensure that communities saw themselves reflected in government legislation. To make the point, I told the prime minister that I would not attend Ottawa's Black History Month event that year if he did not sit down with Black politicians from across the country and listen to their concerns. When he asked if I meant he had to cancel the event if such a meeting did not happen, I responded, "No." Of course, he could have the celebration without the meeting, but if there was no meeting I was not going to attend the celebration; that would send a loud enough message.

Lastly, I could take on community meetings that the PM could not attend. The goal, I wrote, was not to speak on his behalf (unless he asked me to), but rather to act as a conduit for information and projects that should be reported back to the PM and his team.

By the end of February, I was waiting around for another meeting in order to review my framework. I felt that the process of reaching agreement about the framework was almost as important as acting on it. With other parliamentary secretaries coming to me with concerns about what was expected of them, I felt like they were depending on me to lead the way, and I was ready to be the leader they were looking for.

I sent another couple of emails asking when a meeting would happen, then wrote again to say that if everyone in the PMO liked what was in the framework, they could simply give me the go-ahead. But I needed some sort of endorsement. I thought back to ReSolve Research Solutions and how detrimental it would have been to move forward blindly or without team support on major projects. It just did not make any sense to me. I had been on the job long enough by then, and had listened to the concerns of enough members of caucus, to know that each element of the framework was necessary. I patiently waited for some kind of a response—either no, or yes, or maybe. At some point, I went ahead and implemented some of the elements on my own. If necessary, I would ask for forgiveness later.

Around the same time, I received a call from the Prime Minister's Office inviting me to join the Canadian delegation that would accompany Trudeau to Washington in early March on his first official visit to the United States. No need for an evening gown: I was told I would not be attending the state dinner. But I would be invited to meet the president during the welcoming event on the White House South Lawn and to attend a lunch with Senator John Kerry. Right. This is what the prime minister had meant when he said, "Done!"

Wow! It was really happening. I had been practising what I would say when I met President Obama steadily ever since I'd watched him being sworn into office in early 2009: "Hello, Mr. President. It is an honour to meet you." Each time, I teared up before I got to the end. He was the personification of every dream of greatness told to little Black girls or little Black boys—living proof that we could be anything. Now the parliamentary secretary to the prime minister of Canada was going to meet President Barack Obama. Little me from Grenada. ME. Talk about tears.

It was cold and dreary when we flew out of Ottawa on the morning of March 9, but it was glorious weather when we landed in Washington. The sun was shining as brightly as it had the day after President Obama won the 2008 election, when it seemed to me as if a whole new version of the sun had risen. I put on a bright fuchsia dress, made by one of my favourite Grenadian designers, and headed to the White House. As I walked along the path to the South Lawn, I looked up at the balcony—that's where Olivia Pope and Fitz, from the television show *Scandal*, always stood when they were stealing a few moments with each other. I might have mumbled that out loud and I definitely pointed to the balcony. The White House staff accompanying me likely wondered if Canada had legalized marijuana early.

I located other members of my group by the yellow pins on their lapels that indicated that we were allowed to stand in front of the "golden rope" erected on the lawn. I checked out three different spots along the rope before settling in directly behind the place tags on the ground that marked where Michelle Obama and Sophie Grégoire-Trudeau would stand. I dug my heels into the soft earth of the lawn so that no one could push me out of my spot, and waited.

When the top-level delegation of Canadian ministers and government officials arrived, they stood directly in front of the glorious golden rope group, obstructing my view. By the time the president and first lady, the prime minister and Madame Grégoire-Trudeau arrived, I could hardly see a thing. The four shook hands and chatted and smiled with the top-level folks, ignoring all of us "golden ropers," and then the president and prime minister walked directly to the stage. I was devastated. *Really, B?* (I say B with all kinds of respect on it.) *How you gonna play me like that? Walk directly to the stage, huh?*

Well, at least I was there, and so I took some selfies with the first lady and Madame Grégoire-Trudeau in the background. I got some shots of the PM at the microphone and some pictures of the president too. People started texting me to let me know that they could see me in my fuchsia dress on television. I continued to take pictures until someone behind me said, "Celina, here he is!"

Here who is?

I fumbled my phone into my pocket and lifted my head just in time to see President Obama a couple feet away from me. What in God's name was happening? The moment I had been waiting for had arrived and I almost missed it because I had been so busy taking pictures and acting the fool. When the president finally stood in front of me, I couldn't get a word out of my mouth. I had to thank the prime minister for saving my bacon, as I felt him place his hand on my back and introduce me as Celina Caesar-Chavannes, his parliamentary secretary.

I got it out at last. "Hello, Mr. President. It is such an honour to meet you."

Then the president said, "Is he doing a good job?" *He* was asking *me* about the prime minister. I was not prepared for conversation—I had only practised saying hello! When I remained silent, he added, "If he isn't, you let me know." At last I was able to mumble something in response—I don't know what—and he walked away. I thought I was going to pass out on the South Lawn. I kicked myself. I should have said, "Yes! Please give me your number and I will call to let you know if he is doing a good job." I got my phone out again to take some more pictures, but the euphoria of the moment was interrupted by a text from Vidal: "Put your phone away. You are still on TV!" I put it away, composed myself and beamed.

That evening my brother Ryan texted me to ask why I'd dissed the president when I met him. What? I hadn't dissed him. Are you crazy? But, when I watched the coverage, I noticed that at the end of our interaction, the president had gone in to give me a hug and I'd stepped back. I could not believe it. I really had dissed the president. Then I remembered that I'd noticed Prime Minister Trudeau's official photographer trying to capture a picture of us and I'd stepped back to ensure I was facing into the lens. My vanity cost me a hug from Obama!

As I stood on the South Lawn beaming in the wake of meeting the president, yet trying my best to be dignified in case the cameras were still on me, my phone buzzed furiously. I stealthily pulled it out again and read a message from Susan Smith, a principal at Bluesky Strategy Group and co-founder of Canada 2020, a progressive think tank, asking if I was going to the event with Michelle Obama and Sophie Grégoire-Trudeau. "No," I texted back, jokingly requesting to be her plus one. She replied, "Get in a cab and meet me here." She did not have to ask twice.

When I arrived, Susan took me to sit with some remarkable women, including Vicki Heyman, the wife of the US ambassador to Canada, Zita Cobb, owner of the Fogo Island Inn in Newfoundland, and many others. While waiting for the guests of honour to arrive, I basically burbled to these impressive women about how I'd crossed the last item off my bucket list when I met the president. One of them asked me, "Now that you have completed your list, what are you going to do—add more items to it?" The question took me aback. What *was* I going to do now that my list was complete? I thought for a moment and then replied, "I don't want to add anyone else. I guess I want to be the person that someone else puts on their bucket list and wishes to meet." That might have sounded like ego talking to the person who asked, but what I meant was that I wanted to be the kind of person someone else *could* look up to, a role model they could aspire to surpass by becoming their most authentic self. The same journey I was on.

After Mrs. Obama and Mrs. Grégoire-Trudeau arrived and made their remarks, I was standing around with all the bigwig ladies I'd just met as the two guests of honour came to greet them. I watched, amazed, as my new acquaintances chatted with Michelle Obama as if they were old friends, and realized that most of them were old friends! While I hadn't been invited to this gathering, still I mustered my courage and stepped to the front of the group, extending my hand to Michelle Obama. "Hello, Mrs. Obama," I said. "It is such an honour to meet you."

Well, I kid you not. This magnificent, tall, gorgeous woman stepped back on one foot (shod in a black kitten-heeled shoe), checked me out from top to bottom, then said, as she pointed at me with her perfectly manicured finger, "Huh! I remember you. My husband was giving you some love this morning." I froze, unsure if she was joking or not. I didn't want to wait until girlfriend pulled off her earrings and slid off her heels to find out. Michelle is from Chicago, and while I would usually never bet against myself, she could whoop my ass, and, out of respect, I would have to let her. I looked down at my outstretched, unmanicured fingers, politely shook her hand, and retreated out of sight.

I laughed at myself all the way to the next event. I couldn't believe that I'd just had a moment with Michelle Obama. You might

assume it was painful. I beg to differ. It was epic, and left me fanta-
sizing about how she might bring it up with President Obama later
that evening. (I know, I know, but fantasy by its nature is not reality, so here goes.)

MO: Hey Barack.
BO: Yes, darling.
MO: Do you remember that lady in the stunning fuchsia dress
from this morning? At the South Lawn event with Justin
and Sophie and the other Canadians.
BO: Absolutely! That was a fun moment.
MO: [muttering] Fun my ass.
BO: Pardon me? What did you say, my love?
MO: I just said that she looked like she had a little sass!
BO: Yes, she did. You know she's a member of the Canadian
Parliament, appointed by Justin as his parliamentary
secretary.
MO: [muttering, again] Really? I wish I knew that before I gave
her the once over.
BO: Sorry, darling, I missed what you just said.
MO: I was just thinking that we really should invite her and her
family over.
BO: That is a great idea. Let me make some calls.

You can expect that Michelle Obama and I will laugh about this
story at some point. And when we do, I will also tell her that I learned
another life lesson from those beautifully manicured hands of hers,
an extension of the one I tried to give Desiray when I explained how
unrealistic the notion of work/life balance is. Since I met Mrs. Obama,
I always take the time to manicure my nails. Each time, this simple act
of grooming provides me with fifteen minutes to half an hour of

me-time. A few moments to nurture and take care of me. The more coats you add, the longer you have to yourself. Short of holding a glass of wine, there is not much you can do with your nails wet; in effect, you have given yourself permission to refuse all demands from others, tend to yourself and take a moment to blossom. With a little bottle of nail polish, I could signal to everyone around me that the do-not-disturb sign has been hung. Thank you, Mrs. Obama.

As incredible as the trip was, in big ways and small, it was also a bitter reality check. Though he did introduce me to the president, the prime minister did not say one word to me the entire time. I had not been asked to take any meetings or assigned any duties. I felt out of place and useless; it seemed as if the only reason I was in Washington was so Trudeau could fulfill his promise to me. Thrilled as I'd been to meet the president, I felt guilty about the cost incurred by Canadian taxpayers to satisfy a whim I'd expressed for lack of anything else to say in my one meeting with the prime minister.

And there were so many awkward, uncomfortable moments on the trip. Everywhere we went in Washington, we travelled by motorcade. In one instance, the minister of fisheries, Hunter Tootoo, was directed to the minivan I was riding in. I was in there by myself, with lots of room, so I certainly did not mind. But at the next stop a staffer opened the door, ushered the minister out and profusely apologized for putting him in "that" vehicle. Why was the van so terrible for him, but perfectly acceptable for me? I know that the staffer's job was to maintain protocol, and I guess protocol meant that a minister wasn't supposed to be riding with a mere parliamentary secretary. But it felt bad to be treated as though I was a contaminant of some kind.

Worse was taking my lonely van ride in the motorcade to a speech Trudeau was giving at a university the day after the state dinner. When we arrived, I got out of the van and, since I didn't know where I was going, I followed the other members of the delegation into the venue's elevator with the prime minister and his retinue. Suddenly they were all looking at me as if I was a complete stranger. Finally, Gerry Butts said, kindly, "Celina, you're not supposed to be here," and held the door as I got off. I didn't have the nerve to ask where I was actually supposed to be. The lump that formed in my throat kept growing as I found a set of stairs to take me to the main auditorium, but I somehow managed not to cry. After the speech, the motorcade left for the next event without me. In some respect, I was relieved. I needed some time alone after the embarrassment of the elevator. Although I could have taken the bus, I walked back to the hotel, stopping at a Payless to buy two pairs of shoes. Trivial, I know, but satisfying.

I guess my place in the scheme of things should have been clear to me on the flight down to Washington: I was the only elected official seated in the back section of the plane, on my own in a row facing a walled-off section reserved for the prime minister, the ministers and senior staff. The media were back there too, but I was carefully separated from them as well. On the flight home, Trudeau came out to chat with junior staffers who were sitting on the opposite side of the plane from me. I sat up straight and leaned a little forward so it would have been easy for him to make eye contact—I was alone again in an island of empty seats so it wouldn't have been hard to spot me—but no such luck. His jokes were reserved for the staffers, his waves for the media.

It was the first instance in my time in government that I truly felt like a Black woman. Clearly, I have been Black and female all my life, but isolated in my space on the plane, I experienced a familiar, yet unfamiliar feeling—if that makes any sense. I felt my posture weaken and the shape of my face change in a way I remembered from my childhood. It had been the way my father's expression and bearing had changed the night he came home from his job and vowed that he would start his own business rather than put up with more racism at work. His face had looked so drawn its flesh seemed sunken. I hated seeing him like that. Now here was my face forming those same contours, my body disappearing into the seat. I shook myself, trying to dismiss the feeling. *Stop being so sensitive, Celina. You're not being treated this way because you're a Black woman, but because you're the new kid on the block.* Thinking this did not stop the tears from falling, but I had to believe it was true, and for maybe a little while longer I did.

A week after the state visit, on March 18, 2016, I woke up in my Ottawa condo to my phone buzzing. This is not uncommon. My phone buzzes. A lot. But normally not *that* early in the morning.

In a daze, I rolled over and picked it up. I could hardly focus on the names of the people who were emailing and texting. I squinted. "Congratulations," one message said. "Front page and above the fold, well done," said another. "Is that you?" another asked.

In that moment, I realized that an interview I'd done with Jane Taber of the *Globe and Mail*, part of a series of profiles she was doing of new Liberal MPs, had landed on the front page. I'd expected the article to be on page five or six of the lifestyles section, not the front page. I texted Jane to be sure. "Is your article on the front page?" She texted back that yes, it was.

Huh. As I was recovering from the plane ride home from Washington, I felt like the timing of the article was perfect. It outlined my life struggles on the way to becoming the parliamentary secretary to the prime minister, showing me what I already knew but kept forgetting: how much I had sacrificed to get to that point, that I had every right to be in the position and that I did not steal the job or take it from someone else. No one flew across the country to meet with me or considered asking me to join the Liberal team. I worked my ass off to get there.

It also reminded me that to whom much is given, much is expected. So many people had helped me get to Ottawa, it was not good enough that I just *be* there, struggling to stay on my feet. I needed to share the experience with others—the good, the bad and the ugly. I had not been elected to sit on the sidelines, but to enter the political arena and assert myself on behalf of others.

At the end of that month, on Youth Day on the Hill, I offered Kyra, a seventeen-year-old young woman from Goderich, Ontario, the opportunity to shadow me for the morning. We met at 7:30 a.m., and together decided to skip the day's opening remarks and go on our own little adventure. We went to the House of Commons, took pictures in the PM's and the Speaker's chairs and toured the government lobby. I then accompanied her to the third floor of Centre Block to see the Prime Minister's Office. Even though I had been in Ottawa since November, attended Question Period prep every day, and clearly stood out in the crowd of MPs, a guard stopped us as we walked towards the office to ask why I was there. The unfamiliar familiar feeling started up in my gut, but I calmly told him that I was parliamentary secretary to the PM and was taking my young friend on a Youth Day tour. He took a closer look, and this time he seemed to recognize me. He let us pass.

Kyra took pictures of everything around her, thrilled to be there. As we were about to leave, the PM's executive assistant, Tommy Desfossés, surprised us by allowing Kyra to venture into the PM's office, sit in his desk chair, and have her picture taken there. I was not only happy for her, but felt that I was finally doing what I was supposed to do with my access—encourage young women with political aspirations. If we want to change politics by adding women, they might as well get a picture of themselves in the chair. Kyra now has that picture. Maybe one day she will also have the job.

Despite my increased profile after the newspaper article, my role as parliamentary secretary to the prime minister was continuing to cause me grief. Or, rather, my non-role.

I was still going back and forth with members of the senior team in the PMO on the framework I'd come up with. I puttered along until mid-April when, again, I decided that I had had enough. I'd had one five-minute meeting with the prime minister since our introductory session. To be effective as his parliamentary secretary, I needed to be on the same page as he was. I was not. I fully understood that I would never get the full attention of the PM, who was extremely busy. I'd only asked for fifteen minutes a month, with an agenda sent to him in advance, to ensure that we were in tune. Apparently, that was too much. I hadn't yet been asked to attend any events on his behalf, something I could have easily done to lighten his load. I was continuing to work with other parliamentary secretaries to ensure they had better relationships with their ministers, knowing full well that the relationship I had with mine was not the greatest.

I loved my work as the MP for Whitby. We'd taken over some tough immigration cases left unfinished by the previous member, in which people were about to be deported and families torn apart, often completing them with positive results. I didn't need a symbolic role as the Black woman who sat at the right hand of the PM. It was barely symbolic by this point! It also bothered me that I was earning an extra $16,000 in salary. Since I was basically doing nothing much to justify the title, I felt it was a waste of taxpayers' money. My psychiatrist and I were still adjusting my medication and even though he warned me that all the tweaks could make me irritable and that

I shouldn't fire off any more resignation letters, I was growing angry again. I sent an email to Katie Telford and Gerald Butts.

I'll quote it in full to show how much I was at my wit's end: "We need to have a meeting to discuss my role going forward. The way I am being treated by the PMO is absolutely disrespectful, and dare I say racist and sexist. This situation is absolutely terrible. I am blatantly treated differently than other PSs. If I have done something wrong, this is not high school, talk to me about it. Don't try to punish me, by not including me. This situation needs immediate attention."

I hit send and regretted it immediately. I followed it with an immediate apology to Gerry and Katie, and sent another directly to the prime minister. What the fuck was happening to me? I felt like I was always looking over my shoulder and that my senses were always tingling about various injustices. I now realize I had named what was happening in the email, but at the time I immediately blamed myself for using the word "racism" so carelessly. Surely I had to endure a lot more of such treatment before I could show that the pattern of racism existed?

Isn't that what we are supposed to do? Pile up irrefutable evidence of bad behaviour against us before redemption is granted? Cradle the burden of racism in our arms until it is bold enough to rear its ugly head so blatantly no one can ignore it? Microaggressions, such as I was experiencing, did not count. They were too subtle to prove that they had even happened, let alone that they'd had an effect on the recipient. Wasn't that correct?

I thought I had stayed immune to racism's effects for so long—all the way through school and as an entrepreneur. Why was my immune system so compromised now? Maybe the state of my mental health had weakened my system like kryptonite. On the other hand, maybe racism had caused my disease, and anxiety and depression were the symptoms. Or maybe it wasn't racism at all.

I knew one thing for sure, whatever "it" was, it was not only driving me crazy, it felt like "it" was killing me.

I lay low for the next couple of months, concentrating on doing what I had to do and trying not to obsess about how I could be doing things better.

In August 2016, I met with the prime minister to speak with him about the importance of Canada recognizing the United Nations' International Decade for People of African Descent (2015–2024), which was adopted by the General Assembly on December 23, 2013. It was a recognition of the need to promote and protect the human rights of people of African descent along with their full and equal participation in all aspects of society. This was, and still is, a tremendously important resolution, but ultimately its significance will be determined by whether it engenders positive policy and programming that leads to tangible improvement in people's lives. I told the prime minister I had gathered with a group of federal and provincial Black political leaders a week earlier in Toronto with the goal of formalizing a plan to help members of our community. As a country we finally had to come to grips with systemic racism; we believed a national recognition of the resolution could provide a framework for that to happen, especially in the areas of justice, recognition and development. Given the issues supercharging the activism of groups like Black Lives Matter, it was crucial that the federal government and its members respected and recognized the contributions of Black communities to Canada.

After hearing from many experts, our group of Black politicians had decided to move forward with three main initiatives shaped by equity-based analysis, rather than the gender-based analysis that the Trudeau Liberal government relied on in its focus on the rights of women and girls. First was a push to have provincial and federal governments recognize the Decade and undertake efforts to promote recognition, justice and community development. Second, we wanted to advocate for an apology from the federal government to Black communities in Canada for historical incidents of racism and segregation whose long shadows were still reinforcing systemic racism and oppression. Lastly, we wanted to encourage more government procurement opportunities for Black-owned small- and medium-sized businesses. The prime minister seemed eager to learn more and do more in this territory, and I grew excited by the possibilities. It seemed like I had finally found a place where we could work together.

In September, when the PM couldn't attend the opening ceremonies of the National Museum of African American History and Culture in Washington, I was asked, for the first time, to attend an international event on his behalf. The next, and final, time I was asked to represent him was at the inauguration ceremony of the Republic of Ghana's new president, Nana Akufo-Addo, in early January 2017. I wondered then whether I was only being asked to attend Black events on his behalf, and once again I had to dismiss the uneasy feeling that thought gave me. *Just be grateful that you have the job and you are at the table?* Isn't that what I was supposed to do?

I kept being surprised by how daunted I felt not only by the political games on Parliament Hill, but by the actual space. Each time I ran into a woman of colour or a Black staffer, they told me that they, too, struggled with feeling excluded or being met with sexist, racist or microaggressive behaviour. I hated that they felt this way. Soon, every time I passed a young woman in the hallway, I would slip her a note with my personal cell phone number on it and invite her to call me. If I was having such a hard time adjusting to life on the Hill, knowing full well that I could not be fired by anyone but the electorate, how were these women dealing with it all? I would see them with their big, super curly Afros, or dreads or braids, and their extra-dark velvety skin, and reach out to them to let them know they had an ally. On Sunday nights we arranged phone calls or Google hangouts so we could discuss what had happened during the past week in a safe and protected space. We strategized together on how to fill in the gaps we saw in how the government was rolling out policy, especially when the development of those policies excluded the voices of Black women. We laughed over some episodes and cried over others and, most of all, we had each other's backs. The sisterhood we built in those calls and meetings has been long-lasting.

But I did not always succeed in protecting my young mentees, who included my own staff members. When my Whitby office manager, Stacey Berry, and I attended a meeting with an Ontario provincial minister and the CEO of a multi-billion-dollar corporation, she felt the same ice-cold reception first hand that I had experienced in many such meetings. As usual, we got there early enough to find our seats and say our hellos to the other people in the room, most of them men. Some refused to look at us as we greeted them and others ignored our presence completely. We, nonetheless, remained pleasant.

When the minister and the CEO arrived, the men in the room gathered around. As we approached to say our own hellos, they closed ranks so we could not join the circle and tightening up so much that neither the minister nor the CEO could even see us. Stacey's face fell. I couldn't tell if she was about to cry out of her own hurt or from mortification that she hadn't protected me from such a snub. She was about to shoulder a path into the circle, when I gently placed my hand on her arm and told her that we were going to sit back down. "I know you're upset," I said. "I am, too. But you need to remember one important thing. This meeting can't start without us." I smiled. "Whether they choose to acknowledge us now or later, they need us."

When the minister finally was able to break through the circle of men, he came to greet me warmly. When he introduced me to the CEO by name and included my titles, I could see the other men's expressions change. Suddenly they were all interested in engaging, but I had no energy for them now. Instead I asked the minister and CEO, "Shall we start?"

This was me calling on the lessons in patience and forbearance I had learned in the years I was running my business. More than once I had arrived for a meeting with a new client only to be ignored. I would sit in the lobby and quietly wait. I was being paid for my time, after all. Also, in those early years, I knew my clients weren't expecting someone who looked like me. Remember, I deliberately hadn't put my image on any of our printed promotional materials or on our website, so I wouldn't be prejudged for my gender or race. Once, a client only briefly glanced at me when I arrived for our meeting, then told me to wait my turn. I went back to reception and sat down. When he burst back into the lobby complaining that the person he was supposed to meet was late, I spoke up. "No, I'm not. You told me that you didn't have the time for me. Do you have time now?" The look on his face was priceless. He clearly was not expecting a well-dressed, young Black woman to be the owner of a research management company.

When we hold positions that traditionally have not been occupied by people who look like us, and enter spaces where we have been historically few in number, the people who inhabit those realms often don't even see us. In business, I had to learn how to occupy such spaces with poise and confidence, and I did so by channelling the three-year-old me, the one who walked around naked singing at the top of her lungs. To her boldness, I added a couple of lessons my friend Shannon had taught me when I was struggling with my marriage. She told me that the ability to look at yourself in the mirror, without the filters, the clothing, make-up or accessories, and to appreciate what is there—not criticize all the lumps and bumps, the parts that are too big or too small—boosts your confidence, and she was right. But it takes practice. Even now, every time I step out of the shower, I take the time to look at myself in a full-length mirror and appreciate me. We often turn to others to validate us in their space, instead of doing it for ourselves in our own space. Especially in our own skin.

Shannon also taught me I needed to value myself in other ways. One day at work, she actually asked me what underwear I was wearing. (Yes, really.) I did not need to look. I bought them in jumbo packs at Walmart. You know the kind in the plastic Ziploc bags that are folded and taped together so the manufacturer can squeeze more in?

"Throw those away!" she said in disgust. "From now on, you purchase yourself some matching sets. You are worth the investment, aren't you?"

She was right. Why would I take the time to admire all the chocolatey goodness the good Lord had blessed me with and then put on some dingy underwear? I admit I took a deep breath at the prices, but I started to purchase matching sets. Then I gave Vidal the assignment of buying them for me, once a month, as part of our "getting back together strategy." Pleasing Vidal was part of the plan, but I was also wearing them to please me. To reinforce that I was worth the investment.

As I managed to deal with some of the situations politics handed me, I slowly realized that I'd had ten years of practice in how to be in spaces that had excluded people who looked like me before I ever ended up in politics. Although I was having a difficult time, I had built myself a foundation to stand on. I just needed to get my footing back.

Also, if I was going to be different in politics, as I vowed I would be to every voter I'd met on every doorstep, I could not be a fraud. I really couldn't pretend my way through this. I needed to be candid about the good times and the not so good times—as transparent as I was about my voting record and how I spent my time. It was not enough to post pictures on social media and have Sunday meetings with Black Hill staffers. I needed to use the opportunity politics afforded me to do some good.

On World Suicide Prevention Day in September 2016, a terrible storm was brewing in Ontario. I posted on Facebook that although stormy weather was coming, just like it does from time to time in our lives, the storm would eventually roll away and everything would be okay. A few days later, a reporter from Huffington Post got in touch to ask if I would write a blog expanding on my post. I decided it was time to describe my depression in 2014 and my crisis in January. I never would have imagined the impact the post would have as it went viral. The more I was asked about my depression, the more I spoke about it openly, and the more openly I spoke about it, the more I would run into people who were grateful that I did.

After talking about depression during a keynote speech at a Mississauga hotel, an elderly Black woman, dressed in a staff uniform, approached me with tears in her eyes. I started to panic. All Black children are taught to revere our elders, but elder Black women have a very special place in my heart. I thought she was crying because she was disappointed that I had revealed my struggles, that I had allowed myself to appear weak in front of a room full of people. Speaking about mental health in the Black community was still taboo, and I wanted that to change. We could not continue to teach our children to be twice as good, study twice as hard, and practise twice as long, without understanding that it was not a sustainable way to live your life. I did not want the next generation to suffer in silence. But she wasn't coming to chastise me. When she reached me, she took my hands in hers and said, "Thank you." Her eyes were soft, and seemed almost solid black, the whites dark and rusty-red from tears. I could see the hard work, pain and struggle in every line of her face. Still holding on to my hands, she told me, "Every day, for years, I would wake up with the sun and stare out the window until the moon appeared. I did not go anywhere. I lost my good job. I stayed a prisoner in my home and in my mind. I did not know what was wrong with me. I stayed there, watching the sun and the moon for years. Thank you for talking." Now my tears fell too, and we hugged for what seemed like an eternity in the back hallway of that west-end hotel. When I'd shared my story, I'd shown her she was not alone, that it was okay to not be okay.

Later, however, I received a private message from another woman who had heard the speech. She told me she thought it was great that I felt comfortable enough to tell my story, but she feared that if she told hers, she would lose her job or lose her children or both. I knew then that it wasn't enough to speak up about my own experiences. Many other stories needed to be heard, many other situations needed to be talked about and a multitude of voices needed to be amplified.

During the following weeks, I spent time opening up to my caucus colleagues about these issues and talking about what we, as a government, could do. I felt comfortable speaking there because everyone in the room was sworn to secrecy. When discussing another piece of legislation earlier that year, I told my colleagues about my experiences at Sunnybrook. We needed to do more. I went to Jane Philpott, who was the minister of health, and asked her what support she needed to get mental health funding into the next federal budget. She told me I needed to speak up for it. "I cannot be the only one who asks," she said.

"How much do you need?"

"Three billion dollars," she said.

"Come on, Jane! Let's be bold and ask for five billion. That way every young person across the country who needs help can get help."

At our next caucus meeting, I stood up, along with other colleagues, and asked for $5 billion towards mental health. The 2017 federal budget included $5 billion earmarked for mental health funding as part of the provincial-territorial health transfer. Although some provincial leaders were hesitant about receiving earmarked funds related to services that were outside of the federal jurisdiction, all the provinces eventually signed on and used the funds to increase access to services for youth under the age of twenty-five.

All right. With that one win, I'd proved to myself that I was more than capable of making change through politics. It was time to stop playing small and safe. It was time to decide if I was truly ready to go big and start being 100 percent Celina. And if I was going to be 100 percent Celina, I needed to use all the tools in my toolbox, including my perceived character flaws of being impulsive, impatient and naïve. I vowed to stop trying to cuss less and restrain my quick temper. In some way, these flaws were my superpowers, though I knew I would have to strike a careful balance between using them too much and not using them at all. But to be authentic in politics, I couldn't pretend anymore that I'd become some careful, subdued, agreeable version of myself. Otherwise, I would never find the courage I needed to speak up and clap back, finding the resilience to weather the storm and the wisdom to know what to do when using my powers got me in trouble. As it would.

eleven

IN CHARGE OF MYSELF

IN DISCUSSING HOW A person can be happy in their career in an essay called "How Will You Measure Your Life," Clayton M. Christensen, a professor at Harvard Business School, wrote that "the most powerful motivator isn't money; it's the opportunity to learn, grow in responsibilities, contribute to others and be recognized for achievements." I was finally starting to remember that how I measured my life, especially my life in politics, had nothing to do with how the PMO or the prime minister treated me or whether they recognized my work. During the first year of my mandate, I kept waiting for someone else to define my purpose, to "give" me the opportunity to learn, grow, contribute and be recognized. But I was the only person who had control over that. And increasingly I began to take back that control. I needed to remember how and why I got into politics, and the answer to both questions was the people.

When in November 2016 Donald Trump was elected to the office that Barack Obama had held, I knew I couldn't stay on even in the minimal role I was playing as parliamentary secretary to the PM. I wrote a letter to Trudeau on the weekend after the US election telling him that I knew that diplomacy had to continue between our two countries, but that going forward, he couldn't rely on me to play a US-facing role: I didn't have the diplomatic capacity to risk being put in front of that man. I had a bigger thing to ask him too. I reminded him that I had a Black son, who he had met at my house the night of the by-election. I told him that yes, we were in Canada, and yes, we had our own problems with racism, but my children and I, and all of Canada, needed him to stand up against the hateful rhetoric that would, without a doubt, spill over the border and affect our lives too. I knew I was putting him on the spot. Even if he was underutilizing me, he couldn't be seen to just drop me, given that I was the only Black female face in his government. I knew that I would still be valuable in helping with the recognition of the UN Decade for People of African Descent. I'd also heard that he and the strategists in the PMO were planning a mini-shuffle of Cabinet, and thought there might be another place in government for me.

Rumours of a shuffle grew louder in December 2016, at which time I asked the PMO whether it would be useful, given that I had built relationships with the other parliamentary secretaries, for me to prepare a report for him on their various talents, abilities and matches and mismatches with their ministers. I suggested it could better inform his thinking when it came to finding new roles for people. I actually created an Excel spreadsheet in which I described each parliamentary secretary's relationship with their minister and recommended whether they should be moved or stay put or even become a minister themselves. I have no idea whether anyone in a position of power consulted my spreadsheet, but some of the moves that were made in January 2017 mirrored my recommendations. Including one for me: I became the parliamentary secretary for the minister of international development and La Francophonie. I was never replaced as parliamentary secretary to the PM—the role was dropped altogether.

I was ecstatic, though I was careful not to show just how happy I was to my new minister, Marie-Claude Bibeau, whose previous parliamentary secretary, Karina Gould, had just joined her in Cabinet as the minister of democratic institutions—becoming, at twenty-nine, the youngest female minister in Canadian history (and in 2018, the first sitting Cabinet minister to have a baby while in office). I made sure to remind Madame Bibeau that I was the person who had helped build momentum over mental health funding in caucus, and was a total neophyte in the area of international development: there was no way I was gunning for her job. At last, I was learning a thing or two about how the political game was played.

And with this portfolio I could be really useful. After being quickly brought up to speed on various files, I began representing the government of Canada, and our newly released Feminist International Assistance Policy, with unapologetic enthusiasm all over the world. The focus of my work was on improving the lives of girls and women, most of whom looked like me, many of whom lived in places like the one in which I'd been born, and who were struggling with all kinds of disadvantages that Canadian funding and support could help address. I had been a baby left behind when my parents seized the opportunity to come to Canada to make a better economic life for us; if that had never happened, I might have lived a life just like theirs, and that fuelled my enthusiasm for the work. I found myself sharing hugs and stories and tears everywhere I travelled—and my jewellery, too, which I found myself handing to the young women I met.

The development story is the greatest story Canada never tells. We have people across our country and around the world doing amazing work in difficult situations. Then, when disaster strikes, they double down and do more. I was proud that our feminist policy was complementing their work and that women and girls were at the centre of the programs we funded—a direct result of the government listening to recommendations from national and international stakeholders as to what would make the most impact in terms of raising people out of poverty and leaving no one behind. They already knew what we were just putting into practice. Placing women and girls in the centre of policy is not just the right thing to do, it's the economically smart thing to do. According to a 2015 McKinsey Global Institute report entitled, "How advancing women's equality can add $12 trillion to global growth," when women and girls are given the tools to reach their full potential and succeed, their efforts can add anywhere from $12 to $28 trillion to our global GDP. It was not about empowering them—women are born empowered—but about leveraging what they had in order to improve their lives. Our funding was tied to programs that involved women and girls in the decision-making, execution and the evaluation of the projects we backed. I also loved that in my new role, everything I spoke about and supported from the stage at national and international events was in opposition to the rhetoric and acts of Trump's new administration, busy cutting funding to any NGO or government who wouldn't get behind its anti-abortion stance. For the first time in my political life, I felt like the entire government of Canada was standing on the stages with me, boldly promoting women's rights as human rights. When people pushed back against the policy in certain jurisdictions around the world, I stood up and spoke even stronger.

But I was also, always, honest about the state of affairs in Canada as well. The national shame of missing and murdered Indigenous women and girls was a salient example, but other countries also knew that debates were happening in Canada that would result in one province, Quebec, passing a law forbidding public employees from wearing religious artifacts to work. We had as much work to do as a country as others did, and I was glad to be a part of the international conversation about these issues.

But, oh, it was a learning curve.

One of the trips I took was to Japan to attend the fiftieth anniversary meeting of the Asian Development Bank. I had never been anywhere in Asia and I was warned in my briefings that "cultural differences" meant that being a Black woman might not work in my favour and the meetings might not be as warm and receptive as I hoped. None of that dampened my excitement over the trip. Just as I had done when I was running my own company and had to make a business trip somewhere beyond our normal reach, I decided to bring my two daughters with me (we didn't really have the money to spare, but I didn't want them to miss such an opportunity).

At the airport we were greeted by a liaison officer from Japan's Ministry of Finance and a representative from the Canadian embassy. After we cleared customs, we were off on a whirlwind, four-day trip in which I had several meetings in Yokohama and Tokyo with government representatives from Fiji, Bhutan, Samoa and other countries in the region. The two most important items on my agenda, though, were bilateral meetings with Takehiko Nakao, the president of the Asia Development Bank in Yokohama, and Katsunobu Katō, the Japanese minister of women's empowerment and minister of state for gender equality in Tokyo.

Before I met with Mr. Nakao, I got together with David Murchison, Canada's executive director for the Asian Development Bank (ADB), along with other members of the Canadian delegation (which included some people from Global Affairs and some who worked for the bank), at the Intercontinental Hotel. We discussed Canada's financial commitment to the ADB as part of the Canadian government's larger pledge of $2 billion in the global fight against climate change. In the middle of the session, I received a text from my daughters letting me know that they were heading to a nearby mall and then on to other tourist destinations. I texted back that they should have fun and be safe, but after I put away my phone, I must have seemed distracted because a member of the delegation asked, "Is everything all right?"

"Oh, yes. For sure!" I exclaimed. "I was just wondering whether I gave my daughters enough money for the day. I left them with seventy thousand yen." I looked around to see everyone looking back at me with surprise—or was it pity? "That's over eight hundred dollars!" one of the women finally said, clearly trying not to laugh. I shook my head, pulled out my phone, and texted the girls to tell them not to spend all the money. Interesting how I didn't hear back from them on that one. They were usually so good at replying to their mother.

As we left our session and headed to the main ballroom of the hotel, I noticed a big display of copies of a book called *Banking on the Future of Asia and the Pacific: 50 Years of the Asian Development Bank*. I grabbed one and placed it in my purse. In breaks throughout the day, I scanned the contents, hoping to gain a better understanding of the bank. I also made sure to read the foreword, written by Mr. Nakao, and I watched videos on YouTube of talks he'd given. It was easy to see his understanding and passion for the region and its people, and also how proud he was of this historical account of the bank he governed.

My fifteen-minute meeting with him was scheduled from 5:25 to 5:40 p.m. When I got to the door of the room, I saw two rows of five to eight chairs set up facing each other dead centre in the intimidatingly large space. At the top of the two rows were two chairs where Mr. Nakao and I would sit, with the Canadian delegates on my side and the Japanese delegates on his. This was the meeting where I would announce Canada's $200 million commitment towards the second phase of the Canadian Climate Fund for the Private Sector in Asia, which I would follow up the next day with a speech to a larger crowd. The investment was intended to build on the success of the initial Canadian Climate Fund, which had allowed the bank to test innovative approaches to climate finance. We knew that governments could not fund climate action alone. We needed the private sector to make investments as well as share their knowledge and expertise if we were to have a shot at achieving the climate goals we committed to at COP 21.

I took a deep breath, and headed straight for Mr. Nakao, about to offer him the firm handshake we politicians and businesspeople are taught to give. Before our hands met, he briskly reminded me that he only had fifteen minutes for the meeting.

Totally okay by me, I did not say. *I only planned to be here for fifteen minutes myself. I am just as hungry as you are and cannot wait to eat something at the reception when this meeting is over.* I thought this without rolling my eyes, which at the time seemed a small, but necessary, victory.

After we took our seats, I covered the usual talking points about Canada's relationship with the bank and Mr. Nakao responded with the usual appreciation for the bank's relationship with Canada. Yawn! I hated this type of formulaic to-and-fro, so bureaucratic and banal. Eventually, Mr. Nakao went to hand me a copy of the bank's history, signalling the end of the meeting. I held my hand up in protest. "No thanks," I said. Time stopped. The faces of the Japanese delegation expressed pure disappointment at my rudeness. The faces of the Canadian delegation showed pure horror. There wasn't a non-bulging eye in the room.

I slowly leaned over to unzip my bag and pulled out my copy of the book. "No thank you," I repeated. "I have my own copy. Will you sign it for me?"

The collective sigh of relief must have been felt clear across Yokohama. Mr. Nakao beamed at me and graciously signed the book.

Impression made! #BlackGirlMagic! He and I chatted as if we were old friends for another ten to fifteen minutes, well past our time allowance. After we were done, we walked together to the reception.

The meeting with Minister Katsunobu Katō was so important I was briefed at breakfast by the ambassador himself, Ian Burney. Katō was known to be a close ally of the prime minister of Japan, Shinzō Abe, and the pressure was on me to ensure the encounter went well. This time I did not have a book to pull out of my bag, but I did my homework as best I could.

Again, the Japanese sat on one side of the table and the Canadians on the other. Minister Katō and I were placed across from each other, with small versions of our respective country flags in front of us. Katō made his opening remarks—about the value his government placed on Japan's relationship with Canada—and I returned his pleasantries. Good grief. How could I get to the real conversation, the one when we finally put away the talking points, bypassed the bureaucratic ping-pong and connect as people? The light bulb went off. We *were* just people. I pushed my notes to the side. Out of the corner of my eye, I could see the ambassador shuffle in his seat a little. Was he nervous? I hope not.

"Mr. Katō," I said, smiling at him. "You have four daughters, right?"

He responded that yes he did.

"Well, my two daughters are running around Tokyo right now, spending way too much money because I incorrectly calculated the exchange. When we really think about it, everything that we are doing in this room is about them, isn't it?"

He leaned forward. "Please, let your daughters stay and spend as much money as possible!" Then he laughed, and the meeting finally started.

In such moments, I remembered that the cornerstone of our democracy is our humanity. No matter our political affiliation or influence, we are just people who happen to work in politics. Our diplomats handle so much of the load of our relationships with other countries every single day. The best impact a visiting politician like me could make, I thought, was building personal, human, connections, and that rarely came in a briefing package.

At last I was learning to trust that I could be as "politically" savvy in politics as I had been in business. One of the lessons I'd learned is to pay attention to people and appreciate the differences that make every one of us unique. For instance, anyone who paid attention to me at a social gathering might not realize I am not too fond of crowds, and would much prefer to sip my wine, leaning in a corner, and watch others interact. But I consider myself a trained extrovert who can put on the smiles when I need to survive a reception or "meet and greet."

I had studied Mr. Nakao and Mr. Katō in order to be effective in my job, for sure, but I also did it because I was impressed by them, and was interested in how they'd succeeded in their respective fields. I wanted to get a sense of what made them tick. I study myself just as much as I study other people. The way I speak, my hand movements, the way I walk into a room, the way I stand in a room, the way I sit in certain situations versus others, the way I smile, the way I nod, if and when to furrow my brow and whether or not I allow my heels to click, clack on the floor. I have taken the time to study which of my movements make people nervous and which make them feel comfortable. Depending on the mood and the matter of the situation, I adjust.

The management of one's presence in the world is an art. Figuring out your strengths and weaknesses, your abilities, style and values helps you identify what type of contribution you can make to the world. I know that I am valuable to the organizations and the spaces that I occupy, even though I suffer through periods of self-doubt. The point of learning the ways your behaviour affects others is not to become a sort of master manipulator in order to get your own way. Taking the time to truly understand yourself and why you behave the way you do opens the door to understanding, kindness, empathy and compassion towards others. And so often the effort to make lasting, beneficial change in this world rests on treating yourself and others with kindness and respect.

Not that any of this is easy. While I was finding firmer footing with every success in my new brief in International Development, I continued to face a barrage of microaggressions on the Hill, and beyond, that made me question whether I would ever belong there. They ranged from being asked why I was walking down a particular hall, to being warned by a woman in the bathroom not to steal the wallet she had left on the ledge by the door, to being denied access to a government buildings, including my own office. Even on my travels to places where the racial mix was much different than Canada's, I was used to people not seeing me. Once, while travelling as the head of delegation to an international conference, I arrived early for a meeting with the vice president of another country. "Who is the head of delegation?" the vice president's staffer asked my team. They pointed at me. The staffer looked right through me and asked, again, "Who is the head of delegation? The parliamentary secretary?"

I sighed the kind of sigh that makes you remember you have clavicles. "I am the head of delegation and the parliamentary secretary. Is the vice president ready to start?" There was no point in dwelling on it. I needed to be professional and keep things moving along.

When one of my Liberal colleagues told me while we were

waiting for the Parliament Hill bus that he would give anything to run his fingers through my hair, I told him, very seriously, that "touching my hair would be the worst fucking mistake you could ever make in your goddamn life." He decided he would walk, and I got on the bus.

Situations like this were a weekly occurrence, and though they made me uncomfortable, I was able to use my voice to deal with them. But on March 22, 2017, when a PhD student named Judy Grant, who came to the Hill as part of the University of Toronto's Women in House delegation, had her hair searched by security without explicit consent, I was both hurt and furious. The Women in House program is designed to give women from diverse backgrounds the opportunity to come to the Parliament and shadow an MP, and Judy and another woman from U of T were joining me. When neither of my guests showed up in the reception room where we were to meet, I asked other members of the program if they had seen them. Yes, they had. One of the two missing women had had an issue gaining entrance to the building and both of them were still at security.

I headed straight for the checkpoint, where I found two Black women looking distraught. Judy Grant had her hair in large, long dreadlocks, some of them tied up in a bun. She was in the middle of explaining to the security guard who'd insisted on searching her hair how inappropriate it was for someone to do such a thing, especially without warning. It was a devastating and embarrassing experience for her, and equally for me. I work in the House, but the House belongs to her. It belongs to the people of Canada. One of the security guards was extremely apologetic, but the guard who had done the search was not. One ironic aspect of this terrible situation: Judy was a police officer who was completing her PhD in the area of profiling and cultural search procedures. I couldn't make this stuff up even if I tried.

This incident brought home to me that it was all very well to travel the world speaking boldly about women's rights as human rights, but what was I going to do here in Canada? The issue of mental health was something everyone of all backgrounds could get on board with, even if some stigma still existed. Tackling subjects related to equity and justice, racism and intersectionality, especially in caucus, was much tougher. I wanted my colleagues to really understand why experiencing microaggressions is like a death by a thousand cuts—how what is said, and how it is said, impacts people. I wanted what happened to Judy never to happen again, and for that to be the outcome, my colleagues had to understand that a trespass had been committed by a security guard who insisted that she was just doing her job.

Although the government House leader and Speaker of the House were informed of the event, and vowed to make necessary changes, I worried about the incident to the end of that sitting, and on through the summer break while I was at work back in my constituency. I was part of a Liberal government that had sold itself as better than what came before, as the voice of sunshine and progress and open dialogue, as the face of Canada. Though I supported what we were striving for, when it came to these kinds of issues, I didn't feel much sun, light or air. I'd tried hard to dismiss my own uneasy feelings about the ways I was being treated as a Black woman in Ottawa and get on with it, which is certainly what some in the Black community thought you should do when you joined this club: don't get identified as *that* kind of representative of the community—the one who can't have a conversation without talking about racism—or they'll pigeonhole you and, worse, never invite the rest of us in. A Black woman in politics was supposed to be nice, sit nice, dress nice, remain humble, and be glad that she was "allowed" a seat at the table. But I was already failing at all that.

At the end of the summer of 2017, I reached the watershed moment where I finally realized that if I didn't step up, no one else was going to. Every summer we had a fall caucus retreat. This year, the women's caucus was being held the day before the retreat started, which really pissed me off, because it meant I had to miss my children's first day back at school. Also, what was with a supposedly feminist government that didn't put the women's caucus meeting on the main agenda?

And then, when I got to the meeting and heard Maryam Monsef, the minister for women and gender equality, speak, she told us that her primary focus for the following sitting was going to be on promoting the interests of Muslim women. I shook my head in disbelief. While travelling through Canada earlier in the year, she said, she'd heard stories that Muslim women were being denied job opportunities and access to services because of the way they dressed or the names on their résumés. That was true, of course. I knew the prejudice faced by Muslim women. I had heard the stories about them being overlooked from business colleagues. However, this minister's job was to ensure equity for all women, especially those belonging to equity-seeking groups. Her ministry's mission was to investigate and develop legislation and policies to mitigate the disadvantages all marginalized women faced, especially women of colour, and yet here she was announcing that she'd chosen to prioritize one group. After she came off the stage, I asked her if I'd heard her correctly when she said that she was going to focus "primarily" on Muslim women. She told me I had. When I asked what her rationale was, she replied that she needed to act because Muslims in Canada were being targeted with violence, and she reminded me of the Quebec City mosque shooting in January 2017. As if I needed reminding—the whole country had been shocked. She also insisted that she needed to act because Muslim women, in particular, were denied employment and opportunities because they wore a hijab.

"So are Muslim women who are denied opportunities for employment more important than Black girls who are removed from school because their hair is too puffy?" I asked.

She did not respond.

I continued. "Well, if you are going to be involved in putting forward initiatives for one equity-seeking group, don't you need to also understand what other groups are facing and put forward the most comprehensive policy?"

Was it possible that the minister, along with so many others, didn't understand what *all* women face on a day-to-day basis, especially Black women? It's true that in the mainstream, conversation about everything from body shaming to sexual assault was mostly limited to the experiences of white women. Progressive people agreed that talking about a woman's baby bump or other body parts was unacceptable. The rest of us were still pretty invisible in the discourse. Do a quick Google image search for "professional hair" and you come up with pictures of white women with straight hair in the latest styles. Search "unprofessional hair" and the results are largely photos of Black women with braids and Afros. I decided that it was not enough to defend Judy and her dreadlocks at the security desk. I needed to defend us all.

Before Question Period begins every day, MPs have an opportunity to make a statement about a topic of their choice. Right after that women's caucus meeting I requested a time slot in which I would speak about issues affecting Black women. I only had a minute allotted to me and I had to get it right. I began to write, and rewrite, practising in front of the mirror and with my family in order to perfect my words. Then I realized it wasn't enough to make the speech, I also needed to make a statement and I decided to braid my hair so my words would have maximum impact. But there was a little wrinkle. The date I'd been given was Monday, September 18. We'd only get back from the UK, where we were delivering Desiray to her first year of law studies at the University of Leicester, on the Sunday before I had to get back to Ottawa. It would be next to impossible to get an appointment on a Sunday night to get my hair braided. Then I got lucky: a friend's stylist was willing to do my hair. We drove straight from the airport to the appointment.

As I stood on the platform waiting for the train the next morning, I was nervous. Had an MP ever worn braids in the House of Commons? I felt like all eyes were on me. Why did I always have to go overboard? My phone vibrated and I checked my texts to see that the chief government whip was wondering if I could postpone my speech until the Wednesday session. What could I say? *Sorry. No. I braided my hair for this speech and I need to get it over with today so that people do not ask questions about my braids, touch my hair, or stare at me for the whole of the next two days wondering what is up with me.* Of course, I couldn't say that, so I agreed to wait.

Around the same time, the minister of environment, Catherine McKenna, was in the news because a Conservative MP had called her "climate Barbie" on social media. Catherine, like me and other female members, had dealt with different types of body shaming since we got to Ottawa, and we were all reaching the point where we'd had enough. I decided I had to take the advice I'd given Maryam Monsef. Even though my one-minute speech was designed to raise awareness on issues related to Black identity, I felt it wasn't enough to speak solely about Black hair, when I knew that all women and girls were shamed because of their appearance. When Wednesday finally arrived, I'd rewritten my speech one more time and I was ready.

When it was my turn to speak, I rose. "Mr. Speaker," I said, "this week I have my hair in braids, much like I had throughout my childhood. However, Mr. Speaker, it has come to my attention that there are young girls here in Canada, and other parts of the world, who are removed from school, or shamed, because of their hairstyle. Mr. Speaker, body shaming of a woman, in any form, from the top of her head to the soles of her feet is wrong. Irrespective of her hairstyle, the size of her thighs, the size of her hips, the size of her baby bump, the size of her breasts or the size of her lips. What makes us unique makes us beautiful. So Mr. Speaker, I will continue to rock these braids for three reasons. One, because—and you have to agree—they are dope! Two, in solidarity with women who have been shamed based on any part of their appearance. And third, and most importantly, in solidarity with the young girls and women who look like me and those who don't. I want them to know that their braids, dreads, super curly Afro puffs, weaves, hijabs, headscarves, and all other varieties of hairstyles, belong in schools, the work place, the boardroom and yes, even here, on Parliament Hill. Thank you Mr. Speaker."

At the end, my voice cracked with emotion. I was speaking up for myself as well as speaking up for others. When I started in politics, I wore my hair long and straight. When I first decided to cut it into a short bob, my staff told me I shouldn't do it. They stressed that I needed to wear my hair exactly the same way for the next four years: "That is how it's done. You want people to know who you are and changing your hairstyle confuses people." I corrected them. That is how it had to be done in a system that was largely inhabited by white men. I was not a white man, so those rules didn't apply to me. By the time I left Ottawa, I had worn it in a different style pretty much every week. I'd cut it into a short bob again, had it shaved on one side, shaved it completely off, wore it natural and every other style in between just to prove the point. To some men in the House, and even to some of the women, the issue I was addressing in my speech may have sounded trivial, but the overwhelming national and international response confirmed that it wasn't. And soon, Oprah's magazine, O, was calling, wanting to feature me in an upcoming issue about people who were standing up and making a difference.

While being interviewed by David Letterman on his Netflix show, *My Next Guest Needs No Introduction*, President Obama said: "Part of the ability to lead doesn't have to do with legislation, it doesn't have to do with regulations, it has to do with shaping attitude, shaping culture [and] increasing awareness." His words described the purpose I'd finally found in politics. I could review acts of legislation and vote on them with the 337 other people present, and did, but the ability to speak up about issues that brought pain to people was not just my responsibility, it had become my motivation and my calling. I'd found the perfect intersection of my past pain and present purpose. Politics gave me the platform to amplify the voices of the quiet little Black girls who felt and saw injustices and could not say anything. It gave me the platform to speak to young students who were struggling to connect with their immigrant parents, while carving out a space for themselves in the world. And it gave me an opportunity to tell women that I saw their pain and hurt, as well as their beauty and strength.

The problem was that for most of my time in office so far, I'd felt like one of the turtles riding the East Australian Current in *Finding Nemo*. I was trying to keep up with the flow and move with the others in Parliament. I was meeting with my constituents in the riding and those who came to my office in Ottawa, and had been paying attention to the situations in their lives that were causing them grief and anxiety. But if I wanted to understand the root cause of at least some of the problems they were having, and help them, I could not do it if I was rushing by, trying to stay with the pack. If I was passionate about the people I served, I needed to take the time to really listen. I would need to step fully out of the rushing current and form my own space.

As I started to speak out on issues, I felt as if I had stuck one foot outside the current into the calm waters where I was meant to be. But I couldn't stay straddled in this position for very long, one foot in, one foot out. It was painful. Even with what seemed to me like the half-assed way I'd been going about things, I faced an onslaught of negative messages from social media and received death threats against me and my children. I was being sued by a constituent who felt her immigration case was not proceeding fast enough and going through mediation with a staff member who wanted closure after she quit working for me. I realized that there was no turning back now, no path of least resistance. It was my responsibility to shape attitudes with my words, shape culture with my actions and increase awareness through my representation. And if representation truly mattered, I needed to represent something that mattered to me, and that was my community. Politics afforded me the opportunity to reconcile my pain with my purpose, realize my worth and build back my self-esteem. I wanted to help others do the same.

twelve

BLACK COFFEE, NO SUGAR, NO CREAM

IN JANUARY 2018, I SPENT weeks working on a letter, to be published in the Huffington Post on the eve of Black History Month, paying tribute to all the Black women who had been calling out injustice and standing up for issues long before I came on the scene. I wrote it out of love and respect, but also out of some guilt that a person like me, coming so late to the political struggle, was attracting attention because of my position on Parliament Hill. I want to quote it in full here, still out of love and respect, and because it marked such an important moment of understanding for me.

"A Love Letter to Black Women"

Dear Sisters,

I know that it has been a while since I spoke to you. I seem to have just popped on the scene. Over the last twenty or so years, I have been busy raising a family and growing a business, and we have lost touch. I have not been to the barbecues, community meetings or get-togethers in my "busy-ness." Now, I know what you are thinking, "Well, Celina. We have all been busy, and yet some of us still attended the community meetings and gatherings." Yes, I know. And that is why we (I) owe you a debt of gratitude. You stayed connected, where I did not. You sacrificed your energy, time and spirit, and we (I) owe you.

That is why I am writing. To tell you that even though we may have been distant, and I may seem far away, I love you and #ISeeYou. I have tried to reach out through my posts and blogs and speeches and the work I do, behind the scenes, related to policy. I have tried to break the status quo and talk about mental health issues, microaggressions, and the fact that body shaming includes our hair, the size of our thighs, the size of our hips and the size of our lips.

I may not be doing everything you want, as fast as you want. I am trying my best. It is no excuse, but from time to time, my depression and anxiety get the best of me, as I try to navigate this political beast that is very new territory for me. But the outreach was my way of saying that I see you, and through this position, I see you clearer than ever.

I see you Elders. You paved the way. You have lessons to teach and skills to pass down, if only we would listen. Your wisdom runs deep, because it is connected to this land, our homelands, and the motherland. #ISeeYou

I see you Moms. Single or otherwise. Holding it down for your children. Trying to protect them from the streets, and the institutions that keep them down and funnel them into prisons and foster care. I see you praying to God HE doesn't get stopped and carded, and SHE doesn't have somebody put her hair in elastic bands because it is too puffy. Both actions, damaging to their little souls. I pray too. #ISeeYou

I see you Wifey. Loving so deeply and strongly that it hurts. Because you have a partner that you want to inspire, protect and support, yet want to show the door every given day, and Sunday. (I have one at home too. Love him fiercely one minute then want to throw him out the next. Yet when I look into his eyes, all I see is love and my #rideordie). #ISeeYou

I see you Corporate. Holding it down. Producing the results. Bringing the strategy to management, then to fruition, all while being second guessed, passed over for promotion, and silenced when you face aggressive behaviour. I know what that is like. #ISeeYou

I see you Entrepreneur. Trying to make a dollar out of fifteen cents. Trying to get your hustle going. Putting it out there in the hopes that it will be successful and brilliant and everything you imagined. Hoping that they do not steal your idea(s), or pass your brilliance off as their own. Trying to get loans that may never come through, investors that cannot see your vision and naysayers trying to hold you down. #ISeeYou

I see you Activist and Protester. Yes, I am speaking to you @BLM_TO and others like you. You. Doing what this democracy affords you the freedom to do, yet you are met with hate and resistance. You with your brilliant minds and passionate hearts, who know your history, have done your research, who occupy and protest not just for the Black community, but for Indigenous rights, LGBTQ2 rights, and simply put, human rights. #ISeeYou

I see you Journalists, Policy Advisors and News Anchors/Bloggers/ Deliverers. We do not always see eye to eye. Do we have to? You need to hold my feet to the fire. You need to keep me accountable. That is your job. That is your calling. Don't water it down or go easy on me because we are sisters. Go hard, because you want me to produce the best policy for everyone, and I want YOU to be the best damn person in your field. #ISeeYou

I see you Book Store Owner, Historian, Educator and Author. I see you documenting and preserving our history and telling the stories of our present. It is a story that is erased from the consciousness of the world, and your work will be your legacy. It is important. Our people are storytellers and you are the keepers of this beautiful gift. #ISeeYou

I see You. Grinding every day, no matter the occupation or task. Hustling and grinding. Grinding and hustling. Being twice as good, twice as fast, twice as everything, because that is what we were taught. That is the only way we can succeed. I also see that it comes at a cost. The wear and tear. The exhaustion. The mental drain. I see that you are tired. And yet still you rise.

My sisters, in the face of all this you rise, and I see you. I see your
brilliance and courage and unconditional love.

I see you with your black velvet, dark chocolate, jamocha almond,
caramel latte (with a sprinkle of freckle) and all shades of skin in between,
that, when it is kissed by the light, makes your melanin shine brighter
than the sun. #ISeeYou

I see you when you walk into a room and the air has no choice but to
gravitate to you, as you suck the oxygen out of the space. #ISeeYou

I see you with your curves and shape. The ones that have a price tag
now, but yours have been divinely bestowed, rightfully placed, blessed
and cursed at the same time. #ISeeYou

I see you saying that everything is going to be all right. I see you
supporting me, even in our distance. I see you praying for me and
keeping me in your thoughts.

I see you. I thank you. I love you. And this Black History Month,
it is my privilege to honour you.

Love and Hugs,

Celina
@MPCelina

The irony was that my love letter appeared the day after I received
another overt and painful personal lesson in invisibility. On January 30,
the prime minister had gathered select Cabinet ministers and Black
community leaders to stand behind him in the foyer of the House
of Commons as he announced that Canada would recognize the
United Nations International Decade for People of African Descent
and also committed his government to creating a better future for
Black Canadians. At his side stood Ahmed Hussen, the first Somali-
Canadian to be elected to the House and the first to become a Cabinet

minister, having been put in charge of Immigration, Refugees and Citizenship early in 2017. Though I had been the one to flag this opportunity, and moral obligation, for the prime minister twice in 2016, I had heard nothing from him or anyone in the PMO since, which was awkward given that I heard regularly from the community members the government was consulting. They knew more about what my party was planning than I did.

It had gotten so awkward that in June 2017 I'd sent yet another fruitless email to Gerald Butts, along with a handwritten note to the prime minister, to remind them that, as a Black female, I brought a unique perspective to this issue. I also mentioned that they needed to reach out to more than one organization in order to consult Black communities. In my email I specifically mentioned an instance in which I'd found out about a meeting that had happened a few weeks earlier from community members who wondered why I wasn't there, just so that Gerry would know that some solidarity existed among the people trying to move the agenda of recognition, justice and development for Black people forward. I reassured him that I knew the issue was bigger than me and that I wasn't going to make a huge fuss about being excluded. Ahmed was more than capable of championing the road to official recognition of the Decade, I wrote, but surely the input of a Black woman should be pertinent too.

I did not receive a response (a familiar pattern). On the morning of January 30, I put on a mint green dress with a gigantic bow at the neck, designed to make me hard to miss, and stood at the back of the crowd that gathered in the foyer as the prime minister announced that Canada would be among the first countries to recognize the Decade. I was thrilled for my community and for Canada, but as usual I couldn't stop the tears from running down my face. Adam Vaughan had come to stand beside me and handed me some Kleenex. He knew all too well what had happened and had always been an ally.

I wiped my eyes and then I smiled like everyone else. There was no point in crying over being excluded from this one battle when there was much more war to fight.

The Huffington Post piece came out the next day, February 1, at the beginning of Black History Month. (It was also posted to ByBlacks.com, an online magazine started by Camille and Roger Dundas of Whitby, which highlights Black businesses and stories of success in Black communities, and was printed in *Share Newspaper*, a Toronto-based Black community newspaper.) I had chosen to write to Black women specifically, and not to male community activists like my own husband, because I knew that they faced the completely undermining combination of both racism *and* sexism— or "misogynoir," a term coined by queer Black feminist Moya Bailey. Members of my own government had schooled me in the term even as it pledged feminism and diversity as strengths.

On the same day, the government announced that it was going to spend the month highlighting Black women—a fitting and long overdue honour. Our stories of strength, courage and vision were celebrated with hundreds of events throughout the country; more than fifty MPs held such events in their region. In the House of Commons, members made seventeen special statements to call out amazing Black women. The day also saw Canada Post issuing stamps honouring Lincoln Alexander and Kathleen (Kay) Livingstone, two prominent Black Canadians who shattered barriers for all people of colour in Canada. On February 12, Black Canadians representing dozens of communities across the country came to Parliament Hill to meet with MPs from all political parties to discuss their pertinent issues and ask for government attention, funding, and support. This annual day of action had begun in 2016, with a meeting I'd suggested between Black elected officials and the prime minister. A first.

—

In his book, *Faces at the Bottom of the Well: The Permanence of Racism*, Derrick Bell, the first tenured Black professor at Harvard Law School, wrote about Dr. Martin Luther King Jr.'s struggle to remain committed to the "courageous struggle whatever the circumstances or the odds." He went on to say that "part of that struggle was the need to speak the truth as he [Dr. King] viewed it even when that truth alienated rather than unified, upset minds rather than calmed hearts, and subjected the speaker to general censure rather than acclaim." During the early months of 2018, I would live this reality, after I called out a prominent opposition politician for his actions only to have my own colleagues, media and members of the public express their disappointment in me for doing so. I knew full well that I couldn't take a shot at shattering the status quo if I was afraid to get cut. The glass was going to fall somewhere and if I was the one closest to it, I could expect to bleed. And bleed I did.

In late February, our government released its 2018 federal budget. For the first time in the country's 151 years of existence, a federal budget included an allocation designed to help create equity in Black communities. I was surprised to see $19 million dedicated to Black youth and mental health, $23 million to develop an anti-racism plan and $6.7 million for the creation of a centre for collection of disaggregated racial and gender data that would help the government create equitable policy. I was surprised by these details because I had not been involved in any conversations about this budget allocation. I had also objected to the lack of broad consultation with Black communities and the relatively minimal number of dollars. At the Black caucus meeting that followed the budget announcement, my colleagues told me that I should get on board because at last we were putting money behind such pledges. I could promote that, I agreed, even though I wished that the budget allocation was a lot higher.

In response to the funding, the former Conservative leadership candidate and sitting MP Maxime Bernier tweeted, "I thought the ultimate goal of fighting discrimination was to create a colour-blind society where everyone is treated the same. Not to set some Canadians apart as being 'racialized.' What's the purpose of this awful jargon? To create more division for the Liberals to exploit?"

I could not believe it.

I responded with a quote retweet that ended with an invitation to the man to straighten out his head. "@MaximeBernier do some research, or a Google search, as to why stating colour blindness as a defence actually contributes to racism. Please check your privilege and be quiet. Since our gvt't likes research, here is some evidence: theguardian.com/commentisfree/ . . ."

Twitter erupted. It seemed like everyone and their dog was upset, not with Bernier, but with me for calling out his privilege. Soon Rebel Media, a right-wing Canadian online publication, said I "might" be the "most racist MP" in Canada, a weirdly soft word choice for Ezra Levant's outfit. Nonetheless, it was enough to activate their hordes of social media bottom-feeding trolls. There was no way they were going to let a Black female MP tell a privileged white male MP the truth. In their twisted view of the universe, I was not supposed to be challenging the views of prominent male members of Parliament. I was supposed to be grateful I had the job, and just sit back and stay quiet.

I actually could not understand why so many people were angry with me and so few were calling out Maxime Bernier, a failed contender for the leadership of the Conservative Party of Canada, when he described a long-overdue investment in an underserved community as divisive. Well, I *could* understand it: he'd blown a dog whistle designed to be heard by his right-wing base. Still, he'd been elected to serve in Canada's Parliament: How did he get away with such irresponsible views? Didn't the very nature of the job require him to understand that many equity-seeking groups need government assistance and resources to help create equitable communities? I hadn't been paying much attention to the race to replace Stephen Harper, I have to admit. I didn't know Bernier was one of those guys who wanted to be in government in order to tell us we need as little in the way of government as possible—even as taxpayers paid him a salary to look out for them.

The more I reflected on this last question, the angrier I got. Bernier was being described as the victim of my angry Black womanness. Pundits opined about white privilege and their disappointment in me for pointing it out. I was being depicted as the culprit in this exchange for speaking out against his narrow-minded, unjust attitude. I could not look at my social media without scrolling through hundreds and hundreds of offensive messages. I won't repeat any of them here because I don't wish to give them any further space, but they made me sick and scared and worried for my family and my country. I had predicted that Trump's election would embolden haters everywhere, and the prediction had come true. It was horrible to be the target of such a gaslighting attack. In an attempt to create some breathing room for myself, I tweeted another message to Bernier, saying that it hadn't been cool for me to tell him to be quiet and inviting him to have a chat with me. But since I wouldn't apologize for telling him to check his privilege, he refused and the controversy roared on.

I needed to put my business hat on and figure out what I needed to do to get back on the right side of this issue in the minds of Canadians. The first step was not to back down. On March 7, 2018, I was supposed to deliver an International Women's Day speech at a "Women Who Lead" event at Toronto's Empire Club on behalf of Maryam Monsef, the minister of women and gender equality. The job was straightforward: all I had to do was to read the words written for and vetted by her. But, given everything that was going on, I was a bag of nerves at the thought of standing up in front of a largely white crowd of business people. Vidal came with me and tried to keep me calm, but as predicted, he and I were the only Black couple there. During the private reception before the event, I was a little reassured when many people from different sectors, ages and backgrounds approached me to offer their congratulations for standing up to Bernier. And the one Brown person in attendance, who turned out to be the event sponsor, Chandran Fernando, founder of Matrix360, a talent management and workplace strategy firm for equity and diversity in the real estate industry, came up to me, grinning. "You gave it to Maxime Bernier!" he said, and gave me a big hug. The hug was just what I needed to melt the nerves away.

As I stepped on stage, I realized that if I did not talk about body shaming, microaggressions or the obvious workings of racism here, I was doing a disservice to the community I represented. Not just the Black community, but all the racialized and marginalized communities across the country: women, people of colour, including Black and Indigenous folks, persons with disabilities, religious minorities, those with different sexual orientation. Everyone with an intersecting identity needed their voices amplified.

We often hear in Canada that "diversity is our strength," but is it? Diversity is ubiquitous; it is all around us. *Inclusion* is a choice. Inclusion is what will make our country stronger, but achieving inclusion requires consistent and deliberate work. As the anti-Black racism protests of 2020 brought home so urgently, rolling across the whole globe in response to the modern-day lynching of George Floyd, and in Toronto, the untimely death of Regis Korchinski-Paquet, who fell to her death from her apartment balcony after the police came to do a mental-health check, we have such a long way to go.

Although the spaces we occupy are diverse, they are not truly inclusive. Imagine the rewards that will follow from building a country in which each person has the opportunity to bring 100 percent of their authentic selves to their lives and work. Imagine the cultural wealth, the literal wealth, and the innovation flowing free in such a place. Much as all my new critics liked to deny it, we needed—we *need*—systemic change in order to ensure our institutions are barrier-free. Systemic racism flows from policies that reinforce the inequities between us—policies created in the context of systemic racism in the first place: one reinforces the other. That's why we have to keep the pressure up on our lawmakers at every level of government; they're the ones who set the frame and the laws that can dismantle racist policies. But there are some smaller changes that would help mitigate the microaggressions people face on a day-to-day basis. For example, in most workspaces and restaurants, people are still required to choose between a male and a female washroom. Do we really care about the gender assignment of washrooms? In my humble opinion, use whichever toilet you want, just remember to wash your hands.

When Black women and girls are ostracized and criticized for the ways we wear our natural hair, it makes me wonder just how interested we are in being inclusive. I wonder the same thing when I think about the laws we now have in this country that discriminate against public employees who wear religious paraphernalia. We have deteriorating or non-existent infrastructure in Indigenous communities, which inhibits people from reaching their maximum potential while living on and off the land they have occupied for centuries. All these things make it plain that we are *supposed* to choose a washroom carefully, straighten our hair so we don't upset anyone, and take off our religious items when we go to our public-facing job in case they offend the narrow-minded; if our community does not have clean running water we're supposed to just move to the city.

Every time someone is faced with the demand to lose a piece of themselves in order to accommodate those with the power to enforce that demand, our businesses, schools and communities—our whole country—loses. We lose the benefit of 100 percent of that person's contribution. Instead, they give us 90 percent, then 80 percent, then 70 percent and on down, until they are so weathered by the daily context within which they exist, they have no choice but to step away. These are awkward conversations to have, but they need to be had. Loudly, and in public.

As I delivered the minister's speech about all the ways our government was trying to enact policies and legislation to improve the lives of girls and women at home and abroad, and asking all the people in the room to reflect on what their own feminism looked like, the usual butterflies in my stomach once again turned into cheerleaders. I needed to include my own call to action. Since I was already in boiling water with the Bernier situation, what did I have to lose? At the end of the minister's speech, I added this: "I cannot leave this stage without acknowledging that over the past few days it has been particularly challenging for myself in the role I have. I have heard individuals say that I might be a one-term MP because I continue to speak up about issues. And I accept that. I accept it because my feminism requires me to be bold. It requires me to have uncomfortable conversations and to speak my truth. It requires me to smash and challenge the status quo.

"But my feminism isn't for everybody. Not everyone likes black coffee, no sugar, no cream." Here I heard the sound of one person clapping, and glanced down to see that the applause was coming not from Vidal, who was being circumspect, but from my new ally Chandran Fernando.

"So I implore you," I continued, "I implore you to be bold in your definition of your feminism. We have an army of young girls and boys here in Canada who are expecting no less from you."

I was never so glad to be done a speech, and never so glad to have strayed from the script.

After the speech, I headed straight to the airport to fly to Nova Scotia to attend, with Finance Minister Bill Morneau, the unveiling of Canada's new ten-dollar bill honouring Viola Desmond, a civil rights activist from the province. I hoped that my colleagues and I in the party's Black caucus had played a small part in the choice. We'd been sitting together at dinner a couple years earlier during a party retreat in Saguenay, Quebec, when Morneau came over and sat down with us. When he realized we were having a meeting, he asked if he could stay. When we agreed, he told us that they were about to select a woman to feature on the ten-dollar bill and asked for our suggestions. We all told him that Viola Desmond should be the one. As he got up to leave, I pulled him aside and made one final plea from the only Black woman present. In the end, many thousands of Canadians weighed in on the choice, but I was proud that our Black caucus (a parliamentary group that hadn't existed before the 2015 election) had played its part.

The edition of *O, The Oprah Magazine* that singled me out for speaking up against body shaming was released the following week, but even the magic of Oprah Winfrey couldn't tame the controversy still raging around me.

As the Bernier feud attracted national media attention, a prominent Ottawa journalist, Robert Fife, claimed on a CPAC show that systemic racism did not exist in Canada because high-school students of different races hung out together all the time. In response, on March 24, 2018, another Canadian journalist who wrote for Buzzfeed, Ishmael N. Daro, tweeted, "Robert Fife, the Ottawa bureau chief of the nation's paper of record, does not seem to know what systemic racism even means. He thinks it's about whether teenagers of different backgrounds hang out together."

I quote retweeted Daro along with a response on Twitter at 12:02 a.m. on March 26: "To suggest that systemic racism does not exist, makes me question your ability to investigate stories of the Canadian experience without bias." I mean, really: how could Robert Fife accurately report stories of marginalized Canadians and Canadians of colour for the *Globe and Mail* if he doubted the existence of racism?

Later that night, Brian Lilley, another Canadian journalist, posted that, "Liberal MP sees racism everywhere. Is @MPCelina going too far in attacking @RobertFife? Read and RT bit.ly/2IQVD69 #cdnpoli."

Had I attacked Robert Fife? In my opinion, I'd just asked a legitimate question about Fife's ability to accurately report on the lived experiences of people of colour in Canada. Secondly, do I see racism everywhere? Not necessarily, but you better believe I am going to call out bullshit when I read, see, or hear it. Lilley's tweet started another Twitter firestorm. At 9:19 the next evening, having stared at way too much of that firestorm sitting alone in my Ottawa condo, I sent out this message: "So tired of being attacked as a racist b/c I question racism or speak up against it. The label does not belong to me. I will not sit & let others say what they wish, because they feel they can get away with it, or others are too cowardly to object. I will speak up #NotToday."

I *was* tired, and I also felt myself spiralling into the dark place I never wanted to go again. I put my phone down and decided that it was best to stay away from social media for the rest of the night, if not the rest of my life.

At seven the next morning a knock at my door woke me up. I was so groggy I felt almost drunk. I peered through the peephole and there was Vidal, my rock and the love of my life. I burst into tears as I fell into his arms. "What are you doing here?" I asked.

"I left Whitby at three-thirty to be here for you." Vidal knew that his wife was about to spiral and that he needed to catch her when she fell. He carried me into the bedroom, lay down with me and allowed me to cry. He said nothing. He did not ask me to stop or take it easy. He knew that I needed to let it out. All of it. The frustration and anger and exhaustion. I cried until there was nothing left. Then he got me up and led me to the shower. "You need to get ready now, my baby, and go to work," he whispered. When I was dressed and ready, he walked me to my first meeting; only his love and support kept me upright. I thought I could handle everything that was being thrown at me, but by that point I felt as if I had no fight left.

Since I had put away my phone, I didn't know that others had picked up my fight. Andray Domise, a community activist who writes for *Maclean's*, had been chatting with Vidal as Vidal headed for Ottawa, and decided to send a message of support via social media. At 8:28 a.m., Adam Vaughan tweeted a thread of solidarity, including #HereForCelina in every one. "Before anyone wants to discount racism," he wrote in his first tweet, "check the attacks attached to Celina's posts." He then composed an alphabet of individual tweets, outlining the reasons why Fife's comments were incorrect. Under Lilley's post, he described how systemic racism exists in Canada. He included personal stories to drive home his points, along with quotes from various thought leaders. Soon others started adding their thoughts, using the hashtag.

Vidal was waiting for me when I finished my scheduled morning meetings, and told me that I was trending on social media. My stomach instantly sank. I stopped walking. "Why?" I asked, as I trembled with fear. I was staying away from my phone on purpose. I wanted the whole thing to go away.

"No, no, babe. It's a good thing. People are supporting you. Adam and Andray started a hashtag, #HereForCelina, and it's trending in Canada."

I fumbled to pull out my phone. Hundreds of messages from Canadians and people around the world appeared on my social media pages; there were texts and emails. I trembled even more as the tears rolled. "I am not crazy. I am not wrong. I am on the right side of history." I think I even said that out loud.

Later that afternoon, prominent members of the Black community called to tell me that, in addition to posting messages with #HereForCelina on social media, they had started a letter-writing campaign to the PM, his Cabinet ministers and all Liberal members of Parliament asking them to support me. They had had enough. As one of them said, "You have put yourself out there long enough. Others need to get on board. Canadians are supporting you. American journalists are supporting you. Your caucus needs to do their part."

They were right: only Adam and a couple of others had supported me publicly through the weeks after the Bernier exchange. Bernier had attacked the Liberal's budget, giving them a perfect opportunity to show their mettle and their commitment to diversity. Yet during our Ontario caucus meetings, some members indicated that talking about gender, race and intersectionality did not resonate when they knocked on doors in their constituencies. One of them said that people in his suburban riding asked him, instead, "What are you Liberals doing for our white sons?"

I was not expecting much support from them in tackling issues specific to the Black community, but it did not take long for the letter-writing campaign to bear fruit. That evening, at about six, I received a call from Mike Power, who had been my liaison in the PMO when I was the PM's parliamentary secretary, asking me if I was okay and whether I needed anything. He indicated that the prime minister wanted to meet with me before our national caucus meeting the next day. My blood started to boil. Really? *Now* they were asking if I was okay? When #HereForCelina had gone viral?

Where had the PM, the PMO and Liberals been for the last three weeks? Where were their tweets or support during that period?

As annoyed as I was, I remained calm. There was no point in turning into the "Mad Black Woman" and giving them any more ammunition to use against me. Staring at Vidal, I told Mike that yes, I was okay and, in fact, I had everything I needed (right there in the presence of my husband), and agreed to meet with the prime minister. The fact that he wanted to meet before national caucus meant that he really didn't want to talk. My Ontario caucus ran from eight to ten o'clock and national caucus, which he attended, started at ten. When exactly were we supposed to have this conversation?

Vidal and I decided to go out for dinner that night to Whalesbone on Elgin, my favourite local restaurant. I knew everyone in the place, as I ate there by myself at least three or four times a week when I was in Ottawa. We toasted how the day had turned out, laughed and counted our blessings. Everything was better when we were together. Even though he was carrying a full load at home—looking after the children during the week, finishing his doctoral studies and working as the dean of the Police Education and Innovation Centre in Durham—he'd flown to me in the night like my superman. After dinner, we went back to my apartment and I was able to sleep in his arms for a few hours before he got in the car and headed back home.

The next morning, I left Ontario caucus ten minutes early and made the five-minute walk to Parliament Hill to see the PM. We had maybe three minutes together, which, at this point, was about as much as I could handle and felt like more of my time than he deserved.

As frustrated, outraged and demoralized as I was by the entire Bernier/media episode, I was more frustrated, outraged and demoralized by the lack of response from my own political party. Even if they wanted to keep their distance from me—the woman who had raised the topic of white privilege—someone should have defended our budget's investment in the Black community. It would have signalled that it wasn't only "the Black woman" who was offended and rejected Bernier's views, but that the entire government was. If they even briefly glanced at the comments bombarding my feeds, they would have seen that they were under assault too.

Before Black community members started to write letters, no one from the party or the PMO had called me to see how I was doing or if I needed support. I knew that at different times they had reached out to other members, Iqra Khalid for one, who were experiencing issues and threats, but not to me. I mentioned before that one of the rules I try to live by is "If you don't ask, you don't get." And it's true, I didn't ask for their help. I accept full responsibility for this. But when did I have the time to ask? Why did I even need to ask when I was dealing with a public outpouring of hate visible on the internet, trying to insulate my family from it all and continue to handle my job?

In my most cynical heart of hearts, I figured that the party hadn't extended a lifeline to me because someone somewhere had done the political calculus, and figured that their majority was secure in the next election (though no one in politics is able to foretell the shit that's going to come down in the future!). As a consequence, they decided they didn't need to defend the apparently controversial MP of a riding they didn't need to win. And, given that I didn't hold my tongue when it came to Liberal failings either, maybe they wouldn't mind if I didn't come back to the House of Commons.

Still, all the vitriol was also affecting my role as parliamentary secretary to the international development minister and the organizations that counted on me to support their work. Whenever I posted about a development organization or project, the trolls and bots would flood their timelines with racist and sexist comments too. No matter what they thought of me, shouldn't the party have wanted to shut that down as fast as possible? It felt like I was the only one worried about how the fire I was drawing on a regular basis was affecting the ministry. When, in September 2018, I received a call from the PMO extending my term with International Development, they seemed completely surprised when I said no.

I easily resisted attempts by a few people in the PMO to persuade me to stay, but then Jane Philpott called. I was tickled. Jane, who had been shuffled from one increasingly difficult ministry to another in Cabinet, was often the person the Liberals called upon when they needed a tricky situation handled. I loved Jane. She was not only a colleague, but a confidante. Smart, empathetic and humble—she was everything you would want in a minister of the Crown. "Jane, don't you have anything better to do than call me?" I said, when I picked up, and laughed. "Quit doing their dirty work. You know why I am saying no." She could not disagree, given that she knew what I had been going through. I told her, though, that she could tell the PMO they didn't have to worry about one thing, at least—I was not going to disclose my frustrations and why I was leaving.

On the morning in September 2018 when the new list of parliamentary secretaries was released with my name not on it, the prime minister asked to meet with me in my riding after he made a funding announcement at Ontario Tech University in Oshawa. He asked me why I resigned, and, as usual, I was blunt: "I resigned because you did not value me enough to give me a simple phone call or ask a member of your team to find out if I was okay." One phone call from anyone in the PMO at the height of the Bernier controversy—it didn't have to be him—to say that they saw me. A call to say that they understood that the community I represented in Whitby was 70 percent white and to offer their help to fix this attempt to mischaracterize me as a racist. A call to say that they wanted to support a member of the team who was facing the full force of political backlash, a backlash that was spilling over onto the ministry I was supposed to serve. A call to say that they valued the work I was doing.

The prime minister responded that no one called because I did not ask for help. Then he said that I was such a strong, independent woman, he didn't think I needed it.

Right. A strong Black woman like me, with a big mouth like mine, wouldn't possibly need help; we were all so fierce and scary.

At that point, it became abundantly clear that the awareness I was trying to bring to the rest of the country about microaggressions and racism had not registered with my own organization or its leader. The prime minister's experience, largely shaped by his privilege, blinded him to how completely inappropriate his comment was. (When the whole controversy over his dressing up in blackface emerged in the 2019 election campaign, I thought I should have seen that one coming.) I didn't even try to correct him.

After this encounter, I decided I needed to give an interview to someone I trusted about why I'd left the role with International Development. That person was Charelle Evelyn, the managing editor of the *Hill Times*. When I first saw her in the press gallery, I thought I was seeing things. People of colour were so rare in the gallery that spotting a Black woman had me looking around to see if anyone else saw her too. Maryam Monsef caught my eye, pointed to the gallery and smiled, confirming that, in fact, Charelle was real. I was careful in the interview to keep my promise to Jane, dropping only hints as to why I'd turned down the offer to stay on. In her piece, Charelle wrote that my decision to leave had been "brewing for some time" and quoted me saying that I found it difficult to leave because it was a job that I "thoroughly enjoyed." I described my resignation as the "smartest, most strategic decision for me and my family at this time," but I did mention that the "constant need to analyze and second-guess oneself gets exhausting." Anyone reading closely, and with some knowledge of me, would know that I was referring to the microaggression and racism I experienced within my own party.

But a bigger seed of doubt had been planted by my most recent interaction with the prime minister. I'd left the role of parliamentary secretary, but did I actually want to stay on in politics or with the Liberal Party? I was unsure. The past three years had been amazing in terms of the work I was able to accomplish, but my desire to do the job right meant I continually had to challenge attitudes in my own party. Fighting the opposition was one thing, but fighting Liberals was something I did not want to have to do.

On November 14, 2018, I noticed that my schedule for the day included a lunch with an elder Black woman, a former politician I'd met only once before. She'd requested a chat. The next election was a little less than a year away and I was excited about meeting her and receiving the wisdom she would surely impart to a younger Black female politician who had made some noise on behalf of the community and, as a result, had been publicly tossed and turned in the political arena.

We met at a coffee shop in Whitby. After the necessary pleasantries were out of the way, she leaned in and I did too. But what she had in mind wasn't a cozy session in which she would praise me for my accomplishments as a newbie politician and encourage me to keep the faith. No, her message was that if I wanted to remain a member of the Liberal Party of Canada and run in the 2019 election, I needed to "figure out what type of Liberal I was going to be." I was shocked.

She went on to explain. My rebuke of Bernier, she said, was actually a "mark" against me, because in that kind of situation, where the issue was racism, the old adage that "all publicity is good publicity" did not apply to me. That was not all. The first mark against me, she said, was criticizing the prime minister when he'd said that the 2015 Cabinet looked like Canada.

I felt like I'd entered the Upside-Down-from-*Stranger Things* version of Sally Walker's office. I needed to straighten her out. I told her that I had been right to criticize the Cabinet because it did *not* look like Canada, and I would do the same again. I wanted to ask her if she had nothing better to do for the past three years than to tally up the "marks" against me. I restrained myself, but she had even more digs to get in before she gave me the bill for lunch.

She told me that my impact in government had been minimal at best, that I could have had greater impact if I had been friendlier with people in the Prime Minister's Office, and that I would regret the bridges I had burned. Fuck me. I just wanted to get out of there. But I stayed put. No matter how painful it may be to listen to your elders, you do. Patiently and respectfully. More or less.

"I may not have had the impact you had when you were minister of . . . what were you minister of again?" I finally said. I went on before she could answer. "But rest assured that if even one person feels less alone, more resilient or walks with their Afro puffs a little higher because of what I have done while I was here, it has been more than worth it. And I know for sure that more than one person feels this way, and that is all that matters."

I paid that bill, then made sure that no one in my office submitted it as a reimbursable expense. I did not want any more Canadian tax dollars spent on this former politician. I did not want me, or anyone else, to owe her anything.

After that lunch, I wrote the following on Facebook:

Today I had a conversation with someone I truly respect. However, I left the conversation feeling hurt and misunderstood, and I wanted to share some of my thoughts.

When we use the hashtag #AddWomenChangePolitics, it means that when you add women, things will change. However, this can only be true if the women you add are willing to be the change they wish to see, otherwise you have #AddWomenMaintainTheStatusQuo.

I recognize, quite clearly, that I am not your typical politician. I speak my mind (sometimes to my own detriment—human beings do that from time to time), I am transparent (my constituents get what they see) and I am willing to have the uncomfortable conversations that many will shy away from. I am not afraid, and I will not be held hostage by votes.

I also recognize that I represent the Liberals. However, I was not elected by the Liberal Party of Canada. I was elected by the people of Whitby, and it is to the people of Whitby that my allegiance lies. Clearly, based on the conversation I had today, some do not like that, and I am totally cool with it.

At the end of the day, I am here to serve the various communities I represent, which are all contained within Whitby. Women, men, people of all ages, dispositions, races, religions and ethnicities, marginalized populations, people who feel disenfranchised by the political process, etc. They all live in Whitby, and as such, I represent each with passion and vigour.

I do things differently. Sometimes it is not about right or wrong, correct or incorrect, it is just different. I will leave you with this. On David Letterman's Netflix show, *My Next Guest Needs No Introduction*, Barack Obama says that, "Part of the ability to lead doesn't have to do with legislation or regulations, it has to do with shaping attitude, shaping culture [and] increasing awareness." I hope that my contributions to politics, thus far, have helped to move the needle in that direction.

If we want politics to change, we may have to change how we do politics.

Love and hugs,

C.

Nina Simone's song "You've Got to Learn" will be playing during this scene in the Netflix biopic of my life. I'd learned to show a happy face and to pocket my pride, but I'd also learned "to leave the table when love's no longer being served."

I was at a point in my life where I finally understood how valuable I was. Not just to the Liberal Party and politics, but to my community and family. If you do not understand how valuable you are, you will always accept what is given to you. One of the first rules of business is that you should never accept the first offer. It is a hard lesson to learn because most of us are grateful to have received any offer at all. In the workplace, however, the first offer is usually the lowball one—the place the employer starts so that when you counter, you will reach a mutually amenable deal. But how do you know what to offer as a counter? We (meaning women in particular) are often humble people who find quantifying our skills and experience— our worth—daunting. But you need to make the effort. And you need to ask, of any situation in your life, are you getting as much out as you are putting in? Are you getting more? Are you getting less? Friends, lovers, community service, even reading this book— is it worth your time?

If you are not getting as much out of any of them as you are putting in, it may be time to walk away. This is one of the hardest lessons I've learned. But, once I was able to understand my worth, and the value I bring to other people, it became easier to love myself more, create and nurture lasting and loving relationships, and also to walk away when love was no longer being served.

thirteen

AN INDEPENDENT WOMAN

AS I WRITE THIS, TRYING to identify the patterns in what was a chaotic and overwhelming period of my life, it may sound like I had perfect insight at all times about what was happening to me in Ottawa.

Not at all. In the moment, any flashes of clarity were quickly clouded by the insidious nature of acts of racism, sexism, microaggression and other forms of discrimination. They creep into the crevices of your mind in a way that makes you feel like you are going crazy. Somehow, as it had with Bernier, the onus of the act falls on the victim, while the culprit slides away. *Did that just happen? Did anyone else hear what that person said to me?*

I had never felt so much like a "woman," a "Black person" and a "Black woman" until I entered politics. I tried to address this, even to make light of it, in speeches, where I'd look down at my chest and exclaim in mock-surprise, "Oh my, I have boobs!" I'd hold out my hands, and stare at them, saying, "Oh my, I am Black too." But I found it hard to articulate the reasons for the deep, underlying discomfort I felt for most of those four years I was in Ottawa. I've recounted some of the events that felt like explicit assaults, but it was so much more than that.

In an issue of *Variety* published in April 2019, I read an open letter to the CBS television network from Whitney Davis, a Black former executive at the company who at first had pursued a journalistic and then a creative role at the network, but ended up working as its director of entertainment diversity and inclusion. The final episode that sparked her resignation was a large-scale investigation into the company culture that had allowed the former CEO, Leslie Moonves, to get away with sexual harassment and exploitation of female employees for years. Two outside law firms were hired to interview hundreds of staff, Davis among them, and they had given her the impression that their exploration of the company's toxic culture would be wide-ranging. She cooperated fully, happy that at last there was a safe place in which she could detail the casually accepted racism that, in particular, permeated the creative side of the business. She hoped for real change, and when real change was denied—Moonves was let go, but none of the other toxic cultural issues were addressed—she got out of there. But leaving wasn't enough; she felt she had to go public with her own experiences because that might be the only way to pressure CBS to address what she called its "white problem."

The examples in her open letter were so familiar to me I felt myself inadvertently nodding at each one. Even the denial of her experiences by the culprits she called out was familiar to me. Davis's letter helped me name for myself the ways in which the mind games caused by racism are both powerful and debilitating. Her truth allowed me to come to terms with my own.

Despite its lip service to the value of diversity and the diverse viewership it counted on for its success, CBS was not a diverse workplace. Neither was our federal bureaucracy. I could understand the lack of diversity in the House. Becoming an MP required a person to agree to run, seek the nomination, be the candidate and then win the election. There were a lot of factors that were outside of one's control.

But hiring within the federal system was a much more straightforward, manageable process. Though I knew there were more than enough qualified Black people to fill these positions, when I looked across the federal departments for Black faces, I saw none in the senior positions of deputy minister or assistant deputy minister. In fact, since confederation there had only ever been one Black ADM and four Black heads of mission; the first Black woman was appointed to that role in 2018. Additionally, although there is no tally of the number of Black-owned businesses with procurement opportunities with the Government of Canada, I would bet that those numbers are negligible too. Was it only me, or did the government that touted diversity as a strength have a "white problem"?

Davis described how when she and another young Black woman held the two lowliest positions in the CBS newsroom, their white colleagues couldn't keep their names straight. She wrote it off to the fact that she and the other Black woman were not important enough for anyone to take the trouble to remember. She figured it was more about status than race, and it likely happened to young white people in junior positions too. But when she and her boss were the only two Black people working at the executive level in the entertainment division—their brief: diversity and inclusion issues and talent-spotting to try to rectify the "white problem"—other executives still couldn't tell them apart.

I, too, had run into people who could not remember if I was me or some other political Black woman. I got mixed up with Mitzie Hunter, for instance, who was the only other dark-skinned woman in Canadian politics during my mandate. The context should have been a clue: she was an Ontario MPP (provincial not federal) representing Scarborough-Guildwood (not Whitby) who worked in

Toronto (not Ottawa). Not to mention we looked nothing alike. Still, colleagues greeted me as Mitzie on multiple occasions. One man addressed me two or three separate times as Mitzie, even though I corrected each of his mistakes. Once a Liberal colleague tagged me in a photo on social media at an event "we" had attended. I wouldn't have given it much thought, except I did not attend the event. It was Mitzie, not me! Davis wrote, "I don't think most people understand just how demeaning these daily micro-aggressions are. Or maybe they do and don't care." I could not agree with her more.

I want to include one more example from Davis, who described what happened after a senior producer used the "n" word in front of her. When she reported it to her boss, he told her she needed to grow a "thicker skin." Thicker skin? We are Black women. We were born with thick skin.

Our strong reaction to such slurs, and to other racist, sexist and homophobic behaviour towards us and others has nothing to do with the thinness of our skin and everything to do with how the system treats us and dismisses us. Do people think that the Black women who succeed against the odds and ascend to the heights could possibly have thin skin? From the day we're born, our mothers tell us that we have to be twice as good as the other children. My mother in particular was relentless on this subject. We have to work twice as hard and be twice as smart. Everything we do needs to be doubled because we have two strikes against us already: we are girls and we are Black. We can't afford to be thin-skinned. This is the reality of growing up Black.

In sharing her experience, Davis helped make real all the things I still worried were figments of my imagination. Her story spoke to me, and let me know that my experiences were not made up, but accurate reflections of my time in politics. These are not experiences shared by a few, but by many people of colour. Those in power and authority, who are usually white and male, can make us feel that the way we are experiencing their oppression is invalid. They can make us feel that we are too sensitive—that we are just taking "things" the wrong way. We are supposed to get over it, move on and stop making such a big fuss. But we are not the problem. We really aren't.

There are a few more twists and turns in my political journey still to share. Just as I was wrapping up work on this book, teasing out the final thoughts I had to share, I came across a graphic that struck me dumb. It was called "The 'Problem' Woman of Colour in the Workplace," and it described the beginning, middle and the end of my life as an MP so clearly it took my breath away. What I experienced is actually so commonplace, an artist was able to make a step-by-step roadmap out of it. (The version I saw was adapted by a Quebec NGO, the Centre for Community Organizations, with permission from the original source, a US-based human rights organization called Safehouse Progressive Alliance for Nonviolence.)

In it, a woman of colour lands in a workplace where the leadership is white. Everyone is pleased with themselves over her hiring and the woman herself feels "welcomed, needed, and happy." Then a phase called "reality" sets in as she begins to see and then to point out failings and issues inside the organization. She's careful to "work within the organization's structures and policies" even as she "pushes for accountability." After all, she wants to keep her job and keep doing the work she was hired to do.

No, none of those things are happening here, the leaders respond, and even if they are, surely he's the one with the insight to fix them. How can they be asked to correct something they can't perceive? They look around for support that they are blameless and in that effort "People of Colour are pitted against one another."

Next comes the retaliation phase in which the organization decides that really the only problem they have is her. The organization "targets her" but claims they are doing so because "she is not qualified or 'not a good fit.'"

Exit, woman of colour.

I wish I'd seen that graphic before I waded into January 2019. It might have made what followed a little more comprehensible and, because of that, a little less painful to live through.

I was completely surprised when the Speaker of the House asked me to deliver one of the toasts at his annual Robbie Burns dinner at the end of January. I wasn't Scottish. I had no romantic attachment to Canada's colonial history. I wasn't much of a fan of Burns, a white man who was a womanizer and got away with things that most people of colour, especially Black men, would not be able to get away with and keep walking around with their skins intact. But my audience would be Cabinet ministers, MPs from across all parties, and some of the Ottawa elite, and I couldn't resist the opportunity.

When I got up to deliver the ritual toast called "the Reply to the Laddies" (after Jane Philpott had toasted the poet himself and Rob Nicholson had finished his address to "the Lassies"), in true Celina fashion, I spoke about white privilege, race and the toll of being a woman of colour in politics. At the time, I didn't know the story behind Jody Wilson-Raybould's recent move to Veterans Affairs, just that both she and Jane Philpott had new portfolios. But, after detailing all of the women Robbie had slept with and all of the children they bore as a result, I made a crack about the shuffling of two prominent women ministers. "All of his penile philanthropy leads me to believe that Burns may not have just been his last name, but also the feeling you got when you lay with him," I said, then joked that Jane, on account of her medical practice, must know all about that feeling, and might have also felt a bit of a burn at being moved three times over the course of three years into increasingly difficult portfolios. "Speaking of Jody Wilson-Raybould," I continued, "if Robbie Burns was a member of our government, she would have been asked to remove him from our Parliament, not just our caucus. . . . If she didn't succeed, she would have been fired. And if she succeeded in removing Robbie Burns from Parliament, well, she would have been fired. You can't have an Indian doing that to the white man." That was close to the bone, but the PMO had always been eager to point out that Wilson-Raybould was the first Indigenous woman to hold the position of minister of justice, yet had just moved her to Veterans Affairs in what everybody viewed as a demotion, replacing her at Justice with a white man.

I realized there was a lot more behind her move than I'd guessed when, after my speech, the press started to hound me for details they assumed I had to know—forgetting what else they knew about me, which is that I had resigned as a parliamentary secretary four months earlier and likely wasn't in good standing with the PMO. On the scent of the SNC-Lavalin story, they dissected my speech for clues, and even criticized me for withholding the truth when I told them I had no idea what they were talking about. To me, it was just another day in the life of a woman of colour. You do something wrong and you are reprimanded. You do something right and you are reprimanded. I did not know about the issues with Jody and the prime minister. Until that point, I'd barely spoken with her. In my speech, I'd simply stated the truth as I knew it, not knowing how true it was.

Within weeks, the story broke that Wilson-Raybould was moved from the post she'd held for three years because she refused to intervene in a criminal case involving the Quebec-based global engineering firm SNC-Lavalin. In a statement, she indicated that she had come under "consistent and sustained" pressure—including veiled threats—from the PMO, the Privy Council Office and the finance minister's office to halt the criminal prosecution and that she was moved from her portfolio when she did not agree to do so.

After she went public, the *Globe and Mail* reported that some Liberal colleagues were displeased with Jody for her lack of discretion and had anonymously attacked her character, painting her as someone who was not a team player. That angered and appalled me. In those few weeks of the SNC-Lavalin scandal, I posted messages on Twitter like little breadcrumbs, leaving a record of events. On February 10, I tweeted, "As someone on the inside, who knows @Puglaas, I can tell you that she is fierce, smart and unapologetic. When women speak up and out, they are always going to be labelled. Go ahead. Label away. We are not going anywhere. #IAmWithHer #StandUp #ISeeYou."

In the era of #MeToo and #TimesUp, the Liberal Party had positioned itself as the party that would "believe her." Liberals liked to portray themselves as the ones who stood by women when they disclosed interactions with others that caused them to feel pressured or uncomfortable or victimized. I believed in that principle, just as much as I believed Jody. So it was easy for me to publicly support her when other members of the party were turning away. I found it interesting that the party would "believe women" when it was convenient for them and leave them when it wasn't.

By this point, I knew that I would not—should not—run again, but the guilt of leaving a job I was good at, and people I cared about, made the decision torturous. Even though, at my regular riding town halls, we argued about various issues colourfully, I knew that the people of Whitby respected me as their representative and I respected them. They appreciated me as a straight-shooting MP who didn't bullshit or play favourites. Everybody who came into my office was sure to get the truth from me. I was not going to shoo them away, saying that I would "take their concern under consideration." There was nothing to consider. Either I was going to do something about it or I wasn't. Still, even when I wasn't going to take on their issues, I tried to make sure that a constituent or stakeholder never left my office feeling badly. I would take the time to map out ways to make their idea better, present some other options for their consideration, and leave the door open for future meetings. But I also made it clear that I would not sit still for abuse because I was afraid to lose their vote. You could not come into my office or approach my staff in a hostile or belligerent manner. You would be shown the door or hear a dial tone. The fact that a voter was paying my salary with their taxes did not give them the right to treat me or my people with disrespect. I loved each and every member of my team and I panicked at the thought that some of them might no longer have a job.

I told my husband and a couple of close associates first. They supported my decision not to run, but when I added that I was considering sitting as an Independent MP for the rest of my term, they thought that would be a bad look for the party. With much hesitation, I agreed; I supported many of the government's overarching policies and initiatives, and I did not want to undermine those if I could help it. My Ottawa staff advised that I should do the PMO and the chief government whip the courtesy of informing them of my decision before I made it public. Again, I agreed, and on the morning of February 12, 2019, I sent a note to each man's office.

I was startled to receive an immediate call from the PMO to say that the prime minister wanted to speak with me later that day. As if I had not learned anything over the past three years, I thought he might want to say that he was truly sorry to hear that I was not running again, and ask me to reconsider. But February 12 was also the day Jody Wilson-Raybould resigned from Cabinet. When Trudeau called at nine-thirty that night, it was to tell me that he wanted me to wait to make my announcement because the news that I was leaving his caucus and politics would adversely affect him—he "could not have two powerful women of colour announce they are leaving at the same time."

I responded as carefully as I was able. I said, "I hope you can appreciate, not today, or tomorrow or a year from now, the impact that the past year has had on my family. Again, not today or tomorrow, but at some point."

With those words, the prime minister lost it. "Oh my God, Celina. Oh my God. I can't believe that you are telling *me* to understand!" He insisted I should appreciate *him* for supporting me in the by-election. He pretty much yelled that he was tired of people reminding him of his privilege, and ranted on about how he and his family had also been affected. I had put my phone on speaker, as I usually did when I was having work conversations at home. Vidal was within earshot, and as Trudeau spoke, he could see me growing tense, and he was too. I started to pace the living room, the only safe space for me to move in the house we'd just moved into. (We were in the middle of major renovations, the floors torn up and walls knocked down, fixtures sheeted in plastic.) The more Justin spoke the angrier I got. I started to pace up the stairs, through the construction zone, back down the stairs and into the living room, again and again.

The manner in which he was speaking to me took me back to my childhood, when my mother would correct me forcefully for behaviour I didn't think was wrong and I would take it because I had no other choice. I let him rant away. But when he was done speaking, I made him understand that I was not a child he could correct, or even the Celina he had "helped" in the by-election. I was not taking this from him. "Motherfucker, who the fuck do you think you are speaking to?" I slammed the words in his ear so hard, I am sure that everyone in the room with him heard me.

Good grief. I've heard that people who swear are very smart. By the end of my monologue, I'd dropped the f-bomb enough times to make me a fucking genius. Why should I be grateful? I'd worked my ass off in his government for three years. I hadn't even raised the issue of his privilege with him, though now I pointed out that I was well aware that his family had paid a price for his political ambitions, but his had RCMP protection, whereas mine had none, even though both families had received death threats.

The next thing I heard from him was a tearful apology.

I had no time for it. "Are you done?" I asked. He mumbled something inaudible. "Good!" I responded, and hung up the phone. Vidal and I stared at each other for a moment in shock. Did I just use a dictionary full of expletives with the leader of a G7 country and then hang up on him? Better fuckin' believe I did. But Vidal knew that we needed to be calm and think about the situation. He said, "You are not going to like what I have to say, but I think you should honour his request, and wait to make the announcement." Vidal slept on the couch that night.

That phone conversation played and replayed in my mind for days afterward. I wondered if Scott Brison, the former president of the treasury board who had stepped down and out of politics a week earlier, had received a similar berating. From the way he'd looked in the news coverage of his resignation, I bet he hadn't.

Still, I wavered between Vidal's advice and my pride. In the end, I gave the prime minister a pass, deciding that I would postpone my announcement until March 2. I sent him a note to that effect the next morning. When I hadn't heard back from the PMO the following day—at least acknowledging my decision to postpone, if not expressing any appreciation for it—I left another breadcrumb on Twitter. "T-14 When you ask someone to do you a favour, and that favour is completed, be grateful and say thank you."

Within two hours, Brett Thalmann, the director of administration and special projects within the PMO, emailed. "Hey Celina, I wanted to make sure you knew that the PM did see your email from yesterday and appreciated it very much. Thank you for agreeing to delay the announcement. I was also hoping we could meet next week when you are back in Ottawa as I would like to get your advice on a few things. Can you let me know what times would work for you? I'd be happy to come to your office or we can meet at PMO. Whatever your preference is. Thanks again and I look forward to catching up with you in person."

I wrote back: "With all due respect, Brett, fuck right off." I had been giving the PMO advice for years, and nobody listened. Why the hell did they want to talk to me now? To tell me how to slam the door on my own ass as I left?

Bits of the PM's rant kept coming back to me. Even when you feel you are fully justified in losing your temper, somehow it seems necessary to replay the scene in your head, looking for where it could have gone differently. Now I remembered the long minutes he'd spent telling me about the work he had done for the Black community, including on the federal recognition of the International Decade for People of African Descent. He'd at last explained why I had not been included in the planning for marking the Decade. During the meeting in 2016 in which I'd flagged the Decade for him, I'd mentioned that I did not want to be "central" going forward. By excluding me, he insisted he had been respecting my wishes.

He was correct, sort of. What I had told him was that I did not want to be the one person in government speaking "for" Black communities. Communities have been speaking for themselves for years. When he'd asked me for my thoughts about how to proceed,

I advised him that the government should consult the community broadly—elders who had been doing this work for a long time, but also young people who needed to be engaged. He could establish community consultations, but he also needed to reach marginalized Black Canadians either by telephone or with an online survey. On February 15, I tweeted "Not central ≠ Excluded." Only he would know what I meant, if he happened to look, but Twitter had turned into my version of keeping a public record. I needed the record to show that Trudeau had made the decision to exclude me. I hadn't excluded myself.

On the evening of February 16, I received a phone message from a Liberal MP, panicked about a tweet he'd sent out that had called me a "penis." (Of all the words to use, *this* was the best he could come up with?) He called again on Sunday morning, and this time he got me. He wanted to apologize, he said. The tweet wasn't his fault. A friend of his had taken his phone and sent it. Really?

After he hung up, I posted, "All of a sudden everyone wants to have a conversation?? Calling me at 9:30pm on a Tuesday evening or 10:30am on a Sunday morning to play me like a fool is not a winning strategy. I. Am. Not. A. Pawn. In. Your. Game. Come correct or don't come at all. #NotToday."

My husband was not having it, either, and tweeted, "@MPCelina you have just proven that you are not a pawn, you are the Queen." We were both so tired of all the games and so relieved that I'd made the decision to leave politics. In one sentence, my husband promoted me from pawn to queen, enabling me to make any move I wanted.

I went to the next national caucus meeting on February 20, 2019, the following week intending to tell my colleagues that I wouldn't be running in the next election and that I had been thinking of withdrawing from the party to sit as an Independent as a head's up, and out of respect for them. I stood in line waiting for my turn at the microphone, listening to all the expressions of solidarity and support being extended to the prime minister over the SNC-Lavalin affair by the other MPs—it was now so bad his principal secretary, Gerald Butts, had been forced to resign a week earlier. My frustration must have been showing on my face because Frank Baylis, a first-time MP I respected who had also been an entrepreneur in the medical field, pulled me out of the queue to talk with me. Although he did not know about the phone call, he knew I was upset and unsure about staying on in politics, and I am sure he read my face in the way most Black men can when a Black woman is angry. He told me not to let the actions of the prime minister get to me. He reminded me that in caucus my role had always been to try to pull the team forward towards a goal, and I shouldn't stop now. I trusted Frank. A natural leader, he was so thoughtful that every conversation we had made me think more deeply myself. If he advised that I needed to calm down before I spoke, he was probably right.

I got back in line and when it was my turn, I told my colleagues that while I wasn't going to run again, I would stay a Liberal because the people in this room had taught me grace. I would stay a Liberal for the greater good of the team and for the grace that they showed me, which had allowed me to be bold and to speak up. More importantly, I would stay for the 37 million Canadians who sent us to Parliament to serve them.

During the remainder of the caucus meeting, I thought long and hard about grace, and about the ability to forgive and have compassion. I reviewed the events of the past few weeks, especially the pressure the SNC-Lavalin scandal had put on everyone in the room. When the meeting was done, I went to stand in another line, this one made up of MPs wishing for a moment of the PM's time. I waited patiently as other members shook his hand, gave him hugs and in other ways showed him that they were on his side. As I watched, I couldn't help but wonder if he had ever spoken to any of them the way he'd spoken to me. I also wondered if any of them had ever had cause to cuss him out in the epic fashion I had.

Finally, the others were gone and it was my turn. I knew the conversation would be awkward, but during the caucus meeting, the prime minister had talked about the importance of togetherness, of respect and of the value he placed on the team. Other MPs had spoken eloquently on these subjects too. I was sure that he, too, would want to put the telephone call behind us and move on.

"I know that our last conversation was not the greatest—"

The look on his face stopped me before I could finish the sentence. It told me that he had no time for me because he was angry. All the talk about team and togetherness applied to everyone but me. I did not know how to carry on in the face of that so I turned and left the room. It struck me forcibly as I walked away that this man held power and I did not know whether he intended to use it against me. What exactly did he mean when he'd said my decision to not run again would have "impact"? I was so disillusioned I felt sick.

I retreated to my desk in the chamber. On Wednesdays ahead of Question Period, the doors to the House of Commons didn't open until two o'clock, and the space was quiet. I needed that quiet to meditate and centre myself again. When Question Period started— the cameras rolling, media and spectators in their galleries—a figure crouched just behind me and whispered in my ear, "I am sorry. I should not have responded to you in that way after caucus."

Did he mean to make it right with these words? Why couldn't he at least say them to my face? Three years of dismissal, offensive behaviour and disregard worked against me even believing him. The tears I had been holding in since the end of the caucus meeting started to stream out. I left the chamber, found a quiet room, and collapsed.

Jane Philpott and Mark Holland, who represented the riding of Ajax, next door to my own, found me. Mark blurted that he wanted to help because I was not in "good shape."

Poor man. I yelled at him. "This is not about my depression," I said. "I am not crazy. You can't continue to treat me like this and then call me crazy. Jane, please tell him I am not crazy!" She did just that. She'd been standing up to the prime minister herself, in solidarity with Jody.

But I also realized that we were all accomplices in the prime minister's behaviour. Despite what I'd been thinking about grace and my previous wash of fellow feeling for my colleagues, we had all seen him verbally admonish MPs who expressed ideas in caucus that ran counter to his own. We'd made excuses for him or said nothing. When other Liberals felt that to best represent the people in their ridings they needed to vote against the government and then were removed from their duties in committee, we said nothing. When colleagues said that they were experiencing intimidation from fellow colleagues, we said nothing.

I thought about all the times I should have stood up for my colleagues, but didn't. It turned out I did not have enough strength to fight for my colleagues on the inside and for the Canadians I promised to fight for who lived outside the political bubble. I had to choose my battles, and fighting Liberals to save Liberals was not mine. I would need to forgive myself for this.

On the monitors in the room, we saw that, in the chamber, Jody Wilson-Raybould was standing on a point of order to explain why she had abstained from a vote calling for a public inquiry into the SNC-Lavalin affair. She indicated that she abstained because the vote had to do with her personally, and that she hoped that at some point she would have the opportunity to speak her truth. I drew strength from her words.

—

When I went home to Whitby that weekend, I plugged into the true source of my energy. I went to a couple of scheduled events in the riding, but spent the majority of my time with friends and my family. On Monday morning, February 25, I felt ready to return to work.

I caught the 7:15 train for Ottawa. I sat with an older couple who were just returning from a trip to the Galápagos Islands and a woman who owned a company in Belleville. We laughed together for the whole four-hour journey, exchanging stories about travelling and life. I told the couple they should write a travel blog and they told me I had to take a trip to Madagascar. I was sad to see them go when they got off in Smiths Falls.

In Ottawa, I dropped off my suitcase and looked at the schedule. I had Question Period, a couple of meetings and then a panel for CARICOM's Day on the Hill, to discuss the legacy of Caribbean-Canada relations. I scanned the panel details for the questions the moderator would ask so I could prepare my thoughts. It was then that I noticed that the prime minister was going to attend. I immediately felt sick and rushed to the bathroom. After I rinsed my mouth, I texted my assistant to ask her to confirm that the PM really was attending. She did, and he was. I then called the organizer, Sherry Tross, the high commissioner of St. Kitts and Nevis, and asked her for more specific details. We had votes scheduled that evening, so there was a chance I would miss the PM. No, she said, even if I left early, the PM and I would cross paths on the stage. I thanked her and hung up, my chest even tighter and my stomach now in knots. I put my coat on, grabbed my bag and walked to West Block. I thought I would sit in the chamber for a while before Question Period, but as I took my place, I was immediately overwhelmed. I felt just like I had the previous Wednesday. I texted Jane Philpott and she met me in the government lobby, adjacent to the

House. She took one look at me and told me to head back home. I was on the 2:30 p.m. train.

The next day, I scheduled a video call with my psychiatrist. I knew if I waited too long to talk with him, I would go into that dark place I wanted with all my heart to avoid. In advance of the call, I'd provided him with a breakdown of all that had happened to that point. I had also taken the time to call some of the white male colleagues who had decided not to run in the next election and asked them what it had been like for them to break the news to the prime minister. All of them said that he had treated them well. One went so far as to say that the "easiest part of the entire decision was talking with the PM."

I asked my psychiatrist why he thought there was such a difference in the way the PM had reacted to me. Maybe, my psychiatrist said, the prime minister felt that a white man leaving politics was part of the regular course of things, whereas a Black woman leaving reflected badly on him as a leader. Thinking back, that is more or less what Trudeau had said to me. But my psychiatrist didn't think the prime minister was driven by political considerations—which is how the PM had framed it to me. He called it discrimination. That was powerful to hear. He also suggested that I should think about why the PM had knelt behind me to whisper his second apology. Could it be that in his eyes I now had enough power that he was afraid to look me in the face? That all the hard experiences I had been through had made me strong? He advised me not to have any communication or contact with the prime minister except in public places when I couldn't avoid it, and he told me I should stop thinking I could "fix" the relationship by trying to be reasonable. There was nothing reasonable about the situation I was in.

When I got off the call, I felt better. He'd confirmed everything I was feeling and reassured me that I wasn't "crazy" to feel it.

Echoing what Serena Williams said in her recent Nike commercial, which I'd watched on the train ride home and tweeted about as soon as I finished it: "We feel crazy, second guess ourself, underestimating our power, and make changes to satisfy the fragile ego. Show them crazy. #mood." I was tired of appeasing fragile male egos in politics. Racism and sexism undeniably exist on Parliament Hill.

Though I'd left my trail of breadcrumbs on Twitter, I had not told anyone save for my closest circle about my recent interactions with the prime minister, and I announced my resignation publicly on March 02, 2019 as promised without mentioning the PM's reaction. Little did I know that Jane Philpott, one of Justin Trudeau's most trusted ministers, would announce her resignation from Cabinet on March 4, 2019, citing a lack of confidence in the prime minister's handling of the SNC-Lavalin affair. So, three days after Jane's resignation, during what was supposed to be a speech of contrition to the country over the scandal, the prime minister said, "I believe real leadership is about listening, learning and compassion. . . . Central to my leadership is fostering an environment where my ministers, caucus and staff feel comfortable coming to me when they have concerns."

I could not believe those words were coming out of his mouth.

He went on to say that Jody Wilson-Raybould had never come to see him about her concerns about the SNC case. I went from incredulous to furious. If I were her, I would not have taken my concerns to the prime minister either. At that point, I felt I owed it to the electorate and my colleagues to correct the portrait he was painting of his leadership style. So I tweeted about the differences between how I was treated and how he claimed to treat his caucus and staff, and then I told my story to Laura Stone of the *Globe and Mail*.

The Ontario caucus met next on the morning of March 20, 2019, and the session was painful to sit through. My colleagues were focused on their disappointment with Jane's actions and they let her have it to the point of reducing her to tears. Most of them seemed to believe that the right thing for Jane to have done was to put her party above her principles. What happened to the idea that we were elected because we said we would do politics differently?

Every now and again, somebody would lump me into their tirade of disappointment. The charge against me was that when I called out the prime minister in public, I'd gone against the entire caucus. They did not want me there, any more than they wanted Jane. I realized in that moment that I didn't care what they thought. I still believed that the Liberal Party comes closest among all the federal parties to putting forth policies in the best interests of the people I was fighting to serve, but I could no longer be part of the herd mentality that party politics induces.

After Ontario caucus, I went directly to the Speaker's office and asked for a new seat assignment away from the government benches. I stayed there, keeping a low profile, until just before the afternoon Question Period session was to begin.

At two, I took a seat at my new desk in the far southwest corner of the House of Commons. I was shivering, not from cold but from nerves. It is one thing to know what to do and another thing to do it. And maybe sitting by myself in a far corner was just a little too close to my childhood of being seen and not heard when the adults gathered, careful not to draw any of the kind of attention that would lead to trouble. I kept my head down and tried not to make eye contact with anyone. I hoped that if I made myself as small as possible, for a little while nobody would notice that I had made the decision to leave the Liberal caucus and sit as an Independent MP.

Of course, members of the opposition soon clocked where I was sitting, but when they came over to offer their support, I shooed them away. I did not want to be alone, but I was not one of them.

The press gallery noticed too, and out of the corner of my eye I saw reporters staring down at me with interest from the balcony above. The news would be out soon.

Then Frank Baylis sat down beside me. "I am not going to let you sit here by yourself," he said. "You don't deserve this. You did so much for us and for Canadians. We needed to fight for you and we didn't. I will stay with you." Now I wanted to cry, but I had no energy left to make tears.

As I continued to sit in my corner, through that afternoon and evening marathon of votes on the 2019 budget, I had time to try to get used to my new situation and to reflect on how it had come to this. At least I hadn't waited to be kicked out of the party (which would happen to Jody and Jane two weeks later). I had deliberately taken my fate into my own hands, having realized how untenable it was for me to try to continue to speak up for my community, and myself, in this party.

As the news spread, messages started to come in on social media. One of them, from a constituent of mine called MJ, read: "I did not vote for you to be an Independent. Disappointed that you did not stick in the Liberal party. . . . Sorry times."

I tried not to respond, but the temptation was too great. "Sorry about that MJ. I appreciate the note."

The reply was instantaneous. "Well I am liberal in my way of approaching the world. So loyalty and sticking in the party would have been what I would have done. Can I share an example to give you food for thought: I am a catholic and of course right now the church has tremendous issues and changes to make. I am not leaving my way of faith over these changes. My hope is to make changes from within. I wish you the best but disappointed."

There was much to unpack in those few short lines. First of all, I'd had to stop going to my Catholic church in Whitby myself when

I stood up, with my Liberal colleagues, for a woman's right to choose, and also made clear that I was pro LGBTQ2+ and a supporter of medical assistance in dying. When the other parishioners protested my presence, and the presence of my family, I had to weigh my devotion to a religion that could not deal with all of me. MJ's chastisement actually reaffirmed my decision to sit as an Independent member. Sticking with the party for the sake of sticking with the party was not my way of doing business. It was absolutely not the way I wanted to represent the people who'd elected me. I'd had to choose whether to subordinate my values and principles to the party or do what I believed was right. Put that way, the choice was straightforward.

My decision to leave was about politics, but it was also about whether I thought it was worth it to try to keep navigating spaces that are not accustomed to including people like me. To survive in such places, we need to carve out our own niches, because we do not fit into the pre-designed and pre-defined boxes. We disrupt the narrative that underpins the rules by which we play. That takes work and, even when it totally wears you out, it still needs to be done. You need to be relentlessly strategic and smart, because you are so often working against the way "things have always been done."

I had worked diligently to advance issues that are often whispered about but not acted upon: mental illness, microaggressions, racism, equity and justice. I did not do this to be "a voice" for anyone—everyone has their own voice—but because I was conscientious about amplifying the voices of those who are often excluded from the political process—people who aren't dyed Liberal red or Tory blue or NDP orange or any other political colour. I was not going to dismiss the people who elected me to appease a party that disrespected me. If I'd stayed on as a Liberal, I would have had to settle. I would not have been able to look my children in the eye or carry on confidently acting according to my beliefs. MJ, who had reached out to remind me that it was important to be loyal, had reminded me, instead, that I should never settle.

My actions—in particular the interview I did with the *Globe and Mail* in which I spoke out about the PM's behaviour towards me—hurt many of my colleagues and supporters. That was not my intention. But my honesty shouldn't have surprised anyone. From day one in Ottawa, I rarely acted as a bobblehead who read the party lines verbatim. I used my own research and experience to complement the messaging, and came up with my own words as they pertained to the issue and to the people of Whitby. Why would I drink the party Kool-Aid when the world was flowing with great wine?

I was the exact opposite of the "Liberal" MJ identified with. Whether in a place of employment, a classroom, a community or a relationship, I believe we should never be expected to accept bad behaviour or stay put when we know we should leave.

I had embarked on a mission to be different in politics and do politics differently. Taking my place as an Independent was the realization of that mission—and marked my final realization that I have been independent all my life.

There is no time. Like the present. I changed this phrase and added the period in between because the past and future don't exist—we only have now. We only have the present.

As much as I have tried to live in the present, it does not come easy. I often find myself holding on to past hurts and thinking about next steps, all the while neglecting the present moment.

At the beginning of my political journey, I was challenged by the burden of responsibility. It was lonely. Very little in the space reflected who I was, or the contribution of people who looked like me to this country. I walked through hallways under the frozen glares of white men, most of whom seemed disgruntled to see me. A history of structural violence was baked right into Parliament's stones; the halls and offices and meeting rooms, even the House—our national symbol of democracy—made me feel strange and uneasy. Maybe in 2020 with people, including me and my children, having taken to the streets in spite of a global Covid-19 pandemic in order to protest anti-Black racism, we've moved the needle enough so that it isn't just the BIPOC community who understands what I mean.

There is a history of policy enacted and implemented by the Parliament of Canada that has made life difficult for people of colour, that has supported the creation of social institutions that prevented some of our citizens from meeting their basic needs, let alone fulfilling their dreams. I felt that history. I was acutely aware that the space was not made for me as I signed my name into history under the ornately framed picture of the Fathers of Confederation on the day of my swearing-in. I knew even then that it was going to be a long four years.

Then, after writing my first blog in the Huffington Post about my mental health issues, I started to realize that my burden was lessened whenever I used my voice to speak about uncomfortable issues. The heaviness was still there, but I started to understand that the burden of responsibility I was feeling was not a burden at all—it was an opportunity for me to embrace the present and use my position to stir the pot. I loved using my voice to speak about micro-aggressions, body shaming and systemic racism. It was my responsibility, I realized, to bring to the forefront of mainstream politics the whispered conversations people of colour, and in particular Black women, had at water coolers every day. I love my community, and I loved the ability to share their stories in a way that could take the burden off them, to help to create better schools, communities, work spaces and political institutions where we, too, can be comfortable. The community of women who walked with me and those that came before me had paved a way into that space. We are not going to create or build sustainable change for equity-seeking groups if we are constantly afraid to speak the truth. Most importantly, we cannot get to a place of reconciliation if we shy away from speaking truth to power.

CONCLUSION

SOMETIMES I WONDER WHAT WOULD have happened if I had kept my big mouth closed, settled politely into politics, and rode that wave all the way to the lifetime pension? Would I have minded people calling me "the Honourable Celina Caesar-Chavannes" for the rest of my life? Absolutely not. Would I mind that I would have had to call myself dishonourable because I had not stayed true to myself? Absolutely.

It was the right decision, but, still, I felt enormous sadness in the months that followed my decision to leave. Not regret—I still have no time for regrets. If I had never stood for office, I might not have learned how important it is to operate from a place of unapologetic authenticity. Politics led me to a place where I could at last use my voice. It reintroduced me to the three-year-old Celina who did not know what fear was. She loved herself, sang at the top of her lungs and didn't care what anyone said about her, her body or her voice, which cracked more often than it held a note.

But the challenge I knew I now faced was how to live like that for the rest of my life.

That's what I've been doing since leaving politics—digging into transforming myself from a fairly selfish, competitive and money-conscious entrepreneur into a person who cares more about people than titles, more about impact than rhetoric, and more about using my voice for good, and not about spewing pre-written platitudes from unfamiliar pulpits. How do I continue to act on what I learned?

How do you live your best life when you are unsure about what to do next? It's quite possible that I still don't know.

In August 2019, with just a few months to go before the fall election and the end of my tenure, I spent the day packing up my constituency office with the help of my staff. Just as I walked in the door at home, Stacey Berry, my trusted office manager, called. She had something to tell me, she said, and it had to be in person. This was odd, because during all the hours we spent packing up four years of our political lives, we'd spoken of all sorts of issues—except what was keeping me up at night: the thought of her and my other Whitby staff no longer having jobs.

When the people who worked for me in Ottawa found out in March that I was not seeking re-election, they'd easily moved on to other positions. My interns were all returning to school in September. Ang, who came out of retirement to join me in Whitby, could easily return to retirement. But the future prospects for Stacey and my immigration specialist, Christel Ilunga, were not clear. I'd hired Christel right after the 2015 election, and she had stayed by my side through the thick of it. After months of trying to find the right person to fill the job of constituency manager, I'd taken the advice of Margarett Best, a former minister with the government of Ontario, who had hired Stacey while she was in office, and given Stacey a chance. She was brilliant and detail-oriented, and knew exactly how to look after my interests and the work of the constituency. With Christel and Stacey in Whitby, I had never had to worry about a thing. I told her to come right over, and when she got to the house, we settled down in the front sitting room, full of late afternoon light. Maybe she had come up with a wonderful plan that would soon have us working together again. I wanted that too. But, no, what she wanted to deliver face-to-face was an answer she had heard to a prayer she had made for me.

"Your crown has been bought and paid for," she told me, quoting Maya Angelou, who herself was paying tribute to words by James Baldwin. "Put it on your head and wear it. You did your job, and you did it well. Now put your crown on and wear it proudly. What happens next will come. You do not have to chase it. You do not need to ask for it. You deserve it. Just be patient."

No surprise to those of you who have come this far with me: I burst into tears. I don't know if I was crying because of her telling me to wear my crown or at the thought of having to sit patiently until "the next thing" arrived. I am a go-getter. A doer. How could I stay resigned to doing nothing but wait for a revelation with a crown atop my head?

"So how long do you think I will have to wait?" I asked.

We both burst out laughing. There she was, eloquently, earnestly, relaying the message she received on my behalf from her God, and I was asking about the timeline. But she forgave me: Stacey knew how hard it was to put "Celina" and "patience" in the same sentence.

I needed a drink after that and immediately opened a bottle of champagne. Why? Why the fuck not? This was the end of something, and the beginning of something else, and even if I did put on my crown and wait, who knew when the answer would come and what it would be. I pulled some seasoned salmon out of the fridge and told Stacey to call Christel. If this was the end, we were all going to celebrate together. After Christel got there, we laughed, talked, cried, drank—well, Christel doesn't drink, but at least there was salmon for her to eat—for hours. To say that I love these two women is an understatement. They started as employees and became family, and now we were at the end of our road together. I had vowed long ago never to regret anything, but this came pretty damn close.

—

So here I was: forty-six years old, a mother of three, unemployed, Black and female. Don't get me wrong. I was content with my decision to leave politics, but in order to figure out what came next, I needed to take time to reflect.

One of the things I had to reflect on was how beautiful but rare those late summer hours of laughter and reminiscing with Stacey and Christel were. In my life to that point, and especially while I was in politics, I rarely called up girlfriends and asked for their help or got together to laugh, drink and eat, taking a time out from our struggles. Now the fact that I had never reached out to anyone struck me as sad. I had been so busy running through life that I hadn't taken the time to gather a village of such friends around me. Just as organizations select a board of directors to act as a sounding board and provide strategic direction, we, too, need a team of advisors to get us through the tough, the good—well, any kind of times. I had assumed that being independent meant being alone. But independence isn't synonymous with loneliness. I realized that in the times when I felt most lonely, I shouldn't have made so much effort to "protect my independence." I should have pulled those that I loved closer to me.

Maybe I had been too embarrassed to admit I needed help or arrogant enough to believe I could handle it best by myself. My inability to reach out might also have been related to the guilt and shame I felt for having never been part of any activist movement—I did wonder what right I had to ask the community to help me. For so long I had kept to myself to protect my secrets and my traumas; I know I feared that connecting with anyone on more than a superficial level would potentially expose me. The truth of it is that I could have connected more, across the board, in politics. There was actually no point in hiding my secrets. The effort just closed me off from others.

So, although I did have a lot of support—so clear during the #HereForCelina moment—I still felt alone. I let the idea of being the "only Black female member of Parliament" get in my head and form a protective barrier. While I *was* the only Black female in federal politics at the time, I was not the only Black female experiencing loneliness at work. There are countless "only" ones in the world, and if I'd sought them out, their experience could have helped to guide me through some difficult circumstances. Sitting and stewing in my "1-only-ness" just pushed me further into my own head, which was not a very stable place to be. Between my struggles with depression and anxiety and the battle to control my competitive drive to be better than others—to be the best—I had turned further in on myself. I think that's why Whitney Davis's open letter in *Variety* hit me so strongly: it was one of the first times I let someone else's experience breach the walls I put up around me. But I hadn't needed Davis's article to validate my experiences. Any woman of colour could have done that. Any person who has felt marginalized or "alone at the top" could have done that.

So what did I need help with? It wasn't any particular "thing." I was strong, and I was bold, and I could deal with most of the issues that came up. What I really needed to hear from others was some of the ways they navigated the darkness that precedes the unknown. The "unknown" happens every time we are about to do something daring, that moment when the butterflies in our stomachs are telling us that there is something to fear. Even now, each time I am asked to speak in public, the person introducing me finds a way to describe me, or my actions in business or politics, as "fearless." That is so untrue. I am even afraid in the moment before I go on the stage and for another few beats after I get to the microphone. My three-year-old self runs away and leaves me standing there trying to figure out my next move. Serves me right though. I never write my speeches. I either jot notes on a piece of paper a couple hours before the event, or in the car on the way, or I ask people when I get there what they're interested in, and wing it from there. Sounds dangerous, but once I'm over the fright, I thrive on it.

Every leap I took in business or every viral political moment involved some amount of fear—that feeling of standing on the edge of a cliff before you do something daring. Fear is crucial to our survival as human beings. Fear is necessary. I was not fearless, I just didn't allow fear to stop me from doing what needed to be done. Some of the time.

If I am perfectly honest, a combination of my fear and the exhilaration I felt in resisting the status quo has allowed me to accomplish a lot. I've already mentioned *Faces at the Bottom of the Well*, one of my favourite books. In it, Derrick Bell writes of a woman named Mrs. MacDonald who lived in the American Deep South during the Jim Crow era. She knew she could never defeat the racist power structures around her on her own. Engaging in small but persistent acts of resistance against them was her goal. Such acts add up. Whether it was changing the words in a speech to be more provocative or speaking out against racism, I made my own acts of resistance in politics, and I still do. On their own, none of my acts can change systems that have existed for longer than Canada has been a country, but I want to rattle the barriers at every opportunity. Each persistent and sustained act of resistance, each moment of defiance, attacks what Bell describes as the "permanence" of the racism and sexism that permeate our institutions. Understanding this reassured me that my time in politics had been valuable.

In every situation, I was motivated by the responsibility to represent my community—the people who looked like me and the ones who did not. People say that "representation matters." Seeing someone who looks like you in politics, in business, in academia—anywhere—helps you realize it's possible to get there too. However, if representation matters, the representative person sitting at the table needs to be fighting for something that matters to them. If nothing matters to them, why are they there? If they are not going to speak up for issues, why are they there? Especially in public office and public service, they should be vocal on important issues, pushing the powers-that-be to be bolder and advocating for interests that might be outside of their own but promote the greater good. If they don't, they should get out of the way and allow someone who will take their place. If they are only there for the title, the paycheque, the status or the photo op, how does "representation" really matter?

It took me a while to get my feet under me, but I finally realized that if I was going to be at the political table, I had to speak to the subjects that mattered to people in a meaningful way. I needed to be disruptive—in word, in action and in appearance—in order to get through to people and get them thinking differently about privilege, racism or mental health. For change to happen, lots of people need to be prodded out of their comfort zones, and I found I didn't hesitate to raise the uncomfortable topics.

My last act as an MP was to introduce Bill C-468, an act to amend the Employment Equity Act. It was designed to remove the barriers that had stood in the way of Black people rising to the top of the federal public service. In those dying days before the 42nd Parliament was dissolved, so much was deemed urgent that I thought it might not be possible to get the bill on the record. However, with the help of some Conservative colleagues, especially Colin Carrie and Opposition House Leader Candice Bergen, the bill was ready in a matter of weeks.

I rose in the House for the last time on June 20, 2019, and, from my spot beside Jody Wilson-Raybould, who had joined me in my independent corner and who seconded the bill, I thanked all involved. "I came to this place to be a voice for all the people

I represent, to raise awareness on issues, to move the status quo and to remove barriers," I said. "This bill represents the voices of those both past and present in the federal system. It is my hope that it will examine and help remove the barriers that prevent them, especially those from the Black community, from achieving success and promotion within the system. Their voices are reflected in this bill, and it is my honour to bring their voices to this place."

Although the bill did die on the order paper at the end of the term, I was satisfied to have placed the need for change on the record. In February 2020, after the Liberals were re-elected with a minority, both Bill Matthews, the deputy minister of public services and procurement, and Treasury Board President Jean-Yves Duclos announced their commitment to removing barriers and improving opportunities for Black employees.

In addition to growing my village, using my fear for good and representing what matters to me, I have needed to reinforce a couple more truths after I left politics. The first is that life is not a competition. There is no point in comparing myself to those who came before me or those who will come after me. I am my own benchmark. Trying to act like someone else is an exercise in futility if what you want most is to become a better person, to live authentically and to use your voice for good. The goal is to try to be the better version of you.

When young people say that they want to be me some day, I am quick to tell them that it is a terrible goal. "Set better goals," I say. "What is the point of aspiring to be me when I have been so candid about my failings? Create the best version of yourself by learning from your own failures, rather attempting to become a carbon copy of someone who already exists."

Politics had been a painfully beautiful experience—somewhat like childbirth, where you forget how difficult it was to the point of getting lured into doing it again. I appreciate that in a country of 37 million people, only a fraction of a percentage point of us have been members of Parliament; I am grateful for the honour and thankful for the experience.

I appreciate this even more now that I've taken the time to look inward, and to tell the story of my life over the past four-and-a-half decades. Every moment, I realize, was built on the previous one. Every success was built off a previous failure, and every joy heightened from previous pain. There have been times when I've questioned *everything* about myself, every decision I made and every action I took.

This year of self-reflection has been painful, too, but it was what I needed to do to end up here—to appreciate the impact of the awkward and painful moments and to dismiss the noise that resulted when I stood up for what I believed in.

I realize that some of my decisions may not be what others would have made. And that is okay. I stayed silent in the face of assault, just as I stayed silent in my first couple of years of politics, in order to survive.

The last truth I came to is that my journey does not have a destination (well, except the final one). There is no achieving an ultimate state of authenticity, any more than there is a final destination called "becoming a leader." When you define yourself as "the leader," you inevitably begin to defend your positions as if there is no other option, worried that if you respond flexibly to the demands of the day people may call you "inconsistent." The fallacy of believing that you have *arrived* at leadership or authenticity is that you risk turning away from the opportunity to learn in the moment, to change your position or your reaction to a given situation.

Many who have witnessed me trying my best to speak and act from an authentic place have asked me if being authentic "works" in business or in politics. That is a difficult question to answer, because authenticity is a struggle. Don't get me wrong. It is not a struggle because I don't know how to be authentic. That I do know! It is a struggle because authenticity is just as multi-faceted as the idea of leadership. I can't be always singing the one note. I need to take different approaches to the different situations and challenges that arise. So do we all. Some situations require us to be quiet. Sometimes we need to speak audibly and clearly. Other times we are required to shout and take to the streets.

Authenticity is a process of discovering how to use every part of you to make any given situation whole. This includes using your perceived weaknesses and flaws, the parts that embarrass or shame you. We often hide those parts and show the world only a portion of who we really are. That never works out in the end. I could not be anything different, even if I tried. I needed to embrace my anger, and the sound of my own voice, as much as I embraced the desire to do good—*in order* to do good—in the world.

From childhood, I realize, I was never sure if anyone could hear me no matter how noisy I was. Chasing this desire to have my voice heard, I have had ups and downs. That said, I have learned from the experience, and it is my hope that in sharing what I learned I can help transform lives, communities and our world, and strengthen our humanity by sharing our truths.

Before I entered politics at forty-one years of age, I let others or my circumstances define me, much as I wish that wasn't the case. Inside that political bubble in Ottawa, alone at night in my little apartment after daunting, desperate days, I was forced to re-examine everything about myself. To break all the hidden pieces apart and see what made me tick. To have had that long period of reckoning and struggle with my strengths and weaknesses, traumas, secrets and true sources of joy was what allowed me to survive one setback after another, and not just find success, but purpose.

Six years after I took my first train to Ottawa, I not only know who Celina is, but I appreciate her as well. Specifically, I appreciate the "flaws" that have allowed me to grow independent, resilient and authentic. For the first two years in politics, I was so afraid of being labelled an "Angry Black Woman" that I tried to be as polite as possible in order to fit into the "politician" mould. Those days are over. I have embraced all of me. And I won't look back.

On March 21, 2019, I looked out the window at the Ottawa streets and knew I had to leave them behind. But on that day, and every day thereafter, I have had to look in the mirror and face myself. I now see the reflection of someone who is not perfect, but has formed a more perfect union with her self. A woman who is not content with staying quiet, going with the flow and blending in, but who is outspoken, audacious and unique.

Can you hear me now?

ACKNOWLEDGEMENTS

I want to thank, especially, the people who came before me and the people in my lifetime who have given me so much, including the ability to speak confidently and unapologetically. To my ancestors, who had the wildest dreams I now live—thank you. My gratitude, also, to the confident women in my life, who inspire and tell the most wonderful stories, especially Cousin Marie, our family's griot. Thank you for believing in me and sharing my story. I appreciate you.

To those who think their ideas are too small, their voice too soft and who doubt their capacity to run, I will tell you what I tell the moms who approach me thinking they can't take politics on: don't sell yourself short. Think of how your skills in life could transform politics rather than how you need to transform yourself to fit the way politics are done. When you run a campaign, you need to manage different people on your campaign team, and manage the different personalities in your constituency. No one does this better than moms! We give different chores and responsibilities to our children based on their skills and abilities. We know that one child is going to feel like you're asking too much of them, while the other feels like they've been given too little responsibility because you don't believe they're old enough to help. This is the same as managing any team, but particularly a political campaign team of volunteers! Mothers know how to make their children feel included and important, and that their contribution to the family is valued.

Use those skills to run a political campaign. As well, every mother has that one child who likes her and will vote for her no matter what (that's my Johnny), one child who will vote for her, but will require some convincing (that's my Desiray) and one child who will like her, but will vote her off the island so fast her head will spin (that's my Candice). We all have the capacity to use the skills and experience we have to change the world. Let's do that.

I want to acknowledge those who believed in me even when I did not believe that this crazy idea of politics would work. My gratitude goes to the young people who dream of a better world and work towards that goal. To Brianne, Dilara, Jordyn, Onome, Olivia, Heba, Arezoo, Sydnie, Calille, Rhayelle, Raisha, Jaida and Alicia, and others who want to change the world, I will reiterate what I wrote in the first version of my resignation letter: "I also know that I have no right to ask what I am about to ask, but I will do it anyway. I am going to ask women, of all backgrounds to run, and run in packs. Get your girlfriends and their girlfriends and run like we have never run before. My experience in politics has demonstrated to me that there is capacity to change political structures from the inside, but only if we are there in numbers. The treatment I have received from the leadership in my own party is disappointing and regrettable, and I apologize for leaving before I had an opportunity to make any change, but I trust that women, especially women of colour and other Black women, who are way stronger and braver than I am, will finish this job. I know that our country will be better for it."

To those described as "voiceless" or in need of empowerment—often the poorest and most vulnerable among us—you do not need anyone to be your voice. You already have one. It may be a whisper that is ignored, but it exists. You also do not need anyone to *make* you empowered, you already are. You just need the right tools to maximize that empowerment. And most certainly, you do not need a McKinsey report to tell you that when women are given the tools to achieve their maximum potential they can add $12 trillion dollars to the global GDP. Or to tell you that, in the United States alone, the racial wealth gap will cost $1.5 trillion by 2028. This is the economic power of those often described as voiceless and lacking empowerment. Women, people of colour, Indigenous people, LGBTQ2S persons, people with disabilities, poor people and others on the margins of society: can you imagine what your collective strength will achieve when demanding social changes or challenging political will?

To the people of Canada, and beyond, your value is not determined by your title and leadership does not require a title. The power has always belonged to the people. It is time that people realize their power. It is not enough to hear my voice. We need to hear you, too.

INDEX

CELINA CAESAR-CHAVANNES is an equity and inclusion advocate and leadership consultant, and a former Member of Parliament who served as parliamentary secretary to Prime Minister Justin Trudeau and to the Minister of International Development et la Francophonie. During her political career, Celina advocated for people suffering with mental illness and was given the Champion of Mental Health Parliamentarian Award in May 2017 by the Canadian Alliance on Mental Illness and Mental Health. That year she was also named one of the Global 100 Under 40 Most Influential People of African Descent (Politics & Governance category) and Black Parliamentarian of the Year. After she stepped away from the Liberal Party to sit as an independent member in 2019, Celina was picked as one of *Chatelaine Magazine*'s Women of the Year. Before entering politics, she was a successful entrepreneur, launching and growing an award-winning research management consulting firm, with a particular focus on neurological conditions. Celina was the recipient of both the Toronto Board of Trade's Business Entrepreneur of the Year for 2012 and the 2007 Black Business and Professional Association's Harry Jerome Young Entrepreneur Award. Celina holds an MBA in Healthcare Management from the University of Phoenix as well as an Executive MBA from the Rotman School of Management. She lives in Whitby, Ontario, with her three children, and her husband, Vidal Chavannes.

CELINA CAESAR-CHAVANNES is an equity and inclusion advocate and leadership consultant, and a former Member of Parliament who served as parliamentary secretary to Prime Minister Justin Trudeau and to the Minister of International Development et la Francophonie. During her political career, Celina advocated for people suffering with mental illness and was given the Champion of Mental Health Parliamentarian Award in May 2017 by the Canadian Alliance on Mental Illness and Mental Health. That year she was also named one of the Global 100 Under 40 Most Influential People of African Descent (Politics & Governance category) and Black Parliamentarian of the Year. After she stepped away from the Liberal Party to sit as an independent member in 2019, Celina was picked as one of *Chatelaine Magazine*'s Women of the Year. Before entering politics, she was a successful entrepreneur, launching and growing an award-winning research management consulting firm, with a particular focus on neurological conditions. Celina was the recipient of both the Toronto Board of Trade's Business Entrepreneur of the Year for 2012 and the 2007 Black Business and Professional Association's Harry Jerome Young Entrepreneur Award. Celina holds an MBA in Healthcare Management from the University of Phoenix as well as an Executive MBA from the Rotman School of Management. She lives in Whitby, Ontario, with her three children, and her husband, Vidal Chavannes.

D0934609

THE SEXUAL CODE

WOLFGANG WICKLER

THE
SEXUAL CODE

*The Social Behavior of Animals
and Men*

With an Introduction by KONRAD LORENZ
Illustrated by HERMANN KACHER

Doubleday & Company, Inc., Garden City, New York, 1972

Library of Congress Catalog Card Number 76–157593
Translation Copyright © 1972 by Doubleday & Company, Inc.
All Rights Reserved
Printed in the United States of America
First Edition

Wolfgang Wickler is Professor of Zoology at Munich University and a noted ethologist who has spent years in the study of animal and human behavior. Professor Wickler is the author of numerous journal articles and books including *Mimicry*, previously published in the United States; he also serves as editor of the *Journal of Comparative Ethology*, published in Berlin.

Professor Wickler's continuing research in animal social behavior leads him often to Eastern Africa for field studies; presently he is investigating the ecological and evolutionary implications of animal monogamy, in continuation of his study of animal family relationships upon which THE SEXUAL CODE is based.

CONTENTS

PART III

PART IV

INTRODUCTION

Konrad Lorenz

I have very good reasons for attaching great topical interest and great value to this book by my long-standing friend and colleague. These reasons are of a general nature and I shall have to go far back in order to explain them. But I believe that this may help the reader, and especially those readers who are not very familiar with biology, to appreciate the work more fully.

Every species of animal and plant has adapted itself to its environment in a process of adjustment lasting eons; in a sense each species is the image of its environment. The form of the horse's hoof is just as much an image of the steppe it treads as the impression it leaves is an image of the hoof. The process by which a species adapts to an extraspecific reality is a *one-sided* process only if this reality is determined by the immovable laws of inorganic nature. The fin of the fish, its undulating motion, and the streamlined shape of the fish body are an image of the water and of its physical characteristics, which the presence of fish has in no way affected. A species of living thing generally only causes limited changes in the inorganic world. Admittedly corals can alter entire coastlines and themselves build up the reefs on which they settle; plants can turn large expanses of water into land; burrowing rodents can cause landslides, etc. But all these effects are negligible compared to the extent that every animal or plant species influences its *living* environment. All species that live together in the same place are necessarily adapted *to one another* and are dependent on one another, even if they appear to be hostile, as in the relationship between the eater and the eaten. The hoofed animals that graze there and the hard grass of the steppe very largely owe their present form and mode of life to their reciprocal adaptation to each other. As students of phylogeny well know, a kind of armed competition has been taking place between the two since the early Tertiary Age; the grass acquired a harder and harder armor of silicates in order to be eaten less easily, while the grazing animals developed ever stronger teeth and enamel crowns in order to overcome the plants' defenses. For their part, the grazing animals are useful to the grass, by preventing the steppe from turning into forest. Naturally they are not the only partners in this community of life; both are, for instance, dependent on soil bacteria, which break up animal excretions, dead plants, and dead animals into substances that in turn nourish the plants. The final source of energy that keeps everything in motion is the sun, whose rays enable the plants to synthesize nourishing carbohydrates from carbon dioxide. This type of living community, or biocoenosis, involving innumerable species of animals and plants, is like an extraordinarily complicated piece of machinery in which everything interlocks with everything else and the loss of even the tiniest, apparently useless little cogwheel would cause unforeseeable destruction. Above all, of course, it is any sudden change that leads to the collapse of a biocoenosis; apart from rare natural disasters, these are caused almost exclusively by *man*.

Man upsets the equilibrium in which biocoenoses exist because he evolves at a very much faster rate than any other living thing. While the changes in body structure and mode of life to which living things are subject in the course of their phylogenetic development are all based on the same processes of mutation and recombination of genes, and on natural selection, man, thanks to his capacity of conceptual thought and speech, has become able to transmit to posterity the experiences and inventions of individuals as well as the insights that individuals have gained in their own life. So man is the only living thing with the ability to transmit acquired characteristics; the word "transmit" must, however, be taken in the original, juridical sense of heritage here, and not in the genetic sense more familiar to modern biologists.

Man has changed the biocoenosis in which he lives more than any other living thing. He has created his own environment and has scarcely allowed any species of animal or plant to survive other than those whose usefulness to his own well-being was immediately apparent. Unfortunately only a dwindling minority of the holders of political and economic power today knows enough about the character of biocoenoses and their dependence as a whole on the parts of which they are made up. This is why man is well on the way, or rather hell-bent, to destroying the community of life in and on which he lives.

If the fruits of the tree of knowledge drove man from Paradise, that is because he plucked them while they were unripe and has nowhere near digested them yet. Instead, they have given him spiritual indigestion so that all his opinions and ideals pass through him too quickly. It has led to that curious race of man against himself that is our curse and that leads to high blood pressure, cirrhosis of the liver, heart attacks, and premature death. Yet, paradoxically, the majority of people consider this to be progress. Briefly, man has succeeded in transforming his world in such a way that he has made himself unhappy in it and has indeed become *guilt*-laden. So in fact the story in the Bible is quite true.

The problems that beset us today are *ethical* problems.

The reason they are so difficult to solve is that it is quite impossible to discover firm criteria in the kaleidoscopic world of man with its lightning changes. As long as mankind still evolved more slowly it was easier, and at least people *believed* they had some idea of what was good and what was bad. But the devil lies by definition, and the serpent's promise that men would know good from evil once they had eaten from the tree of knowledge proved the most disgraceful lie of all. Men seem to know this less and less the farther their so-called knowledge advances. But this was not inevitable; it is so chiefly because the devil has given man a far too inflated opinion of himself, which prevents him from knowing *himself*. There are no such obstacles, however, to his knowledge of the world around him. Knowledge is power, and man has gained great power over the universe around him, but not over himself and his own behavior. This is a highly dangerous state of affairs.

Proverbially, pride comes before a fall, and man in his pride is only too eager to see himself not as a part of nature but as something at the opposite pole, if not actually superior to nature. Indeed, the term "nature" is itself a product of this pernicious attitude. The delusion of man and nature as opposites has resulted in senseless questionings. A great deal of fruitless effort has been devoted to discussing what is or is not "natural" to man.

By being contrasted to a number of entirely different things as its polar opposite, the concept of "natural" is being robbed of any pertinence or definition. One moment it is mankind as a whole as opposed to nature; the next it is only man's spirit; then his culture; or, finally, "unnatural," the abnormal in the sense of something diseased, is considered the opposite of nature. Accordingly, the term "natural" also assumes a series of entirely different meanings. First, "natural" can mean the nonspiritual—as in Klage's *Der Geist als Widersacher der Seele* (*The Spirit as Enemy of the Soul*); second, it can mean all that is peculiar to

man, not on the basis of cultural tradition but because of
the hereditary factors of our species; third, it is simply
equated with "healthy."

The value judgments made on the content of this scin-
tillating concept are, of course, even more muddled and
contradictory. According to Kantian moral philosophy,
everything natural is of indifferent value; the best action is
free of all value if it is born of natural inclination and not
of categoric self-analysis. Civilization has imposed on man
the need to control some of his instincts, and this has led,
through excessive exaggeration in certain pietistic and puri-
tanical cultural circles, to the appalling delusion that all
natural drives are *ipso facto* inspired by the devil, especially
if they give pleasure. Yet, on the other hand, it is considered
a legitimate excuse for highly reprehensible behavior patterns if they are "natural." In terms of the object of their
drives, some otherwise upstanding men consider themselves
free of all moral responsibility. The English proverb runs
"all is fair in love and war"; so the loved one can be
treated just like an enemy. Few people blamed Goethe
for seducing, betraying, and—if truth be told—killing
Friederike von Sesenheim in the most shameful manner.

Unfortunately this confusion in the concept of what is
natural, due to the fallacy of opposites, is so familiar to us
all now that we are scarcely able to see what misleading
and dangerous results it has. Arnold Gehlen cut through
the Gordian knot with the opposite phrase that man is by
nature a civilized being. Broca's area in the supramarginal
gyrus of the left temporal lobe, where praxis and gnosis,
experience and knowledge, collaborate in such wonderful
fashion and form the basis of conceptual thought and
speech, is just as much a physical and natural organ of
man as his lungs or kidneys, although there are no comparable organs in the animal kingdom. And nothing is more
natural than disease! No living system is free from these
disturbances to its function, and small, disease-breeding or-

ganisms are just as much part of the realm of nature as man himself.

In order to solve the problems that are currently troubling us and to obviate the dangers looming from all sides we need a *new ethics*, springing from a mode of thought quite different from that concept of opposites we have just criticized. This mode of thought, which sees man not as a contrapuntal opposite but as *part* of a single universe based on natural laws, is not new. Its statements and methods are those that have been accepted in biology since the days of Charles Darwin. This approach to the universe also posits values—and pairs of opposites. The widespread idea that science is "value-free" is entirely misleading. The biologist knows that in the course of phylogeny, the new, that has never existed before, is constantly being created, and that it is more than the original elements from which it sprang; so he also recognizes the existence of lower and higher stages of organic being. And with the knowledge that every organic system can step out of order, i.e., fall ill and die, the biologist is also aware of the opposites of health and disease.

The question of what is a lower and what a higher stage is just as meaningful as the other question of whether a course of life is diseased or healthy. When we consider passages of human civilized life we often find ourselves in the position of having to decide these questions. The reply to the second question is particularly difficult and lays great responsibility on us. For health and disease are concepts that can only be defined in the context of the living area of the organism in question. Sickle-cell anemia, a hereditary malformation of the red blood corpuscles, not only reduces their number but also their ability to carry oxygen. In a pure genetic, "homozygous" state, the tendency to sickle-cell formation is a so-called lethal factor, and, even if it exists in a "heterozygous" (split gene) state, it severely affects man in his normal environment: Even the heterozygous sickle-cell anemic person is "ill" in northern latitudes. In certain regions of Africa, however, which are particularly plagued by malaria, *he* is healthy while the possessor of "normal" blood corpuscles inevitably falls ill. For, curiously enough, the destructive malaria plasmodia cannot penetrate the malformed blood corpuscles; so their possessors are immune against the disease that makes residence in these parts impossible to any "healthy" person.

This makes it very clear that the almost synonymous attributes "healthy" or "adaptive" (meaningful in terms of the survival of the species) can only be applied in relation to a definite living area and a definite structure or function. In the case of phylogenetically evolved structure and functions of prehuman living things, this condition is still relatively easy to fulfill; but it becomes very difficult if we want to decide on the culturally based norms of human social behavior. The increasingly rapid alteration of his environment that man brings about by his culture and above all by his technology means that the traditional behavior norms of a culture can lose their adaptive powers almost "overnight"; moreover, other norms, that only recently were quite unadaptive, abnormal, and hostile to survival can henceforth serve the preservation of the individual and the community. Patriotic and militant enthusiasm for national ideals was still an essential behavior norm a few centuries ago, whereas today it is entirely reprehensible. A profound skepticism of time-honored ideals used to be harmful, whereas today it is essential to our survival.

This state of affairs, which is becoming more acute from decade to decade, has caused great ethical and moral confusion. The young generation of extremists believes that it must completely throw overboard all the traditions that have been handed down by its parents, and arrogantly deludes itself that it can construct a whole new civilization quite by itself. It does not realize that in terms of the history of civilization it is doing its best to regress to the level of a hypothetical pre-Stone Age or, in ontogenetic terms, to the stage of development of a pre-Struwelpeter. The older generation confronts the young with outraged rejection, seeing itself, not unjustifiably, as the sole defender of civilization; but by so doing it is also insisting, unawares, on dragging on traditions that have long since become outdated and are, if anything, detrimental now. The danger of a particularly narrow-minded form of fascism looms over America.

In no area of human life is the confusion and perplexity so great as in the sexual field. The primordial and proverbial power of the sexual drives is very liable to bring the behavior of the individual into conflict with the demands the community imposes on him. That is why, in all human cultures, sexual life in particular is regulated by very definite traditional norms, whose prime intention is quite obviously to bring up the children to be healthy and culturally mature members of society. It is still a truth valid for all cultures that the family is the elementary unit of every nation and civilization. These norms differ very widely in different cultural circles, from which we may deduce that man has devised no detailed, phylogenetically adaptive program for building up a family. But at the same time all the families of all the nations also have a whole number of traits in common, which clearly indicates the presence of certain common, culturally independent human and instinctive fundamentals.

There is scarcely another field of human social behavior where the idea of the so-called "natural" has been used in such contradictory fashion as that of love and family life. Either it is used as a pseudo-legitimate excuse for reprehensible behavior and as a passport to uncivilized excesses, or it serves to devaluate, if not forbid, healthy behavior patterns necessary to the survival of the species. There are few fields where clarification of this kind is as essential to the continuity of our civilization. The answer to the question whether a certain behavior norm, which seems pernicious or even abnormal to the older generation, which is more closely tied to tradition, may not in fact be system-preserving and therefore "healthy" in the present social environment, can be just as important as the answer to the reverse question, whether traditional behavior norms, which seem to have stood the test of age-old custom, are not extremely harmful under present conditions.

The solution to the question whether a certain behavior norm is healthy or diseased, whether it is beneficial or harmful to the survival of mankind and his civilization, is closely related, although by no means identical, to the question of good and evil. Certainly, the preservation of the living system of mankind and his civilization is a *value*, and we have a great ethical responsibility to uphold it. Certainly everything that can tend to the destruction of this value is undoubtedly bad. But we bear an even greater responsibility, namely for all that could still *become* of our descendants, in what will, God willing, be a better future. The great organic process of becoming, that has transformed unicellulars into multicellulars and animals into men from pre-Cambrian times, is continuing, so we firmly believe, in human civilization. We are duty bound to preserve it, above all because this is essential to its further evolution.

It was the encyclical *Humanae vitae* that occasioned this book. For the encyclical very clearly shows where theology is deficient in knowledge of nature and why the instructions it has given under the aegis of natural laws are suspect. This does not mean that the instructions are necessarily wrong—merely that they are questionable and therefore impose no obligation. Primarily this is because, even where they call on the nature of man, they in fact spring from an *idea* of man that is derived from a static concept of nature, in which history and evolution have no part. The same once applied to natural science. But a constant confrontation with nature forced natural science into a dynamic, historical mode of thought. For evolution exists, and the nature of man, to which ethical norms relate, moves with it.

It lies in the nature of man that he can do more than he may. Natural science and in particular biology can indicate what is biologically useful to man, and can check whether the ethical norms set up by others agree with the laws of biology. If they do not, usually it is because they derive from an abstract, metaphysical view of the nature of man; then a reason has to be found why people reach different conclusions—according to whether they start from the physical or the metaphysical nature of man. One test is the evidence about nonhuman beings, since it is assumed that they cannot act against their nature. If these organisms act otherwise than expected, the false expectation must be due to an error of method. It would be mere arbitrariness rather than method, and a question not of science but of ideology —and therefore outside the realm of any real discussion— to attempt to conceal this error by holding that the damage that man, by his fall, has also done to nonhuman creation is responsible for the fact that this creation does not live up to the nominal value of man's expectations. This does not, however, mean that such ideas are wrong; but neither does it allow one to discover whether they are right. All such discussions should be concerned with the behavior of man and of animals and with comparisons of the two, not with humanized, anthropomorphic observations of animals or an animalized, theomorphic view of man. Biologists and ethologists have brought to light facts that surprised the moral theologians. It is to be expected that the latter will re-examine their views in the light of these facts.

Humanae vitae requires that human behavior be subordinated to the purposes of nature, declares that it is a sin if personal relations are not subordinated to (licit) bodily behavior, and transforms a number of biological laws into ethical ones. This can only be done on a metaphysical basis. As long as this basis is circumvented, the requirement cannot be understood properly; it is, therefore, not an ethical requirement—unless it pertains to an ethics of mystery.

I have not attempted to list theological authorities that have proved wrong; rather I have tried to show as clearly as possible how one can arrive at scientific statements on the behavior on animals. The reconstruction of phylogenetic developments is of major importance here. The methodology for this was originally created for the forms of organs (morphology). This is why I used it first for comparative studies of organs, then applied it to simple forms of behavior—such as locomotion and foraging—and only then, after a few necessary amendments, applied it to social be-

havior and communication among animals.[123]* My knowledge of the behavior of many of the animals discussed
here is due to ten years of research work at the Max
Planck Institut für Verhaltensphysiologie (Max Planck Institute of Behavior Physiology) and long observation of
tropical animals in the wild. I have to thank my teacher
and friend, Dr. Konrad Lorenz, for making this possible.

Theology and natural law

A number of theologians tend to react almost allergically
to scientific discoveries that alter our image of mankind,
even though many theological views largely coincide with
those of biology. For example, it would contravene the
teachings both of biology and theology to assume that
natural drives have no good use. Theology teaches that
God created nature and it was good. But both sciences also
teach that it is not true that automatically *only* what is
fitting and good comes about in the world. The biologist
knows that changes in the environment can make new demands on a living thing to which its existing system of
construction and function are not adapted. In some cases
a single organism or an entire species can founder on this
unfitness. Moreover, among higher animals and even more
among men, the functional plan of behavior is not already
determined at the egg stage but can and must be completed
in the course of the individual's life, through experience
and learning; and here too it may happen that the living
thing learns something wrong. The theologian knows that
evil impairs nature, which was created good, and that man
at least is able to act contrary to the will of the Creator.
So both sciences accept that man can act in accordance

---

* Where appropriate I have indicated recent specialist literature by
means of small numbers in the text that correspond to the numbers
in the bibliography, in order to give the interested reader the opportunity to go deeper into certain individual questions.

with nature or against nature, do good or evil. Consequently, both must try to establish criteria as to what is "natural" or "good." If we assume that the created world is the realization of divine ideas and that the Creator orders nonrational creatures in terms of the purpose he has set them by the law of nature, then "natural" and "good" can be equated in the realm of nonrational creatures. If this is meant to imply anything at all for man, who is endowed with reason, then it is that "to do evil" means the same as "to act contrary to (human) nature."

Since they agree on so many things, it is astonishing how often scientists and theologians still contradict each other, massively contradict each other in fact. In some fields the contradiction is increasing rather than diminishing, although one would expect the opposite if our knowledge really is advancing. The most recent important document of the teaching authority of the Catholic Church, the encyclical *Humanae vitae*, has been subject to more contradiction by natural scientists than any other. This is strange, considering that the document is directly concerned with "a teaching founded on the Natural Law." This "Natural Law" relates to reproduction and the conjugal life of human sexual partners, so it is also of extreme interest to biologists. It was formulated rather like this: Although reproduction also serves to unite the partners, besides serving procreation, these two meanings are inseparably connected, so that each marriage act is open to the transmission of life. I consider this the correct version, translated into biological terms, of what in theological language reads as follows: *That teaching . . . is founded upon the inseparable connection, willed by God and unable to be broken by man on his own initiative, between the two meanings of the conjugal act: the unitive meaning and the procreative meaning.* True, this is immediately preceded by: *No believer will wish to deny that the teaching authority of the Church is competent to interpret even the natural moral law.* So the encyclical is not only concerned with a natural law but also with its interpretation.

But the quarrel is obviously not sparked off by the interpretation alone, but by the somewhat unusual situation that this law of nature was laid down not by biologists but by theologians who, however, have omitted to tell how they came by it. This is why natural scientists and medical men competent in this field are now trying to examine the natural law in question. It is probably common knowledge by now that they have not yet been able to verify it, that is to say, that they seriously doubt whether there is any such natural law.

Specialists are not the only ones interested in this problem. In fact, there are countless laymen into whose daily conjugal life the Church has intervened heavily with its instructions. Many people find themselves simply incapable of following these instructions. Yet they are not satisfied with a purely emotional disagreement, as I have found from frequent conversations with engineers, teachers, soldiers, students, theologians, and university professors, but they try to form their own judgment in the controversy. Where theological statements of immediate interest contradict those of natural science and medicine, it is indeed up to the "consumer" to decide which to believe. Naturally he cannot hope to master all the knowledge of the two branches of science—normally not even scientists can do so. But what he can do is examine the methods that lead to the different conclusions. According to theological teaching, he is in fact obliged to do so; he cannot avoid the decision, which he must then somehow substantiate to himself, since "whatsoever is not of faith is sin," even if one blindly obeys the instructions of the Church.

No doubt it may seem bad manners to find fault with another instead of putting one's own house in order. Yet it is permissible here, not because we want to reprimand the theologians, but in order to get closer to the truth. Biologists and theologians are both concerned with the law of nature. And even if what they are seeking is not necessarily identical, it does at least coincide in part. At least the man who hears the instructions of the moral theologians and who inquires into natural laws is the same person. If he should now elaborate a stringent method for exploring natural laws and arrive at findings that do not coincide with the statements of theology, he will have to doubt the latter. It is no secret that many statements on man made by theologians and learned churchmen have become very suspect, whether they deal with the relationship between man and animal or with original sin.

But who made it all become suspect? It was those theologians and learned churchmen who did not know their method. This is fairly easy to demonstrate.

The first pages of the Bible give two accounts of the Creation with contradictory details. The first lists the following sequence of creation: heaven and earth, plants, animals, man; but the second states explicitly that man was created before the plants and the animals. It is quite legitimate for the natural scientist to examine the discrepancy and to clarify the different points described; at least one of the two statements must be wrong factually. But quite apart from the question of fact, very different basic attitudes to the accounts of the Creation are possible, and this is decisive for our discussion and many similar debates. On the one hand we could point to the striking discrepancies in details, thereby exposing the whole thing as hearsay if not deception. The *sine qua non* of this entirely legitimate method is distrust. But distrust is unfitting in the eye of God; he demands faith. And this gives rise to the other basic attitude one can take, which assumes that the two accounts with their different details were given deliberately, as an indication that it is not the details that count but something more general that can be expressed one way or another. So the contradictory details would be expressly

meant to prevent the reader from paying too much attention to superficial details and contenting himself with them.
Accordingly theology says the Bible is not a manual of
natural science but contains the tidings, clothed in a particular form of language, *that* God created the world, but
not *how* he created it.

But the natural scientist is particularly interested in the
how. And he will soon find that in this respect neither of the
two divergent accounts of the Creation is correct. This
makes many people doubt whether there is any truth at
all in the account of the Creation and whether it would not
be more advisable, if not necessary, for the natural scientist
to dismiss the Bible entirely. But anyone who gives way to
this doubt, be he natural scientist or theologian, is clinging
to details like a Pharisee and is overlooking the possibility
that the natural scientist may have found yet another way
of putting it, that expresses the essentials equally well. The
more such methods of portrayal there are, the easier it
should be clearly to distinguish the essential from the inessential.

Unfortunately the theologians have overlooked this again
and again. In order to remove any doubts people might
have and to sustain man's faith, theologians have tried to
defend the Bible against natural scientists, i.e., to compile
scientific counterarguments. Of course it can happen for a
natural scientist to assert that he has disproved that the
world was created by God; but he cannot put this forward
as a scientific finding, for his methods cannot yield any such
thing. The believer must not let himself be shaken by such
statements. The theological doctrine of the salvation is not
under attack by natural science; anyone who wants to defend it in spite of this would be falsely accusing natural
science of trespassing outside its territory—but this would
mean he himself was trespassing in the opposite direction
by trying to prove the doctrine of salvation with scientific
arguments. That is a rather tragic confusion. But it is not

the business of theology to decide whether scientific evidence is conclusive.

A tragic case of mistaken method having grievous results that still vex us today is the traditional teaching of the Catholic Church on monogenism, i.e., the doctrine that all mankind is descended from a single parent couple. Genesis only mentions the creation of orders of animals (birds, fish, etc.), not of individuals; similarly it says: "Let us make man." The doctrine of a single pair of progenitors cannot be deduced from the Biblical account of the Creation. The Church accounts for it in other ways too, for instance basing it on the theological doctrine of original sin; here the Church states dogmatically that the sin of Adam was passed down to all his descendants by descent, not by imitation; "original sin is transmitted through propagation." Hence the theologians deduced that the whole of mankind is descended from a single human couple. Admittedly this is not strict dogma but merely a "theologically certain doctrine" that can be revised as soon as there are sufficient grounds to do so. But these grounds existed from the outset, even within theology. Several notable theologians are now disputing the fact, that for theological reasons, monogenism must be encouraged under any circumstances, as was believed for a long time.[37] But there is no need to be a theologian to see that the assertion that all mankind descends from one pair of progenitors is a cogent biological statement. In principle, natural science can check such statements; whether our researches have furnished enough evidence for us to do so now is another question. But in any case it is a statement that belongs in principle to the field of natural science. So it is up to the natural sciences to decide whether it is correct. Theology is neither willing nor able to make positive statements in the field of natural science that are binding on the conscience of the faithful. Yet here theology is actually submitting a dogmatic statement to the judgment of natural science, thus risking that the statement will be refuted. Since theological statements lie outside the field of natural science, the statement on monogenism must be untheological. The duty of the theologian is to preach the doctrine of salvation, and here they must keep their statements independent of the current state of knowledge of natural science; otherwise, whether they wish it or not, they will become advocates of the theses of natural science. So it was not only untheological but in fact illogical for Pope Paul VI to declare, as recently as July 1966:

> *Thus it is quite clear that you* (the twelve theologians who had come to Rome for a symposium on original sin) *will regard the explanations of original sin given by some modern authors as irreconcilable with genuine Catholic doctrine. Starting out from the undemonstrated hypothesis of polygenism, they deny, more or less clearly, that the sin from which this great trash heap of ills in mankind is derived was first of all the disobedience of Adam, "the first man," a figure of the man to come—a sin that was committed at the beginning of history. As a consequence, such explanations do not agree with the teaching of Sacred Scripture, Sacred Tradition, and the Church's magisterium, according to which the sin of the first man is transmitted to all his descendants not through imitation but through propagation. . . . The theory of evolution will not seem acceptable to you whenever it is not decisively in accord with the immediate creation of each and every human soul by God, and whenever it does not regard as decisively important for the fate of mankind the disobedience of Adam, the universal first parent.*

The reference to the "undemonstrated hypothesis" betrays uncertainty of scientific method; the Pope is drawing limits to knowledge in the realm of natural science: *These limits are marked out by the living magisterium of the Church, which is the proximate norm of truth for all the faithful . . .*

In the context of the above mistake of method, the Pope's instructions to medical men in the encyclical *Humanae vitae* are, to say the least, misleading: *In this way scientists and especially Catholic scientists will contribute to demonstrate the fact that, as the Church teaches, "a true contradiction cannot exist between the divine laws pertaining to the transmission of life and those pertaining to the fostering of authentic conjugal love."* Natural scientists cannot prove that a theological doctrine must be right. Even if the Pope's wish is granted, namely that *medical science succeeded in providing a sufficiently secure basis for a regulation of birth, founded on the observance of natural rhythms* to determine the likelihood of conception more and more exactly, this is still no proof of the accuracy of any Church doctrine. There can be differences between natural laws and what theology has proclaimed as divine law. The theologians' explanations of nature and, in particular, the nature of man, are so impregnated with outdated scientific views that it requires natural scientists to work out what the theological nucleus of these explanations is.[93] But half of all the scientists history has produced are alive today. And our knowledge is growing apace. Of course, theology will always have to speak in the language of the times if it wants to be understood; but it must also develop alongside the insights of natural science if it does not want to be misunderstood in the future. It will have to take note of the fact that not only is man changing the world, but he is changing it more and more rapidly.

This is why it behooves the theologian to take an interest in the bases of the natural law in question (if it is one) too. And he does. The papal encyclical on birth control is subject to more controversy, even within Catholic theology, than any other. Unfortunately, the often rather heated dispute suffers greatly from ignorance of facts, without which one simply cannot work or argue. On the whole these facts are, however, widely accessible—except in theological textbooks; and, moreover, the subject is by no means one of dry academic scholarship but on the contrary very entertaining, because it deals with the family life and social life of all kinds of animals for whom man has a great deal of interest and affection in any case. I hope I will be able to offer at least entertainment to some, and food for thought to as many others as possible in this attempt to collate what the ethologist has to say on the question of reproduction and pair-bonding.

In the case of the more important animals, I have given both the English and the scientific name (in parentheses and italics), since different writers tend to christen exotic animals with various imaginative names that make it difficult to identify them.

I have concentrated on a few striking examples in each section; usually there are also a number of other familiar examples. This is not meant as a handbook, however, but as a definite scheme of argument. I trust the reader will credit me with giving examples from which one can generalize. Distrustful readers can check this from the bibliography. The earlier examples include more details on the life of the relevant animal species in order to indicate other biological connections; the later ones, for the sake of simplicity, concentrate on the elements of behavior under discussion. The word "marriage" as used here is purely descriptive and denotes the bond between partners of different sex; it is also applied to animals. This is common practice in scientific literature addressed to the layman too and it is intended neither to deny man the special, supernatural features of his form of marriage nor to falsely attribute them to animals.

The book is divided into four parts. The first deals with the predicate value of natural laws, the second with the specific natural laws of reproduction, the third with the natural law of pair-bonding in the context of reproduction, and the fourth with a few conclusions important to man.

Sternberg, May 1969   Wolfgang Wickler

THE SEXUAL CODE

I

1. Natural Inclination and Conscience

> *But beware instinct . . .*
> *Instinct is a great matter.*
>
> Shakespeare

Like Falstaff in Part 1 of *Henry IV* (Act 2, Scene 4), many people use instinct as an excuse for actions of which they are ashamed later, or at least actions of which their fellow men do not approve. Does behavior research, which is bringing more and more instinctive behavior to light for man too, therefore provide collective excuses for every situation in life? Is it true that we are well on the way to blaming failures on demons again—not, of course, on demons and evil spirits hovering somewhere in the world about us, but on demons within ourselves? If there is any truth in the notion that our traditional set of instincts is no longer adapted to the demands of the mass societies of today, if, as Konrad Lorenz says, what we call the voice of temptation is in fact the discrepancy between the demands of modern civilization and the instinctive drives that were created for age-old, perhaps prehuman conditions of life but which still cling to us today as a hereditary historical burden—do we not then have a good excuse? Cain did indeed slay Abel; but were not his aggressive drives really to blame?

This kind of argument seems to forget that, like the fratricidal Cain, perhaps Peter, who used his sword on the

servant of the Caiph, also acted instinctively. If we can
hold the polygamous tendency of man responsible for a
broken marriage, we can equally well hold an instinctive
tendency to monogamy responsible for marital fidelity, or
the brood-tending drive responsible for maternal devotion,
and so on. The reference to instincts can serve to extenuate
reprehensible behavior as well as praiseworthy actions,
although, of course, the latter usually need no excuse. The
only question is what this "extenuation" really means.

Our judges and spiritual advisers, when they deliberate
on guilt and sin, are not the only ones to be plagued by
the worry that motor drives in man, which take effect along
with conscious decisions, could put in question the responsibility of the individual. The same did and still does worry
those who want to or ought to propound positive moral
norms. Schiller's words are often quoted in this context:
"I like to serve my friends, but unfortunately I do so out
of inclination; and so it often worries me that I am not
really moral." These words allude to the fact that actions
that have been performed *against* natural inclinations are
nearly always considered worth particular merit. Lorenz
has repeatedly pointed out that in their choice of friends
people prefer those whose friendly behavior does not spring
from purely rational considerations but from natural affection alone. He explains this as follows:

> *The man who behaves socially from natural inclination
> normally makes few demands on the controlling mechanism
> of his own moral responsibility. Thus, in times of stress, he
> has huge reserves of moral strength to draw upon; while the
> man who even in everyday life has constantly to exert all
> his moral strength in order to curb his natural inclinations
> into a semblance of normal social behavior is very likely to
> break down completely in case of additional stress. . . . It
> is no paradox but plain common sense that we use two dif-
> ferent standards for judging the deeds of a man and the man
> himself.*[75] In any case, then, "plain common sense" obvi-

ously trusts the "instinctive" good deed no less than the categorical imperative.

The case of a child who has fallen into the water is often quoted as an example. We expect everyone to be prepared to jump in after the child "without thinking twice." A moment of thought would suggest the same course of action, but by then the child would have drowned. So we can say in favor of instinctive action that it is quicker off the mark than action guided by reason. But we could also quote the tragic case of the hero, who shoots without second thought out of a natural inclination to help a friend in danger, but overlooks a few details that would have shown him that in this particular case his shot will put the friend into even greater danger if not kill him.

Since man can find himself in a great many more different situations than were provided for in his instinctive behavior, he cannot avoid having recourse to reason at times to decide whether he may follow his instinctive natural inclination or not. And I believe man knows this, and that basically he does not evaluate an action according to whether or not it corresponds to natural inclination but according to whether reason came into it at all in the first place. This brings us to a—perhaps unexpected—technical problem. How does one tell whether a man has had recourse to reason? If one knows what the natural inclination is, and he acts against it, then one can be almost sure that he considered his course of action beforehand. But if he acts according to his natural inclination, then he may have had recourse to reason beforehand, or he may not. And since one simply cannot know for sure, a certain asymmetry necessarily creeps into the evaluation of action; we tend to favor those that overcome natural inclinations and to lump these natural inclinations together as the "beast within." This attitude is very odd, not to say suspicious. For it assumes that man is wrongly constructed—so wrongly that, in order to act well, he must constantly fight against his makeup. This does not make sense in biological or theological terms, since at least the natural endeavor to preserve the species must be good. So the problem of how nature and ethics go together is particularly acute in the field of reproductive behavior.

We may begin with the basic general assumption that in principle it is immoral for man simply to act without reflection, even if the outcome is good. That is why the example of the child who has fallen into the water is misleading, if not dangerous. For it merely shows that it *can* be good to follow natural inclinations; but it does not show that unreflected action is good as such. Here the distinction is confused by the haste with which the action should take place in this special situation. If one took the time to consider whether to jump in after the child or not, and then jumped, this would be entirely meritorious, although perhaps less effective. Precisely today, when man is always rushed in any case and often seduced into senseless hasty action, we must not discredit reflection merely because it takes time. Of course, no man can consider all the possible principles involved before each individual action. This is why we need guidelines, norms, that have come into being through the same consideration of principles. Actions that are performed against the natural inclination are only considered worth particular merit because they make it abundantly clear that the person had recourse to reason first, not simply because the action was counter to his natural inclination. It is no less meritorious if reason has commanded him to follow his natural inclination. Instinctive action is morally neutral; what is of value is the decision made by reason or conscience, by the final authority whose decisions each man must follow without fail. And this is by no means a new insight. "For whatsoever is not of faith is sin," says Paul (Rom. 14:23). Evidently Paul is not concerned whether objectively seen the action was right or wrong.

So it is no excuse to call on the aggressive drive or other drives. We must not make them into demons, nor must we ignore them if they have been proved to exist. If they should actually prove themselves liable to do good, then it is the man who fails to do this good, who withholds or even cuts off this opportunity from others, who is acting immorally.

2. Ethology

Ethology and ethics

The scientific term for behavior research is "ethology" in Anglo-American parlance. The word derives from the Greek ἔθος, which denotes custom or usage. Our words "ethics" and "ethos" derive from the Greek ἦθος, meaning "good custom." So the scientific terms ethology and ethics sound more similar phonetically than they are in meaning. Ethology is not the doctrine of ethics. Yet the findings of behavior research overlap into the field of ethics, in the form of subsidiary quantities. This is very easy to show in the field of reproduction. For the preservation of the human species is both an ethical and a biological good for which we must strive. It is ensured by biological mechanisms and human laws. On a purely biological plane, all that serves to preserve the species has a positive value. But we cannot simply transpose this to the ethical plane, as the following simple reasoning will show.

For many species of animal, a considerable measure of intraspecific aggression, i.e., aggression directed against conspecifics (members of one's own species), is very advantageous; in very simple terms it leads to the extension of the species over all available and suitable living spaces, including the less good "second- and third-rate" ones, and it favors the fittest at the cost of the less fit. The fitter individual is the greatest opponent of the one who is merely fit. Let us assume that this also applied to the ancestor of man and that we are now living in an environment that demands far less aggression toward our fellow men than we produce. Then the balance between the natural characteristics of man and the demands of the environment in which he lives is upset, perhaps so much so that it is a threat to the survival of the species "man."

Now man has the ability—and perhaps even the duty—to regulate such imbalances. On principle this can be done in two ways: Either he himself changes or he changes the environment. Indeed, in most fields man acts rather ruthlessly toward his environment in order to satisfy his own needs (for comfort, better food, more rapid transportation, more leisure, etc.). In purely biological terms, he could take the simplest way to ensure the survival of his species. So biologically it would be legitimate to consider whether suitable changes to the environment could not create a situation in which man can once again make use of as much aggression against his fellow men as he has at his disposal. It is indeed possible that man owes his higher evolution to precisely such a violent rivalry between groups of pre-men or primitive men. But we must also take into account that on the biological plane the relative number of offspring counts, but not each single individual, and the individual counts the less the younger it is. The moment we consider the preservation of each individual human life as a necessary ethical good, we have raised a demand that is not very common on the biological plane. And this demand excludes certain corrective measures that seem inherently suitable for re-establishing the disturbed balance between man and his environment.

Yet we will prefer those corrective measures that seem most in harmony with the nature of man and the laws of nature in general, if we consider the laws of nature as part of the revelation of the will of the Creator. We cannot discover the corporal nature of man solely from observa-

tions of man. For one thing, it would require experiments
that are not allowed to be performed on man, and for which
other, more suitable creatures must therefore serve as guinea
pigs. Second, man has a long phylogenetic history that—
like all history—has left traces in its current end product.
Its origins can only be shown by a comparison of many
other creatures, which could enable us to reconstruct the
phylogenetic development of man.

According to Teilhard de Chardin, the true nature of
man is not to be found in his animal past but in his spiritual
future. However much we may agree with this, we cannot
accept the possible inference that we should accordingly
concentrate on the spiritual future of man and leave his
animal past to the past. For this past is still very demonstrably present. So, for instance, in spite of all deliberate
decisions to have a child, however responsibly they may be
expressed and freely decided, there is a very close correlation in both man and animals between frequency of
conception and seasons or temperatures of the environment;
this can be shown by statistics published in 1966 by the
U. S. Department of Health, Education, and Welfare. In
West Germany, Sweden, and England the maximum frequency of conception occurs from May to July, the minimum between November and February. Other minor factors
also play a role here, as the following may show. On November 9, 1965 there was a power failure in New York
lasting one night; there were no lights, no movies, no television, no theater. For a short period, nine months later, the
clinics noted a rise in births of 33 to 35 percent. In December 1966 a great flood shut many Venetians in their
houses; just nine months later, in the first half of August
1967, 45 percent more babies were born in Venice than
usual. From January 26 to 31, 1967, a heavy snowstorm
in Chicago paralyzed shops and traffic. Nine months later
the normal birth count rose by 30 to 40 percent. In the small

mountain town of Somerset, Kentucky, the community aerial for television reception for the seven thousand inhabitants was switched off for a month owing to a legal dispute; nine months later, in January 1969, the number of babies born in the hospital reportedly rose to three times the normal count.

It is not just excusable but even called for today to speculate on the appetite for news. Newspapers, radio, television, and the underlying appetite for novelty, for interesting news from the whole world, are extremely necessary, among other things because they report the news from those distant parts to which we have more or less deliberately extended our influence. Not to see, not to find out what we are achieving (with the decrees that are issued, the medicines that are brought on the market, the aid to development that goes out to other parts of the world) is to reduce our sense of responsibility. The dangerous outcome of this became clearest during the Second World War. In his diary of the years 1946–49, Max Frisch describes the "difference which consists in whether I drop bombs on such and such a model, which lies there under the chasing clouds, half pathetic, half boring and paltry, or whether I too stand down there, open my pocket knife, and go up to a man, a single man, whose face I shall see. . . . I cannot believe myself capable of the latter. As for the former, and here lies the difference, I am not at all sure."

Like long-range weapons that can aim outside our field of vision, every action or effect that goes outside the direct range of our conceptual world must be compensated for by reports back; for these reports bridge the spatial gap between us and the events and give us the possibility of control and responsible behavior. That is to say, we must apply our technical progress equally on all fields; narrowness is dangerous here too. Compensatory measures are now required in many fields. The criterion is obviously always whether a natural equilibrium can be maintained or re-established. In any case, there is always more than one factor to take into account. We must think in systems. Ethics also demands this; ethics is not keyed to the individual alone, but also to the preservation and functioning of society. So the limits to the free play of the personality are the legitimate interests of the community. When ethics gives guidelines for behavior, they will be dependent on the current state of knowledge of the complex connections between the well-being of the individual and that of society. As our knowledge of the laws of nature grows, so too does the number of ways of eliminating disturbances in the corporate life of individuals and of finding a way out when legitimate interests come into conflict. For example, it is biologically advantageous that individuals age and die. An immortal living being is certainly no contradiction in terms, for the most simple living things, those that are in many ways closest to the primitive state, are still potentially immortal today. True, they perish in great numbers owing to outside influences of the most varied kinds, but not through age. But if we want a rapid evolution toward ever more advantageous forms of life, then each population must bring its capacity for reproduction and means of varying its heritage into play as fully as possible, i.e., bear as many offspring as possible, all slightly different from one another, tested under real-life conditions. If, however, there are only a certain number of possible places to live, they must not remain permanently occupied by existing individuals, for then there would be no room for new developments. Necessary as it is for the individual to assert himself and remain alive, it is equally necessary at some point to withdraw from circulation a model that has already been tested, so that the population can survive in the competition with neighboring populations. Since the same rules apply to the automobile industry, this vocabulary is quite apposite.

Ethology and medicine

If a biologically predetermined, natural behavior exists for man, then anyone who wants to alter or influence human behavior must know it. This is best shown by a comparison with medicine, which also attempts to influence the biological functions of man. In both cases it is a question of removing deviations from the norm. Where this norm comes from, how the medical man knows the constitution of a healthy man, and what therefore counts as diseased, or how one can tell what behavior is right and what therefore is wrong or in need of correction, shall remain out of the discussion here. We must only remember that the norm is not merely a question of the majority, that is to say, of what could if need be described as "normal." Even if 90 percent of mankind suffered from diabetes, we would not say that they were "healthy" diabetics. Moral theology has made occasional attempts to substantiate the idea that monogamy is the norm for mankind by arguing that it predominates among most peoples and that there is a "trend toward monogamy," as Thielicke puts it, in the history of mankind. Quite apart from whether or not such statements are true, they cannot be used to set up an ethical norm. We could apply the same method to show that most people lie, that closer and closer contacts between more and more people produce a "trend toward lying"; then we would have to declare that lying is an ethical norm.

Accordingly, we will assume that the medical man knows what a healthy person is. So illnesses are deviations from this norm, and it is necessary to redress them. The most ancient method of doing so is by exorcism: "Thou shalt become healthy." Exorcism and faith healing are still practiced today, but they are not very reliable cures. Causal analyses of diseased states that allow the doctor to recognize

foci of infection and organic malfunctionings and to treat
them specifically have a much better success rate. Naturally,
an exact knowledge of the functional connections also enables the doctor to make a healthy person ill or a sick
person even more so. Ethically the method is neutral; it
can be used for good or evil.

Similarly, we will assume that it is known how a man
should rightly behave. Most deviations from this standard,
experience has shown, occur in the realm of social behavior.
The method that is still most widely used today to correct
or prevent such deviations consists in the adjuration "Thou
shalt love thy neighbor as thyself." Again, the results of
this method leave much to be desired and tend rather to
encourage an attempt to make an exact causal analysis of
the disturbed system and its functional structure here too.
At best, the outcome will once again be a neutral scheme
of possible treatments, which will also enable one to elicit
other things besides the valid norm. For the sake of experiments and in order to discover generally valid laws, researchers also study animal behavior in comparison to that
of man. They can even test methods of influence on suitable
animals, not because man "is nothing but an animal," but
because he has some verifiable features in common with
animals. Medical men successfully experiment with medicines on mice, without thereby asserting that man is a
rodent. Furthermore, neither the medical men nor the behavior researchers can transfer their finding on one animal
species to another animal species or to man. All they can
transfer is working hypotheses, certain predictions; and these
always have to be checked again. Similarly, experiments on
animals only allow the researcher to predict the probable
effect of new medicines on man; and the predictions can
sometimes be wrong in spite of the most stringent test
conditions.

How to make predictions that will be as accurate as
possible is a question of method that will be discussed in
the following chapter.

3. How Can We Discover a Law of Nature?

This is a question of method, and one that is very topical
in many of the sciences today. It arises whenever a scientific statement becomes doubtful. The source of these doubts
is not so important. If one "has a kind of feeling" that a
statement is wrong, one can always check how it came to
be made at all. This also means checking on the funda-
mental facts and the way the statement was deduced from
these facts. But one can also examine the question of method
for its own sake and find out what statements a new methodic process would produce. The method is tested as to
the truth of its finding. Truth in this sense is the agreement
between different statements or, for example, between logic
and facts. We do not want to stray into philosophy, however,
but simply to discuss facts of nature. In this context, "nature" is first and foremost the part or aspect of creation
that is accessible to the working methods of natural science.
Later, when we are discussing man, we will also take into
account those parts of human nature that are not accessible
to the methods of natural science, but are accessible to
our own immediate experience. Natural science is an em-
pirical science; the truth of its findings are determined by
verification. According to Weizsäcker, this results in propo-
sitions that, admittedly, are unproven axioms, but that are
generally accepted as true. A biological statement is true if
it is applicable to the living thing, if it is in conformity
with its nature. The statement must indeed conform with

the nature of the living thing; it would obviously be nonsense to assert that a statement was true but did not agree with nature because the living things were wrong.

There are, however, various scientific methods of testing one and the same fact. Moreover, there are statements about man that stem from different sciences and were therefore discovered by different methods. Since mistakes can creep into every scientific working process, it may happen that such statements are irreconcilable with one another. This has one great advantage. It is the only way of calling attention to the fact that one of the statements may be wrong. Accordingly, both statements will have to be verified as to method, and in the end we may legitimately hope to have advanced a step farther in our knowledge. When methods are not questioned we are in the realm of ideology.

It is characteristic of behavior research that it does not confine itself to studying certain parts of living things, such as hormones or sensory organs, or certain biological abilities, such as hibernation or cell division. Rather it attempts to find out how the different animal species, as they exist today, do in fact exist. It examines the living animal, if possible in its natural habitat. It asks what the consequences are in terms of the continuance of the species, if the individuals defend territories, live in well-organized states, have innate responses to certain environmental stimuli, acquire personal experiences, and in given cases transmit them to others, etc. Behavior research tries to explain why some closely related animal species have considerable differences in behavior—why, for instance, some animal species severely wound or even kill one another in intraspecific fights, while others do not in spite of possessing dangerous weapons. This also requires a study of history; the researcher must know why the individual behavior patterns of fighting, courtship, etc., have changed in the course of phylogeny, and how they develop during the growth to maturity of the individuals. All these factors force the researcher away from the isolated detail and toward systematic thought. For example, he could ask what would happen if chimpanzees were forced to live on a treeless seashore, or just why it seems such a ridiculous idea for a cow to lie in wait in front of a rabbit burrow, catch a rabbit, and then devour it. It has been demonstrated again and again that different species of living things exploit entirely different living conditions and that they are equipped to do so in very specific ways, like the fish for swimming, the bird for flying, or the mole for burrowing in the ground. But it is also clear that identical abilities are developed independently of one another and existing coincidences can disappear again. The penguin is a bird, but it cannot fly; instead, it can swim as well as the whale—and yet neither is a fish. Birds, insects, and bats can fly, but they have developed this ability independently from one another.

So there are two fundamentally different methods of comparison: the *comparison of relationships* and the *comparison of abilities*. The first examines how the same organ can produce different things (for instance, a front leg can become a bird's wing or a bird's wing can become a flipper, in the case of the penguin). The comparison of abilities examines the coincidence that different organs can produce (for instance, a wing can come from a front leg among birds and bats, or from a dorsal skin projection among insects). As far as the method is concerned, characteristic behavior patterns can be treated in the same way as organs, for it has been shown that although their form is largely traditional, it also depends on the function of the behavior pattern in question and gradually changes if the behavior pattern changes its function.

If we want to know how a certain organ or behavior pattern has arrived at its present form in the course of phylogeny, we must look at its forerunners, which means that we must adhere strictly to the same organ or the same behavior pattern. It is no use comparing insect wings in order to understand where the bird wing comes from. But a comparison between bird and insect wings does help us to understand what is essential to the function of a wing. Obviously this is not so much a question of whether the wing is made of bones and feathers or of chitin. Since this methodic approach is very important, we will clarify it by yet another technical example. One and the same automobile factory can develop as different models as private automobiles, trucks, and buses; in the same way, the "mammal" factory can develop moles, gazelles, and squirrels. That these very different models all come from the same factory is not apparent at a glance; but it can be determined by a close examination of their structure. On the other hand, very different factories produce almost identical types of vehicles, such as buses; similarly, very different classes of animals have produced living things able to fly. Although they often look rather similar from the outside, a careful analysis of their construction will show that these largely analogous models come from different factories. So if we want to know what is characteristic of the principle of the bus, the best way to find out is to compare buses from different factories. Then we will find differences typical of the different factories that are obviously inessential (such as the method of wheel suspension, whether the engine is in front or behind, or which way the windshield wipers work); we will also find analogies that exist in spite of the different methods of construction typical of each factory, and that are therefore essential to the construction of such a thing as a bus at all.

In the same way, the anatomist compares organs that are largely analogous but that have evolved quite independently, like the eye of the vertebrates and the eye of the octopus. Externally they are extraordinarily similar, yet they prove to be two quite separate "inventions." The octopus eye developed as a skin depression, and the sensory processes of the retina are directed toward the eye lens; by contrast, the eye of the vertebrate is a projection of the brain, and the light-sensitive cells point away from the lens, i.e., the

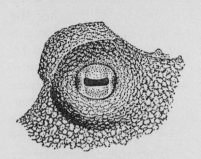

Two cases where almost identical organs of sight came about in the animal kingdom. Left, the eye of the octopus; right, the eye of a mammal (goat).

retina is inverted. The details of the structure are unimportant to the function; what is important are the component parts typical of the lens eye, such as lens, iris, vitreous humor, and retina.

The behavior researcher compares animal abilities in the same way, for instance reproduction or fighting, or the different types of animal society, such as permanent pair-bonds or compact larger groups. And if we want to know what is essential to pair-bonding, then we will have to compare animals that are as different as possible, that have "invented" monogamy independently from one another. This method will yield the natural laws that the lens eye obeys as well as the natural laws of pair-bonding, or marriage. It is only when one has perceived these laws that one can attempt to apply them and make them prevail by the methods peculiar to man.

II

4. Relative Masculinity and Femininity

Every living cell is potentially male and female and can react as a male or a female according to the predominant influences. The incidence of a particular sex can be determined by the genes, which are often situated in the so-called sex chromosomes; but it can also depend on external influences. In the first case we say that the development of male or female tendencies is genetically determined, and in the second that it is determined by modification. A cell becomes male or female according to which of these two tendencies predominates in its development. It is important to note here that this predominance is only in comparison with another cell in which the opposite tendency predominates. Even among very simple organisms such as algae, which have threadlike rows of cells one behind the other, one can observe that during copulation the cells of one thread act as males with regard to the cells of a second thread, but as females with regard to the cells of a third thread. The mark of male behavior here is that the cell actively crawls or swims over to the other; the female cell remains passive. So sexual differentiation is not absolute; there must be differences in the "strength" of the sex within each male or female, so that a cell that is normally female can behave like a male with regard to a more strongly differentiated female cell. This has now been proved true for many species, although the necessary tests are usually extremely complicated; in some cases it required almost ten years of work with pure-bred pedigrees.

There is one unicellular animal species in which one can tell at a glance the sex and the strength of each individual cell's development. This is a little flagellate, related to the *Polymastigina* and called *Trichonympha*, which lives in the

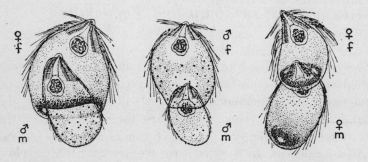

Each individual of the flagellate *Trichonympha* either has a stronger female (♀) or a stronger male (♂) differentiation, but can react both as a female (f) and as a male (m). So a male animal can play the role of female (center, ♂ f) toward a stronger male, and a female animal can play the role of male toward a more female animal (right, ♀ m). Left, "normal" mating between individuals whose sex is clearly differentiated.

intestines of the wood-eating American cockroach. As with many unicellulars, the individuals fuse entirely in the sexual act. In this case the male individual follows the female and penetrates her from behind through a special zone of plasma. This process resembles closely the penetration of a thread of semen into an animal egg. A typical *Trichonympha* female is recognizable by the number of little dark pigment spots arranged in a dense ring on her rear cell section. The male, by contrast, has only a few of these little dots distributed freely over the entire body of the cell. But there are all manner of transitions between the two extremes, and one can determine how strongly developed the female tendency of such a unicellular individual is by the number of dark dots. During a typical copulation, an individual with only a few dots penetrates one with a dense ring of dots, as shown in the illustration; so it is playing the part of the male. But it will be forced into the female role if it meets up with an individual with even fewer dots on its plasma, who will in turn take over the male role.

In the same way, a rather weakly developed female can act as a male when faced by a strongly developed animal. It can even happen that three individuals copulate with one another, the middle one penetrating the first one as a male, while at the same time serving as female for the third one.[15]

This kind of relative sexuality does not occur only among lower plants (algae, fungi) and unicellular animals, but also among fairly highly developed animals. Among segmented worms, to which our earthworm also belongs, the large related class of marine segmented bristleworms (*Polychaeta*) includes the species *Ophryotrocha puerilis*. These animals gradually grow from the larval stage into ever longer worms. The longer the worm is, the more segments it has, and any worm with more than twenty segments to its body is a female. The familiar experiment of cutting one of these animals down to five or ten front segments turns the animal into a male until it again develops the number of segments typical of a female. But the experiment works only if one feeds the animals badly at the same time; and, if one continues to do so, the worms will remain male, even if they have already grown too long for males. This worm demonstrates a typical instance of protandria or "provisional masculinity"; at first the individuals are male and then they become female. The experiment shows something else too: If one keeps two fully grown females together in a culture bowl, one of them will soon become male and fertilize the eggs of its partner. This transformation is effected by a substance emanating from the eggs that are still in the body of the female. The animal with the most eggs will assert its influence and thereby force the other to act as the male. After the eggs are liberated it can, of course, now occur that the other animal will produce more eggs more quickly; then they will exchange roles. This is possible because, in each segment, the animals form indifferent sex cells, which can become eggs or sperms depending on the external circumstances influencing them.[41]

Zoology textbooks also mention the worm *Bonellia viridis*, which lives hidden in rock crevices in the Mediterranean and North Atlantic. The fertilized eggs produce free-swimming larvae that are still of indifferent sex. The larvae grow up, settle somewhere, and become females with a thick body several centimeters long and a proboscis almost a meter long with which the animals search for food in the vicinity. If one of the free-swimming larvae comes upon the proboscis of a female, it will settle there too, and in the course of four days it will turn into a male; then it separates from the proboscis again and wanders into the sexual canals of the female where it remains and—often together with other males—proceeds to fertilize her. It develops into a male so rapidly because the animals scarcely need to grow during this process—the males only reach a size of about one millimeter. The process of larvae that are not yet sexually determined turning into males through influences emanating from a female is actually quite widespread among invertebrates. Among one species of wood louse, the sawbug *Ione*, which is a parasite living in pairs on the gills of a ghost shrimp (*Callianassa*), the larva becomes a female if it settles directly on a host gill. But the next larva to settle on this female becomes a male; if, however, it is removed and put on the next gill, it too will become a female. Other wood lice have only old females and young males, because each individual is a male when young and later turns female. Similarly, the offspring of the small slipper-limpet *Crepidula* is male while it is still living alone. When it reaches a certain size it settles somewhere and changes into a female. The young animal settles on a conspecific that has already settled, and so we find rows of up to twelve animals sitting one on top of the other. The last arrivals are always male and remain so for a very long time, since the female animals sitting underneath them emanate an influence—presumably some substance—that keeps the young animals in the male state for the long period.[41]

So the final development into male or female is determined by outside influences among these lower animals too. However, the sexual differentiation affects many organs of the body, so that in the end the animal cannot revert in the same way as the *Ophryotrocha* could. Besides bodily structure, the physiological processes of the body and its behavior are also affected by the development of one or the other sex. Of these, the body structure is of course the most rigid, while behavior is the most variable factor. It can happen that even among animals who are indubitably male or female according to their bodily structure, each individual can still display the behavior of both sexes. Even birds, who have no penis and only copulate by pressing the rims of their cloacae firmly against each other, can still copulate inversely, i.e., the female can hop on the male, behave like a male, and copulate. In this case it is possible for a bird to actually fertilize another, as happens among pigeons.

On closer examination, it will become apparent that even among mammals, male and female behavior is often not as precisely demarcated and distributed among different individuals as is normally thought. We tend to connect very definite roles with the concepts of "male" and "female," not only in the act of mating but in every facet of social life. Often we take the idea of roles from our own cultural sphere and transfer it to the animal world without realizing it. In extreme cases this leads to talking about perversities among animals, simply because the observed behavior would be called perverse if it occurred among humans.

The Bighorn sheep (*Ovis canadensis*) offer a good example of how relative male and female behavior can be among mammals. The sheep live in the Rocky Mountains either in small or fairly large herds. The most experienced members lead the herd to the feeding places known to be most favorable in the respective season; these sites can often be separated by up to twenty miles, so that no individual would find them by itself. For this reason alone it is more profitable for the sheep to assemble in herds.

Outside the rutting season, the animals live in herds consisting of males only or of females with their young and a few smaller males. What is curious about these animals is that between the extremes of rams over eight years old and lambs less than a year old one finds every possible transition in age, but no other differences whatsoever. There is no clear distinction of sex; the bodily form, the structure of

Age groups of male mountain sheep, from left to right: 8–16, 6–8, 3–6, 2½, 1½ years of age; far right, a fully grown female with the weakest horns.

the horns, and the color of the coat are the same for both sexes. Since the males become bigger and heavier, the typical female is absent from this pattern. Geist has examined the social behavior of mountain sheep in depth[35] and found that even the males often cannot recognize a female as such. In addition, the females are only of interest to the males in the rutting season.

The social life of these mountain sheep demonstrates a large number of clearly distinct behavioral patterns, such as presentation of horns, pawing with the forelegs, mounting, butting, battle leaps, pursual, sniffing, and baring the lips (*Flehmen*). So the more one is inclined to class behavior patterns according to sexual roles, the more one will be astonished to find that *both* sexes play two roles, either that of the male or that of the young male. Outside the rutting season the females behave like young males, during the rutting season like aggressive older males. The female is in heat only two days a year and will let herself be mounted only if she is defeated by a stronger ram. Subordinate rams behave in the same way. This means that male animals behave aggressively toward subordinate animals, but behave like a female in heat toward their superiors. Females in heat attack rams, females not in heat retreat from attacking rams. Young rams and females in heat automatically prefer the proximity of strong rams with powerful horns. So, day in, day out, the high-ranking rams always have animals around them who behave like females in heat, either because they really are, or because they are inferior males. (If the high-ranking male simply fought them with all his strength, he would also drive away all the females in heat around him and would lose the chance to reproduce.) The strong ram must tolerate this behavior of females in heat, so the lower-ranking rams have a chance of remaining unmolested by their much stronger rivals by camouflaging themselves with the behavior of females in heat. This very aggressive behavior incites high-ranking rams to mount them, which explains why rams also mount lower-ranking members of the same sex. Since young animals and females who are not in heat evade male attacks, one finds herds of female animals and young ones who remain apart from the group of males outside the rutting season. The aggressive behavior is always present, however, in the group of males, above all among low-ranking males; as we have seen, the high-ranking males are obliged to tolerate this. So the group of males offers the rams an opportunity for aggressive and sexual activity. Females who are not in heat avoid both. But when in heat they seek out the groups of rams of their own accord.

So these mountain sheep treat conspecifics differently according to their grade, which is dependent not on sex but on size and ranking order. There is a line of development leading from the lamb to the high-ranking ram, and the female animals (♀) behave exactly as though they were in fact males (♂) whose development was retarded. Since they alternate between being in heat and not in heat, they also alternate between the behavior of a male and that of a young animal several times in the course of their life. This can be shown schematically:

Typical behavior

EVASION	ATTACK	MOUNTING
♂ — lamb $\longrightarrow$	low-ranking ♂ $\longrightarrow$	high-ranking ♂
♀ — lamb		
$\downarrow$		
not in heat ♀ $\leftrightarrow$	in heat ♀	

We can say that the only fully developed mountain sheep are the powerful rams, for they alone, within five to seven years after attaining sexual maturity, reach the final stage of fully mature physical structure and behavior possible to this species. Even when they are sexually mature, the females remain at an early stage of development, corresponding to that of the young ram.

There are examples showing that behavior patterns typical of one sex can also appear as a kind of transitional stage at certain moments in the youth or later development of the other sex among many species of animal. Careful observation will show that this can take different forms even among closely related animals. Half-grown male bullfinches, for instance, display purely female behavior up to the first winter; they make nest-building motions (although the adult male bullfinch does not take part in building the nest) and even utter mating calls. But female bullfinches of the same age do not behave like males. By contrast, both sexes of young tree sparrows display male and female behavior; one can recognize the males only from their juvenile song. But young tropical finches never exhibit the behavior of the other sex.

In the social behavior of mountain sheep, female behavior evidently counts as of low rank, male as of high rank. This is not only so among sheep. Among tropical cichlids of species that have clearly differentiated sexual behavior, if one keeps only individuals of the same sex together—females only, for instance—one will always observe that one of the animals, usually the strongest, will act like a male, dig a spawning hole, display, and try to entice the other females there. On the other hand, if one keeps only males together, one of them will soon occupy a spawning territory and attack the others violently. One of the attacked can then assume the female role, follow the displaying animal to his spawning hole, and even make spawning motions there. In the case of a rather unusual cichlid, *Tilapia macrochir,* whose males deposit the sperm wrapped up as though in a parcel (spermatophore) when the female has liberated her eggs,[121] two males were observed "spawning" with each other, one wearing the male display dress, the other in female dress. Naturally neither of the two spawned, but both deposited their spermatophores.

It is fairly common in the animal kingdom for female sexual behavior to occur only in connection with submission, as with mountain sheep. Of course this is not apparent until one has come to know the animals well and has let both sexes live together at will. It is fairly rare today for us to allow our domestic animals to mate freely; usually man intervenes to control mating, in extreme cases by means of artificial insemination. Some breeds of domestic animal, such as highly bred dogs and horses, are incapable of copulating at all without the helping hand of man. But the owner also keeps a watchful eye on less highly bred horses, often enclosing the mares in a paddock by themselves and only bringing them a selected stallion at certain times. Unpleasant incidents can occur during this kind of "free herd-copulation," because the mare of highest rank takes over the role of stallion and attacks the new, genuine stallion without mercy or keeps all "his" mares from him. Among monkeys kept in captivity, if the only old male is absent due to death or accident, a fully grown female can take his place; this occurs particularly among macaque monkeys. Even if there is a lower-ranking male in the group dominated by this female, he will not often manage to mate with the female of higher rank than himself, so that she remains without progeny for the time being.

The fact that subordinate animals often play the role of female can sometimes lead to curious behavior. Among cichlids, we have often seen the loser give up his poster-colored display dress (which can happen in the space of a few seconds thanks to the physiological color changes peculiar to these fish) after a violent conflict between two males. Yet he does not follow this by trying to escape from the aquarium; rather he swims after the victor. This would seem the silliest thing he could do, since he risked a new thrashing. In fact it is the best thing he could do; for to pursue the territory owner without threatening him is typical female behavior; at most it incites the victor to court and lead the loser to his nest.

Naturally, subordinate females also play the female role,

often in very intensive fashion. This is why a male hama-dryas baboon always achieves success if he violently attacks and bites a female who strays from the band. Afterward he simply turns around and goes back, and the rep-rimanded female follows him closely "at heel." Here again one could ask why she did not make a wide berth around the "angry" male after his attack or even try to flee from him. In fact, in such cases the aggression of the highest-ranking animal can promote the cohesion of the group, even when it is not directed against outsiders but against members of the group.

The same, incidentally, applies to the parent-child bond. Young ducklings who follow their mother cannot be pre-vented from doing so by punishment disincentives—they will only follow all the more eagerly. Admittedly this is an experimental situation and the punishment is not meted out by the mother. But similar factors seem to me to play a role in the weaning efforts of monkey mothers; they actually turn aggressive toward their young, but they have little success at first and are only successful later because the young monkey eventually joins up with other members of the group, particularly with its contemporaries.

We can see how closely related aggression, ranking be-havior, and sexual behavior are by observing how easily one can turn into the other. The "furious" copulation of various mammals, for instance sea elephants, baboons, macaques, pit-tailed macaques, and chimpanzees, is well known. In each case an enraged male mounts any member of the same species in sight at the time and makes copu-latory motions or actually copulates with it. The animals also do this if man puts them into a state of furious ex-citement, for example, if a man shows a caged monkey a delicacy but does not give it to him. Chimpanzees react by storming around the cage in a fury, with erect penis. Rage copulations do not occur if the animals are put in a state of fear. So aggression can easily turn into mating behavior among males. By contrast, females in a sexual mood take cover in "coyness" toward the male; they wait or come back if the male does not follow and incite him to pursue and mount them by repeatedly fleeing a short distance away. We will discuss in detail on pp. 206f. how subordinate males often act out female mating behavior in face of a higher-ranking conspecific.

5. Behavior Precedes Body Structure

It is easier to reply to the question why male sexual behavior tends more toward aggression, whereas female sexual behavior is more closely bound up with submission or flight if one rephrases it as follows: What has male sexual behavior to do with aggression, female sexual behavior with flight? "Aggression" derives from the Latin verb *aggredior,* which in English means to go up to, to approach, to attack. Among very simple organisms, which are bisexual but whose sex cannot be determined externally, it is the individual who moves toward another to copulate with it who is considered male. We have mentioned the flagellate algae as an example of this (see p. 24). On this level, then, it is all simply a question of definition. We call the more aggressive individual the male. But higher organisms no longer consist merely of one cell, which is also the gamete, but have a body that is clearly separated from the gametes. In the context of reproduction, this body can help to bring the gametes as close together as possible.

Sponges and many molluscs draw in the sperms with the currents of water; so the eggs remain "in place," i.e., in the mother animal, while the sperm have to travel. The sperm will be more likely to reach their destination if the animal does not simply liberate them anywhere but brings them close to the egg cells, which are either within the mother animal or liberated too. In the latter case eggs and sperm must be ejected at the same time; this is achieved by a synchronization of the sexual animals that involves their hormones, senses, and locomotive abilities.

The marine ragworm (*Nereis*) rises to the surface of the North Sea in the nights around April 15. Then the worms assemble and eject eggs and sperms en masse. At this time their eyes, antennae, and other sensory organs also grow much larger. After this reproductive journey, they die. By contrast, the palolo worm (*Eunice*), a bristleworm living in coral-reef hollows of the tropical seas, ties off the rear half of its body where the male or female sexual products are located. This rear end leaves the front of the body, swims to the surface of the water to meet other such independent body halves and to empty out its sexual products, and then dies. The remaining front half, however, regenerates a new rear end. This process is synchronized according to the phases of the moon (during these predictable lunar phases the Samoans collect great quantities of the swarming segments of worm; they regard them as a delicacy). The main segment of the worm with head and brain takes no part whatsoever in sexual life. The tied-off rear end of a closely related worm (*Autolytus*) does not die off but regenerates a new head, thus becoming an independent new individual. So nature has many different ways of bringing the gametes together. And anyone interested in the natural laws of "copulation" and "reproduction" in general must have some knowledge of these processes. Since there are something over a million animal species in creation, of which only 6 percent are vertebrates, the so-called lower animals must also be taken into account.

Water is a fairly good method of transport for sperms, but many are still lost, and if different species of animals liberate eggs at the same time, too many sperms will meet up with the wrong eggs. So even marine animals have "invented" copulation, which later became very important for terrestrial animals. In copulation, the actual act of mating or coition, the sperms are once again brought to the egg cells: The entire male animal seeks out a female and deposits the sperms on her, externally or by introducing them into her body. The male marine horse-hair worm (*Gordius aquaticus*, found in European streams) deposits the sperm beside the female genital aperture and in the course of two days the sperm wander into her sexual passages of their own accord. The dog leech (*Erpobdella*) deposits the sperm, packed in spermatophores, anywhere on its partner. A fluid from the packet of sperm eats its way through skin and muscles into the cavity of the body, where the sperm then swirl around. Some reach the eggs, but most are eaten up beforehand by resistance cells as though they were invading viruses. Among velvet worms (*Peripatus*), who are land dwellers, the male crawls onto the female without any preliminaries and attaches a spermatophore anywhere. The resistance cells of the female eat a hole into her body and into the wall of the spermatophores below the place where they are attached, so that again the sperm can swim around in the blood of the female until they reach the ovaries where they fertilize the eggs. In spite of their curious form of copulation, these animals are by no means primitive; for instance, the young develop inside the female, are nourished by the mother through the placenta and finally, fairly large and well-developed by now, are born alive.

Bedbugs (*Cimex*) copulate in a similar fashion. The male pierces a hole into the female's back by means of a spike situated in front of his penis and ejaculates the sperm into the hole. Many other flat bugs do the same—although the females have well-developed sexual organs which, however, they never use for copulation. Instead, the females have a special tissue on the part of their body where the male is most likely to pierce; this tissue absorbs the sperm and then conducts them on into the bloodstream. In fact one bug, called *Xylocoris*, finally evolved a new aperture, of complex structure, on the female's back, into which the male copulates.[14]

The ancestors of these animals once mated "normally," using the appropriate female sexual aperture. Then a sexual aberration occurred among some species that would have had to be termed unnatural at first, with regard to the existing copulatory organs of the two partners. In this case, however, evolution did not eradicate the aberration; on the contrary, it became normalized. Even the animal's bodily structure adapted itself to "extragenital copulation." Comparative studies of variously specialized species now enable us to reconstruct this piece of phylogenetic evolution without too much trouble. If anything was unnatural here, it was our habit of thinking in static norms. *One simply cannot deduce, on the basis of body structure and the forms of organs, binding norms for the future behavior patterns for which these organs are used;* nor, therefore, for example, can one assert that ventroventral copulation is the only form of copulation natural to man *on the basis of the site of the organs.* (Incidentally, the ability of sperm ejected into the female's abdominal cavity outside her sexual passages to find their way to the eggs and to fertilize them has not disappeared even among the most highly developed animals. For instance, this "intraperitoneal insemination" can occur among hens, rabbits, and cattle.)

6. The Development of Genital Organs

The example of bugs taught us that changes in behavior can entail changes in body structure. This is not only so for bugs. Normally we imagine that copulation occurs when the male introduces a penis into the sexual aperture of the female. But totally different kinds of copulation and genital organs also occur. Whether one calls it mating or not when the male deposits a packet of sperm on the outside of the female is a question of definition. This is in fact a borderline case; for although it is very common in the animal kingdom to deposit spermatophores, the accompanying circumstances can be very different. Among beetlemites (*Oribatei*) and certain springtails (*Collembola*), the males deposit large quantities of stemmed spermatophores anywhere on the ground, with no relation to the female, so that they look like fungoid growths. If the female comes upon one of these "gardens of love" she will pick a few spermatophores with her cloacal aperture. Even when they meet, males and females make no sign of recognition. But with another kind of springtail (*Dicyrtomina*), the male at least takes cognizance of the female. He deposits his drops of stemmed sperm around the female like a stockade, so that she is bound to happen upon one of them when she moves. The male bristly millipede (*Pselaphognate-Polyxenoidea*), one of the smallest groups of millipedes, deposits its sperm drops without coming into contact with the female; but he spins "guidelines" of threads that catch the attention of any female in the vicinity and lead her to the sperm drops. The fifty-legged centipede (*Lithobius*), the bristletail (*Machilidae*), and the silverfish (*Lepisma*) have evolved very enterprising "web games" that help guide the female to the spermatophore—they are in no way less complex than the foreplay to pairing and copulating of higher animals.[98]

Among vertebrates, the males of our native newts also deposit spermatophores in front of the females in their pools in springtime. Then they entice the females to crawl over the spermatophores by waggling their tail, thereby directing a scent, and at the same time walking slowly backward. Scorpions grasp their female by the pincers, deposit a spermatophore on the ground and then, moving backward, pull the female over it so that she can pick up the spermatophore with her cloacal aperture. In this form of copulation, the sexual apertures of the animals do not come into contact; yet the sperm reach the eggs by way of the female's sexual passages.

There are other methods too. The males of the small, blind garden centipede *Scutigerella* also deposit a stemmed drop of sperm. The female, who encounters it at some stage, bites the drop off its stem, but instead of swallowing the sperm, she stores it in special cheek pouches. Then, when she lays eggs, she takes each individual egg into her mouth and smears it with a small portion of semen. The females of the small, segmented marine tarpon (*Megalops*) bite off the sperm-bearing segments of the males who swarm around them, and devour them; the sperm penetrate through the gut, reach the body cavity, and then swim over to the eggs and fertilize them. To ask whether or not this can be called copulation is not as important as to realize that many paths can lead to fertilization and that in each case definite behavioral traits determine the direction in which organs and physiological processes will evolve in order to make fertilization possible. This is so even if the female is "snappish" and eats parts of the male. Among vertebrates, a number of cichlids (e.g., *Haplochromis*) have evolved a method of oral insemination similar to that of the *Scutigerella* I described. The females take the eggs into their mouth to hatch them before the males come to inseminate them. Now, the males have colorful egg "dummies" on the pelvic fins, and the females try to take these "painted" eggs into their mouth too. At the same moment, the male ejaculates and the female, trying vainly to get at the egg snares, instead receives the sperm in her mouth; the sperm joins the eggs in her mouth cavity and subsequently inseminates them. Here too I have been able to show by comparative studies how a "behavioral anomaly" is not corrected in nature but compensated by the modification of other behavior patterns and organs; it becomes a new norm.[120, 125]

In every case where the sexual partners come into direct contact during copulation, which parts of their body will turn into copulating organs depends entirely on the partners' relative positions and on their behavior. Cuttlefish and octopuses mate with the partners facing one another; the mouth areas of the *sepia* touch but the octopuses sit far apart. In both cases, the male deposites a spermatophore directly on the tentacle (to the left of his abdomen) that has been specially modified for this, and then uses this same tentacle to introduce it into the female cloacal aperture. The males of most spiders ejaculate a drop of sperm onto a small web especially constructed for this purpose. Then they take the sperm into a leg converted into a copulating organ— the so-called "pedipalp" or mandible antenna—seek out a female, and pump the sperm into her cloacal aperture with the pedipalp. So in effect they copulate "with their hands." Among fish, the sexual partners of egg-laying toothed carps (*Cyprinidae*) synchronize very carefully and then eject eggs and sperm at the same time. During this process the female rolls up the front part of her anal fin into a cone and puts

it around the anal fin of the male; the eggs and sperm
are kept together in this channel. In a related group of
toothed carps (*Poecilidae*), which give birth to live young,
the males probably rolled up the anal fin originally too.
The males of species still in existence today have anal fins
that are fairly specialized in this direction. Their few remaining finrays are folded against one another during the
mating time, and this produces a groove just in front of the
sexual aperture on which a ventral fin can lie like a lid.
The whole serves as a copulating organ, whose tip is introduced into the female sexual aperture. The copulating organ
of the Southeast Asian toothed carp (*Phallostethidae*) is
made up of parts of the thorax and shoulder girdles and the
first pair of ribs. The males of the shark and rock have
formed copulating organs out of the rear part of the pairs of
ventral fins, and some species of grope (*Scorpaenidae*) and
Brotulidae have a "penis," i.e., a fleshy extension of the
genital papilla, which they use for copulation.

Quite independently from one another, very different
groups of animals have evolved a penis of the kind we find
so normal as the male organ of copulation. For instance,
while the dog leech I described deposits sperm packets on
the outside of the female, the medicinal leech (*Hirudo*)
has a penis for copulating with the female; during copulation, the couple lies abdomen against abdomen. The whirl-
worm has a penis, and so do snails, who are hybrids. Some
mites deposit spermatophores; others transfer them to the
female sexual aperture with their mandible antennae. Others
again have a penis. The mite *Pyemotis*, which feeds on
caterpillars, gives birth to live young who are already sexually mature. The young males remain attached to the
mother after birth, sting her, suck out some of her body
juices, and then wait for a young female. They take no
notice of other brothers who are born, but if a sister should
appear in the genital duct, one of the brothers will grab
her, drag her out, and copulate immediately.[52] Among

spiders, the harvestman (*Opiliones*) has a penis, and ventro-ventral copulation is typical of some species. A very complex penis structure and a similarly complicated female genital organ is often so characteristic of higher insects that taxonomists use these organs to differentiate the species. In the great fish kingdom, there are also a few species with penis (see above); among amphibians there is at the most one case, namely the African tree toad (*Nectophrynoïdes*). These are the only amphibian toads to bring fully formed young into the world; but no one has seen them mate yet. Reptiles, lizards, snakes, tortoises, and crocodiles usually have a fairly specialized penis. An exception is the famous tuatara (*Sphenodon*), a member of a very ancient order of reptiles. During copulation, tuatarae press the rims of their cloaca firmly against each other. Most birds copulate in the same way, for only very few (e.g., the ostrich and the goose) have a penis. Male mammals all have a penis, although its form and structure can vary a great deal.

This list suffices to make it clear that the penis was very often "invented" as an organ of copulation in the animal kingdom, even among higher vertebrates. The copulating organs of tortoises, crocodiles, and mammals have one common origin; those of lizards and snakes have another. The latter have a double penis, made up of two halves that act separately and are inverted for copulation like the finger of a glove. In terms of the methods of copulation described above, all this shows that the male organ of copulation is also a subsequently evolved, auxiliary structure, which appeared on those animals whose behavior during the act of mating called for it. Again, body structure follows in the wake of behavior. Accordingly, the homogenous term "penis" refers at most to a same function in each case; in fact, the organ of copulation evolved out of quite different existing bodily organs and in entirely different ways. This is why it can also have various secondary functions. Among some flatworms, the penis comes out of the oral aperture, is equipped with spikes and poison glands and, besides copulation, is also used to catch prey (e.g., among the *Prorhynchus*). Some types of flatworm introduce the penis into the female sexual aperture, others sting the female with it anywhere on her body. This method has also been evolved by several other species in the animal kingdom.

The naïve notion that animal behavior conforms to the organs the respective animals evolve must therefore be corrected as follows: the evolution of organs conforms to *existing behavior*. This is just as easy to show for many other organs besides the sexual ones. Hence we can deduce the following very important general law: *Behavior patterns are the pacemakers of evolution*.

The relative strength and rank of the two sexes have played an important part in determining the mating position that was adopted. The superior pursuer mounted his partner from behind. The differing copulating positions of many lower animals have not yet been studied in terms of relative rank, but such studies would no doubt teach us a great deal more. Many female insects sit on the male during copulation. As far as mammals and men are concerned, they do not copulate in a certain way because they have a penis, but they have a penis because the mating behavior of their penisless ancestors foretold the evolution of such an organ. By virtue of this, the male genital organ has taken over all the functions involving the behavior that gave rise to the evolution of this organ. This is why the penis of some flatworms is used for catching prey. What functions the penis of mammals and men can fulfill besides copulation will be discussed in the following chapter. Here we need only point out that it is wrong to assert, as people sometimes do, that only man mates in the ventro-ventral position with the partners facing each other. In fact this position already occurs among lower animals, such as leeches, harvestmen, centipedes, North Sea shrimps, and common crabs; among fish such as the ray, among mammals such as the whale, and among monkeys such as dwarf chimpanzees or bonobos (*Pan [Satyricus] paniscus*). However, it is very likely that man is the only one to use this mating position—which was no doubt made possible to him for other biological reasons—in order to strengthen the profound personal relationship between the sexes.

7. Apparent Homosexual Behavior

In the context of ranking order, sexual behavior patterns are often independent of the sex of the participants. It can sometimes happen that female animals will mount each other, just as males do. But the concept of homosexuality is misplaced in this case, although it is often used for it—perhaps because the observer is not fully aware of the circumstances that have led to such behavior. We should only speak of homosexuality if an individual clearly prefers conspecifics of the same sex within a sexual context. The word "prefers" is important here, for it presumes that conspecifics of the opposite sex would be just as accessible to the individual. If this is not the case, we could be dealing with a so-called blocked drive, which is worked off on the wrong object for lack of anything better. Here too the precise choice of word is important: If no conspecific of different sex is available, the observed homosexual activity *can* be an ersatz satisfaction of a drive—but it can also be genuine homosexuality. Under these circumstances, it is difficult, if at all possible, to decide. It is equally difficult to interpret an individual case of apparent "homosexual" behavior exactly. Once again it could simply be a question of rank demonstration. Here, as in every realm, to use a concept carelessly only creates confusion. In the framework of our theme, we are not concerned with the interpretation of the behavior patterns we have just discussed; rather it is a question of describing regularly recurrent types of behavior.

From what we have already said it becomes clear that

when male baboons mount each other, this need not be homosexual behavior but could also be a demonstration of

"Playful" mounting between young hamadryas baboons.

rank. The same applies to female baboons who mount each other. When a subordinate male assumes the role of a female in face of the victor, because this role is also a sign

Copulation of the hamadryas baboon and (right) a superior baboon mounting an adult subordinate one as a gesture of dominance.

of submission, we are dealing once again with a demonstration of rank and not with homosexuality. The examples of
relative sexuality described earlier are not instances of homosexuality either.

Similarly, a high-ranking female hamadryas baboon mounts
a lower-ranking female.

Apparent homosexual behavior can also occur when the
active individual cannot distinguish male from female,
either because of special contingencies or on principle. That
animals can make mistakes, even in questions of sex, will
surprise no one. There are in fact cases where the sexes
really are indistinguishable. This may seem nonsensical if
one starts from the assumption that it is essential for an
animal to find its sexual partner and to be able to distinguish it from a conspecific, at least during the mating season
and for those animals who copulate, i.e., actually seek out
a partner rather than simply liberate their sexual products
together in a great swarm. Among the already mentioned
flat bugs, the species *Afrocimex* proves that there are other
possibilities too. These animals have evolved a form of
extragenital copulation in which the male bores a hole
through the back of the female with his genital apparatus

and deposits the sperm there. He also treats all other males in the same way, i.e., the males copulate in this way with all members of the same species. Their ancestors could at least feel or tell by the genitals whether their partner was male or female at the beginning of copulation. But today these bugs bypass the female genitals during copulation and this obviates the possibility of control. Now if the male produces enough sperm, it may happen that he simply distributes them among all the available members of his own species—the *Hesperoctenes* species even distributes them among the larvae of both sexes. This means that the wastage is greater, but it also means that the females get as many sperm as they require to fertilize their eggs. But it seems that this is still not the whole story. Just like the females, the males too have a special body tissue under their back, which absorbs the sperm and conducts them on into the body.[14] Naturally, the sperm never reach ovaries in the body of the male but are distributed throughout, even in the legs and head. Presumably this copulation among males is not simply a breakdown in nature but has some special value. Further investigation is necessary here too.

Bugs are only one example of how extravagant organisms are with their sperm. Egg cells are carefully stored, not because they correspond to a higher level of being but simply as a matter of economy, for the egg cells are often full of nourishing substances for the embryo; these substances must eventually be mustered by the mother's body and "cost" more than the plain gamete. Sperm, by contrast, have no "material value" worth mentioning. Our native red stag uses ejaculated fluid (which almost certainly contains a large number of sperm) in order to mark out his territory. He spurts it on his coat and antlers with erect penis and then smears streaks onto twigs and branches as scent marks![11] The North American wapiti or elk (*Cervus canadensis*) also uses sperm for marking. If two territorial neighbors do this, it is, of course, not homosexual behavior.

No more can one call the curious behavior of the sperm of South American marsupials such as the opossum homosexual: The sperm of these animals lay themselves one against the other in pairs as though they wanted to copulate before they are brought into the female sexual passages. The biological significance of this mating of sperm is not known.

8. The Phallus as a Sign of Rank and Threat

Besides copulation, the mammal penis is also used for urinating, and urine in turn quite frequently serves to mark
out a territory. In the case of social animals, the marking
out of territory is always the affair of the highest-ranking
animal. We can determine their rank by the degree of frequency with which, for instance, olingos (*Bassarycion*)
mark out their habitats at certain points. If one removes
the highest-ranking animal, the next will move into his place
and also take over his typical frequency of marking. But
animals do not only mark out territory; a stallion, for example, marks the pile of droppings of a mare, and some
species mark the subordinate member of the same species
or the female they are courting directly. The Asian marten
(*Nyctereutes*) sprays his female with his urine, and wild
rabbits, porpoises, scaly anteaters (*Manis*), the large Pata-
gonian Cavy (*Dolichotis*), the acouchy (*Myoprocta*), and
the North American porcupine (*Erethizon*) spurt a powerful
spray of urine onto their partner with erect penis. In given
cases the partner shoots back, so that a brief urine-spraying
duel can develop.

The fact that the penis is erect for this suggests a common
behavioral root for urine marking and copulation; for marking, the urine is usually ejaculated sporadically too, while
for simple urinating it flows regularly. Marking paths with
urine is known among half monkeys, such as slim lorises
(*Loris*), slow lorises (*Nycticebus*) and lemurs; the mon-

A young squirrel monkey presents its genitals in order
to impress.

goose lemur also marks his female with urine. These animals are predominantly scent-oriented and most of them are
nocturnal. But the higher monkeys are diurnal and largely
orient themselves with their eyes. This is why the erect
penis becomes a direct signal rather than the scent marks
emanating from it. We can follow the transition very well
in the case of South American squirrel monkeys (*Saimiri*).
These monkeys impress one another by straddling their
hind legs and displaying their erect genitalia. This gesture
serves to threaten individuals foreign to the group—including their own mirror images—and as the most important
demonstration of rank within the group.[90] Occasionally a
little drop of urine is also emitted in the process, but it is
not significant. The same display of the genitals also occurs
among capuchin monkeys (*Cebus*). Urine emission disappears entirely among the even more highly developed old
world monkeys in this situation, but the penis is very clearly
displayed. Since these monkeys—unlike many lemurs—no
longer follow scent traces in fixed territories but often
wander about freely in nomadic fashion, they use genital
display as a demonstration toward others of the current

Doguera baboon "on guard."

boundaries of the group. The males openly sit "on guard," often turning their back to the group. The penis is extended far out, and this alone makes it very conspicuous, as with savannah baboons (*Papio*), whose penis is scarcely visible when drawn in. The genitals of African monkeys of the genus *Cercopithecus* have become extremely colorful for this signal function: the penis can turn bright red, the scrotum a luminous blue. The color combination can vary from species to species and it is one of the brightest body colors found among mammals. This use of the genitals is not directly related to the sexual drive. It can occur independently of sexual behavior patterns and is occasionally to be seen among, for instance, young squirrel monkeys a few days old in the appropriate social situation.

We also find an emphatic exhibition of the male genitals without sexual connotations among humans. Greek hoplites and Etruscan warriors wore greaves, helmets, and breastplates, but left their genitals uncovered. When they had slain an enemy, they cut off his penis. Haberland still found this custom, which used to be widespread, in southern Ethiopia a few years ago.[39]

The penis as trophy of victory was soon replaced by images. Even today almost all the tribes of southern Ethiopia wear a simple phallic ornament made of light shining

Phallic brow ornament made of metal worn by a southern Ethiopian as insignia of rank.

metal on their brow; it is called "Kalatsha" and is thought the most important of ritual objects. Originally it was a sign that the wearer had killed an adult male opponent and was now allowed to start a family. Most of the Galla tribes adopted it as an insignia of rank that only high priests and holders of special honors were allowed to wear. The king of the great southern Ethiopian kingdom, Kaffa, used to wear on his brow a three-part phallus, which was at first interpreted as a crown. Divinities of very high rank, such as Ammun Rê in Egypt, Tlaloc in Mexico, and Shiva in India are also represented with erect phallus.

Besides being displayed on a man or even on his hut as an insignia of rank, we find the phallus on the phallic figures that are described as ithyphallic (i.e., with erect phallus). The most familiar are probably the ithyphallic stone hermes that Herodotus described as an ancient tradition. One still finds figures of the same type, worked in wood, on the Sunda Islands today. From exact details of the sites of the finds and from reports by the respective peoples or their priests, as well as from the prayers of consecration and supplication connected with the erection and veneration of such figures, the following amazing coincidences with the monkeys "on guard" have emerged:

1. These figures are guards. They stand at the entrance of villages, houses, and temples as well as on graves and property boundaries.
2. They always stand with their back to the guarded object and display their genitals to the outside.
3. Often the phallus is painted in conspicuous colors, for instance red.
4. These guards protect against demons of various kinds, against earthly and supernatural enemies, and against the spirits of the dead, i.e., always against beings whom man treats as members of his own kind. On wooden figures of this sort, which are still made in southern Bali, the threatening phallus is accompanied by a clearly defined threatening expression.

In no case I know of are these guards aimed against predators' vermin. Instead they are opposed to those spirits and demons whom man holds responsible for the appearance of vermin and animals that damage crops, which is why they also stand on fields. In Bali, ithyphallic straw figures were placed on the rice fields. But the further the old function of the phallus as sign of rank and threat fell into disuse, the more these guards against threats to fertility were made into direct promoters of fertility and symbols of fertility, especially since the threatening organ is also a reproductive organ and this reproductive function is familiar to man.

Left: straw guardian the height of a man from a rice field near Sanur. Center: wood-carving of a guard ("Mo-emmedi"), height 44 cm.; both made in Bali in 1968. Right: wooden house guard ("Siraha"), height 150 cm., from Nias.

The phallic signal acquired this significance from the observer. The same applies to the very simplified guard figures on which arms and legs, and eventually even the rump and head, were often left out, so that the phallus alone remained as a "mushroom stone." Sometimes, secondary human outlines were added on the shaft, and this is the origin of the naked stone figures with "hat."

The more abstract shapes are allowed to become, the more objects we will find that seem to resemble them for various reasons and also have a phallic effect. Menhirs, monoliths, obelisks, Etruscan tombstones, Islamic prayer towers, and southern German bulbous spires have all been

Left: Korean "stone god," height 150 cm.; Right: stone
sculpture from Guatemala, height 31 cm.

interpreted as phallic. Recent tests and spontaneous oral
accounts showed that many men see lipsticks as phallic
symbols; accordingly, lipstick advertisements have deliberately been rendered more sexual. Even psychoanalysts are
in danger of overlooking the fact that the phallus has two
meanings—which are biologically related but can be separated: Primarily the phallus is a symbol of power; it only
became a symbol of fertility secondarily, on the roundabout
route of its possible associations in the human mind. So it
would be one-sided to relate the phallus only to the sexual
realm. Many exhibitionists are disturbed not in their sexual
life but in their integration into society; they do not want
to incite their opponent to sexual activity but to frighten
him.[81]

We do not know how far the conspicuous penis guards
of primitive peoples who go naked (e.g., in New Guinea
and the Congo) also serve as a symbol of rank or defense
against spirits. What *is* known is that in Indonesia the phallus is used to drive away evil spirits; island dwellers who

believe that wind and waterspouts are provoked by evil spirits take their bared phallus in their hand and point it in the relevant direction to drive away the evil spirit.[101]

There are countless other details that could be recorded on this theme; I have noted some of them in other books.[122, 124] Here I am only concerned with showing how a comparison of the behavior of as many species as possible can also throw light on the darker sides of human behavior.

9. Social Stress

Whenever the problem of overpopulation is raised, the question of food also moves into the foreground. This is justified insofar as the food supply sets a definite limit to population. There have been extensive calculations concerning this limit, and efforts—usually based on theoretic considerations—are being made to find out just how far the limit can be stretched if all the food reserves known to man are exploited. In addition, attempts to raise the yield of grain and other crops are being made as are efforts to make seaweed, plankton, and other unusual plants palatable to man. This too can stretch the limit but it postpones the problem rather than solving it. Perhaps we can afford to do so if we hope to acquire enough knowledge during this period of respite to be able to find a real, final solution to the problem of overpopulation.

But we cannot afford to overlook the fact that the density of population also has another limit, and one that is perhaps lower than the "starvation line." Men are not machines that can be crowded together as closely as the electricity supply permits—always taking care, here too, to dissipate the work heat. Unlike machines, men get on one another's nerves, not only when a density that entails food problems has been reached, but much sooner. This is another of the many things man has in common with animals.

Many people are, no doubt, familiar with the very different effects of full and empty buses. In an empty bus, the few passengers distribute themselves in an entirely "un-forced" way, sometimes leaving a whole row of seats free, look quite at ease on the whole, and react to one another or the conductor in a fairly friendly fashion. In a crowded bus, free seats are, of course, limited, and the passengers look much less comfortable and react in a much more ir-ritable way. Many try to ignore their closest neighbors as far as possible, as though the only resort were to take as little notice as possible of the fact that the neighbor has already moved much too close for comfort. And yet it would be very easy to supply all these passengers with sand-wiches on a longer journey. One could transport more pas-sengers in airplanes if the passengers allowed themselves to be herded together more densely. The first class is not more expensive because there is more to eat but primarily because everyone has more room. So we do not pay only for food but also for the distance between us and our neigh-bor. The same applies to the constant demand for living space. The higher the pressure of the population density, the more "money power" will have to be spent on keeping one's neighbor at a distance.

Hutt and Vaizey have made careful studies of the effects of overcrowding in playrooms on children between the ages of three and eight.[46] Each child was observed in three playgroups of different sizes, with up to five playmates, with six to ten, or with more than ten other children. The playroom was always the same size, nine meters by six meters. The tests showed that the number of social con-tacts between the children decreased the more densely the room was "populated," although this was when there were in fact the most opportunities for social contacts. So the children avoided one another. When there were more than eleven children, quarreling increased noticeably, as, inci-dentally, did the abuse and destruction of toys, which is interpreted as an open expression of aggressive tendencies worked off on the toy instead of the neighbor. This indicated that man has certain regulating mechanisms that are dependent on population density and influence his behavior. It is striking that children with brain damage are much more likely to react aggressively under the same conditions, and they have a clear advantage if they play together with normal children in an overcrowded room.

In a quite general context, people feel distinctly uncomfortable when they cannot keep the desired distance from their neighbors. What is this sense of discomfort? Various kinds of experiments on social animals in recent years have suggested the kinds of factors that could be responsible. At least the tests showed which organic functions are altered by population density. There are far more of these than one might have supposed. The organic changes also show what aspects of behavior, hormones, growth, maturation, etc., are interdependent and consequently also affected in extreme situations. But it is not even necessary to wait for extremes; all these functions are always affected to some degree, no matter under which conditions the living thing happens to live at the moment, whether alone, with a few of its own kind, or with very many. Since we have no reason to assume that man can escape these effects, we should ask ourselves how far our present behavior is dependent on such environmental influences, rather than proceed from potential future conditions.

Tests on various living things, plants as well as animals, have shown that under natural conditions the size of a population regulates itself automatically. "Automatically" here means with the assistance of predators, infections, lack of food, etc., i.e., by methods that man likes to describe as "cruel." It is known, for example, that in the so-called "mouse years," when mice multiply at an unusually high rate, mouse-eaters also bring forth more young, so that the mice are under greater enemy pressure. Where man sees to the mass increase of an individual species, as in the great pine plantations, there is great danger that the corresponding enemies, here the pine-eaters, will soon gain the upper hand. Predators and parasites could be included in the general concept of "enemy" here. But these enemies do not gain unlimited power either, since they themselves begin to perish when their victims decrease in number.

No living thing can multiply to an unlimited extent. Each great tit must find an insect approximately every two and a half seconds, even in winter, to cover its food requirements. So in places where there are few insects, correspondingly few great tits can survive. Many animals mark out territories for themselves and defend them against their own kind; thus they create a "garden" for themselves from which they can draw their food supply.

This has been well documented for the willow ptarmigan (*Lagopus lagopus*) of Scotland.[28] From autumn to the following summer, the cocks defend territories in which each cock tolerates only one hen. These territories are situated in areas of heathland, for the ptarmigans eat the berries and shoots of the plants there. If one removes the territory owners, for instance by shooting them, they are soon replaced by animals who were previously outside the heathland. So there are "reserve cocks." But not in summer. Individuals who have no territory have no chance of surviving until the next autumn or of reproducing. The only thing, of course, that prevents them from so doing, is the lucky owners of territory. So they are by no means sick or ailing individuals who could not defend a territory in any case or who are on the mortality list. On the other hand, the yield per unit area does in fact influence the size of a territory. When some areas of heath were made to yield more by the use of artificial manure, the willow ptarmigan cocks were satisfied with smaller territories, which meant that more cocks could settle on the same area and begin to breed. So the food supply does not directly affect the population density in this case; indeed, it would be impractical if all the animals who could not eat their fill simply died. As long as all the ptarmigans have to fight for the little food available, they will at least all receive a little; but perhaps they would all get too little, and then none would survive in the end. So it is more advantageous to the species to ensure the support of the territory owners by a system of territories and to sacrifice only those individuals who have no "real estate" to support them. Admittedly this often seems cruel, because each individual "egoistically" sees to its own needs and—from the human point of view, of course—is therefore responsible for the death of inferior rivals.

But this social behavior is important to the preservation of the species. And it sets limits to the population density. One cannot make an unlimited number of ptarmigans breed, even on extremely well-fertilized areas of heath. Even in the Land of Cockaigne, not as many common or brown rats would reach adulthood as there is room for. This was tested by making an abundant food and water supply available to a group of brown rats living in a large enclosure. Although eventually one could have expected a population of five thousand young rats, the group did not reach a size of more than 150. Another example: If two pairs of chaffinches are kept in a cage, only one will breed in spite of good feeding. The reasons for such "population regulations" were studied on various animal species in recent years. What the animals suffer from, although they have enough to eat, is called stress. The factors that produce stress are described by some researchers as stressors. In general, stress is characterized by the fact that it can be elicited by many different causes, for instance cold, loss of blood, infection, overpopulation, etc. This suggests that stress is a generalized, unspecific reaction on the part of the organism. If we limit our considerations of stress to the reaction provoked by members of the same species—although it could equally well be provoked by something else—we can speak of "social stress." It has been found that all stress is characterized by the fact that the suprarenal gland cortex produces more hormones than usual, which means that there are fewer growth, thyroid, and sex hormones in the body than in the normal state. The effects of this on population increase have been chiefly tested on mice, rats, rabbits, and tree shrews, because these animals can be kept in captivity and bred so easily.

The tree shrew (*Tupaia*) is a very interesting animal from Southeast Asia, whom we shall come back to in another context (see p. 162). It has proved a very good test subject for the problem under discussion here since it allows one to determine the effects of stress externally. Accordingly one can test the same individuals in different situations. For the other species we have mentioned, we only know of inner signs of stress so far; so one has to kill the individuals and examine their organs, which means that each animal can only be tested once. But every disturbance to the tree shrew makes its tail hairs stand on end, so that the tail becomes conspicuously bushy (normally these hairs lie flat so that the tail looks smooth and slender). D. von Holst worked out elaborate tests[44] that demonstrated that the bristling of the tail hair is evidence of a general excitement typical of stress that can be elicited by any kind of disturbance such as sudden noise, the sight of an unknown object, battle with its own species, capture by the test organizer, etc. Each tree shrew bristles its tail hairs for a certain percentage of the twelve-hour day, and this value remains equal for months, as long as the animal lives in the respective situation. Every change in its environment leads to a new "bristling value" of the tail hair, which again remains constant for the duration of the new situation. If an animal is placed in a cage with an unknown conspecific of the same sex, a short battle will ensue, ending with the submission of one of the animals. From then on the two rivals behave almost the same, but their tail-bristling values differ considerably: The victor almost never bristles his tail, while the loser bristles his almost all day but stops if the victor is removed from the cage.

Von Holst has been able to discover the following connections by dint of careful comparative studies: Young animals who have a high tail-bristling value evidently grow more slowly than their brothers or sisters in an undisturbed environment. Even with adult animals, the body weight varies with the tail-bristling value; if this value rises by about 60 percent, the animal can lose a third of its weight within a few days. Adults regain their original weight again when the disturbance ceases; but young animals, whose growth beyond puberty was inhibited by disturbance, never reach the typical adult body weight and remain lighter. Maximal excitement (indicated by continual bristling) always leads to the death of the respective animal, sometimes even in the space of a few hours.

With young male tree shrews whose tail hair stands on end for more than 40 percent of twelve hours, the testicles do not, as they normally would, pass through the inguinal canal into the scrotum but remain in the body. Moreover, the scrotum skin does not turn dark. If the animals are removed from the environment disturbing them, it will take about a week before the scrotum changes color and the testicles enter the scrotum through the abdominal wall. With adult males who bristle their tail hair more than 70 percent of the time, the testicles move back into the abdominal cavity. The scrotum regresses, loses its dark color, and is hardly visible after about two weeks. The weight of the testicles decreases and sperm production ceases. Things only return to normal when the situation of stress ceases.

Female tree shrews living under conditions where their tail hairs stand on end for half the day do not produce offspring; when the bristling value drops, they bear offspring again. However, if the female has suffered this disturbance for many months, the progeny of the next three litters can still die of starvation because the mother will still not have produced enough milk for them. Even when she eventually produces the normal amount of milk, the progeny of the next litters will starve, and this is because the female "forgets" the feeding times. Not until the fifth or even later litter will the young animals be reared normally. So social stress can have quite considerable after-effects, even if it appears on the surface to have been overcome.

Even lesser situations of stress, which only elicit a tail-bristling value of 20 percent of the normal timespan of twelve hours, are sufficient to prevent the rearing of offspring. The females give birth normally, have enough milk for the young, and suckle them too. Yet, within a few hours of the birth, any animal from the group, sometimes the mother herself, will go into the nest, take out a young one and, undeterred by its furious noise and desperate struggles, partially or wholly devour it. This cannibalism stops as soon as the tail-bristling value falls below 20 percent. The reason is not some mysterious maternal instinct to spare the offspring from growing up in a bad world, but more probably the deficiency of a gland secretion. Adults have a gland in the region of the thorax between the forelegs with whose secretion the mothers mark the young shortly after birth, by rubbing the gland against them. This scent mark keeps all members of the species, including complete strangers, away from the young. Situations of stress, when the sympathetic nervous system of the animal becomes excessively active, produce a number of effects besides tail-bristling; one of these is the absence of the gland secretion. So the young are not marked and other adult tree shrews are not prevented from devouring them.

Female tree shrews exhibit yet another behavioral change under moderate social stress: They try to "mate" with members of their group in male fashion. They pursue an individual, lick his genital region, mount him, massage his flanks with their forelegs, and perform thrusting movements with their thorax. This behavior dies down with the disappearance of the stress.

All these effects of social stress can be explained in terms of the well-known collaboration between the central nervous system and the hormone system. But this is not so important here. What we must note is the variety of effects social environment has on the social behavior of animals, above all on the processes related to population or birth control.

If tree shrews live too densely, they can keep the population count constant; but, strictly speaking, this is not always achieved by birth control. For offspring are in fact born, even though they are then devoured—because of excessive population density—or starve to death. What can, however, be described as birth control is the so-called "Bruce effect" found among many animal species. The Bruce effect is the termination of a pregnancy that has already begun. The fertilized eggs of the embryos that have developed in the uterus of the mother are destroyed, and this can still happen in the last days before birth. Over half the pregnancies of wild rabbits in New Zealand are terminated in this way. Normally the young are born after eighteen to thirty days of pregnancy and weigh forty or forty-five grams; but they can still be resorbed in the womb after twenty days. When this happens the mother's body hardly loses any nutritive substances—much less, at any rate, than it would in a miscarriage. The more densely the rabbits have to live, the more young rabbits never see the light of day. Young females resorb more embryos than old ones. And if the highest-ranking females in a rabbit population have six or seven litters a year, and the lower-ranking ones less, this too is due in part to social stress that naturally affects younger, low-ranking animals more seriously.

The tests of Parkes and Bruce[88] have shown that the population density of mice and some other rodents can be regulated a step earlier, by means of the so-called "pregnancy block." In the first four days after mating, female mice react very sensitively to foreign males, i.e., to males other than the one with whom they have mated. If one removes this male and puts another male in with the mated female, she will not become pregnant. But by the fifth day after conception this effect appears only in some females, and by the sixth day it disappears entirely; if one does not replace the male until then, the female will become pregnant in the normal way. Similarly, female mice still become pregnant if they are completely isolated from males, even if this is done immediately after they have mated. So the male is no longer necessary after mating to bring about pregnancy. Yet his presence does have some effect, for if one does not replace the male, but instead adds a strange male to the pair, the female will become pregnant normally again. This means that although neither of the males mates with the female now, the male who originally mated with her can remove the effects of the strange male by his presence alone.

But how does the female mouse recognize "her" mate? This is not a difficult question to answer: by smell, for mice largely orient themselves by their nose. Indeed, there is no need to introduce a strange male to the mated female; it is enough for the female to smell him, the best means being by placing the droppings from the cage of any male into the female's cage. And this male need not even be sexually active; he could even be a eunuch. The operative scent is contained in the male's urine. It is probably a mixed substance, whose composition varies from male to male. The female must be able to smell the substance; female mice whose organ of smell has been removed do not react to strange males. Moreover, the female has to be exposed to the scent for quite a time. Sometimes twelve hours are enough; but the reaction gradually increases in strength in the course of two days. This is why one can prevent a pregnancy block by separating the "right" male from the female for only twenty-four hours and then putting him back again; even if a strange male or his smell has been acting on the female during the whole of this time, she will still become pregnant.

The gradual buildup of the female's reaction suggests that hormones play a part here. Also, it has been found that the foreign smell—which the female must, of course, recognize as foreign—that is carried via the hypothalamus (a region of the midbrain) and the pituitary gland (hypophysis) prevents the release of hormones necessary for the fertilized egg to embed itself in the uterine mucous membrane of the female. So one can remove the pregnancy-blocking effect of the foreign smell by giving the female the appropriate hormones. But normally, when a female has mated, the smell of a strange male will mean that eggs that are already inseminated do not become embedded but are ejected from the womb.

Here we must stress that this is not the only effect of olfactory stimuli to affect the reproduction of mice. By virtue of their sense of smell, the animals can distinguish castrated from noncastrated members of the species, and females in heat from those who are not; very often experience plays a part here, so that very young, virgin animals are not yet able to make these distinctions or so that particular smells that the animals came to know in their youth are preferred later. Moveover, mice in exclusively female groups stop being periodically in heat, but if they are joined by a male, or even the smell of a male, almost all females will immediately start a cycle again. Each of these effects is being studied individually with increasing precision. So far, we have only a hazy notion of how it all works and interconnects in the normal life of wild mice, uninfluenced by experiments. Nor can we expect a regulation of the population density of mice accompanied by the nervous and hormonal reactions we have described except in extreme cases.

Yet it is important to know about these effects of social situations on the creation of new life.

Tree shrews eat their newborn young, rabbits resorb the half-formed embryos, mice do not even allow the fertilized eggs to become embedded. What all these cases have in common is that new individuals who already exist are annihilated again. In other realms of nature, the offspring are not treated with kid gloves either. While the South Sea albatross brings up one young bird every two years, the Central European goldcrest has two clutches of ten eggs each year, i.e., twenty young. Yet, as far as we know, neither species is increasing or decreasing. In consequence, as with all animals, each parent pair must in the course of its life be rearing exactly two young, who will take the place of the parent animals when they die. All offspring beyond this die, one way or another, depending on the species. Apparently the carp lays one million eggs, but most of the young are devoured by predators while still at the larva stage. Similarly, more than a quarter of all young rooks that hatch perish in the nest for unknown reasons. It is easy to understand why many animal species ensure themselves against inevitable but also quite unpredictable accidents by overproduction of progeny; for floods can destroy nests, periods of bad weather can make it more difficult to find food so that many young starve, diseases can break out, etc. Some species seem to make provision for such eventualities: The common buzzard brings more young into the world than it can later feed, so that a few, usually the weaker ones, always die. But if there is an unusually large number of mice in one year, the buzzard can exploit this by rearing a corresponding number of progeny; so he does not miss his opportunity. The "nestlings" can, therefore, act as reserve young, useful to the species either when food conditions are particularly favorable or if the other young birds should die. In addition this means that if there are too many young, natural selection will choose in favor of the fittest. What is less easy to understand is the behavior of the sea eagle, who lays two eggs and hatches them but never brings up more than one nestling, namely the one to hatch first. The eggs are laid at an interval of three or four days, and accordingly the young hatch at an interval of three or four days. As soon as the second chick hatches, the older one sits on it, not by mistake or out of clumsiness but quite deliberately. Even if one rescues the smaller chick and feeds it, the elder one will come up at once and crawl around continuously until it is again sitting on the smaller chick, who is thus cut off from the food and smothered, i.e., actually murdered.[74] We cannot as yet tell exactly why the sea eagle does not abandon the idea of laying a second egg from the start, although there are a number of possible reasons that have not yet been fully investigated. What is certain is that almost all animal species produce a marked excess of offspring, which is very quickly reduced again. Although the losses are quite considerable, we can usually understand why so many young animals have to be sacrificed.

It is not clear, however, why the production of young is cut short, so to speak, in the cases of the tree shrew, rabbits, and mice that we have described. No doubt, if the young are devoured or destroyed in the womb, there is no great material loss and the building material stays "in the family." But an inquirer into the natural laws governing the transmission of life would surely be perplexed by the fact that these offspring are destroyed without much inhibition, yet copulation still takes place.

10. Regression

Psychologists are well aware of the occurrence of reversions to childish behavior among humans. These states appear quite commonly as reactions to stress, difficulties in life, and failures in general. One such reaction is bed-wetting. These temporary or permanent returns to earlier behavior are called regressions.[21] But the individual never reverts entirely to an infantile stage and all its behavior patterns, only to some aspects of it. A quite general deduction we can make from regressions is that infantile behavior patterns still exist in adults; normally they are not in evidence, yet they have by no means been eradicated in the course of a subject's life. This is also shown by the fact that certain brain diseases can cause behavior patterns typical of infants to reappear. Here, however, they are caused by an organic illness, in which case they are not called regressions but are pathological disinhibition phenomena related to the breakdown of certain parts of the brain or brain functions. By contrast regressions are not so obviously pathological.

Experienced animal observers have long since noticed that regressions occur not only among humans but also among warm-blooded animals. Presumably regressions are common among cold-blooded animals too, and even among invertebrate lower animals. But in order to uncover such behavior one must know the animals in question very well. We usually only know domestic animals, who are almost exclusively warm-blooded, so well.

Regressions very often seem quite normal on the surface; in fact, the further one analyzes the total behavior of the respective species, the more normal it will appear. Why do regressions exist? What good do they do the animal? The best way to find an answer to this question is to try to determine the age from which regressions actually appear. Surely it is not quite suddenly, overnight. For they are not new patterns of behavior but have been there for a long time, living underground, so to speak, only to break through again at some later date. It would only be expected then that childish behavior patterns would appear more frequently during childhood, less frequently later, and then ever more rarely without ever quite disappearing. Although no systematic tests have been evolved to date, enough cases have become known in the course of time to confirm this view.

Young kangaroos always flee into the mother's pouch at first; but the older they are the less often they will do so. In situations of danger, however, even sexually mature animals will still flee to the mother and hide at least their

Left: newborn kangaroo at the mother's teat (pouch not shown). Right: A fully grown giant kangaroo may still flee to its mother's pouch in cases of danger.

head in the pouch. Baboon babies cling to the mother almost continually and ride on her back; older offspring flee to the mother when they are threatened and cling tightly to her; and if he is scared, even a grown male baboon will rush up to another friendly baboon and clutch hold of him.

Regressions among adults are known to have been elicited by massive provocation in some cases. For instance, tree sparrows who have flown slap into a windowpane and are stunned or very dazed can sit around for hours, sometimes for days, without a sound and "gape" at the human with open beak; this enables one to provide them with food. When their condition improves, the gaping behavior disappears.[97] Childish patterns of behavior are not directed only at man. Adult male robins and linnets have been observed feeding another male who had a broken leg; normally two males will fight each other, as these males had done too before one of them had an accident. A fully grown frigate bird and a gannet were found in a large breeding colony of sea birds, each with only one wing, together with a large but blind white pelican. They were all several years old. None of these birds could catch its own food, so they must have been fed by other members of the colony for years.[1, 71] In the Bronx Zoo some years ago an accident cut off the beak of a female jay in such a way that the animal could not eat by herself. She begged just like a nestling for two years, even turning to members of different species in her cage, and was fed by a small capped jay throughout this time.

In all these cases the individual who still begged like a child, although adult, had suffered bodily harm. It had had a shock, or met with an accident, and was about as helpless compared to its normal contemporaries as a nestling is compared to adults. But forms of behavior that could be described as regressions can also appear when nothing has befallen the individual directly but something has altered in its environment.

Young storks who are almost fledged wander about their nest flapping their wings, but they stop this as soon as the parent birds return. The behavior typical of older birds is evidently inhibited then and gives way to more juvenile behavior when the superior parents are present. This is particularly striking with some small birds who have been brought up by a human whom they now look upon as their parent. At first the hungry nestlings simply gape with open beak and beg at their foster parent just as though he were their real parent. Later they manage to eat by themselves, picking food from the ground. Gaping and picking are two quite distinct behavior patterns at this stage, and picking is the later one to develop. Normally the gaping behavior is inhibited or blocked by the picking so that it disappears as soon as the animals can pick properly. What is interesting here is the transitional stage, i.e., the phase in the juvenile bird's development when picking is just beginning. At that point, so long as they are left to themselves, the juvenile birds may be able to pick up food quite well and so be able to get enough to eat. But if their human foster parent is in the vicinity, they gape and beg at him again. Even if he does not react, they will continue to gape. A bird of this kind, that has already fed itself for days in the absence of its foster parent, would rather starve than feed itself when the foster parent returns. Lorenz, Meyer-Holzapfel, and other ethologists have observed this repeatedly.

Within an animal society with members of different rank, regressions occur most often among inferior animals. This becomes very clear when one individual suddenly falls in ranking order. An adult hound can suddenly display the typical behavior of a whelp toward a superior rival, throwing himself on his back, whining, and urinating a little. As we all know, from the moment of sexual maturity a normal hound urinates against trees and posts with his back leg raised.

Other examples of adults exhibiting childish behavior in

the face of higher-ranking members of their species will be discussed later (see p. 131). Since this childish behavior makes the higher-ranking members of the species feel they are being approached as parents, any potential aggression they might feel is subdued. So regressions can protect an individual from attack. They are widespread among social animals and have an important function: to deflect social threats. When they achieve this they are, of course, not pathological phenomena. Exhibited by a child, regression has the function of eliciting brood-tending activities without which the child could not thrive. Regression protects juveniles who act thus, although not as frequently as before, from stronger members of the group, because the brood-tending attitude it elicits inhibits aggression. In this context of inhibiting aggression, the same actions can survive in adults too, although springing from an entirely different motive, as shown on p. 133. For instance, begging between the partners of a pair can be a form of greeting or a behavior pattern that strengthens the pair-bond. Such regressions mean that the animal is resorting to signals from childhood in the interests of communication in newly developed social behavior patterns. Seen in this light, these behavior patterns have also been termed "symbolic actions." How have they acquired the connotation of pathological? Probably because they are seen most often where they occur most often. And this is in abnormal situations of captivity when an inferior animal cannot avoid higher-ranking members of the group; so he remains entrenched in conciliatory childish behavior. In brief, then: When such behavior is expressed occasionally it is quite normal; when it becomes a permanent behavior pattern we may be dealing with an unnatural situation and the individual himself is not necessarily abnormal.

11. Psychic Castration

When higher-ranking animals, such as stork parents, inhibit the adult behavior patterns of young animals, these behavior patterns may still have matured in the juvenile animal before they actually appear. At least this is so if the young stay with their parents. But if one isolates the young, these behavior patterns could appear comparatively earlier. Then we can describe the young animals reared separately from their parents not as early developers but as uninhibited. Indeed, examples are known that could be explained in this way. However, there are other possible explanations too.

Inversely, one can also postpone the appearance of adult behavior in the young animal by prolonging parental care. Young butcher birds gape at their foster parent for up to six months beyond the normal time if he continues to provide them with food. An even more striking example: In a colony of cattle egrets in captivity provided with ample food, Otto Koenig has produced phenomena that he describes half in earnest half in jest as "spoiled hippies" (*Wohlstandsverwahrlosung*).[59] Even on attaining sexual maturity, the young egrets still gape at their parents and beg for food (and are still fed, for begging young egrets are very insistent and the parents must feed them if they want peace). It can even happen that the young egrets beg their parents for food and then pass it on to their own young! Meanwhile the whole family continues to sleep in the eyrie. By the next spring the young egrets want to brood too, in the same place where they grew up themselves, and they build their nest on top of that of their parents. The young egret will choose as his partner an animal as familiar to him as possible, i.e., one with whom he has always been together, and this will be either one of his sisters or his mother. But the father has no intention of giving up his rights, and the son can only play husband as long as his stronger father is absent from the nest. So these egrets do not learn all the things a young heron normally learns when he has separated from his parents and has to "stand on his own feet."

The case of cattle egrets is particularly striking because they generally mature very early, much earlier than other herons. Under normal conditions they are capable of brooding quite independently by the time they are a year old; other herons can brood only after two years. But in this caged colony they never became self-sufficient. Nevertheless there were no fights, for the cattle egret is the most social of herons and never quarrels with good friends. All the members of this colony knew one another well, however, since they could not possibly escape from one another. So it was possible to create a compact group that displayed a number of characteristics we already know of from animals who normally live in similarly compact troops. Here the colony was held together artificially, externally by the enclosure and also by the large supply of food. In the wild, however, it costs considerable time to find food for three or four large young cattle egrets. The parents have to stay away from the eyrie for increasingly long periods of time, and the young gradually begin to seek their own prey during the period of waiting.

One other feature is worth note. A normal heron displays several very striking color markings in the pairing season: The bill, which is normally yellow, becomes glowing orange at the tip and red at the root, and the skin of the nose is often a bright blue-red. The legs are also red. But in the parent-child group in the eyrie, some of the young retained their everyday coloring. This allows us to conclude that they never attained the state of excitement normally related to the beginning of the reproductive period, a failure which may be connected with hormonal disturbances characteristic of situations of stress.

During our discussion of symptoms of stress we mentioned that lower-ranking animals could be "repressed" by a group of higher-ranking animals of the same sex and then remain in a state corresponding to that of juveniles who have not yet reached sexual maturity. This could also be regarded as regression, yet it is not so much a display of typical childish behavior as it is the absence of normal adult behavior. With male tree shrews, sexual behavior disappears entirely under these conditions, the testicles move back into the body cavity, and sperm production ceases. And young stags who are already sexually mature but have high-ranking old males above them in the herd do not manage to mate nor do they show any inclination to do so. Similarly, in bands of hamadryas baboons, only the highest-ranking male is sexually active. But among stags, a one-year-old brocket begins to rut and be fertile as soon as the older rivals have been eliminated.

This effect of repressing sexual behavior is not limited to male animals; it can be even more in evidence among the females, especially when they have a regular reproductive cycle. It is known that if the females of various species of monkey are put into a strange band of monkeys, they will not come in heat for a fairly long time, in given cases not until they have reacquired a fixed position in the ranking order. One can observe the same phenomenon among even the lowest vertebrates, fish, when the said species lives in compact social bands. This is the case with the *Tropheus* cichlid from Lake Tanganyika (see p. 199): Here too the females stop spawning regularly if they are put in an unknown shoal and kept there.

This phenomenon, namely that animals who have sometimes already been sexually active are forced back by social circumstances into a state corresponding to that of an animal who has not yet reached sexual maturity, has been called "psychic castration." The expression is not a very happy one since it is misleading. Castration is an operation that cannot be revoked. Here, by contrast, sexual activity is only repressed; it returns as soon as the animal is freed from the situation in question.

Sexual repression in younger social animals results in the stronger and therefore higher-ranking animals becoming more likely to bear offspring. We have already described the case of rabbits, where the lower-ranking and younger females often resorb the embryo again. A more familiar example is that of animals living in packs where only the highest-ranking male copulates with the females, so that in effect he becomes the father of most of the offspring. Here it makes no difference if other males are excluded from reproduction; but if females are excluded, the number of offspring will drop. Perhaps this is why females are less prone to psychic castration than males.

It is not hard to understand this in biological terms, for barren females bring no advantage to most species; they are wasted, in a sense. This does not apply where there is a division of labor, as in insect states where barren females, the workers, do most of the work. Their gonads are kept inactive by certain substances emanating from the queen; so this is a kind of social castration too, but one that is reversible to a degree. For if the queen dies, the gonads of some workers can begin to function again. In insect states, however, the exclusion of female animals, which entails the absence of offspring, is offset by an incredibly high production of offspring by the queen, who can lay as many eggs on her own as all the other female workers could together.

The loss of offspring due to other forms of specialization on the part of the female animals is made up in this fashion. But it is only possible if the differently specialized individuals are kept firmly together in a functional community. This is rarely the case in the animal kingdom, so that it is also rare for nature to permit females to have no offspring.

It is a different matter for males. Often their time is not nearly fully occupied by the business of reproduction; moreover, they supply and make available their necessary contribution, the sperm, in excessive amounts. So it would do no harm if many of the males were excluded from reproduction. But would it be useful? Where is the advantage of high-ranking males keeping their lower-ranking rivals from reproducing? Might there not easily be, among these subordinate individuals, some who have a combination of genes that would benefit the species? This benefit could only be proved in terms of biological fitness. And that is tested not by means of a gene card but by the success that an individual achieves in its life. Of course, genes are not the only factor that contributes to success, but they do play a decisive part. If anything can be proved to have stood the test, then it is the genes of those individuals who have "made it" in life, who have survived all the perils of enemy attack, starvation, competition, etc. And it is quite reasonable to assume that to multiply this heritage that has been tested as far as possible in the "trial by fire" of life, even at the price of other, as yet untried, combinations of genes, must be advantageous to the species. Psychic castration can, therefore, bring advantages, but this is not to say that there cannot also be disadvantages attached to it, which may even predominate in certain circumstances. Indeed, the existence of a "council of elders" among baboons shows that the baboons have overcome the system of giving a monopoly of reproduction to the most successful individuals (see pp. 191f.). One disadvantage of psychic castration is that it sometimes leads to a superior member of the species being overprivileged; but this implies that only one of the participants is already at a disadvantage. Indeed, it would be a rather arbitrary display of emotion were we to consider the following with either satisfaction or horror:

Paper wasps of the *Polistes* species form nesting societies in which several sexually mature females build their nests one beside the other. But these females who live together do not all have the same rank; there is a ranking order. This order is built up on the special behavior patterns exhibited in the meeting of two animals, i.e., whenever they feed each other reciprocally (which will be discussed in more detail on p. 153). One of the wasps raises itself up, quivers its antennae at the other, and chews the other's head and thorax. Meanwhile the other wasp cowers and does not move at all or only moves in a very inhibited manner. The wasps whom such encounters prove to be the high-ranking ones now devote themselves exclusively to laying eggs. The lower-ranking individuals only lay a few or no eggs; instead they see to providing food and to the construction of the nest, which they moisten in hot weather. The behavior patterns that the high-ranking wasp exhibits toward the others probably stem from combative behavior. In serious cases—for example, if a strange wasp comes to the nest—this behavior also involves embracing the other wasp with the legs and stinging it. The reason why subordinate wasps lay hardly any eggs is that their gonads are rendered inactive by social repression. Now the same can also happen to the highest-ranking wasp, whom we can call the queen here. For there is a very closely related species, the parasite paper wasp (*Sulcopolistes*), whose females visit a paper wasp's nest and conquer it.[99] The parasite paper wasps begin by defending themselves against the attacks of the nest-owners by slowly embracing one after another, stroking them with their antennae, sitting on them about-face, bending with the abdomen, and dabbing at the neck and waist of their victim with their darting sting. Hereupon, the host wasp stays as quiet as after an encounter with its own high-ranking queen. The queen herself is subdued by the parasite wasp in the same manner. And the effect on her is also to block the activity of her ovaries. She stops laying and reverts to the life of a worker—"reverts" because she had originally built up the nest alone and had reared daughters who then lived with her as subordinate females. But the parasite paper wasp does not go through a worker's existence first; she conquers a paper wasp's nest and has her eggs hatched by her paper wasp hosts and their former queen. This form of social parasitism is very common among social insects.

III

12. Mating, Reproduction, Pair-Bonding, and Brood-Tending

Is it true that animals and humans mate in order to reproduce? Or that parents stay together because this facilitates brood-tending? We can determine whether these statements are in fact laws of nature by observing nature. A survey of conditions among very primitive living things tells us about primeval conditions.

Mating among unicellular animals takes two different forms. Either the copulating partners fuse, or they lay themselves one against the other, exchange parts of the cell nucleus, and then separate again. The biological significance of this process is that the genes, which are always slightly different between individuals, are mixed anew, producing new variations. These slightly divergent variants form the basis for further developments. The same applies in the reproductive behavior of higher animals who recombine their genes. With unicellulars, however, it is to be noted that mating has nothing to do with reproduction; on the contrary, when the partners have fused there are only half as many individuals left as before. When unicellulars reproduce, it is without sexual activity, by division into two (fission). We also find reproduction without sexual activity among fairly highly developed animals, who do not simply divide into two. This is called parthenogenesis (i.e., development of ovum without fertilization into new individual). New offspring develop from the ova of the female without the intervention of a male. Many polyps and various small crustacea such as the water flea (*Daphnia*) reproduce in this manner. So mating and reproduction can co-exist without any necessary connection. The animals we have just named reproduce without mating as long as the environment is favorable; then they produce as many offspring as they can as fast as they can, to make use of the good nutritional possibilities. Reproduction becomes sexual when living conditions deteriorate, for instance when the available space is exhausted. When unicellular animals or crustacea mate, reproduction ceases for a considerable period of time. That is to say, in this case mating and reproduction, each serve a different function: reproduction serves the extension and survival of the species, while mating serves to increase the number of variations within the species and provides the basis for the development of new types and even of new species.

Sexual reproduction is not always tied to mating among vertebrates either. The male water newt deposits a packet of sperm on the lake or pond bottom and the female comes and picks it up with her cloaca. Other examples of sexual activity without contact between the partners are listed on pp. 35ff. On p. 226 we show, conversely, how mating is not necessarily linked to sexual reproduction. So mating and sexual reproduction are also independent in a number of cases. Many species of fish who discharge eggs and sperm anywhere and abandon them to their fate nevertheless live in permanent monogamy; examples are many well-known butterfly fish (*Chaetodon*) of the tropical seas, familiar to all aquarium owners. Since, on the other hand, all animals that mate are certainly not all monogamous, monogamy and mating are also independent. Moreover, both can occur independently of brood-tending. We already find brood-tending among the lower animals that bear offspring anonymously, without contact between the parents. Various starfish tend their brood on the body of the mother; in the case of *Lepasterias*, the offspring develop in the mother's body, as with many shellfish. *Stygiomedusa*, a colored deep-sea jellyfish, gives birth to live offspring ten centimeters long. But the monogamous butterfly fish do not concern themselves with the eggs or larvae they hatch, and some birds who no longer tend their brood, because they have become brood parasites, nevertheless live monogamously, like the African didric cuckoo (*Chrysococcyx caprius*), the cuckoo weaver (*Anomalospiza imberbis*[34]), and probably the black-headed duck (*Heternonetta atricapilla*[119]).

What use, then, is monogamy is these cases? It achieves the same end as the fusion for life of the sexual partners among many lower animals (e.g., the double animal—*Diplozoon*—among sucker worms, and the blood fluke—*Schistosomum*—that causes bilharziasis). In fact, it still occurs among vertebrates, for example deep-sea anglers (*Ceratias*). It means that the sexual partners do not have to search for each other again and again. Any search entails the risk of error, and if animals of different species mistakenly fuse their gametes, they produce hybrids who can be sterile or otherwise affected. More important is the fact that closely related species in particular, who could still bear fertile offspring with one another, are specialized in different ways, with respect to nutrition, habitat, or some other part of their environment. This different specialization allows them to make better use of existing conditions and prevents intra-specific competition. In very simple terms, a species of animal that eats grass can only tolerate a limited number of individuals on a particular pasture ground; should a related species appear that ate leaves from trees, its members could safely co-exist on the pasture since they did not compete with the grass-eaters. But it is important for the grass-eaters to recognize the leaf-eaters, for otherwise they would waste efforts to chase them away as supernumerary grass-eaters.

So each species must distinguish itself externally by recognition signals.

Such signals are also necessary in sexual reproduction, for if hybrids appear, the species will lose its specialization again. The animals must, therefore, be able to recognize a conspecific sexual partner. Here it is enough if one sex is different from species to species, so that the other sex can choose according to the differences. Among many animals, the female is occupied with brood-tending, so she would put herself and her offspring in great danger if she had bright markings. In these cases the males are more striking, and wear a display dress, differing for every species, while it is the female who chooses. The most attractive example of this phenomenon is in the emphasis on contrast among closely related species inhabiting neighboring territories. In places where the species occur side by side and there is a risk of mistaken identity, the recognition signals, songs, or markings contrast more strongly than at the other ends of the area of distribution where only one species occurs. Living things that do not choose and largely leave the meeting of the gametes to chance, suffer from continual hybridization, which spoils any chance of different specializations and the formation of different species. (This is typical of plants, which cannot seek out a sexual partner; although the plant kingdom is much more ancient than the animal kingdom, there are about five times as many species of animal as plant species today.[78]) The display dress, which often differs so much from species to species, prevents mistakes in the choice of sexual partner. The more often an individual reproduces, the more often it will have to choose, and the more risk it runs of making a mistake, especially if the partners only meet briefly, copulate, and then go their way again. The longer they stay together, the easier it is for them to notice and correct an initial mistake. If they stay together permanently, they avoid the need for a new choice and the ensuing risk of error.

Comparisons between certain groups of animals have shown that permanently monogamous animals are indeed protected at least as well if not better from choosing the wrong mate than those of their relatives who do not form lasting pair-bonds. This applies even when the latter have evolved extremely conspicuous display dresses, differing according to species, as recognition signals. It is very clear in the case of tropical cichlids and birds of paradise,[78] and it explains why the male and female of non-pair-bonding species have strikingly differentiated colors and clearly distinct display dresses, while the monogamous species do not as a rule. *Monogamy replaces display dress.* It prevents mistakes in mating and the ensuing waste of time and gametes; that is to say, it preserves the characteristics of the species. This is true of monogamy whether or not the parent animals tend their brood. So monogamy is functionally independent of brood-tending; but it can also serve the interests of brood-tending. One could describe the physical fusion of sexual partners as "physical marriage." But in a genuine, permanent marriage, the individuals remain mobile independently of each other; in a sense they grow together in their behavior while recognizing each other as individuals. A transitional step between the two forms is "local marriage" (*Ortsehe*). Here the partners attach themselves to the same locality or nest but not directly to each other. The Californian blind goby (*Typhlogobius californiensis*) spends its whole life in pairs in the channels a burrowing shrimp digs in the seabed; the male or female of the fish will drive off all rivals of the same sex but tolerate any partner of the opposite sex who has chosen the same habitat. One can replace either the male or the female by another at will. Similarly, the stork is more attached to its eyrie than to its partner: the male stork and female stork are "married" not to each other but each to the nest[38]; they are faithful to a place but not to a partner.

Because mating, reproduction, and pair-bonding have entirely different functions and are largely independent from one another in nature does not, of course, mean that they cannot also be related to one another. The more highly developed animals have combined mating and reproduction and made pair-bonding subserve brood-tending. Eventually, brood-tending and mating are made to promote the interests of pair-bonding, as will be shown in later chapters.

13. Permanent Monogamy

We can distinguish between several different forms of marriage, depending on the number of participants. We speak of single marriage (monogamy) when there are only two partners, and multiple marriage (polygamy) between either one male and several females (polygyny) or between one female and several males (polyandry). Depending on the length of the bond, we also distinguish between seasonal marriages, which can last at most the length of a reproductive season, and permanent marriages that last longer, in extreme cases a whole lifetime. Polygamy in the strict sense of the word means simultaneous bonds with several partners; the male has a harem rather than allying himself with different females one after the other. For polygamous animals, the number of offspring in a population depends on the number of sexually mature females; but with monogamous animals it is the number of firmly paired couples that counts. Over and above such side effects, the various forms of marriage must also be considered as adaptations to particular modes of life. We will not go into this further here; I only want to point out that even within the most closely related species (tropical cichlids, for instance) there are quite different marital forms. If we retrace phylogenetic evolution, we will find that certain conditions lead to a conversion from monogamy to harem marriage and finally to nonmarriage (agamy).

So permanent monogamy is not necessarily a final stage

of development. Polygamy can be structured in a more complex way and can be more highly developed; and, in addition, it can be more beneficial to the care and well-being of the offspring. Investigations into the natural connections between marital forms and modes of life under certain environmental conditions have only just started. We know that in some way each affects the other. We also know that marital form is genetically determined among animals. It would appear to be less so for man, just as man is not genetically committed to a particular environment. From this we may conclude that the different marital forms of different peoples are adapted to their different modes of life and that a marital form that once predominated can give way to another if living conditions demand it. Again, monogamy will not necessarily be the final stage of a line of development. In any case, we would have to start by clarifying the connections between mode of life and type of marriage before demanding from any people that it should change its current form of marriage.

Permanent monogamy is widespread among animals. Examples are cichlids, butterfly fish, small birds, ravens, pigeons, geese, parrots, moles, jackals, dwarf antelopes, whales, marmosets, and gibbons, to mention only a few groups of quite different animals. In each case there are also closely related species who live in polygamy or without pair-bonding (in agamy). So monogamy is not typical of man alone. And the well-known moral theologian who asserted that permanent monogamy, among graylag geese, for instance, belongs to a group of phenomena found among highly developed animals in whom we see incipient manlike traits[22] was being rather careless. Animals who are monogamous in the strictest sense of the word are those who still remain firmly attached to their sexual partner when their gonads are in a state of rest—for instance, in winter—and sexual activity stops entirely. For man, the gonads can usually only become inactive in very old age. So permanent monogamy in this sense of the word is demonstrable for animals, but not for man, where it can only appear vestigially. In extreme cases monogamy among animals can last well into old age, when they are no longer capable of reproducing. It may also happen that one partner dies and the other mates again with a much younger new partner, or that one partner becomes seriously ill. The old or sick animal stops all courtship and sexual activity and the young or healthy partner is often overwhelmed with sexual offers from other members of its species who have not yet mated. Nevertheless it quite often adheres to its mate, which shows clearly that the pair-bond is not based on the sexual activity between the partners. We know examples of this: Bourke's parrots (*Neophema bourkii*), violet-eared waxbills, (*Granatina granatina*), and the bullfinch (*Pyrrhula pyrrhula*). Of course, firm monogamy with a partner who is too old or sick prevents the healthy partner from reproducing too. This shows that pair-bonding is independent of reproduction and can even come into conflict with it. One can forcibly separate such pairs, and sometimes the healthy partner will then mate again. But there are also cases, for instance among the graylag geese, in which the remaining partner stayed alone, hardly ate, and finally died. So it seems that even among animals the pair-bond can endure beyond death. But normally it does not do so, and instead of further abstract discussion we shall now give a few examples describing the usual biological procedure.

Two typical permanently monogamous animals native to Europe are the bearded tit (*Panurus biarmicus*)[58] and the tree sparrow. The bearded tit occurs from southern Europe to Asia, and in the belt of Lake Neusiedl in Austria. Even in its juvenile dress it mates. The partners spend their whole life in very close permanent monogamy and can only be separated by force. The color of the plumage is different for the two sexes, but this is only apparent after the juvenile molts, long after the animals have paired. The young animals soon recognize the sex of their partner by its beak, which is orange-yellow for the young male, but blackish for the female. This color marking appears soon after the young leave the nest. At first they live in flocks of their own age group. At night they sleep close together with plumage fluffed in spheroid shape, but they are rather quarrelsome in daytime. The males in particular hack, peck, and pluck their flight companions at every opportunity. But soon each young bearded tit concentrates his devilry on a certain female; and if she tolerates it willingly, the issue is decided in a very short time: Two or three days later the two sleep closely clumped together at night and not each with its brothers and sisters as before. During cleaning and drinking, foraging, bathing, and sleeping, the one will hardly leave the side of the other, and they continually preen each other's ruffled feathers. If one flies a grass blade farther away, the other will land beside it a moment later. If one loses sight of the other, it will call loudly till they have found each other again. Soon the pair separates from the others and the flight communities break up.

The juvenile full molter begins about two months later, and from now on the pair does not stick together quite so closely. Of course they do not separate, but at least there are no more quarrels if they meet another member of the same species. The pair recognize each other by their voice and the call-bond is enough for them now, so that they can tolerate a separation of a few meters. But the marital partners sleep close together throughout their life. If one dies, the other will fly around excitedly, searching and constantly calling; it will then sit around miserably, but it will become extremely agitated the moment it hears the call of another bearded tit or a sudden rustling in the bulrushes, as though hoping that at last its partner was about to land beside it.[58] Eventually a second marriage can take place, but this bond will not be so firm and can only take place between widowed partners. A partnerless old bird will find no contact with the young flocks formed of sibling communities. The continual quarreling and pecking prevents it from communicating and soon drives it away again. The quarrelsomeness of the young bird, which rises to full strength during puberty, makes it impossible for an old bird to marry a teen-ager. But in flights of adults there is neither courtship nor jealousy. Even widowed birds can make contacts and find new partners here.

So the expression "lifelong monogamy" can easily be misleading. Firstly, of course, the pair-bond does not last a lifetime in the literal sense of the word, for life has already begun in the egg; yet a pair-bond can come into being surprisingly early, although a part of life will already have passed. And often the span from life to death is not very long either. Indeed, it is almost certain that only animals of about the same age mate (as we shall explain in detail on p. 116). Yet it is very rare for both partners to reach a fairly old age; the hawk snatches one, the cat devours the other. This is why one can only find out how permanently monogamous such animals are designed to be by extensive observations or by "protective imprisonment" in aviaries.

The pairs of the Eurasian tree sparrow (*Passer montanus*) are also "lifelong" partners as a rule and have three broods a year. However, it is seldom that a pair is lucky enough to rear young birds together for two consecutive years. Normally one of the two will lose its life one way or another, and the survivor has to mate again. The partners are faithful to each other, particularly the females, who refuse the advances of every other male even when their own partner is ill or wounded. The males, by contrast, although they do not leave their female either, will sometimes take care of widowed neighbors. For widows blatantly prefer males whom they already know to total strangers. "So it can happen that a male has to mate with three females, to build three nests for the next brood, to brood on one clutch already, and yet feed young chicks in three other nests. Such a bird will not have a moment of rest all day long."[20]

Frau Deckert has described the following rather animated episode in the life history of a male tree sparrow whom she ringed with green and therefore called "Green" (the other individuals are also called after the color of their ring[20]). He was ringed as a brooding bird in 1956, and the same year he probably reared three broods in the same nest and probably with the same female. In 1957, "Green" brooded again, in the same cavity under a tiled roof, and also adopted the widow of a neighbor, whose nest lay at a distance of two meters from his own. Principally he helped the widow to build her nest, but only reared the offspring of his first wife, for the widow had none. But both females reared their second brood with the assistance of "Green." Then they both disappeared. In July "Green" courted again and mated with a neighboring widow called "Left Black," who had a hollow twenty meters away but left it to move into "Green's" hollow. They both built the nest, but this female was already beginning to molt and produced no brood. Nevertheless the new pair stayed together till "Left Black" was suddenly missing in October. "Green" now mated with the next nearest neighbor, who was at least three years old, a widow for the fifth time, called "Red," and whose hollow lay forty meters away. At the same time, "Red" also had another wooer and until she decided in favor of "Green" she carried feathers into her old nest with the help of the other male, and into "Green's" nest with the help of "Green." Then she and "Green" spent the nights together in his nest all winter long. In spring 1958, "Red" chose another abandoned nest halfway between her old nest and "Green's" hollow. There they reared three broods together successfully and remained together until February 1959 when "Red" became the prey of a sparrow-hawk. By March "Green" had a new female, with whom he reared and fed another three broods.

Tree sparrows very quickly notice the absence of a father in a neighboring family, and then take care of the widowed female together with her nest cavity and her chicks. The female reacts first by defending her nest against the new male, and for days she drives him away from it with loud clamor; on the other hand, she does allow herself to be mated by this male—for her next brood. This is because all courting males behave like young birds, even, of course, when wooing a female who has never mated. The male sits with ruffled feathers and slightly lowered wings and warbles. During intensive courtship this turns into a hoarse, polyphonic call that cannot be distinguished from the note of the seven-to-fifteen-day-old nestling. If the female comes closer, he ruffles his feathers even further, makes hesitant bows, often still quivers his wings, accompanies the female if she flies off, and remains ruffled in flight. By contrast, when the pair has come to an understanding, the female usually follows the male when they take trips together and comes up close to him when they are roosting. They also find the nest material together. From April on one can see the pair copulate frequently; but they stay firmly together beforehand too when they are not copulating and also remain together outside the brooding period. The partners can recognize each other individually, even by voice alone. And later, long after they have mated, the male still puffs up his feathers occasionally and utters the nestling call. So these rituals very probably have a pair-bonding function; no pair comes into being without them.

Copulation occurs most frequently during the egg-laying period, but occasionally also in the first quarter of the brooding period, and then again shortly before the chicks of the first or second brood are fledged. The male hops up on the female two to seven times in succession while rapidly repeating a characteristic tender "vluug" sound several times. Both sexes utter this sound, the male more frequently than the female, when they fly away from the nest, when they land in the cavity, when they relieve one another in brooding or brood-tending, when they bring nesting material, etc. It is a greeting call, which occurs only in the reproductive period, and which marital partners address exclusively to each other, never to strangers or neighbors. This call can be described as a "tender greeting" that is exchanged between the actively reproductive partners of a pair as soon as they relate specifically to each other, which is, of course, especially during copulation.

14. Ambiguous Social Signals

The examples we have just quoted show that some social signals are not clearly explicit. Even with the guillemot (*Uria aalge*), mating and greeting calls are the same; the partners of the pair greet each other at the nest with the same barking call that the male uses during mating. The mating call is slightly higher pitched than the greeting or contact bark, but there are fluid transitions between the two.[116]

If we want to translate such calls into "human" terms, we will have to watch very carefully to see what their true meaning is. Perhaps, as with the "vluug" of the sparrow, the bark of the guillemot is never anything but a greeting, and the male is simply greeting his female during mating. But the young of the bearded tit have a very quiet nest-begging call, which later turns into the light "didididi . . ." with which the male entices his female into a thickly matted bulrush and indicates that this is where they will build. Do both calls simply mean "here is the nest"? The young bearded tits call "shr shr" as soon as they have left the nest so as to let their parents know where they are and that they are hungry. The male in the dense bulrush also calls "shr shr shr . . . ," whereupon the female comes up very close to him. Does "shr" simply mean "come up close to me"?

Very many of these calls occur in two situations. Are we giving them the right name if we look for what both situations have in common, or is it more accurate to class them according to their specific meaning? This is very difficult to decide.

If several related species of bird have a certain call that only the young utter when they are hungry and that causes the parents to feed them, then we can speak of begging calls. If this call is also used by adult males of one of the species to entice a female, then one must conclude that for this species the begging call has been emancipated. Whether it has then faded into the generalized meaning of "come!" or whether it means "come and feed me" in both cases, and the female merely finds no one to be fed by her in the second case, could be decided by careful observation of all the reactions; in some cases this can be done by imitating the one call in the other situation and similar experiments. We shall come back to this problem later. Here we only want to confirm that the same calls that the young address to their parents also occur between adults. This does not only apply to calls, i.e., acoustic signals. Among nearly all species of pigeon the males entice their partner to the nest by means of special movements. These movements are identical to those that the young bird uses for begging. This becomes particularly striking among pigeon species where the begging behavior of the young birds is clearly distinguishable according to species and the same differences appear in the nest-enticing behavior of the males. In our language, enticing to the nest by the young birds would mean "come here and feed me"; enticing to the nest by the males would mean "come here." So the meaning of the signal has been extended. Now this assertion would presume that the food-begging of the young is in fact the earlier signal. Among pigeons, this is difficult to decide because we always find both meanings in the enticement behavior. But if one compares birds in a wider context, it becomes very clear that the begging of young birds is indeed earlier, for it is far more widespread and always made up of the same elements. This begging only occurs with a different sense for the adult animal among comparatively few species, and then it is usually to entice a sexual partner.

The less probable a posture or locomotive process, the easier it will be to recognize it again. This is very important when there is a suspicion that one and the same posture or movement occurs in two quite different situations. If a bird opens its beak wide, this does not mean much at first, because it does so for yawning, threatening, begging, and perhaps other situations too. What else should it do with its beak but open it? But if a young tropical finch bends forward and down with open beak toward its parents, and turns its head away from the axis of its body, twisting its neck so that it is looking up at its parent from the side, and then makes curious pivoting motions of the head, this is such an extraordinary manner of begging that it alone will show that the bird belongs to the group of tropical finches (see p. 194). Now if a male fire-tail finch (*Staganopleura guttata*) displays in this way in front of an approaching female, we can be quite sure that in this case the childish begging movement has returned in the pair-bond situation and that we really are in presence of the same behavior pattern and not a superficial resemblance.

It is necessary to point this out because anyone who is extremely familiar with a group of animals can recognize simple behavior patterns from small and unobtrusive features; often, however, he omits these details from a more general description for the sake of simplicity, which then makes the layman suspect that he has made his assertions quite arbitrarily. It is no use for the expert to say superciliously that disbelievers can check the facts for themselves; usually they cannot do so because rearing these animals is far too complicated, nor can one expect a layman to observe every one of the animals about whom he wants more information. It is better for the layman to assume that the

Like the diamond finch nestling begging for food (top),
the adult male twists his head with a stem of grass in his
beak when he displays in front of the female.

assertions of the experts are presumably well founded and
that he may therefore believe them. Misinterpretation and
suspicion can only be avoided by exact description. The behavior patterns analyzed in the preceding chapters have
been studied and described with sufficient care for us to
venture more far-reaching comparisons. Where there are
still doubts, they have been noted separately.

15. Measurable Advantages of Monogamy

Pair-bonding is often exploited for brood-tending among higher animals. It seems self-evident that two parent animals can feed and protect their offspring better than one simply because they can share the various tasks. However, seasonal monogamy would be sufficient for this. But we can also show that permanent monogamy leads to better brood-tending results. This is because it gives the animals a chance to acquire experience and this experience will influence their later behavior, as can be proved for animals whose previous history is known. For instance, if one treats American ringdoves (*Streptopelia risoria*) with hormones and keeps the animals in pairs, some twenty-seven out of forty will brood. The reason why thirty percent of doves do not brood, although all the preconditions for it have been fulfilled, lies with the partner, as can be proved by observation of the doves in two consecutive, experimentally produced brood cycles.[10] For the second cycle, each animal is given a new partner. But two groups are formed: In the one, each animal is given a partner who has reacted in just the same way as itself in the first experiment (positively or negatively—i.e., has brooded or not brooded); in the other group each animal is given a partner who has reacted differently—i.e., this group consists only of pairs in which one partner has brooded, the other not. Result: In the first group, one out of nine animals reacted differently from the first time; in the second group it was every fourth. The clear difference shows that the animals really do adjust their behavior under the influence of the behavior of their partner, and—this is important—to not brood in certain cases, whereas they would have brooded with a suitable partner, conditions otherwise being the same (as they had proved in the first brood cycle).

If this is so, it must be advantageous if partners who suit stay together, instead of risking a less suitable partner next time, always assuming that we are dealing with animals who live long enough to survive several periods of reproduction.

This too can be proved. True, only one species of animal has been studied in enough detail in this respect, namely the kittiwake (*Rissa tridactyla*). A colony of this northern species of gull was observed for twelve years by J. Coulson,[16] who found that sixty-four percent of females brooded with the same partner as in the previous year. And only one-third of the animals who changed partners had been forced to do so because their previous partner had died. In other cases the partner was still alive and even lived in the same colony. Then it became evident that for an overwhelming number of animals who had changed partners, the previous brood had been a failure. This is not to say that the animals decided to separate because of the failure; what is far more likely is that the failure of the brood and the separation had the same cause: The animals were not suited.

Pairs who were successful and stayed together began to lay and to brood three to seven days earlier in the next season than other animals of the same age who had changed partners. So older animals usually brooded earlier than young ones. Females who change partners lay fewer eggs in the following year and have less success with their brood—i.e., a lower percentage of eggs develops into fledglings. Animals who changed partners twice in two consecutive years, thus having three different partners in three successive years, were more affected than those who had only changed since the previous time. This demonstrates that reciprocal habituation to a new partner is not the only factor responsible for the lower success rate; for all animals who had changed partner since the previous season would have to adjust to the new partner, whether or not they had also changed partner the year before this. The disturbing after-effects of a change of partner only disappear gradually and can still be traced at least two brood cycles later. Whether the partner had died or had not returned for some other reason does not matter; the adverse effect is the same. So what we are simply calling "adverse effect" depends only on the fact of the change of partner, not on its causes. Naturally it is made up of many different reactions by the partners affecting quite different facets of brooding behavior, as the tests described in the chapter on social stress indicated (see pp. 65f.).

From observations of the kittiwake it has become quite clear that the permanent monogamy of successful partners is advantageous among these animals—i.e., it produces the greatest number of offspring. Yet it is also advantageous to change partners if a pair has no brooding success; for then there is a chance that each will find a suitable partner next time. In this case, the brood success is still less than for a long-paired couple, but notably greater than with an unsuited pair.

With the tree shrew (*Tupaia*) too, harmony between the partners of a pair plays a considerable role in the success of reproduction. Even small remnants of aggression between male and female mean that the female will always eat her young (see p. 66). This is not so for all kinds of animals, but it occurs in some cases. And if harmonious relations between partners can become so important that it is clearly worthwhile not to change partners if an animal is currently living in harmony, then it is only to be expected that there are also special biological developments that facilitate the coming and staying together of the partners of a pair. This is indeed the case, and I will list a few of them here, although only in terms of the connection with permanent pair-bonding and not of the effects on brood success.

16. Pair Formation

The bearded tit is a striking example of how early the animals mate. Early marriage is fairly frequent among birds, but it raises some special problems.

The bullfinch (*Pyrrhula pyrrhula*) lives in permanent monogamy. The beginning of a bullfinch friendship, however, does not lead one to expect this. The unmated bullfinch female flies up to a male, dips her upper body down low, ruffles her ventral feathers, and threatens the male with wide-open beak and hoarse calls of "chooah." At first the male retreats from this stormy wooing, and if he is already paired or otherwise uninterested, actually flies off. And he is right to do so, for the female becomes increasingly furious and pursues her partner wildly; if they are in a cage she will chase him around until he subsides bewildered in a corner. But if the male bullfinch is in fact interested in the female, he soon dares to defy the female's threats. The more self-assured he is and the less he allows himself to be intimidated, the more quickly her aggressive behavior breaks down. Her threats decrease more and more and finally he dares to hop up to her and to touch her beak with his for a split second; then he turns away very markedly and hops slightly to one side. If his partner is in agreement with him, she will soon flirt back in the same way; now they both hop up to each other with ruffled ventral feathers and tail held sideways, touch beaks briefly, turn away and repeat this pattern again and again.

The goldfinch, siskin, serin, and linnet beak-flirt in a similar way and also utter notes of tenderness. The male siskin, goldfinch, and serin go up to their partner during the beak-flirtation ceremony and slowly grasp her beak in their open beak. Now this looks very much like feeding. And feeding is indeed its origin. Even with the bullfinch, the male soon starts to feed the female from his crop when they have both firmly decided on each other. In the meantime the female makes childish begging movements like a dependent young bird. She even makes herself as small as possible, looks up at her partner from below, and gapes at him. In the short pauses while he regurgitates new food from his crop, the female begs, oscillating her body and flapping her wings like a young bird, but without the latter's begging sounds.

Partner feeding becomes necessary during the brooding time. Normally a bullfinch clutch consists of five eggs. When the female has laid the fourth egg she broods for thirteen days. During this time she is fed exclusively by her mate, who appears near the nest with full crop at regular intervals and entices her to come to him; he never feeds her in the nest itself. Partner feeding is the prerogative of the higher-ranking animal, who is normally the male. In exceptional cases, if the male is ailing or temporarily weakened in the molting season, the roles can be reversed and females can feed their males.

So, as these very exact studies by Nicolai[84] show, feeding the young has become partner feeding for the bullfinch while the female broods. In addition, tenderness feeding has come into being outside this period; this has evolved into a beak flirtation without the transmission of food, which serves the partners as greeting.

It is curious that even seven-week-old young birds beak-flirt with one another; this always occurs between nestlings from the same nest, since they already know one another well individually. They affiance themselves with one of their brothers or sisters while still in their juvenile plumage, but do not distinguish according to sex, which is not yet recognizable at this age. So just as many same-sex as opposite-sex pairs are formed. All these young birds exhibit only female behavior and even invite their partner to copulate with them; yet they never achieve copulation, since all the young males also behave in this way. In the course of their life, then, all bullfinches at first behave in typical young bird fashion, i.e., gape and beg the parents for food; later they all behave like females, i.e., make nest-building motions and invite others to mate. Only adult males exhibit typical male behavior, feeding their partner and mating with her. In terms of their partner, females employ elements from their juvenile behavior throughout their life, while males only do so when they are ill. So nestling, female, and male behavior follow in the above sequence. And at each higher stage of development, the animals still dispose of the characteristic behavior repertory of the previous stage, as we saw with the mountain sheep (see p. 28). In a mythical story of the creation of the bullfinch or mountain sheep, the male would probably be created last and not, as in Genesis, the female.

The sibling pairs of bullfinches cling together just as firmly as the adult pairs, but not as long. After some three months, in about August, juvenile molting begins, and with this sexual differences appear, both in plumage markings and in behavior. Now the males begin to feed their partner, but still display in the female mating posture, which in fact still occurs among their fully colored brothers too. These sibling marriages are dissolved by the end of the year, those between members of the same sex sooner than those between opposite sexes, and now each bird seeks out an unrelated partner of the opposite sex. During the period of transition the animals can have double "engagements," one still with a brother or sister and one with the future marriage partner. When the gonads begin to function, the early bonds are finally dissolved, and the former partners of a same-sex marriage now fight each other with particular violence. Marriage between brothers and sisters would, of course, lead to inbreeding, so it must be avoided or dissolved.

Normal as it may seem to us at first glance that a bird such as the bullfinch, who lives in permanent monogamy, should form a firm pair-bond while still young, its biological significance is still not clear. Could the birds not wait a few months and then pair properly, instead of forming a provisional marriage first that has to be dissolved later and replaced by the final marriage? We do not know whether, if one removed the opportunity for sibling bonds, these individuals would later have difficulty in their relations with their marriage partner. It seems very possible, and certainly requires study.

We could of course assume that this very early juvenile pair-bond is a by-product of social behavior, probably connected with the later permanent marriage, but biologically unimportant in itself. Then it would be an amusing incident, hardly worth bothering about. But one cannot dismiss an as yet unexplained phenomenon as unimportant, thereby saving oneself the trouble of further research, if the phenomenon becomes too frequent. Early pair-bonding exists among very different birds, and some birds take quite considerable trouble to effect it; so it must have some value.

There is a very striking example among tropical finches (see p. 194) such as the African violet-eared waxbill (*Granatina granatina*), which also lives in firm pairs. Adult males are a lovely chestnut brown on their back, the females somewhat lighter. Both sexes have a blue band around their brow above the reddish beak and a large round area of color on the cheeks, which is deep violet for males, a lighter violet for females. In addition, the male has a black spot on his throat. The scarcely fledged young bird, who leaves the nest at the age of nineteen days, has a gray beak and is dark grayish brown on top, brownish orange underneath. At first the young bird is still fed by the parents, until the age of about thirty-five days. A few weeks later the young birds molt into their adult dress; they reach full maturity in the ensuing dry season, which lasts some months in Africa, so that they are ready to reproduce at the beginning of the next rainy season. They do not wait until then before seeking their mate, however, but begin before they are thirty-five days old, i.e., while they are still being fed by their parents. In this case, however (unlike with the bullfinch), the formation of same-sex pairs is prevented; for, from the twenty-first day and in the course of about a week, markings of different colors for the two sexes are very rapidly added to the simple juvenile plumage. In this period the animals molt in precisely those areas of their cheeks, upper beak, and throat where the characteristic sexual markings are located; by the time they are thirty-five days old they already display the typical sexual markings on their head, while retaining their juvenile dress on the remainder of their body, and are already firmly paired off. This early molting on the decisive parts of the head ensures pair-bonding with the opposite sex.[85]

The isolated early molting of individual parts of the plumage certainly acts in the interests of early pair-formation and gives us an idea how important this juvenile pair-bonding is (so important, in fact, that a special molter is inserted!). This would not be nearly so striking if the animals had simply shifted the over-all molter into adult dress forward to this time. It would surely have achieved the same result, and in addition it would have been simpler merely to alter the molting date rather than upset the whole molting plan. So why do they do this? Why do they retain their juvenile dress? Presumably, says Nicolai,[85] it has something to do with the fact that quite a few of the firmly paired animals are widowed in the course of a reproductive season, as we have shown with the tree sparrow (see p. 97). From the onset of the first rains, two, three, and even four broods follow one upon the other. The young birds from the first brood would already look like adults if they molted immediately, while the real adults were still busy with the second brood. And an old bird who had lost his partner around this time would be tempted by the large supply of young birds ready to form pairs and might choose one of them as a replacement. But the young bird would not be capable of reproduction yet. So the old bird, if he happened upon an immature "teen-ager," would have to let his reproductive talents go to waste. This can be avoided if teen-agers are recognizable as such, i.e., still wear juvenile dress. The young birds themselves probably place a different value on these markings, since they pair off with each other; but only in cases of necessity do adults resort to a young bird who is not yet fully colored.

These examples show how many different aspects must be considered and how much one must know of the living habits of a species before the fundamentally quite simple questions on which the attentive observer will stumble can be answered. We still need to know much more about these birds before we can determine the biological significance of their early pair-bonding. The same applies to the following species, on whose life in the wild we know even less than we do about the violet-eared waxbill.

Indeed, the violet-eared waxbill is not the only bird to have an isolated early molter on the parts of its plumage that are important for sexual recognition. Its closest relative, the purple grenadier (*G. ianthinogaster*), also lives in pairs and molts in the same way. We find the same in quite different groups of birds, for instance Australian black honey-eaters (*Myzomela nigrita*). Among Asian timalias, the Pekin robin and the silver-eared robin (*Leiothrix lutea* and *Leiothrix argentauris*) molt on their throat and breast while they are still being fed by the parents; they also form early pair-bonds and are monogamous. In the woodpecker family, the tiny, soft-tailed piculets commonly found throughout Africa, South America, and Asia (genus *Picumnus, Sasia*) molt the specifically sexual markings on their head in the same way as the waxbills, as soon as they become independent, but do not molt the rest of their juvenile dress until they are about a year old.

It would seem only natural to assume that it is always important to prevent the pairing of individuals of very dissimilar ages. The bullfinch (see p. 95) achieves this thanks to the extreme quarrelsomeness of the young animals just able to mate, against which adults are powerless. Yet we must check these working hypotheses thoroughly, even if they sound very plausible. This takes a great deal of time and good knowledge of animals. The only method to achieve it is for nature-lovers or bird-watchers, or whatever the researchers who largely work without instruments are often rather disrespectfully called, to observe patiently in the field.

17. Pair-Bonding

It is not only in connection with the coming together of partners that remarkable biological processes take place; the same applies later too, between the partners who stay together. They include certain ceremonies that each individual performs only with its mate or with a closely related member of the family, but not with unknown members of the species.

One such striking ceremony is duet songs, which are typical of monogamous birds whose sex cannot be distinguished externally. In the simplest and probably most primary cases both individuals give voice to the same notes or phrases, echoing each other or singing together in unison. In more specialized cases the partners in their duet utter different phrases or parts of phrases, which can be combined in various ways. This occurs among very different groups of birds—pairs of cranes, screaming sea-eagles, little grebes, and others. Some African shrikes have arrived at an extreme form, for instance the tropical boubous (*Laniarus aethiopicus*), where every pair has its own repertory of several fairly long phrases, which each partner can sing alone but which the pair normally sings with carefully divided roles. As far as we know at present, the duet also contributes toward the spatial coherence of the partners, since each can hear where the other is even when they are hidden in dense undergrowth.

These duets have been evolved quite individually by vari-

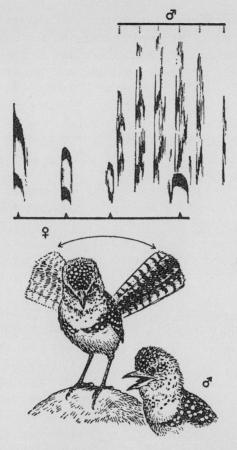

Greeting ceremony of d'Arnaud's barbet (*Trachyphonus d'arnaudii*). Top: sound spectrogram of the duet. The tail-wagging female constantly repeats four notes, the male always adds his hoarse call in the same place; it is shown by the six vertical strokes in the spectrogram.

ous other birds besides songbirds (among whom the shrikes belong), for instance by some of the barbets related to the woodpecker. In recent times the African d'Arnaud's barbet (*Trachyphonus d'arnaudii*) has been studied very carefully. Here the male inserts a hoarse "shrée" call at certain definite intervals in the repeated sequence of the female's calls; this note derives from the nestlings' begging call. The female accompanies the whole duet with conspicuous tail-wagging. We also find duet songs among the highest monkeys, namely the siamang (*Hylobates syndactylus*), a monogamous large gibbon from Sumatra. Research into the origin of these duets and the influence they exert on pair-bonding has only just begun. We shall discuss other behavior patterns typical of the partners of a pair in the following chapters.

18. The Derivation of Billing

Although it is difficult to discern any definite origins in simple motor patterns, we are not entirely helpless in this matter. For instance, it is worth trying to trace their evolution. What use it is if this attempt succeeds will be shown by the following examples, the first of which is the masked lovebird (*Agapornis personata*).[111]

The lovebirds from the African steppes are also called "inseparables," an indication of how closely the pair clings

A budgerigar feeding its young in the nest.

together. The partners can be observed feeding each other throughout the year. Usually the male feeds the female; the reverse is rare. Feeding between partners is important to the survival of the female during the brooding time, for she broods alone, sitting in her nest the whole time and being fed exclusively by the male.

Outside the brooding time, the female eats independently. And yet the male still keeps feeding her. In this phase, feeding has the function of a contact gesture and obviously serves pair-bonding (like allopreening, see p. 145). Partner feeding also occurs in the foreplay to copulation. But here only small bits of food are regurgitated, whereas genuine feeding usually involves large portions.

Partner feeding works only if the other bird is ready to take the food at precisely the same moment. If, for instance, the female looks away even for a moment, the male cannot feed her, so he swallows the food and then has to regurgitate it afresh; probably he can only balance the food in the right position on the tip of the tongue for a second or two. During the transmission of food only the tips of the birds' beaks come into contact, and the food is pushed across with the tongue. The female holds her head erect while the male twists his a little, so that their beaks cross transversely. This is exactly the same position as for feeding

Beak contact as greeting between paired masked lovebirds.

the young, and no doubt feeding between adults is derived from brood-tending behavior. It can happen because the female begs or because the male offers food of his own accord. But the female's begging posture is not entirely the same as the begging position of young birds. When young birds beg, they crouch down, directly facing the parent, who, incidentally, is always the father if they are fledged, because by then the mother takes no more notice of them. Begging young birds stretch their head forward and ruffle their feathers; the wings are raised, and they sometimes make flapping, balancing movements. When an adult female begs, she draws her head back a little and turns it in a half-sideways or sideways position to her partner; it may be that the female does not adopt the normal childish posture because she holds the whip hand in the pair and is now superimposing begging on rank position.

When the male initiates the feeding, he begins to regurgitate the contents of his crop, bends down toward the female, and briefly touches her beak with his, sometimes also pulling the upper part of her beak to him. This brief beak contact, during which the partners turn their heads toward each other for a split second and interlock the tips of their beaks like two links in a chain while inclining their heads at different levels, also occurs on many occasions outside the feeding ceremony, usually while the animals are sitting next to each other or allopreening. In this case it is occurring in a quite neutral situation. We only find billing between partners, not between flock members who are on less familiar terms with one another. Whenever members of the flock come close enough to a pair to disturb it, so that the pair clearly feels importuned, the partners throw brief glances at the disturbers and make rapid preening and evasive movements; and, billing increases, as it does if strangers are introduced into the aviary, or if changes are effected in the environment, or after a great outside danger has passed.

Billing also increases during pair formation and during

greeting if the partners have been separated for some length of time. Quarrels between partners always end with billing; in the middle of a violent beak duel or during a short pause for breath, one bird, usually the male, will suddenly incline his head for billing; the partner immediately agrees, and the quarrel is over. Even if one of the pair has a quarrel with a third bird, the other partner immediately comes up and rams the first on the flank so violently and for so long that it finally turns around for billing; the "arriving" partner shows no interest whatsoever in the object of the quarrel! The appeasing or pair-bond strengthening function of billing is just as evident here as in the relaxed neutral situation we described earlier. Again the beak contact can last a certain time; the tongue may be stuck out a little and the animals may utter noises similar to the nestling sound and make sporadic movements of the head, which we normally see only with young birds. These additional elements are good bases for the conclusion that billing is a part of feeding, or perhaps an extremely abbreviated version of feeding. However, Stamm, to whom we owe these detailed observations,[111] drew the following conclusion: Since the mechanism of the beak does not permit all that many modes of action, although the beak does serve many purposes (eating, cleaning, preening, pecking, fighting), these various behavior modes must necessarily involve such similar movements that one could just as well say that billing derived from allopreening. Admittedly, one must be cautious in interpreting these behavior patterns; nevertheless Stamm is overlooking a whole series of common features here that point clearly to the derivation of billing from feeding. For instance, allopreening is not addressed to the beak of the other, nor does the partner turn its beak toward the other if it wants to be preened; similarly, the sounds and movements of the tongue and head found in billing do not occur during allopreening. This case can show all the details to which one must pay attention. Perhaps one or

THE DERIVATION OF BILLING

another reader will still have lingering doubts. Such doubts can, in part at least, be removed by comparative observations of other birds, on whom one can retrace the derivation more fully, while yet passing through the same transitional steps. The common raven may serve as an example.

The role that the common raven (*Corvus corax*) played in myths and legends as the bird of Wotan suggests that even our ancestors were good observers and had noticed the following: Ravens in general and the common raven in particular are more alert and eager to learn and, if brought up by human hand, more affectionate than most other birds. Indeed, the behavior of the common raven is only tied to instinct to an astonishingly low degree, so that the bird has quite a lot in common with mammals like brown rats or primates who "specialize in nonspecialization." The expressive and social behavior of this most imposing of ravens was recently analyzed in detail by Gwinner.[36] In contrast to jackdaws and rooks, who breed in colonies, the raven is only sociable in youth. At first the fledged young stay with the parents for a remarkable length of time, almost five months, in fact. Then they join into flocks with other groups of brothers and sisters; here they form pairs, who separate from the flock at the beginning of the third year of their life, establish fixed territories, and then remain together for the rest of their lives.

As we said, ravens have less rigid behavior patterns than many other birds, and accordingly we find that behavioral elements from brood-tending or pair-bonding occur in other situations here too. The partners of a pair are not very different in rank, and although the female invitation to copulation is most likely to involve the drive to flee, it also occurs in the male foreplay to copulation, if the courted female has not exhibited it first. The wings are spread out to the side, the folded tail quivers horizontally, and the neck is stretched out horizontally forward. This posture coincides with the extreme submission posture of common ravens, when it occurs together with the sounds uttered by begging young birds. Among jackdaws, this female invitation to copulation is entirely freed from its sexual connotations and has become the usual form of greeting of female to male.

This childish begging behavior, during which ravens squat down, flap their wings, and utter begging sounds, can also occur independently from hunger and no matter whether or not the partner has food to offer; then it serves to appease the partner. The appeasing animal can open its beak wide and, like a young bird begging for food, bring it as close as possible to its partner. Instead of attacking or pecking, the latter then abandons its threatening posture; sometimes it may insert its beak in the wide-open beak of its mate and even make thrusting movements with it as though feeding, although it is not in fact transmitting anything at all. Animals who wish to approach a higher-ranking member of their group also display this begging behavior, often making themselves small and thin at the same time, by sleeking their small feathers, drawing their head in between the shoulders, and bending their legs. In addition, begging behavior always occurs in a pair when the male is feeding the female.

As with the lovebirds we described, the female common raven broods alone and is fed by the male throughout this time; and he will feed her better, the more firmly she sits on the clutch. During this time the male "must" feed his female. But he also does it throughout the year, although not always as frequently. Toward spring, pair-feeding and incipient courtship display increase continually, to reach their highpoint during the nest-building time. Now the female who is fed begs like a young bird and also takes the food like a young bird with her beak twisted in a longitudinal axis of ninety degrees against the feeder's beak. The male, who brings his female small, tasty morsels outside the brooding time too, feeds her continually now. First the food is carefully prepared or fetched ready-prepared from

Common raven feeding its young (left) and greeting by billing (right).

its hiding place; the male stows it in his beak or throat pouch, approaches his partner with splayed steps, often flapping his wings too, and—to the accompaniment of feeding noises—offers her the food. The position of the beak and the soft feeding noise "gro" clearly indicate that this pair-feeding derives from feeding the young. When feeding its young, the beak of the old bird is turned at an angle of ninety degrees against that of the gaping young bird so that the food can be plunged very deep into its throat. This is no longer important during pair-feeding, yet the position remains the same.

The soft "gro" sound with which the old raven summons its young to open their beak and with which the male raven summons his incubating female to take food is not the same only in pair-feeding but occurs throughout the life of raven pairs whenever they make contact with each other. Young birds also say "gro" during their first attempts at walking, but only if the parents are present; and they will utter it more loudly and more rapidly the less steady they are on their feet. So "gro" is not only a feeding sound but also a contact or greeting sound.

Since there are so many similarities between pair-feeding and feeding the young, we may ask whether perhaps among these birds both have the same motivation and are dependent on the same mood. In fact, with the raven in particular there are indications that pair-feeding and feeding the young belong to different moods. Ravens have an extremely varied repertory of usable sounds, consisting of elements they know from birth to which are added sounds they have learned. Like many other songbirds, ravens learn best from those beings to whom they are bound by the strongest individual ties; normally, of course, these are the parents, and especially the father. The bullfinch, for instance, has created traditions of song, songs transmitted from father to son. Gwinner reared a raven, and in the first years he often lured him to the netting of the aviary for feeding with the word "*komm*" (come). The raven spontaneously took over "*komm*" himself for the situation of pair-feeding and later invited his female to accept tasty titbits by saying "*komm.*" We do not want to discuss here what an extraordinary achievement in abstraction it is (although there are parallel cases, in particular among ravens) for the bird to bring this sound into relation with the food-transmittal situation and then to utter it again when he was no longer being fed himself but instead had assumed the role of provider of food. What is more important in our context is that the same raven, when he became a father, always used the normal "gro" feeding sound when feeding his young. *This shows that feeding the young and feeding the partner were two different things for him,* although he used largely identical behavior for both.

But ravens can do more than this. Some pairs can change the pair-feeding ceremony, quite by themselves and to different degrees according to the pair. Gwinner observed several pairs among whom, after a period of married life, the food given by the male to the female was pushed back and forward with the tongue from beak to beak several times, sometimes for more than thirty seconds, until the female took it. So the beak contact had to be extended for this whole period of time, and finally the pairs beak-flirted in the same way even without food. One pair went even further. It sat together with closely linked beaks for minutes on end, without making feeding noises or transmitting food. Another pair of ravens walked around in circles side by side with similarly linked beaks. That this behavior is really an altered form of brood-feeding can only be affirmed so surely because the process of transforming the ritual was observed extremely carefully in these cases. There was ample opportunity for comparative observations, for all the pairs repeatedly used the correct pair-feeding method besides this individual variant. Obviously we are not dealing with a process of maturation typical of the species and dependent on age either, for not all old birds changed the feeding ritual thus or in other similar ways. *Rather we are dealing with rituals "invented" by the birds.* And it is very likely that equally precise observations of other birds, especially parrots, will show us similar series of alterations in brood-tending behavior, which would not only help to remove any remaining doubts on the correctness of our interpretation of

Monk parrot feeding its young (left) and beak-greeting between the partners of a pair (right).

beak contacts and such, but might even bring to light hitherto unnoticed connections with other social greeting ceremonies.

The herring gull (*Larus argentatus*) is also monogamous.

The fate of several pairs was followed over a period of ten years, and this showed an easily overlooked preliminary stage of pair-feeding.

Even outside the nesting place and outside the brooding time, the partners of a pair remain together, in winter too. The pairs are formed in the so-called "clubs" of unpaired gulls, and it is the female who chooses. She pulls in her neck, sticks out her beak and lifts it a little, and then circles slowly around the object of her choice. The male may go off with her immediately or start by strutting about and attacking other males. Occasionally females choose a male who is already mated and try to intervene in an existing pair, which provokes violent aggressive and defensive behavior on the part of the original female. To the careful observer, the term "jealous behavior" seems almost self-evident as a description of her behavior, although one must note that it is not meant to suggest anything about the bird's possible feelings or the form of the behavior. The comparison with human behavior that the term "jealousy" suggests is only intended to make it easier to outline the situation and function of the actions.

If one partner of a pair of herring gulls dies, the other may pair again. The male herring gull also feeds his mate. He regurgitates a little food, which she swallows greedily. Normally she begs for it, particularly during the reproductive season.[114] Careful observation will allow one to discern the inception of pair-formation before mating and pair-feeding have begun. It can be seen by the fact that a gull allows another to take food away from it right in front of its face. It is well-known how incredibly food-jealous gulls in particular are. So pair-bonding begins with not begrudging food to another, which in a sense represents the lowest stage of pair-feeding.

We find the same phenomenon with a quite different group of animals, who are not vertebrates at all—namely, spiders. The few spiders who have any form of social life eat together, i.e., do not begrudge food to other members of their kind. On p. 159 we discuss the societies of these curious social spiders.

We will learn about other forms of social behavior with different functions later. Here we will begin by showing the behavior patterns of the young bird toward the parent animal; this behavior will assume an important part in the relations between adults. Begging and feeding can indeed serve to provide nourishment, for instance in the case of a brooding female, as happens with many if not most parrots. In the first days the male actually feeds the whole family in this way. He brings the female food, which she in turn regurgitates and passes on to the young nestlings. Pair-feeding can also acquire a quite different significance for the pair: wax-wings (*Bombycilla*) are paired from the moment the female takes a berry from the beak of the male who has offered it to her. Among terns (*Sterna*), the marriage contract is sealed as soon as the courting male has offered the female a fish. Actual food provision only plays a subordinate part here.

The courting female of robin redbreasts, whose behavior has been examined in great depth by Lack,[71] utters a shrill, monosyllabic call in front of the male, and then, when he approaches with food, dips her wings and quivers them. Meanwhile her call turns into a rapidly repeated note. Then she is finally fed by the male. It is impossible to distinguish the posture and notes of the female from those of a young robin that is being fed by its parents. But although the female begs quite persistently, and is repeatedly fed by the male, food and appetite only play a negligible role here. On several occasions Lack observed parent robins who wanted to feed their young but were disturbed by observers in the vicinity of their nest. Here the female would turn and beg at the male although her beak was already stuffed full of insects for her young. She was not begging for food but for "moral support," as we would say in human terms (for further examples see p. 189).

Feeding can disappear entirely too, and instead we can have billing or beak-flirtation. In general begging at the partner among adult birds corresponds to the food-begging of newly fledged young birds. Some elements can disappear or others be exaggerated, yet the resemblances are great enough to lead the observer to mistake one for the other at times. For instance, the young begging green-finches one hears in March are in fact courting females. The resemblances can also lead to mistakes by the birds themselves. Among wrens and seagulls, the father coming to the nest with food has been observed hesitating as to how he should respond to the begging of fairly well-developed young birds and then deciding to make an attempt at copulation. With the parasitic jaeger (*Stercorarius parasitusicus*), when a parent animal feeds a young one, the other parent may crouch beside the young bird and be fed too. Familiarity between the individuals seems to play a major role here: The female diamond dove (*Geopelia cuneata*), whose male entices her to his nest by childish behavior, treats this male in the same way as she would treat her young; she takes no notice of her actual young during this time, however, but only of the dove in the nest, whom she knows well.

This emancipation of childish behavior often becomes very apparent among monogamous animals, but it is not confined to them. Childish behavior can also be directed against unknown members of the species, whether the species in question lives in firm pairs or not. It can even evolve further into a social action that is executed in unison by a fairly large number of animals. The following examples will make this clear.

The gray jay (*Perisoreus canadensis*) native of North America lives in pairs; but in winter the jays gather at suitable feeding places in quite large groups. Weaker animals fluff up their feathers, raise their tails, and hop around, squeaking like young birds. In tense situations they quiver their wings and squeak like a young bird begging for food. In face of serious attack by a conspecific they lie down, stretch out their quivering wings on the ground, squeak softly, and stick their beak down into the snow. By doing this they display their black cap on their neck, which looks just like the black face of the nestling, whereas adults have a white face. So the aggressor is confronted with all the signals that characterize young birds. If he still attacked, he would no doubt also do so to his own young, thereby imperiling his own succession.[35]

We owe exact details on the behavior of the European bee-eater (*Merops apiaster*) to Mrs. L. Koenig,[56] who was the first to succeed in rearing these lovely animals in captivity. The bee-eaters breed in horizontal tunnels some meters deep, which they have dug themselves in clay walls. The sexes of these elegant birds are barely distinguishable, since each sex exhibits both male and female behavior toward its partner. These birds often exchange roles at short notice so that one cannot even distinguish male and female behavior patterns. Very often a male who is slightly sexually excited will perform the female mating invitation to his female. Yet only the male seems to feed the female, and always before copulation. He offers her food in the tip of his beak, she takes it, swallows it, and then adopts the invitation to mating position, with outstretched head and usually with eyes closed. The young birds are fed only by the parents at first; as soon as they come out of the brooding tunnel, other adults feed them too. The begging call of the newly fledged young bird is a strange, penetrating, slightly falling "eeeeeeeeeeeeeeeeeeee" sound uttered with wide-open beak. This call serves the old bird as a show of submission when faced with threatening conspecifics. In addition, a bee-eater threatened by a conspecific can gape at it, without a sound, its body bent back. Then the aggressor grasps it by the beak, tugs and shakes it, but never starts the wild beak-

snapping and wing-flapping of a violent fight as it would do
if both animals were equally aggressive. Such fights can
also take the form of real air battles. The defeated bird flees
and is violently pursued by the victor and sometimes attacked again. But the weaker bird can from the start avoid
a fight by resorting to the submission posture drawn from
childish behavior.

Among Indian white-eyes (*Zosterops palpebrosa*) from
the Ganges, partner feeding serves to deflect a threat. According to the observations of Kunkel,[65] these animals appear to live in rather loose pairs; at least they change
partners fairly often. Attacks are fairly common even between partners who already know each other. Compared
with that of many other small birds, the white-eye's pointed
beak is a very dangerous weapon. Both sexes can divert an
attack by their partner by offering it their fully raised
feathers for preening (see p. 146). If the female opens her
beak wide in front of the male, he will quickly introduce
his own in it; sometimes this is preceded by obvious regurgitating movements. If she threatens him with closed beak
"he touches the tip of her beak with his and lets the tip
of his tongue enter her beak." This "tongue kiss" is never
provoked by other than threatening behavior on the part of
the female, and it serves to overcome her contact shyness.
The actual feeding takes place in a moment. Hesitant females can thus be fed by several males. Here too feeding
does not, therefore, serve to keep the partners together but
is an almost anonymous form of appeasing a member of the
species.

The bald ibis (*Geronticus*) greets members of the nesting
colony with begging movements similar to those of the wood
swallow, to whom we shall come back later (see p. 139).

Australian honey-eaters of the *Meliphaga* family use the
wing-quivering of begging young birds in precopulatory
courtship. The males quiver more violently than the females.
But this behavior also serves as a greeting between pairs

who meet at the boundary of their territory. They all quiver their wings for a few seconds and give half-suppressed calls like a begging young bird.[47] This gesture of peace never occurs between the partners of a pair, perhaps because the partners never stray more than a few meters away from each other; since they adhere together so closely they hardly need to greet each other. But among one species, the yellow-tufted honey-eater, *Meliphaga melanops*, begging behavior also occurs apart from its function of greeting, as a genuine social action in their communal group singing, in which up to twenty birds can take part. In its social function, wing-quivering is even more conspicuous than during begging (whence it originally derived), for young honey-eaters beg very "listlessly" and only quiver, with half-spread wings, in exceptional cases (for example, if they are very hungry). *So this childish behavior pattern is more strongly defined among adults than among the young birds themselves;* it has atrophied in the original function from which it derived —by comparison with the greedily begging young of other songbirds—but it is fully preserved in its derived social function and has even developed further.

This suggests that the derived behavior pattern has been emancipated. It becomes very clear in cases where brood-tending has quite disappeared, i.e., feeding the young no longer occurs, whereas partner feeding does. Examples are brood parasite birds, such as some cuckoos who lay their eggs in the nests of other birds and have their young hatched and brought up there.

The American yellow-billed cuckoo (*Coccyzus*) still broods itself and feeds both its young and its partner. The South African didric cuckoo (*Chrysococcyx caprius*), by contrast, does not brood nor does it feed its young, but it does feed its mate.[94] Here, although the cuckoo is non-brood-tending, its readiness to respond to begging in partner relationships has remained unimpaired. Thus it can even happen that an adult cuckoo will feed a young bird of its own species that it happens to come across. This has been observed with Klaas' cuckoo and the bronze cuckoo (*Chrysococcyx klaas* and *Chalcites lucidus*) as well as with the Burmese koel (*Eudynamis scolopacea*),[76] and it is probably not a remnant of brood-tending but rather a partner relationship extended to a young bird.

Instead of "courtship feeding" we should perhaps use the term "greeting feeding," for the male of the small Galapagos "tree finch" (*Camarhynchus parvalus*) and the American yellow-billed cuckoo (*Coccyzus americanus*) feed their females during copulation, and the Javan pheasant-coucal (*Centropus javanicus*) holds an insect during copulation and only gives it to the female afterward—and this can no longer be called courtship. Nor is beak contact absolutely essential to this partner feeding, and each male feeds his

The begging and presentation of fish in a feeding scene between parent and young bird recur in the same form as the prelude to copulation between the partners of a pair of wide-awake terns.

female in the same way as he would feed his young. The tern holds a fish sideways in his beak, and the partner grasps it at the other end and takes it. But even here there are the species' typical differences: The wide-awake tern (*Sterna fuscata*) regurgitates food and lets it drip into its partner's beak, while little terns (*Sterna albifrons*) may link their beaks for feeding and during copulation. The female gull-billed tern (*Gelochelidon nilotica*) may beg out of hunger; then she will allow herself to be fed by the male but not to be mounted by him; but she may also beg as an invitation to copulation, in which case she allows him to mount. In both cases her begging looks just like that of a young bird, but it has different "motives."[73]

Social feeding is important not only between the two partners of a pair. It also occurs in societies to which a fairly large number of adults belong. Again, however, its form is the same as for feeding the young.

19. Harems and Larger Groups

If we allowed it, our domestic fowl would live, like its wild forebears, in social groups with one cock at the head of about five hens. Naturally we scarcely ever see this now. If we forget about the very many different varieties we have bred and about the fat pullets in batteries or young cocks bred in incubators, and quite apart from attempts to blunt their beaks so that they cannot hack one another to bits (how many hens can be crowded into one square meter?)—can we still find cocks quarreling about their hens instead of farmers quarreling among themselves? Can any hens still manage to hatch their eggs out of sight of man? Since we keep our fowl under such extremely artificial conditions we are unable to appreciate the instructive structure of their society. The most we may see of it today is a hen with her chicks.

While the hens are brooding and then while they lead the chicks, they live apart from the other adults. Each hen marks out her own territory and defends it against neighbors; during this time the hens do not react to the entice-ments of a cock. The hen leads her chicks to water and to feeding places; she gathers them together and takes care that no strangers join them. Chicks who stray into the wrong family are pecked and driven off by the hen and her chicks. The hen is particularly watchful if she has to cross an open, unprotected place. If something arouses her suspicion, she will utter a warning call that sends her chicks into cover. She herself always stands in such a way that she can keep the danger in sight. If an enemy approaches, she attacks it violently. While the chicks are eating, the hen stands guard with raised tail and slightly dipped wings. It is rare for her to eat anything herself at this time, and, when she does, the chicks usually come up to her at once. She can also lure them to a tasty morsel directly, by pecking very markedly on the ground, lifting what she has found with her beak, letting it drop again, and then uttering the clucking call everyone knows. When the chicks are about a month old, the hen roosts on a tree with them at night, first flying on to a branch herself and then enticing the chicks to follow her.

This typical maternal behavior disappears as soon as the chicks become independent and leave the mother. Then she joins a cock again and behaves quite differently. Yet in a normal society one sees the behavior we have just described all the time—on the part not of the female but the cock. In fact there are cocks of different rank. The lowest-ranking ones wander around alone, have no territory, and try to rape hens who have strayed too far from their group. Slightly higher-ranking cocks try to establish territories of their own in the domains of high-ranking cocks, but abandon them again as soon as the latter threatens them. When they are about a year old, they gradually manage to assert themselves against the old cocks, which they achieve most easily outside the reproductive season. The high-ranking cocks have fixed territories, within which they dominate all the other cocks. They crow in order to affirm their territory, and do so fairly often, while lower-ranking cocks raise their voices considerably less. (After sunrise the highest-ranking cocks crow up to twenty-eight times in half an hour, the lower-ranking ones only about eight times, the lowest-ranking ones not at all. This is a social effect of rank organization, as shown by the fact that the crowing frequency of low-ranking cocks rises as soon as one removes the highest-ranking cocks.) The highest-ranking cocks always have hens about them. Each defends his hens against his neighbors. Gathering the hens together, he can lead them to feeding and watering places. He guides them very carefully over places without cover. He warns them of impending danger, and then, while the hens are seeking cover,

The cock guards and entices his hens just as the hen guards and entices her chicks.

keeps the object of danger in view. He attacks any cats prowling around. While the hens are eating, he stands guard with raised tail and slightly dipped wings. Only occasionally does he himself eat briefly, and usually a few hens run up to him then. He can also call the hens to him directly, by very conspicuously picking something up from the ground in his beak and dropping it again while calling "cluck cluck." In the evening he is the first to take to the trees, and then calls to the hens to join him.

These parallels in the behavior of the hen and the cock catch the eye at once.[79] But there are similar parallels in the behavior of chicks and hens. Just as the chicks flee to the mother if they are attacked by a strange hen, so the hens whom a wandering cock wants to overcome by force flee to "their" cock. The behavior pattern of the chicken-hen group is echoed in the hen-cock group. This means that the harem society of adults is structured according to the same pattern as that of the mother-child family. This is because the hens can change their social role according to whether they are "head of the family" in a crowd of chicks or members of the harem of a cock. As territory owner, the cock plays the same role toward his hens as the territory-owning hen does to her chicks.

The birds called wood swallows (*Artamus*), which occur in the Indo-Australian region, offer a particularly interesting example of social life. Immelmann recently very carefully

Food-begging, prelude to copulation, and social greeting look the same for the wood swallow too.

observed some species in Australia.[49] Wood swallows cling very closely together in pairs, probably throughout their life; but over and above this they also lead a very highly developed social life. They are extreme examples of contact animals. When they are at rest they always sit closely cuddled up to one another and preen one another's feathers. Several times a day, particularly in the evening, they fly up to great heights in groups and wheel around with loud calls. They do many everyday tasks together in groups, such as foraging, cleaning themselves, attacking other birds, roosting, and even rearing young. The pairs do not establish territorial boundaries to separate them from their neighbors, nor do they brood in colonies, but nest in intimate proximity; neighboring pairs visit one another's nests and later feed the nestlings in turn.

So nestlings and fledglings are provided with food by a number of old birds, and sometimes this continues even after they have become independent. On the other hand, these young birds often also feed their own brothers and sisters from the next brood and in addition take a part in feeding unknown young birds. This behavior survives their whole life long, for adult members of the species may also feed one another. Similarly the young nestlings and fledglings do not beg only at their parents but at all conspecifics, a characteristic they will retain throughout their life. In this way, even ailing individuals can be provided with food by other members of their species.

Young birds who beg spread their wings slightly and raise them a little; older birds raise them almost horizontally. In this position they slowly move the wings up and down, but much more slowly than the quivering movement of most songbirds; in addition, they slowly pivot their head back and forth around the vertical axis.

White-breasted wood swallows (*Artamus leucorhynchus*) also sit close beside their sexual partner before copulation and quiver animatedly with slightly raised and spread wings. This behavior can be repeated several times; in between the male can fly off, catch an insect, and feed it to the female, who once again quivers her wings. What is curious is that the male joins in this childish begging movement when he is feeding her, i.e., he also quivers his wings. Among the black-faced wood swallows, *Artamus cinerëus*, the partners sit far apart, with wings extended to their full width and slightly raised, the one that is turned away from the partner raised slightly higher than the adjacent one and with fanned tail. Both animals perform slow circling movements with their wings and tail, and then they mate.

Sometimes it takes several minutes for the second partner to begin its wing and tail movements. The speed and extension of the movements increase a little, and it is only a minute or two after both birds have reached full speed that they copulate.

This sequence of movement can also occur without being followed by copulation and even outside the brooding time. Then the "prelude to copulation" is solely in the service of the pair-bond. The pattern of movements is derived from brood-tending behavior. Among the white-breasted wood swallow it consists largely of a presentation of food overridden by long and intensive begging. Here, however, unlike during brood-feeding, the feeding partner also quivers its wings and "begs" with them. With the other species, the black-faced wood swallow, wing-quivering has turned into slow, circular movements like rowing, and the presentation of food by the male has almost disappeared in the prelude to mating. So the childish begging behavior has been transformed more thoroughly in the prelude to mating. This species also leads a more highly specialized social life.

We also see begging very frequently in other situations. If a wood swallow lands close beside a member of its kind, it often begs at it briefly, again with exactly the same movements with which a young bird begs. The already seated bird may respond with the same begging movements. Both may content themselves with slight wing-quivering, or they may perform the whole gamut of behavior up to the transmittal of food by the new arrival. Here begging serves as a social gesture of greeting, probably with an appeasing function.

Some courtship movements and nearly all the social behavior of the wood swallow thus derive from the behavior repertory of the young bird. They include not only begging motions but also the contact-call that has developed without gradations from the begging call. The female utters this noise shortly before copulation and during the preliminary feeding by the male; in addition, a bird landing near a conspecific uses it as greeting. Accordingly, the acoustic accompaniment to wing-begging has also developed

Social allopreening of masked lovebirds, a species of parakeet; and of pelicans.

from the young bird's begging, and one can justifiably assert that these animals have exploited childish begging for the pair-bonding ceremony, for the foreplay to copulation, and for general social greeting. The effect on the partner has remained the same too, for in all these situations the begging behavior can incite the partner to real feeding, although admittedly this is rare between adults. Instead it often provokes the partner to hop up to his mate or to allopreen, or even to execute the same begging behavior.

That is to say, adults react to the begging of other adults in more varied ways than to the begging of young animals. So they can discriminate between the two (perhaps simply because adults look different from young birds). This is an indication that begging behavior "means" different things in the relationship between the animals and is "understood" in different ways. Moreover, it occasions different physiological effects—it is "intended" differently according to whether a young bird or an adult is begging. Young birds beg when they are hungry. But the same behavior among adults is independent of the state of satiety of the birds: A newly arriving wood swallow can even beg at the present company by way of greeting if it is already holding food in its beak. This suggests, first, that begging behavior occurs among adults when they are neither hungry nor sexually excited, and that it therefore has a special social function. But at the same time it means that these animals perform social actions that cannot be attributed to any of the normally accepted drives, such as aggression, reproduction, flight, feeding, etc., and that social life therefore contains its own particular drives. Whether one should speak of social drives is disputable, and rightly so insofar as we do not know whether the various social actions of this kind all depend on one and the same drive or on several different social motivations. It is not surprising that these social motivations create no new behavior patterns but exploit already existing ones, for evolution always builds on what already exists.

If a behavior pattern acquires a new or additional biological function, it must always undergo a change in its inner motivation or acquire a new motivation of its own—this latter is also called emancipation. Without this "change of motivation" the behavior pattern could only be used in its original context. In such a case, only a hungry bird could greet its partner or invite it to mate if begging movements always remained motivated by hunger, as with the young bird. For the sake of simplicity we have up to here omitted detailed discussion of this question, but it applies to all cases of derived behavior patterns. If a begging movement can appease or deflect aggression it must be available to a satiated bird too; it cannot be motivated by hunger alone, for otherwise only the hungry could live together peacefully in an animal society.

20. Other Emancipated Brood-Tending Actions

There is no distinction left between begging and food-offering in the beak-flirting of ravens. Among Adélie penguins (*Pygoscelis adeliae*) too, the male holds the beak of the female in his own without giving her food. Among various kinds of cormorants the partners of a pair are in the habit of grasping each other by the beak and tugging and shaking each other back and forth. Sometimes this may look like a quarrel, but it too derives from brood-feeding. Young cormorants plunge their beak deep into the throat of the parent animal and fetch their food from there. The parent bird who is offering the food opens its beak wide, and this often displays in the interior of the beak strong color markings that serve the young bird as a feeding signal. Like others, this signal can also become emancipated and serve the bird again later in life. The female shag (*Phalacrocorax aristotelis*), for instance, entices a shy male by opening her beak wide,[1] thus showing its colored interior, which presumably has a calming and inviting effect because it is the food-presentation signal. But, like chameleons and many other lizards, birds also open their jaws for threatening, and this action may also display striking colors. One can tell from the response of the partner whether the gesture has a threatening and frightening effect or an enticing one, but little investigation has been done in this field.

Nest-building also belongs to brood-tending in the wider

sense of the word. Among some kinds of birds both sexes together build the nest; among others the females do it alone while the males provide the nesting material. A new courtship or greeting gesture has evolved from the presentation of nesting material, as it has from the presentation of food. The male can make simplified nest-building movements in the air in front of the female, with a blade of grass in his beak, even if he is no longer helping with nest-building. The emancipation of this action and its transfer to a new field of function is proven by the fact that, like the partner feeding of cuckoos, it survives even when the original meaning has disappeared. It can also be shown to be emancipated because the relation to the object in question has changed; for example, when a male robin feeds his young he holds several insects in his mouth, but when he feeds his female as a form of greeting he only holds one insect.[71] The male crimson finch (*Neochmia*) holds stiff green blades of grass in his mouth for courtship; his ancestors built their nests from these blades; today, however, crimson finches build their nests out of half-moldy soft blades of grass and have only retained their former preferred object for courtship, which has become emancipated from the old nest-building behavior.[48]

In some cases it is not clear whether or not a behavior pattern that is important in the relations between the partners derives from brood-tending behavior, even if it still occurs there too. The reverse process, namely a shift from pair-bond behavior to parent-child behavior, is also possible.

Everyone must have seen birds allopreening, for instance among pigeons, parrots, herons, and ravens. Of course this does not occur among all species of birds, and there are occasions in which some do it while fairly closely related species do not. It is typical of penguins, albatrosses, storm petrels, cormorants, storks and maraboos, horned screamers, rails, pigeons, parrots, owls, mouse-birds, toucans and, finally, many songbirds. In all it is known of forty-one bird families. In some cases the partners preen each other alternately; in others they do it at the same time. The allopreening looks fairly similar, even when the birds' beaks are as dissimilar as those of parrots and pelicans. The flanks are very rarely allopreened, the breast and back somewhat more often, the various parts of the head always, particularly the back of the head, the throat, and the area around the eyes. These are, admittedly, areas that the birds cannot reach themselves with their beaks, yet there is no reason to assume that species that are not allopreened there suffer any disadvantage because of it. Even species that do allopreen often only do so for a short span of the brooding period; so this behavior is not essential to the care of their feathers. What is its use then? Harrison, who has deeply concerned himself with this, found that the following factors favored the occurrence of allopreening[40]:

1. Confined space, either because of the peculiarities of the nesting place or because the animals move awkwardly on land and therefore use less space than is available.
2. Prolonged separation of partners.
3. Companionship, in the flock or in a large brooding colony, and also in prolonged pair-bonds between two animals.

Confined space, frequent encounters, and unfamiliarity after separation, which can even lead to slight estrangement, are all factors that heighten aggressiveness. And allopreening is indeed closely related to aggressive behavior; sometimes an initial attack ends in allopreening, which then serves as *ersatz* and appeasement. Similarly, the invitation to allopreening is connected with the drive to flight, appeasement, and evasion. Presentation of the raised head or throat feathers, often with the eyes half closed, acts as such an invitation. This gesture cannot only appease aggression but it also reduces the partner's tendency to flight.

Among some species at least (for instance, penguins or relatives of the stormy petrels), allopreening is also very noticeable between parents and their young. But it is doubtful whether allopreening is an emancipated form of brood-tending behavior; in fact, it is not even certain whether it is an independent behavior pattern at all or whether perhaps it is only an action that occurs in conflicts—to express it in human terms. We know that allopreening may occur as an act of confusion or "displacement," but not whether it is ever done deliberately or even what its purpose is.

Actions that occur in its place are also important in the context of the social meaning of allopreening. Among boobies, for instance, there is one species, the brown booby (*Sula leucogaster*), which does not allopreen at all; it is very rare for the red-footed booby (*Sula sula*) to do so, but it is an everyday occurrence for others. Now in those situations where these other species allopreen, the red-footed and the brown boobies offer their partner a twig for building the nest. These little gifts brought back by the returning bird are necessary to the harmonious relations between the partners, as they are among other birds. Eibl-Eibesfeldt has demonstrated this very well: He took a bunch of seaweed (its gift) away from a flightless cormorant (*Nannopterum harrisi*) on the way to his nest; on his arrival empty-handed the bird was immediately driven away by his partner.[28] The invitation to allopreening cannot, of course, be removed from the animal in the same way, but by comparing the situations, particularly among closely related species, we may conclude that this gesture has the same appeasing effect.

21. Termites to Chimpanzees—No Change

The examples we have quoted so far of socially important behavior borrowed from childish behavior referred to birds. For a long time now birds have been the animals on whom most research has been done, and ornithology has always played a leading role in behavior research. Primarily this is because so many bird-lovers never tire of watching their protégés and have thus gained a very wide knowledge of their way of life. Another reason is that in the course of the evolution of vertebrates, from fish through batrachia, reptiles, and birds to mammals and monkeys, behavior has become increasingly more varied and differentiated. Meanwhile fairly long, rigidly established behavioral sequences disintegrated into ever smaller elements that became usable again, both individually and in continually new combinations. Naturally, this often makes it hard to recognize the elements. Among the lowest vertebrates, fish, it is still quite simple. Either they mate or they do not mate; their behavior is characteristic of a particular situation. Among higher mammals, however, the attribution of identical behavioral elements is often extremely difficult. Is pawing the ground with the front legs the beginning of flight, or of digging, or an attempt to cover something with sand, or simply "nervousness"? If all four legs paw in the sequence in which they are moved for running, one could say that pawing was an attempt to flee that had been inhibited for some reason. But if only one leg moves, we have too few points of reference to tell from which behavior pattern the action might derive. In this line of development birds occupy a position where series of movements evidently already serve new functions; and yet these series still represent sufficiently large chunks of former, even longer sequences of movements for one to identify them and affirm with some certainty that a greeting ceremony derives from the begging of the nestling.

This is only a very general argument to explain why people noticed this emancipation of behavioral elements among birds so soon. Naturally we find behavioral patterns of unknown origins among birds too, just as the emancipation of brood-tending behavior also occurs in other classes of animals. It is necessary to show this by examples too; otherwise the reader might get the impression that we were indeed dealing with a natural law, but one that only applied to the bird kingdom.

Among the very varied species of the cichlid family there are, as we mentioned earlier, some that form pairs who adhere firmly together for a long time. The Indian orange chromide (*Etroplus maculatus*) is one of them. The eggs are attached to stones, and both parents guard and fan the eggs until the young hatch, usually after three days. The parents carry in their mouth the freshly hatched larvae to a prepared sand-pit and continue to guard them there for another five or six days. Sometimes larvae are moved to a new sand-pit during this time. Some nine days after hatching, the young begin to swim freely, leave the pit, and follow their parents in a dense swarm. The parents continue to watch over the swarm of young, using their mouths to bring truants back to the swarm, drive off enemies, and move slowly enough all the time for the young to be able to easily keep up with them. The family remains together in this way for another twenty-five days; then the parents' interest in their by now fairly independent young wanes;

they separate from them and can now begin to prepare for a new brood.

From the first day on one can see the free-swimming young, who are some seven millimeters long at first, foraging for food. If the supply becomes short, the swarm will distribute itself over a larger area; if there is ample food, the young stay close by the parents. But in any case they return to them constantly from the first day on, for each young fish swims back to one of the parent animals about once every ten minutes and eats a bite of body mucus from its flank. The orange chromide belongs in fact to those fish who feed their young with an excretion from their own body. In the appropriate phase of the brooding cycle, the mucous cells in the membrane of the parents

The young of the Indian orange chromide eat from the body mucus of the parent. This movement becomes a form of greeting behavior between the partners of a pair.

multiply by more than thirty percent. They are essential to the survival of the young. Young fish who are deprived of them show a very high mortality rate and the survivors remain very backward in physical development and growth.[118] The same applies, incidentally, to a South American cichlid, the famous "discus" fish (*Symphysodon*). It too feeds its young with body mucus in the early days. Since this mucous secretion is stimulated by prolactin,[6] one could even call them "mammal fish," for prolactin is the hormone that stimulates the milk glands of mammals and the secretion of crop milk among pigeons. Milk and crop milk are well-known as essential nourishment for the very young, such as pigeon nestlings.

Whereas with the "discus," the frequency with which the young visit their parents decreases with age, it clearly increases with the orange chromide. When the young are over a month old they snap a bite from their parents every three minutes. Even when the family has dissolved, one still occasionally sees the young, and, more rarely, adults, swimming up to a larger member of their species and snapping at its flank. The partners of a pair do this continually, and in fact this is the only situation in which an orange chromide addresses such behavior to an equal-sized conspecific. So this behavior of the young animals who take something essential to their nourishment from the body of their parents also plays an important part in the pair-bond, both in the time when the pair forms and later during "married life."

We can also find permanent social groups outside the realm of vertebrates—among insects, for example. Whenever social animals are discussed, people usually think first of the famous insect states, those of the termites, ants, and bees. Termites are sometimes called "white ants," but they have nothing to do with the highly developed ants; rather they are fairly primitive insects, closely related to cockroaches. In their states the king survives together with the queen, with whom he founded the state, whereas in the states of *Hymenoptera* ("membranous wings") such as ants, bees, wasps, hornets, and bumblebees, only the queen survives. All insect states are structured according to a very definite system. There is only one animal who sees to reproduction; the others, sometimes numbering hundreds of thousands, serve the state as workers, brood-tenders, soldiers, builders, etc. One of the largest insect states is that of the leaf-eating ant *Atta cephalotes*, whose subterranean nests can extend to a depth of five or six meters in the ground and span a distance of more than one hundred meters. Five or six million animals live here with a queen, who lays twenty million eggs in her lifetime. If she dies, the whole state perishes with her. For nest-building, these animals move some forty tons of soil, construct thousands of chambers, and breed fungi in them on chewed-up leaves. For the defense of the state they have large soldiers; for bringing the pieces of leaf, leaf-carriers; for protecting the carriers, "foot-soldiers"; the foot-soldiers ride on the piece of leaf and drive off the flies that try to attack the busy leaf-

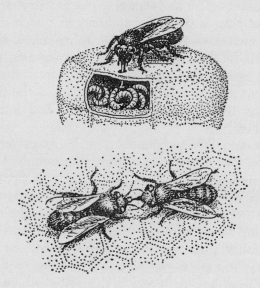

Above: bumblebee feeding the larvae. Below: a worker bee feeding another.

bearer and lay their eggs on his neck.[29] This solidarity among so many and differently specialized individuals has always excited the admiration of observers, and researchers have tried to find out what it is that holds the animals together. They found that there is a nest scent varying from state to state and that the animals drive away or kill any individual with a different nest scent. But this only means that the right nest scent protects from attack. What actually holds them together, as far as we know, is primarily social feeding. The insects continually beg their companions for food and are then fed with a regurgitated drop of food. Two animals can beg at each other too, or try to feed each other reciprocally.

This social mouth-to-mouth feeding derives from brood-tending behavior too, for the insects also feed their larvae mouth-to-mouth. This has come from various successive stages of development. As with the ichneumon fly (*Ichneumonidae*), the mother can sting a grub or other animal and lay an egg in it, or, like the digger wasp (*Sphecoidea*), she can build a chamber in the ground, drag several victims into it, and lay the egg on them. In the most simple case, for instance among potter wasps (*Eumeninae*), these brooding chambers are amply provided with food and are closed up after the mother has laid the egg. We find a higher stage of specialization among some kinds of potter wasp from Africa. Here the mother begins by dragging only one grub into the chamber and laying an egg by it, but she leaves the nest open and brings more grubs from time to time so that the larva is continually provided with new food. Among even more highly specialized kinds, the mother chews the food destined for her larva into a pulp. Since all these species form a very closely related group, it is once again very easy to reconstruct the gradual changes of behavior, finally leading to a "subsocial" behavior that already fulfills many of the requirements of social life although the animals do not live socially yet. When adult, the off-spring scatter. But in the wasp genus called *Stenogaster* there are, besides some species that behave as we have just described, some where the mother animal feeds and rears several young at the same time in one nest; at first the young stay with her and help to feed the next brood. After a while they are replaced by the new brothers and sisters and leave the maternal nest to establish their own. So they are fully developed young wasps by then; some build their own nest immediately next to that of their mother.

Only the true social wasps (*Vespinae*)—i.e., our common black-and-yellow wasps—have succeeded in forming social communities in which most of the individuals spend their whole life—although only as workers, for they are no longer capable of reproduction. Brood-tending feeding has evolved into reciprocal feeding by all the members of a state, and even the larvae are not only fed themselves but also provide drops of saliva rich in nourishing substances that are important to the survival of the whole community. Under certain conditions the larvae can even serve as food reserves for the adults. Normally the wasp larvae hanging head down in the cells are fed with a pulp made up of grubs and other insects that the adult wasps premasticate in their mouths. As soon as the larvae are touched, they release a drop of saliva from their mouth aperture, which the adults swallow greedily. This saliva provides an essential motivation for the adults to go to the larvae, and it is fairly common for wasps to visit their larvae again and again and incite them to excrete saliva without bringing them any food pulp. So one cannot say that the animals are motivated by purely maternal feelings and devote themselves quite selflessly to the larvae. Similarly, it is probably the attraction of the larvae's excretions that causes the young wasps to stay with their mother. And if we are right to assume that the excessive exploitation of the larvae by continually inciting them to excrete new saliva weakens the larvae in a specific fashion and inhibits their development into normal sexual animals, then it becomes clear how strongly the development of the individual and the development of society are interrelated here too.[42] Since we are dealing with natural processes, we need not worry about considerations of right and wrong. It would be more rewarding to consider what this adds to our knowledge of the plan of creation.

In the immediate context of our discussion, it is important to note that wasps and bees have developed this system of states independently of ants; this shows how normal it must be for animals to exploit brood-tending behavior for the construction of a society. Ants have reached an even higher level of individual specialization; we speak of "castes" in their societies. Among honeybees, the different duties in the hive are performed by various old workers, so that each individual passes through a series of different jobs in the course of its life. One or two days after hatching from the cocoon, the female worker begins her job of caring for the larvae; about a week later she spends two weeks or so on general "housework," excretes wax and kneads it in shape for building honeycombs, helps to clean the hive, and also stands guard at the entrance; after this she becomes a forager and brings nectar, pollen, water, resin, etc. to the hive. In case of need she can return to her earlier jobs. But among ants the individuals who do the different jobs are also very different in physique, so they do not, therefore, change jobs. The behavior of the soldiers among leaf-eating ants, for instance, is distinguished by the fact that they never take flight and even attack huge enemies. In order to do so they have developed very large heads and great muscles on their mandibles; but they can no longer eat by themselves with this mouth, so they have to rely on being fed by the female workers. We should really speak of female soldiers too, for these animals are all female in genetic structure, although functionally they are sexless and infertile. They have in fact been sterilized by chemical substances that the queen bee produces. These substances are licked up by the workers and distributed throughout the hive during reciprocal feeding, and their effect is to suppress the development of the reproductive organs. This shows how closely the different behavior patterns are interlinked. The individual animal decides to search for food not because it is or is not hungry; rather it gathers much more food than it can use itself and divides it up among other members of the state. If an ant is hungry it need only beg from a companion. During feeding, both animals act in a community-bonding fashion. The ant that is being fed receives in addition a portion of the substance that makes it into a worker. So this chemical social effect is based on social feeding, which in turn derived from brood-tending feeding.

Such a complex system of social communication and reciprocal influences is, however, liable to what we would call "abuse" in human terms. If an ant can satisfy its hunger by begging from another, a whole group of ants who have fallen on hard times can do the same. But what if they had fallen on hard times because they only had soldiers and had "forgotten" to see to workers? We know what happens then, for we know of species that do precisely that. These are the well-known slave-holding ants found in various ant species. These slave-holding species only have soldier-workers, who cannot eat by themselves. They move in organized columns, often covering long distances, and attack the colony of another species of ant; the workers of the attacked colony usually react by running wildly to and fro and trying to bring the cocoons to safety. But the intruders overcome the workers, take away their cocoons, and carry them home to their own nest. The hatched young do not "know" that they are in the "wrong" nest; they help out just as they would have done at home, working in the state, and looking after the cocoons that are the booty of further raids. The slaves do the building, drag food into it, and look after the eggs and larvae of their robbers. But they have no queen of their own, and gradually the normal death of old age thins out their ranks so that the robbers continually have to see to replacements. For the slaves it obviously makes no difference whether they function as wheels in the machinery of their own state or whether they work as equally responsible wheels in the state of their war-like robbers. These individuals, who are so structured as to react correctly in the interests of the state, are "made" for slavery.

But events need not be quite so warlike. One species of ant without workers of its own can very easily be a parasite on its closest relatives, to whom it is almost identical exter-nally and whose social communication signals are the same. These parasite species are only noticeable because they produce few or no workers, which means that they do not contribute to the preservation of the state on whose po-tential they live. The species have developed as "social parasites from their own ranks," that is to say they have reached a further stage of specialization and broken away from a normal ant species, so that they now live together with and at the cost of this species. The ant state with its perfectly organized care of all individuals belonging to the state is fertile terrain for social parasites; because of the necessary reliability and thus rigidity of its organization the state cannot protect itself against parasites who exploit the state-preserving reactions of the workers in their own interests, while contributing nothing to the preservation of the collective good themselves.[42] Quite different animals can also become parasites in the ant state in this way, for example, mites, bugs, spiders, or beetles.

Of course it may be that the "parasite" for its part offers talents that are of advantage to the species it joins. An example is the cooperation between ants and plant lice.

Plant lice (*aphids*) live off plant juices and excrete the honey as a sugary fluid. They do this increasingly as soon as they are disturbed, flailing about with their long back legs at the same time. It is quite common for an ant to encounter a plant louse and to "disturb" it. The plant louse reacts by waving its legs about and excreting a drop of this sweet substance. For the ant this behavior is the same as when a fellow ant offers a drop of food while greeting with waving antennae. So the ant sees the plant louse as the head of another ant, greets all plant lice by friendly begging, and is fed by all of them. Sometimes the ant also tries to feed this presumed fellow ant and offers the rear end of the plant louse a drop of food—in vain, of course.[54] The mistake on the part of the ants is to the benefit of the plant louse, since ants keep the plant louse colony free of enemies. For the ants, the plant lice are just as much of an advantage as milch cows are to us. The only one to suffer disadvantages from this cohabitation is the plant. The plant louse, who can suck without being annoyed by ants, normally excretes some three cubic millimeters of the sugary fluid per day but excretes three times as much when visited by ants. The fact that one single state of red ants can devour more than a hundred kilograms of the fluid per year gives some idea how this feeding, which has developed from a brood-tending action into a bond holding the society together, and in which the plant lice have become involved as though by accident, affects the plant world, which originally played no part in the social behavior of ants. We cite this example to show that in nature the simple social behavior of one species of animal can entail quite unexpected consequences and can extend its influence to organisms of a quite different type.

The example can also teach us how difficult it is to establish a suitable criterion for what is natural or unnatural. Can it be unnatural that social parasites live in the ant state in nature?

Perhaps the termites can come to our aid again in this train of thought. It is not that they give us the key to what is natural and what is not. But a careful study of the social life of termites might perhaps explain how social parasitism can be avoided. No case of social parasitism is known among termites. They too have social castes that are interdependent, and they too practice reciprocal mouth-

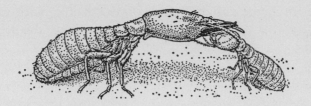

Termite worker feeding one of the large soldiers.

to-mouth feeding among adults—a social bond that derives from brood-tending behavior. For, as we showed for wasps, among the insects closely related to termites there are many species where the mothers care for the eggs and lick them, like the earwig (*Forficula*), and others where the mothers feed the larvae, like some cockroaches. And termites, like social wasps, have made use of this brood-tending behavior as raw material for building up a highly specialized society.

Even among spiders there are species that live socially. Very often, all that is generally known of the life of the spider is that it can be dangerous for the males to come close to a female, for the females are often much larger and treat the male like prey. Not all spiders live in strict solitude; there are some who work together in large groups and get on correspondingly well. In recent years a number of such spiders from Africa have been closely examined, above all a "round" spider (*Achaeranea disparata*) and a cellar spider (*Agelena consociata*[18]).[68] Both build large communal webs on shrubs. If a fairly large prey such as a grasshopper is caught in the web the spiders rush up, carry it away together, and then feed on it together too. Since spiders have a very narrow mouth they cannot devour their food bit by bit; nor do they have chewing mandibles, so they have to suck in their food. This is why they mash up their prey chemically, by spitting digestive juices onto it. The disintegrated predigested prey is then drunk. Individual spiders of the above-named cellar spider family have been made to eat from a radioactively marked prey and then put back on the communal web. After all of them had captured and eaten a new prey together, the radioactivity was traceable in the other animals too. So it must have been spat in the digestive juices of the animal first infected with it and then imbibed by all the others. In fact, the animals eat as though from one large bowl; none of them, so to speak, cooks its own dinner for itself alone. Whether this exchange of substances has any social significance is not yet known. But it is interesting to note that among spiders, who are generally known as greedy and food-jealous animals, a fairly intimate form of social life goes together with a reciprocal grant of food comparable to the early stages of pair-bonding among gulls we described earlier (see p. 128). Admittedly both types of spider form anonymous open societies into which conspecifics from other webs can be admitted without difficulty, and in fact one can even form a new community made up of animals from altogether different webs. It is known that among some other comb-footed spiders of the *Theridion* species, including those native to Europe, the mothers share their meal with their children. One can see a mother with some thirty offspring "eat" from one large fly. And the mother does not only tolerate her young here but even bores a number of holes into the prey for them so that they can eat, for the jaws of the babies are still too weak. When the mother eats alone, she only bores one or two holes. The very small baby spiders are fed mouth-to-mouth by the mother. She regurgitates food from her stomach and offers it to the children in drop form; they come to her one after the other and take the drop from her mouth. The young are cared for in this way from the first day after they hatch from the egg-cocoon until, a few days later, they can take part directly in the mother's meal and later even help the mother to tie up her prey with sticky threads.[9] This collaboration between mother and child is largely the same as the collaboration among adults

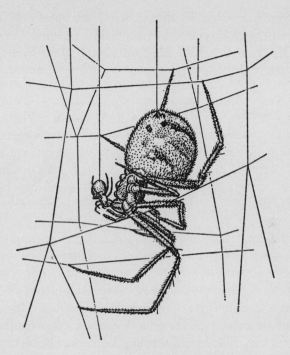

Comb-footed spider mother feeding a young one mouth-to-mouth.

in the related species described earlier, who always live in communities. But hitherto all we know is the correlation between the two; whether social life grew out of brood-tending behavior here too still has to be investigated.

These few examples from the great kingdom of lower animals suffice to show how much even they can tell us about the basic questions of communal social life. Further research in this field is looked forward to with great expectation. Here we will confine ourselves to the observations we have made about fish and birds and now turn to mammals, among whom there are again species that characteristically live in firm pairs or in larger compact groups.

The tree shrews of Southeast Asia, who are very curious animals in many respects, have already become familiar to the reader from the discussion on social stress (see p. 64). In systematic terms they are very primary mammals. In

Tree shrew mates lick each other's snout (right) just as infants do to the mother (left).

contrast to earlier views, they may not after all belong among the close relatives of primates, yet they have some things in common with hares and rabbits. This can be seen, for example, in their brood-tending behavior. Rabbit mothers only visit and suckle their young once every twenty-four hours, tree shrew mothers only once in forty-eight hours! The tree shrew offspring, usually numbering two or three, are quite full up in a few minutes, when they are left to their own devices again for another two days. True, the mother builds a nest for her young, but she does not stay there. She spends the night in the special "parental sleeping nest" together with her mate, with whom she lives in firm monogamy. The young are neither warmed nor covered with nesting material nor cleaned by the mother, and she would not bring them back into the nest if they left it; in fact, they never do so at this stage, and only man or some other disturber could throw them out. Martin, who was probably the first to observe the entire social behavior of these animals carefully,[77] described what happens during the visit of a mother to her young. She stands over the young with straddled legs, and neither looks at them nor licks them. The young lie on their backs diagonally to the mother and suck rapidly. They thrust against the mother's stomach with their front paws. After a short time they move from one teat to the next. After sucking they move forward to the mother's head and lick her mouth, which she inclines down to them. Occasionally the mother offers her mouth directly for licking. After this she leaves them again.

After thirty-three days the young leave the nest, but still return to it in the following three days in cases of danger and at night. After this time they follow their mother into the parental nest and sleep with the parents, until, aged some ninety days, they reach sexual maturity and leave their parents. Shortly before their first excursion out of their own nest the young are occasionally suckled every day. Outside the nest they sometimes suck every six hours, but probably cease to do so entirely as soon as they live in the parental nest. During the transitional phase mouth-licking also occurs more often. At times one young tree shrew sits to the left and another to the right of the mother and they lick up a clear fluid that emerges from the corners of her mouth. Occasionally the young also lick the mouth of the father. When they move into the parental nest, mouth-licking gradually becomes more rare. What its purpose is has not yet been established. Perhaps it provides the young with some nourishing substance or with the necessary digestive bacteria. Or perhaps it provides them with particular olfactory substances. But whatever its significance, it is no doubt an important pattern of behavior between mother and child because it plays such a large part in brood-tending, which has very few other notable features among tree shrews.

Later, this mouth-licking occurs again constantly, but only between the partners of a pair (and probably only when other adults live in the same area). When a male and female who are paired meet, they can sniff at each other just as they sniff at every other member of the species; but here one licks the mouth of the other, just as the children do to their mother. The licking can be initiated by the male or the female, but it is seen more frequently between the parents themselves than between them and the young, who may still live with them. Again it is not certain what its purpose is. Perhaps it serves to transmit scent signals, or it could equally well be a pair-bonding rite.

Intensive reciprocal mouth-licking, in which the young eagerly swallow the maternal saliva, also occurs among golden hamsters (*Mesocricetus*), harvest mice (*Micromys*), spiny mice (*Acomys*), and dormice (*Glis*); they do not live in a state of marriage but sometimes form loose groups. Mouth-licking has never been observed among adults.

One predator that lives in firm monogamy for some years at least is the African black-backed jackal (*Canis mesomelas*); sufficiently protracted studies are still required to determine whether the pair-bond lasts a whole lifetime. Both partners share the brood-tending. As soon as the young begin to eat solid foods the parents go on the hunt and bring prey to the young from far away. They do not carry it in their mouth but presumably in their stomach. While the parents are hunting, the young often play with one another, but they immediately beg at the parents on their return and even venture a little distance to meet them. The young jackal raises its head up steeply toward the mouth of the parent animal and even nuzzles its lips. The parents then regurgitate the food they have brought: whole mice or a rather liquid dark mass that consists of beetles and other insects. Sometimes the young do not wait for the prey to be dropped on the ground but take it out of their parents' mouths, into which they can stick their heads quite far.[123] Adult jackals greet their pair-partner with the same begging gesture, crouching down a little and nudging the lips of the other with their mouth.

The same is known of wolves and domestic dogs. They

Adult jackals (top) and hunting dogs (bottom) nuzzle
the jaws of their partner in greeting in the same way
that their young beg food from adults.

too bring food to their young; the young beg at the parent
by nuzzling its jaws, and adults greet each other in the
same way. But they do not live in firm pairs. So this greeting borrowed from the food-begging of the young animal
can—as with the wood swallow among birds—acquire a general social meaning. This has been studied carefully for
hunting dogs. The African hunting dog (*Lycaon pictus*)
is the predator with the highest success rate in hunting.
Hardly a trip ends in failure. These animals live in packs of
several adults of both sexes (in one carefully studied pack
there were six males, two females, and fifteen young in all,
from two litters).[61] They hunt every morning and evening,
in small groups. As long as the pack still includes dependent
young, the females stay with their offspring and the males
hunt alone. They tear pieces the size of a hand off the prey
and devour them; only the head and skeleton of a thirty-
kilogram gazelle remain after five minutes. Then the hunters
trot home and feed their young by regurgitating the meat in

large portions. When the young are full and will eat no
more the adults eat the meat again themselves. If the young
become hungry again and beg, more food is regurgitated.
Often they regurgitate what they have just begged from one
animal for another begging animal. In this way all the members of the pack are provided with meat. This "meat-spit-
ting" is a very effective brood-tending measure. In a pack
of hunting dogs that had lost all its females through accidents, five males brought up the nine five-week-old young
alone. Such a feeding community also enables the animals
to divide up the work in a society in which some members
at least "earn their living" indirectly at times. When the
pack becomes active again after its night or midday rest,
or before it sets off on the hunt, or when some members of
the pack meet again after a short separation, intense greeting takes place. The animals go up to each other in a tense
attitude, just as they do when other large animals disturb
them in their territory, and then lick each other's face and
nuzzle their nose against the corners of their partner's
mouth in the same way as the young do to the large adults
or hungry adults do to returning hunters. So this begging
behavior is also addressed to members of the pack who are
themselves hungry. But the behavior does not only serve
for food-begging; it is also a greeting, and it removes social
tensions within the group. When the young are five weeks
old they also begin to use this gesture of greeting.[61]

Sea lions (*Zalophus californianus*) live in herds on the
coasts of the Galapagos Islands during the mating season.
The herds always consist of one bull and several females
together with their young. Each male occupies a strip of
coast that he defends against rivals by swimming to and fro
in front of it almost all day long and, when he surfaces at
certain points, loudly barking. Often this means that territorial neighbors emerge next to one another in the shallow
water to strengthen their common boundary. Young animals
who want to go into the deeper water are cut off from it by

the bull, who pushes them back into the shallow waters again. In the evening, the bull drives all his females and young to the shore and is the last to land. Females among themselves only defend their current territory against other members of the harem when they are on dry land. Yet this

Left: greeting between mother and child of Galapagos seals. Right: between male and female Galapagos sea lions.

fairly often leads to disputes. In that case the lord of the harem immediately comes to land and separates the disputants by pushing his way between them and then greeting both sides until the ladies have calmed down again. The greeting consists of waving his outstretched neck from side to side and touching the snouts of the ladies. The females greet one another in the same way, as do mothers their children.[26] Presumably this greeting has derived from the food-begging of the young. But hitherto it has not been fully proved, for young sea lions are not fed by the parent animals. Here, as with the cuckoo (see p. 133), the behavioral pattern may have survived as a social greeting while the original function—i.e., feeding the young—has disappeared; for sea lions are predators, among whom feeding the young is very common; this applies not only to dogs and jackals, as we have seen, but also among smaller predators, such as polecats or mongooses. But the food is not always regurgitated for the young; often it is simply brought to them in the parents' mouths, as with meerkats (*Suricata*), a kind of mongoose that lives in Africa. Here the mother brings the food to her young, offers it to them in her mouth, and then leaps about in front of them until they obey her and take the food from her mouth. Meerkats will eat animal and vegetable foods of the most varied kinds, and in addition they are "food jealous" and try to grab food from the jaws of others. When the mother brings food to the young

A young brown rat snatches a bit of food from its mother.

and then incites them to take it from her she is teaching them which foods are suitable. And indeed this creates eating traditions, for the young learn to choose the diet the mother prefers.[31] Similarly, young squirrels, rats, and other rodents who are just beginning to learn to eat alone try to steal bits of food from the mother's mouth.[28] All this is reminiscent of the snout-nudging that occurs in the greeting of various sea lions. Yet this is only a reference to its possible origins.

This manner of feeding that we have shown among many birds and some predators also occurs among the manlike apes, the chimpanzee, gorilla, and orangutan, who also feed their young mouth-to-mouth with regurgitated food. Even small chimpanzee and gorilla children take bits of food from their mother's hand or even from her mouth. And they also use their own hand or mouth. It is known of gorillas, at lease in captivity, that the mother takes food between her lips and then offers it to her child directly. Chimpanzees do this too, and we know that they also do so in the wild.[72] Even two-year-old children beg at their mother by presenting their pursed lips to her; then the mother pushes a lip full of chewed food directly into their mouth, for chimpanzees have a very wide lower lip, which can be filled with food like a large spoon. As with many birds, and with jackals and hunting dogs, this feeding gesture also appears among adults, namely for greeting purposes, and in particular when two animals have not seen each other for several days, for instance because the pack had split up.

In addition, all chimpanzee mothers gently press their lips onto various parts of the body of their babies and small children (up to the age of one year old). They take the child's hand and touch the palm with their lips. The lips are not pursed for this but remain close to the teeth. The mouth is usually open. Adults touch each other in the same

Mouth-to-mouth baby-feeding (left) and "kiss" of greeting between adult chimpanzees (right).

way, pressing their lips to an arm or a shoulder, at times even to their own hand. A worried child can touch its mother in this way, or even an adult male chimpanzee while he is copulating with the mother. So the kiss of greeting between chimpanzees could also stem from the rather groping contact of the lips which, like mouth-to-mouth feeding, is equally typical of mother-child behavior.

In terms of reciprocal feeding and the social actions derived from it among mammals, there are obvious analogies with the bird behavior we described earlier. The jackal lives in monogamy like the raven and has turned feeding the young into a greeting between partners; meanwhile the actual transmission of food has disappeared, leaving only a ritual. The hunting dog lives in fairly large communities like the wood swallow and treats all the members of the group in the same way as monogamous species treat their mate. The sea lion seems to correspond to the cuckoo, not because it has no brood-tending behavior but insofar as mouth-to-mouth feeding has disappeared here too, while the greeting ritual derived from it has survived. As with birds, however, many other typical brood-tending behavior patterns exist among mammals, and they also play a definite role in social life.

Hungry fawns squeal or utter the somewhat softer contact sound. This brings the mother to them, and she may utter the same sound. Later the same sounds no longer serve to call the mother but to keep mother and child together. The doe in heat also entices the buck with the same sounds.[66] Moreover, she summons him to follow her in the same way as the fawn did, remaining standing in front of him, turning back her raised head, and uttering contact sounds.

If two chamois or goat antelopes of different ranking order come into contact, the lower-ranking animal will usually demonstrate its inferiority "spontaneously." It crouches down, stretches out its head low and horizontally, and occasionally also lifts its nose slightly. In addition it cocks its ears forward and raises its tail above the horizontal. In this posture the chamois slinks or trots to the superior

Fallow-deer doe approaching the buck (top) and low-ranking chamois approaching a higher-ranking doe (below).

partner on bended legs. Animals of all ages and of both sexes do this. Usually they aim for the side of the high-ranking animal, in particular its flanks or head, or more rarely, they come from behind to the rear, i.e., the scrotum for males, the teats for females. Young animals prefer to aim for the body zone of the partner, where the breasts lie on the female, and it can quite often occur that they then subside on their carpal joint ("kneel" on their front legs) and raise their snout conspicuously. This humble attitude is not always released by aggressiveness on the part of the high-ranking animal; often the inferior one will spontaneously go up to the other, in particular among young animals again. These are fairly clear vestiges of child-ish behavior toward the mother, although combined with other elements. For instance, fawns never run to their mother with bended knees nor do they then emphatically cock their ears.[67] If a doe approaches a stronger male she will come with out-stretched head and slightly open snout, while making licking tongue movements, diagonal, upward-thrusting movements with her head, her tail standing on end, and sometimes also uttering a short call. A young fawn coming up to its mother to drink behaves in exactly the same way.

22. The Social Significance of Maternal Signals

Adult African hunting dogs, whose group behavior we described in the previous chapter (see p. 165), use various gestures of greeting or appeasement that derive from childish behavior. The young suck from their mother in a lying,

Young hunting dogs sucking from their mother (left) and adult hound licking the teats of a female in greeting (right).

sitting, or standing position. But, as we showed, they do not only receive milk from her teats but are also provided with meat—in part undigested—regurgitated from the mouth of both parents. They beg for both by nudging with their noses, but do not aim specifically for one or the other. It may happen that they obtain milk by bumping their nose against the lips of the mother, or they may obtain meat by knocking against the middle of her body. Young dogs aged three to five weeks prefer to direct their begging movements at the middle of the mother's body between the front and back legs, and do the same to males too. For her part, the mother invites them to suck either by lying down on her side and offering her large right-hand teats or by walking backward with her head held low some meters in front of the whelps, as for regurgitating food, and then letting them suck.

So mouth and teats have a food-presentation significance. At the same time they have a social significance derived from this. On p. 166 we described how these dogs nuzzle one another's lips in greeting. Besides this we also find adults addressing childlike behavior at the female's teats: During the violent greeting after the midday rest and before departing on the hunt the dogs can lick the female's teats. A remarkable feature of this predator notorious for its cruelty toward its prey is the almost unsurpassed friendliness between the members of a pack. There is no apparent ranking order among them, and instead each tries to outdo the other in displays of humility. For this they use gestures of greeting and appeasement derived from childish behavior. So nuzzling and licking of the mouth and teats are not only interchangeable begging movements, but both are also transferred into the social behavior of adults.[61]

The males of the Indian flying fox (*Pteropus giganteus*), a large, fruit-eating bat with a wingspan of up to eighty centimeters, which lives in large colonies, also lick the female's teats, in particular during the foreplay to copulation. There are no firm pair-bonds among these animals; the females are usually rather on the defensive so that the young males have to make great efforts before managing to mate. This is probably why an element from childish behavior, which can put the female into a tolerant frame of mind, appears during their foreplay to mating.[83]

At first the female bat tries to resist the courting male; but among other animals the female more often tries to run away from the male, and the male can counteract this by childish behavior too. An example are the waterbucks of Uganda. Comparison with related species helps to clarify in which functional context this specific behavior benefits the antelope.

The group of ungulates, which is very rich in species, includes many different forms of corporate life between male, female, and young. The bonds between the sexes range through nearly every possible gradation. We find a minimum of solidarity among giraffes, where not even mother and child remain together for long, and the maximum with some duikers, who are monogamous throughout their life. Among most of the species, however, the sexes only meet for mating. It is very common for the females to live in fairly large herds, together with their young, and for the males either to form their own herds or for each male to defend his own territory. When in heat, the females then come into these territories.

The male who succeeds in mating with most females has most progeny, and is therefore favored by selection. But in each reproductive cycle the females are mated several times; so several males can come in question as the father. The probability of a certain male conceiving his progeny with a particular female naturally increases with the number of potential copulatory acts he himself manages to perform during her cycle. This means that he must do his best to prevent rivals from getting at the female. His primary weapon is his territory, in which no male will tolerate rivals. The boundaries are established beforehand by combat, and even when a female is in a neighboring territory, another male will not try to cross the borders. However, this is only half the problem solved. Since the territorial borders only apply to the males, a female could decide to move in with a neighboring male instead. The males of all species try to prevent the female from doing so by various means. Usually they circle around the female or females—who often arrive in groups—try to bar their way or to impress them, and even threaten them. Among the defassa waterbucks (*Kobus defassa ugandae*), the males hold territories extending from twelve hectares to two square kilometers, each closely bordering on the next, in which young males and all the young females wander about. The calves are also born in the territory of an adult male. During the first two to four weeks of its life the calf remains hidden in a special place; this keeps its mother tied to the area too and thus to the territory of the male where her calf was born. Since the next reproductive cycle begins during this same period, although it only lasts a day, the respective territory-owning male has no difficulties in keeping the female in heat close to him.[110]

The Uganda kob (*Adenota kob thomasi*) is closely related to the defassa waterbuck. But the males' territories are extremely small and only have a diameter of fifteen to thirty meters or even less. They too are closely adjoining, thus creating a male colony of mating territories that is fairly large at the borders and becomes smaller and smaller

A young Uganda kob sucking from its mother (left) and adult bucks in the sequel to copulation (right).

toward the center of the colony, until eventually fifteen or more territories are crowded together in an area of a diameter of about two hundred meters. The females prefer the center of the colony with the smallest territories; most mating occurs in the inner three or four territories. But here the danger of the female moving over to a neighboring male is very great. The Uganda kob bucks counter this by a special behavior. First, no feature of the foreplay of mating of this species looks at all like a threat that could drive off the female; since the foreplay to mating of most antelopes is full of threatening gestures, this "foresight" on the part of the Uganda kob is very striking. In addition, he is the only one to have a special sequel to mating, which can last up to five minutes (copulation itself lasts at most two seconds). While the female stands quiet the buck licks her teats or the inguinal glands, which are directly beside them; he does so by pushing his head either between her straddled back legs or under her abdomen from the side like a suckling calf. This behavior also contributes toward preventing the female from crossing over into neighboring territories and enables the same male to copulate again after a brief pause. Consequently most females only visit three or four males, i.e., much fewer than would be expected at first.[12]

There is no doubt in these cases that the maternal source of milk has a social significance for the adult animals. It can already acquire it for the animal in its early youth. For among mammals, the mother, who at first is the only one to provide food, is therefore also the most important social partner of the newborn animal. Generally, those maternal signals that herald food also acquire the additional significance of marks of protection and security, above all among species who suckle their young for a long time. One can observe this among ungulates. Young antelopes who are suddenly frightened often run to the mother and grasp her teats, even at an age when they would not normally drink from her any more. This "comfort suckling" is also known of the European deer. When the doe, alarmed by a cry of fear from her young, has freed it from an enemy or even fled with it, the young animal will suck briefly and be licked intensively by the mother. Drinking and cleaning are typical of every encounter between mother and offspring in the first three to five months after birth. The doe licks the fawn, particularly around the rear, and this light "massage" intensifies the young animal's search for the teat and desire to drink. Licking reappears later in a different context: After copulation the buck and the doe lie down for a while, then stand up and lick each other reciprocally. This contact behavior corresponds entirely to that of the male Uganda kob after mating; among deer it also serves to keep the partners together, for the buck remains with his doe for a long time, up to nine months.[66]

Young marsupials are born fairly unformed; the offspring of the giant kangaroo are born after only one month of pregnancy. They continue to grow in the pouch, where they sometimes remain for six months and into which they manage to crawl from the birth aperture without help. In the pouch they take the teat into their mouth and cling to it firmly. Later, when they occasionally peer out of the pouch, they still keep the teat in their mouth most of the time. Young kangaroos who have already left the pouch flee back into it at the first sign of danger. But when they have reached a certain size the mother no longer allows her young to return to the pouch; then the young kangaroo confines itself to sticking its head in it (see p. 73). The "comforting effect" of this behavior is not so obvious here, however, since the young are not weaned until after sexual maturity; so it can happen that a female animal already has one young one in her pouch while she herself still sucks from her own mother, and, in the meantime, a "little sister" is already clinging to the other teat. In the foreplay to mating the male sniffs the genital zone and the pouch aperture of the female. He finds special scent glands there which, as far as we know, play a part in mating behavior.

As a rule mammals have scent glands both in the genital region and also beside the teats, whose smell is automatically learned by the baby; later, this scent can become fairly important to mating behavior or even in more general social life.

Man also possesses a scent-producing organ, namely the axillary organ. It is particularly highly developed among women and consists of an extensive complex of scent glands under the arm. This scent organ is not so well-developed among any monkeys, so it is certainly not a mere remnant left to us by our prehuman ancestors, but an evolutionary feature typical of man. This suggests that it is of significance in the social communication between mother and child and between man and woman. Indeed, we already know that olfactory signals play a considerable role for man and that the sensitivity of women to certain scents varies with the menstrual cycle. It would be important to discover more about this, and to compare it with the olfactory signals of animals. Unfortunately this is difficult for us, because we are unable to perceive many chemical stimuli and because analysis of chemical substances is very time-consuming as well as being more awkward than that of sounds or colors, for example. That is why the following examples are probably easier for us to understand, concerned as they are with sight-oriented animals, i.e., those who are guided predominantly by their eyes. But the nose still plays a part, even with man ("He stinks." . . . "This stinks."); only there are clearly visible signals besides the smells.

The young of the gray woolly monkey from South America (*Lagothrix lagotricha*) are suckled for eighteen months. During this time the main purpose of suckling gradually shifts from feeding to comforting. By the age of six months, the young monkey is only suckled before going to sleep and two or three times during the day, usually to console it after some excitement or shock.[127] For a young monkey six weeks old the maternal breast already represents a signal, which the mother uses deliberately when she calls it if it sets off to seek adventure. She lifts her arms and shows it her rather large, full breast. (The young monkeys will also go to other well-known females and occasionally also suckle there.)

It is fairly certain that an olfactory component enters into play here too. The body odor of woolly monkeys is strongest on the breast. In the first four weeks of its life, the baby clings to the dense breast fur of the mother and learns its smell. Later, when the young monkey makes friends with other members of the colony, it begins by seeking out the highest-ranking males and cuddles up against their chest. According to observations made by Williams, the familiar smell of the breast plays an important part both in the relations between mother and child and also in mating, and even in the greeting between adult males. Moreover, the entire living area, in particular that of the adult males of a colony, is marked with "chest rubbing"; the monkey smears saliva on certain places and objects with the lips, and then spreads it around with upward thrusting movements of the chest until eventually his chest is dripping wet. Females do this much less often, the high-ranking ones slightly more often than others. The chest of the male is usually matted and has bark-colored spots from his habit of marking trees.[127]

Many young monkeys of all kinds can be seen sleeping with their mother's teat in their mouth. But even when they are awake, they seek shelter there. If they have strayed far from their mother they rush back to her in face of an often imaginary danger, hold onto her, and grasp a teat with their lips; they do not then suckle, however, but instead twist their head around far enough to be able to see in the direction of the danger. Rheus monkeys, African tree monkeys, and baboons, to mention only a few, all do this. The children often hold the teat in their mouth without sucking even when no danger is looming. This is known of the ring-tailed lemur (*Lemur catta*), a half-ape, too. The maternal teat simply has an appeasement effect. This is why it is difficult to say exactly how long baby monkeys continue to drink from their mother. Observations made in the wild by Jane van Lawick-Goodall[72] have taught us that chimpanzee

A young African vervet seeking shelter at its mother's breast.

babies drink every ninety minutes up to the age of a year and a half. But one still sees six-month-old chimpanzee babies drink much more often, every quarter of an hour, in fact. That is because this is the age when they begin going out on short forays, and since they are still frightened of any number of things, they keep running back to the mother to seek comfort at her breast, often only for a few seconds. They also grasp the teat when a playmate tries to pull them away from their mother or to annoy them in some other way. Three-year-old chimpanzees are still suckled about once an hour. The children are weaned automatically when they are 3½ because the mother is then able to conceive again and her milk dries up. The children still try to drink from the mother a few times and then give up. Sons leave their mother off and on for a few days when they are about six years old. But close relations are maintained between mother and son even when he is adult; the son comes to his mother's aid if she is threatened by other chimpanzees and the mother shares her food with her son.

Among chimpanzees, then, the female breast has a social significance for the child, but not, so far as we know to date, for adults. But there are signs that it has among other monkeys, such as some African tree monkeys, where the female teats are strikingly colored in certain phases of her cycle, no matter whether she has offspring or not. Since monkeys are very sharp observers, one must assume that the males at least learn to value the teat coloring of the female as an indication of her readiness for mating. This has not yet been studied. There is one monkey, however, for whom the female breast has become an unmistakable social signal. This is the red-chested gelada baboon (*Theropithecus gelada*), who is not in fact a baboon at all but more closely related to the African tree monkeys. The importance of the breast as a signal is evident among other primates too. The breast of the female ring-tailed lemur is almost hairless while she is suckling, so that a black patch of skin is visible in her fur, which is otherwise light gray. Among female tree monkeys who have already borne young, the teats always jut out from the fur; they are red and placed so close together that the baby can suck on both at the same time. The red-chested gelada baboon acquired its name from a large hairless patch on its chest. The patch is divided up into two zones by the fur that grows in from the side. The smaller upper zone is like an inverted triangle, with the lower point touching the point of the inverted heart-shaped zone below it. The naked skin varies from pale red to bright blood-red, and surrounding fur is gray brown. The whole effect can become extremely striking, for on the border of the fur the "*décolleté*" is entirely surrounded by wrinkled folds of skin that can turn almost white and then look like a *ruche*. Again both teats lie close together in the lower heart-shaped area and can, according to the phase of the sexual cycle, become bright red in contrast to the paler skin.

The gelada baboon lives in the mountains of Ethiopia at a height of some three or four thousand meters. It forms bands consisting of harem groups, i.e., a male and several females with her young. They seek their food on the high plateaus, preferably while seated. In this position the chest is very conspicuous. We know that these baboons do not merely carry this physical signal about on them and let it have its effect, but exploit it deliberately in face of conspecifics, pushing out their chest at a partner from the group in a similar way to woolly monkeys. Several observations also suggest that they can underline this by pointing their finger at their own breast. Since these animals have not yet been sufficiently well studied, we do not know yet what effect this signal has on the partner—perhaps it is appeasing, or promises protection and comfort. We can assume that the baby is automatically exposed to this signal when it drinks, like the babies of other animal species who are exposed to the scent signals near the teats. What is certain is that the female breast is a socially important signal for adult gelada baboons and that it has even undergone certain changes in the service of this function, namely becoming more conspicuous. It has acquired a new significance without losing the old one, and the new significance is built up on the old.

There are numerous examples to show how the outer form of an organ changes when it acquires an additional function. Organs and the responses addressed to such organs by the members of a species are quite often to a large extent emancipated from their original purpose in the animal kingdom. Nature or the Creator sees no reason not to introduce an existing "invention" elsewhere too if it can be of use there. Often this upsets the attempts at classification of men who would like to separate organs neatly according to their functions. In the end there will presumably be nothing for it but for man to accept the natural order he finds and to adapt his classifications to it.

Originally, no doubt, breast and teats only served to nourish the infant. They have now acquired not only an additional function in social life but have been exploited in other directions too, for instance by bats, in particular the small insect-eating bats. This order of mammals, very rich in different species, includes the group of horseshoe bats (*Rhinolophoidea*), to which the native European horseshoe bat also belongs (*Rhinolophus*). The animals took their name from the curious "sonar" system on their nose, which serves them for ultrasonic echo-location. In general bats only produce one young, which is why they only have one pair of teats. Formerly, mammals had a number of teats, like pigs, arranged in two rows along the abdomen, and the milk gland formed a long milk line. Among many mammals the length of the milk gland together with the number of teats decreases according to the number of young. The remaining teats can be located near the back legs as with cows, goats, horses, and antelopes, or in front on the trunk as with monkeys, elephants, and bats. In fact, horseshoe bats have another pair of teats between their back legs too; the milk gland beneath them has shriveled up, but among some species the teats themselves are very large and jut far out of the fur. These teats have become specialized as dummies; the young bat takes one of them firmly in its mouth and then rests upright against its mother, who is hanging head down. For drinking, it turns around and goes to one of the front teats, which provide milk. The mother can already take the young bat with her on excursions in the first days after birth, when it attaches itself to one of the dummy teats. Young kangaroos hang onto a teat continually too, but they are also attached to the mother by her pouch. The "dry teats" of horseshoe bats no longer serve for feeding, but in a sense replace the pouch, by keeping the young firmly attached to its mother; they have even become specialized in terms of this attachment function.

The basis for this specialization is the fortuitous "transportation by teat" of the offspring, which we also know of various rodents. Female rats, mice, and squirrels who have had a sudden fright often drag their brood along with them for a certain distance simply because the young do not let go of the teats but remain hanging from them. Usually they fall off after a little while and are then brought back into the nest in the mother's mouth. Among one kind of vole, however (*Microtus incertis*), the female is said to sit over the young in cases of danger and to summon them to suck her teats, and then drags off the whole brood while they are suckling. The young of the wood rat (*Neotoma fuscipes*) hold onto the teats so firmly that the mother can make long leaps with them; the milk teeth of these young are bent into special gripping organs, which fit the teats exactly.[27] Since these animals have many offspring, all the teats are used for suckling; horseshoe bats, by contrast, can leave some teats for conversion into organs of transport.

Infant baboons, rhesus monkeys, and langurs do not only cling to the fur of the mother when she sets off but also hold onto a teat with their mouth. These examples show once again how physical structure depends on behavior: When the mother has to take the young with her and they hold onto the teat, the teats, which were originally meant for suckling, can be transformed into organs of transport. But the same also applies to the original function. Female mammals have not become the more important of the two parents in the care of the newborn baby simply because they possess milk glands; rather the milk glands have become fully developed on the female because it is she who is bound most closely to the young, for the males are also equipped with milk glands.

23. Special Behavior Patterns of the Infant Animal

It is common to classify young animals as either nest-huggers (nidicolous) or nest-fleers (nidifugous). Nest-huggers come into the world relatively undeveloped, often with closed eyes, without fur or teeth, and unable to walk. Nest-fleers, by contrast, are so well developed that they can follow the parent animal or even live by themselves. Kangaroos, bats, and monkeys, however, do not fit either of these categories; their young are born unfinished, but they are not placed in a nest; instead they remain on the body of the mother or of other adults, who carry them around. Manlike apes build sleeping nests, but they never leave the young in them. Chimpanzee babies remain in constant contact with the mother's body during the first four or five months following birth![72]

This very close contact between parents and offspring has given rise to several other behavior elements besides the significance of the maternal breast; these elements acquire an important role in later social life. For example, among monkeys, this includes the well-known reciprocal "delousing" or allogrooming. Originally this was a behavior pattern the mother addressed to her child. Among gorillas, three times as much allogrooming occurs between mother and child as between adults. Among chimpanzees, however, it is the reverse—not because chimpanzee mothers care less intensively for their young but because grooming between

Male doguera baboon performing brood-tending ("delousing") on a young one (left); social grooming between
adult female hamadryas baboons (right). The grooming
female has a large estrus-swelling (see pp. 208f.).

adults has increased to a corresponding degree; one-third
of all allogrooming actions among chimpanzees takes place
between adult males and adult females.[95]

This mutual fur-care is known to anyone who has ever
watched zoo monkeys, such as macaques or baboons. A
more exact analysis will show that the "delousing" partners
do not meet haphazardly. Among rhesus monkeys, for instance, it is mothers and their offspring who prefer to
delouse each other, even if the offspring is already adult.
They can be joined by good friends of the mother, and
this creates loose- or tight-knit grooming communities within
the society.[96]

Among adults, allogrooming appears to inhibit attack and
is used in those situations that could easily lead to disputes,
in order to appease a higher-ranking animal; it occurs very
often between the female and her mate during the mating
season. There are distinct postures for the invitation to
allogrooming, but the males can also respond to presentation (see p. 207) by allogrooming. The more fully these
conditions are studied on increasingly numerous species of
monkeys, the more clearly we discern the great social sig-

nificance of this action, which also derives from brood-tending.[63, 109]

The same evolution has occurred independently among the half-apes. They too have converted the maternal grooming of young into an important social action, but they groom predominantly with their teeth, while the higher monkeys use their hands.[51]

When a baboon or macaque mother has weaned her offspring and no longer lets it drink from her breast, one sometimes sees a young one sitting in front of its mother

A young doguera baboon trying to reach the mother's teats.

and stretching its hand out to her breast. I saw doguera baboon children in the wild who reached out for food that the mother had in her mouth or was taking into her mouth. Occasionally they also reached for the mother's face, which was then turned to them. From these gestures there has now developed a "begging gesture," like that of zoo mon-

Hamadryas baboon (above) and chimpanzee stretching out an open hand in "begging."

keys toward visitors. The animals learn to convert the original grasping attempt into a calm, expectant raising of the hand. Macaques living in the wild use this as a begging gesture toward conspecifics; chimpanzees too, both young and adult, stretch out their hand to a member of their species who has food, and some of what they desire is then placed in their hand. Even high-ranking chimpanzee males beg lower-ranking ones who had a lucky hunt for meat.[72] An adult male hamadryas baboon in Munich Zoo did not only employ the usual pasha methods but also used his hand, laid open on the ground in the direction of his female, as an invitation to her to come to him or to stay with him. Chimpanzees eventually command agreement or social support with this gesture; a lower-ranking animal who wants to go past a higher-ranking one to a tree with fruit stretches out its hand to the higher-ranking one and waits until the latter lays its finger on the hand or some other part of the body of the beggar in agreement. Opening up the hand, stretching out the hand, and, finally, pressing the hand, give encouragement or support in tense situations.[72]

It is tempting, although not yet clearly proved, to assume that these manual gestures go back to early childhood when the young one grasps its mother. More exact long-term observations will no doubt tell us more. It is already known that hand-foot contacts act as encouragement and signify agreement and greeting among chimpanzees, as does reciprocal touching of the genitals. The following social behavior patterns are more obviously derived from childhood.

For a mother-hugger like a young monkey it is particularly important to hold on and, if danger threatens and it is far from its mother, to rush back to her immediately and cling to her so that she can carry it with her on her flight. This behavior survives into old age: Adult male baboons and chimpanzees who are scared or faced with danger or an unknown thing that frightens them look around for a friendly comrade, go up to him, and embrace him. Before an attack on an enemy predator or at the onset of a violent quarrel within the herd one can see large male baboons falling around each other's necks uttering soothing sounds. Even the young animal who has been weaned, first seeks refuge with another female and larger males; this can lead to individual friendships, in which gestures of greeting taken from brood-tending behavior play an important role. The success of such friendships is based on the mutual "protective help" that often lasts well into old age. Gestures of embrace and clutching to the breast derive from maternal behavior, which one partner uses in response to the other's search for refuge.

Among hamadryas baboons, other brood-tending elements besides these play a major part in the structure of the harem society.[63] Males also take part in brood-tending (see illustration, p. 187), particularly the young males. Orphans are usually adopted by half-grown males and brought up by them. At the onset of sexual maturity, the males take young females to themselves and treat them like a mother her child: They carry them against their body, take them on their back to jump over crevices in the rocks, guard them, and continually clutch them like a mother her child (males punish adult females with bites if they stray too far). These young females flee to their male protector in case of danger, cuddle up to him like children to their mother, and also call him with the call of the lost child. The male builds up a firm relationship with females who are not yet sexually mature with the help of this mother-child behavior; sexual behavior can remain absent for years, until the female is sexually mature.

By contrast, the young male can take up sexual relations with the females of an existing harem (see p. 227), and it is easier the younger he is. This way of life as an additional male on the borders of a harem group is extremely advantageous, for it means that the young male acquires the varied experience of paths and places of the old pasha and finally takes over the whole harem when the pasha abdicates and gives up his monopoly over the females. Yet the old animal continues to remain in the group, which is now led by the younger male, and he is still of use when situations crop up with which the young baboon cannot yet cope, perhaps because he has never before encountered them. Then the young baboon does not precede the troupe as leader but waits for the grizzled expasha to take over the leadership again. We find the same principle among doguera baboons: These animals have a "council of elders" who are no longer the highest-ranking group leaders and no longer have a prerogative in reproduction.[63]

24. Change of Function of Sexual Behavior

Permanent corporate life between two or more individuals is obviously a recent stage of development and, as always in evolution, the necessary adjustments are not "invented" *ad hoc* but derive from existing behavior. Behavior patterns taken from brood-tending are addressed to conspecifics; they agree neither with aggression against these conspecifics nor with flight behavior before them but are well suited for neutralizing aggression and flight tendencies in a society. Lorenz has stressed *redirected aggression* as another pair-bonding mechanism, which plays a role in the mating behavior of cichlid and graylag geese pairs.[75] Redirection means that the aggressive tendencies of one partner toward the other are deflected from the latter to a third party; the first partner is often infected and joins in too. This "come on, let's both get that one" behavior has some drawbacks, however: It binds two individuals at the price of their good relations with a third one and very often requires that a third be there in the first place. There are cases, again among monogamous cichlids, where a pair disintegrates for lack of such an outside "whipping boy," because the partners now direct their aggressive tendencies at each other after all. Now the different forms of pair-bonding are not mutually exclusive, and the same animal can exhibit both redirected aggression and functionally changed brood-tending actions.

There is a third root of pair-bonding behavior, namely the

sexual relations between the partners. Sexual behavior is also addressed at conspecifics, and it is equally irreconcilable with open attack or open flight. Australian finches offer a good example of the role that functionally changed sexual behavior can play in pair-bonding and social life.

Tropical finches are clearly followers of civilization and are therefore fairly easy to observe in the wild. In addition, they stand out by their very sociable way of life, which aroused the interest of behavior researchers. Immelmann has devoted extensive studies to the eighteen Australian species of this finch, and found, among other facts, the following.[48]

Far from the brooding places the animals live in flocks in which unmated animals of both sexes find their partner. Pair-bonding is usually initiated by the male with his song and preliminary courtship displays. If a male sings to a female who is already mated and at the same time slowly hops up to her, either he is attacked—or the female flees. But a female ready for mating shows her agreement by responding with weak greeting or courting movements. Among the zebra finches (*Taeniopygia guttata*) and the star finch (*Neochimia ruficauda*) pair-formation has taken place as soon as the partners cuddle up to each other or allopreen. In every case it is the female who decides whether to accept the male's advances or not; females who particularly want to mate can also invite the males to court. Most species seem to live monogamously, but the degree of cohesion of the partners varies: Diamond finch, red-eared finch, fire-tail finch, gouldian finch, and crimson finch are largely solitary, and the partners remain fairly independent even in the brooding time; however, among long-tailed and masked finches (*Poephila acuticauda* and *Poephila personata*), both partners always follow each other blindly, even when they are in flocks outside the brooding time. The flocks or groups are most characteristic of the steppe species, least so of the species that live in forests.

Shortly before sunset, the groups dissolve. Group coherence is an advantage for life in dry regions where the animals can only brood at certain times and sometimes have to go far afield to find food, and this coherence contributes much to the reciprocal stimulus and synchronization of the brood-pairs. Most species, therefore, continue to live socially during the brooding season. In many colonies real friendships come into being between pairs of neighbors.

Above all it is the special "social hours" of the day that serve to keep the group together; these periods are partly devoted to a communal search for food. The "socials" of masked amadines are the most highly developed instance. They are held at any desired spot as soon as several pairs from the large brooding colony meet: First the partners of each pair sit together allopreening, at a distance of a few centimeters from the next pair. After several minutes, isolated animals separate from their partner, hop up to a neighboring pair, and begin to "help" preen there. Gradually the whole group comes into motion, new partners keep coming together, and in the end almost every member of the group has preened every other one. This "social," in which six to ten pairs usually take part, lasts from thirty to sixty minutes. Eventually the brood-pairs come together again and the partners fly back to their nest together.

We have already spoken of the social significance of allopreening (see pp. 145ff.). The masked finch displays other special behavior forms during its "socials" too. Each newly arriving pair is greeted by rapid movements of the tail feathers, which quiver up and down vertically; all the pairs greet one another by quivering their tail feathers in this way. But this tail-quivering also occurs in a quite different behavior context, namely at the end of a series of courtship displays as the female invitation to copulation. This invitation to copulation, which is unusual among small birds, is peculiar to all tropical finches. Tail-quivering is widespread in this context, so it is no doubt the earlier behavior.

The tail-quivering of the masked amadine is both a female invitation to copulation and a general social greeting.

Among masked finches it has also become a gesture of greeting; this means that, although it looks identical in the two cases, it serves two entirely different purposes. But there is a difference in the choice of addressee: Between marital partners, tail-quivering occurs at the end of courtship as an invitation to copulation, and the female directs it at her male. As a gesture of greeting within a group, it occurs exclusively between members of the species who are not partners. When marital partners greet each other in a group, they perform a very low courtship bow. For tail-quivering to act as an invitation to copulation, the animals must, therefore, know each other as intimately as only the partners of a pair usually do; otherwise it will have the effect of a greeting. The partners of a pair have evidently chosen a different behavior pattern as greeting—namely the courtship bow—because they always see tail-quivering as an invitation to copulation. But masked finches bred in captivity consider all tail-quivering, even when meant as a greeting, as a summons to copulation. Perhaps this is because they are all compelled to know one another only too well in the confined space in which they live. Hereupon the males try to mate with each female who greets them. What is also striking is that only the female uses tail-quivering as a prelude to copulation, whereas both sexes use it for social greeting. So it can mean two things if done by the female, but if the male does so it can only be a greeting.

How has it happened that what was originally a purely sexual pattern of behavior occurs in group situations at all? So far we have only begun to answer this problem. It is likely that group life as such, which as we know serves the reciprocal stimulus and synchronization of the brood-pairs, is slightly sexual in tone. The "socials" we have described give the animals an opportunity for a kind of social courtship, and individual courtship actions have become freed from this context, which was originally strictly sexual, and become emancipated—now they serve to keep the group together. Some even occur more frequently outside the re-productive season than during the brooding period, so they must have become fairly independent of sexual mood.

The social groups of tropical finches, as we have shown, consist in part of young animals who have not yet mated, but also usually of firm pairs, who stay together outside the brooding season too. And if the solidarity of the group is strengthened by functionally changed sexual behavior patterns, the same applies to the solidarity of the pair. There are some behavior patterns that clearly serve pair-bonding, such as the courtship bow toward the partner, with the tail often turned to the partner too. This bow derives from nest-building behavior; it is a firm component of the foreplay to copulation, but also occurs throughout the year as an exaggerated greeting between the partners of a pair, and in rather weaker form as a general greeting between the members of a group.

The same applies to song, which primarily serves as a form of address to a female. It has a purely sexual significance and in a pair-bond it serves to stimulate and woo the female. Besides this there is the so-called "undirected song," which indicates a very slightly sexual mood, differs from the courting song only in its slowness and the longer intervals between the individual phrases, and is never directed at a conspecific. But among many species it serves to keep the group together. First, it has an infectious effect, so that other males also start to sing, preferably while perched close beside the first singer. Females do this too, and adult males even sit beside young birds who have not yet molted but who already sing. So we are evidently not dealing with "singing lessons." The listening attitude is very strongly marked among spice finches, mannikin finches (*Lonchura*), and some other kinds. While the singer continues its song as though alone, other members of the species sit down in front of and beside it, stretch out their neck till their head is close to the beak of the singer, as though actually lending an ear, and remain motionless in this position for a time. Sometimes the listeners quarrel about the best seat or even stand in a line so that if one bird flies off another can move up. Some singers are clearly favorites, and they are usually closely surrounded, while others almost always sing alone. Females listen only to males, not to their own sex. This behavior is not found among masked amadines.

I have listed in the bibliography other examples of originally sexual behavior patterns that have been transferred to the general social field among birds.[48] The examples quoted here may suffice to clarify the general principle.

The transfer of sexual behavior patterns into the social realm is not, of course, confined to the kingdom of birds. It also occurs from the lowest to the highest vertebrates, i.e., from fish to monkeys. But unlike brood-tending, which is often easy to observe in captivity, higher forms of social life can only be adequately studied in the wild, since the conditions of captivity can falsify normal behavior. But observations in the wild are usually very difficult to achieve, and this is why we have sufficient details of the social behavior of only comparatively few animal species; however, results so far show that this will be an extremely fascinating field of inquiry.

Among fishes, we again know most about a family that the amateur loves very much. These are the cichlids (*Cichlidae*), of whom we have already discussed one representative, the orange chromide (see p. 149). In the last twelve years, we have examined forty-five species of cichlid from twenty-three different families in the Max Planck Institute and have compared their fights, their brood-tending, and their social behavior. Besides the harem-formers, the monogamous, and the nonmonogamous types, we also found a cichlid (*Tropheus moorii*), from Lake Tanganyika, who forms compact groups of several females and males and wanders along the wide, rocky shores of the lake in such shoals. If unknown members of the species come into the vicinity of the shoal, they are attacked and driven off, while the members of the shoal seem to keep peace among themselves. Exact observations under conditions as close to normal as possible in large aquaria showed, however, that members of a shoal are not quite as peaceful among themselves as would seem at first sight. Unless the animals are just taking a siesta, it may even happen that every few minutes one will swim up to another and threaten it with outspread fins. The strongest male does this most frequently. Normally such behavior will not lead to a fight, for the threatened fish reacts by placing itself broadside in front of the aggressor, turning its head diagonally up, dropping its tail and bending it slightly away from the opponent, spreading its pelvic fins out to brake, and gently shaking the tail end of its body from side to side or quivering its entire body. This "tail-beat" (*rütteln*) appeases the partner, who thereupon desists from further attack and swims on its way.

Anyone familiar with the over-all behavior repertory of this fish will have come across the "tail-beat" before, al-

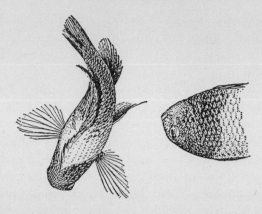

The tail-beating of the *Tropheus* cichlid is both a male display movement and a general social appeasement gesture.

though in a totally different context. Indeed, it is one of
the most frequent behavior patterns of the courting male
and also occurs when he ejects sperm after the female has
deposited the eggs. It occurs as a courtship movement
among many related kinds of cichlid too, but always on
the part of the male and only if he owns a territory, if
he is ready to spawn, and if in addition a female who is
also ripe comes to him. This clearly shows that tail-beating
is a sexual behavior pattern. More distantly related cichlids,
for instance the *Pelmatochromis* species, where it is the
female who courts, have taken these movements very far.
Here the female bends herself into a U-shape and stretches
out to her partner her convex flank, which is marked with
a bright red area of color. This colored mark on her abdomen has a bite-inhibiting effect, as experiments have
shown, and the whole "belly dance" has the effect of appeasing the male, who is generally fairly aggressive. The
relatives of the *Tropheus* cichlid we mentioned also have
a red or yellowish-red spot of color on their flank; in this
case the males are also the ones to do the courting. The
Tropheus cichlid itself is black with a yellowish-red band
of color around the middle that can light up in the space

of seconds if the animal is courting, and disappears again equally rapidly after the reproductive act.

In all the species we have just discussed the sexes are easily distinguished because of this courtship coloring or display dress. But this is not so for *Tropheus,* where the females also have a display dress. They do not in fact court, nor do they need this display dress for their reproductive behavior. But here the typical courtship movement, tail-beating, also serves to create agreement within the group, as we have seen, and in this context the female certainly does need it. Males and females tail-beat as often as they are threatened by fellow members of the group and quite independently of whether there are or are not any animals in the group ready to mate. In addition, appeasement tail-beating occurs among young animals, long before they reach sexual maturity. This proves that tail-beating has become largely if not completely divorced from sexual excitement. Anyone who expects early progeny after the violent "courtship" of these animals will discover this to his disappointment—for it cannot even be said with certainty whether both sexes are in fact represented in the group. I was disappointed too until I understood the circumstances, which comforted me very soon, since the animals did eventually reproduce.

Within the social group, *Tropheus* uses tail-beating in order to inhibit aggression. The male *Tropheus* tail-beats both in a sexual context, i.e., during courtship and insemination, and in a nonsexual context, in order to appease an aggressor. In both cases the movement looks the same. The female *Tropheus,* who does not court, only uses this movement for appeasement in a social context. For the behavior researcher this means that behavior sequences as a whole must be kept in sight if he wants to decide whether the same movement means courtship or appeasement. In addition, he must remember that externally the female resembles the male. This is remarkable because the male and female *Tropheus* often play very different roles in their reproductive behavior and because all cichlids where this is the case have very distinct males and females. The more difference there is between the behavior of male and female, the greater are the sexual differences. Among species where the female alone tends the brood while the males court, fight for a mating territory, and inseminate the eggs, this has led to males and females being described as belonging to different species simply because they look so very different. With *Tropheus* too, only the male courts; the female takes the eggs into her mouth, broods them there for some forty days, and later also takes the young into her mouth in cases of danger, while the male pays no attention to them. But in spite of this great difference in behavior, the sexes look the same. This makes it clear that there must have been a strong evolutionary tendency against the formation of sexual differences. Everything points to the fact that this tendency derived from social life. So far *Tropheus* is the only species of cichlids to lead this kind of social life. In it the male courtship movement plays a special, secondary role; this applies not only to the movement itself but also to the display dress accompanying it. With the help of the physiological color changes that are so common among fish, the display dress can change; yet special color cells must exist for each coloring as well as for the corresponding nerve fibers. That the female *Tropheus* possesses both can only be explained by the fact that she needs both for social life within the group.

It is now possible for us to give a rough estimate of how important this functionally changed courtship movement is to the species. Tail-beating in a social context must be just as important as the great external difference between the sexes is among related species; for this tendency toward distinct sexual differentiation among nonsocially living species is balanced out by the other tendency to eliminate sexual differences among species where tail-beating, which is socially important, occurs. Later we shall cite examples of comparable cases where sexual differentiation can even be eliminated retroactively in the interests of social life. This could also be true of *Tropheus,* i.e., that with its ancestors who did not yet live socially males and females were clearly distinguished from each other and that the females only came to resemble the males afterward. From what we know of these animals now, however, this is unlikely, nor would it make much difference in the problem discussed here in any case. So we find the same principle of sexual behavior forms transferred to the social field even among cold-blooded vertebrates. The following examples will show that the principle is also valid for the most highly developed vertebrates.

The spotted hyena (*Crocuta*) from Africa is a very curious mammal. It is ugly and branded as a coward, and from among the very many different sounds it utters people always stress the "demonic" laughter to which it gives vent when excited. If we add to this the sinister teeth that act like shears and that are capable of breaking apart even the thickest bones, we gradually create a picture of a truly horrible nightmarish monster. This supposed "monster" is in fact very easy to tame and when adult will remain trustworthy as a dog. This alone goes to show that the spotted hyena is a social animal, for only they can attach themselves to man as a substitute parent and accept him as a social companion. (Besides the spotted hyena there is also the striped hyena, but it has none of the following features in common with the spotted hyena.) Studies made in recent years by Kruuk have adjusted the image we had of this animal a little.[70] The spotted hyena is a very social animal; it lives in fixed territories in packs of ten to a hundred individuals, and each pack has a central resting place and hollows in the earth where the young are first lodged. Contrary to popular belief, hyenas do not only eat carrion but also hunt living zebras and gnus. They assemble into a pack of several animals, usually toward evening, after spending the day resting in a mudhole in the shade of a tree or some other protected place. The members of a pack know one another and greet whenever they meet, even when they assemble for the hunt in the evening. The members of a group stay peaceful among themselves when devouring their prey, but if animals from another group come up there will immediately be quarreling or even open warfare.

Since the time of Aristotle, legend has had it that spotted hyenas can change their sex at wish, which is why they laugh so often. Even today the Bantus and some white hunters still believe that these animals are hermaphrodites. The reason for this error is that in fact males and females can hardly be distinguished externally, since their sexual organs look the same from the outside. Older females who have already had several litters have much larger teats than males and the birth opening is enlarged; but this is not very noticeable because it is not located where one would have expected to find it. The females also have two clearly visible scrotum pouches immediately under the anus, just like the males, except that they do not contain testicles but simply fatty and connective tissues.[19] In front of this, on the abdomen, the female has a penis just like the male; because of its somewhat different anatomical construction one should really call it a pseudopenis, but in this context the following is more important: The pseudopenis of the female can hang just like that of the male with its tip almost touching the ground. In addition it can be erected. The skin of the pseudopenis surrounds the birth passage, which therefore opens in front at the tip. This seems highly impractical, for normally young mammals leave the body of the mother by the shortest possible route after they have passed through the pelvis. But hyena babies can only reach the open via a birth passage that curves 180 degrees forward. What is surprising is that these babies are extremely well-developed for a predator. Their eyes are already open,

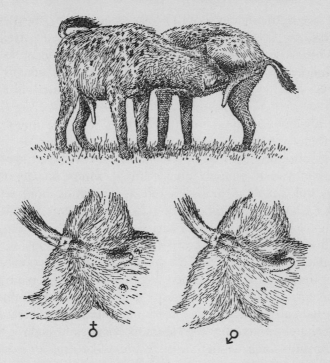

♂ ♀

The external genitals of the male and female spotted hyena look almost the same (below). They play an important role in the socially appeasing greeting ceremony of these animals (above).

they have cut their incisors and canines, and they can walk, albeit somewhat shakily.

Hyenas are probably relatives of the larger cats, which include civets. Among these cats there are several species where the differences in the external male and female genitals are very slight. But the coincidence is never as great as with the spotted hyena. And it is very likely that this coincidence developed in connection with their social life. In any case it plays a large part in it. The external genitals have a decisive importance in the friendly greeting between members of a group.[120]

If two spotted hyenas who know each other meet, they persistently lick and sniff each other's genitals, at the base of which also lie the teats and special scent glands, so that the whole area is socially very significant. This area is displayed conspicuously to the partner: the animal lifts the hind leg nearest its partner and at the same time the penis or pseudopenis juts far out. So at first one cannot tell whether two males, two females, or a male and a female are greeting each other; one also sees this form of greeting between young animals and adults. It has an important appeasing function and is in effect a greeting of peace. A hyena who refuses this greeting to another runs the risk of being violently attacked or driven off.

This greeting derives from the pair-bonding behavior of the male, for the genitals of the female are, of course, not erect during copulation. But the position of the female genitals requires the male to adopt a special posture preparatory to mating, which we need not discuss in detail here either. Before mating the animals also sniff each other's anal zone, which is only vaguely hinted at during greeting. It is evident that part of the male foreplay to mating became a social gesture of greeting for both sexes here and that the reproductive organs play an important part in it. How the form of the females' organs changed for this purpose is not yet known, since no comparative observations have been made on related species of predators.

We know more about comparable greeting ceremonies among various Old World monkeys, i.e., all the monkeys that occur outside the Western Hemisphere. (They are sometimes called small-nosed monkeys in contrast to the wide-nosed monkeys of the New World.) It is presumed that the New World monkeys have retained more primitive traits, and that the Old World monkeys are therefore more modern and more highly developed; all the manlike apes also belong among them. The most familiar from our zoos are the baboons, in whose social behavior sexual signals play a very large part. Most mammal females adopt a typical posture when they invite the male to mate. They turn their hindquarters to him and bend their tail to the side or upward. But anyone who carefully observes a band of baboons will soon discover that by no means every individual who presents in front of another is female, and that the individuals to whom they present also react variously to it. This is because, as has been known for some time, presentation also acts as a gesture of social appeasement or as greeting by a lower-ranking animal to a higher-ranking companion. This greeting can take many different forms. There are all manner of transitions, from a brief swaying of the hindquarters during walking, to a short pause, during which the tail is slightly or very markedly bent to the side, and finally to the most remarkable position of all in which the animal puts its behind directly under the other's nose, looks at it backward over its shoulder, and sometimes even bends its forelegs and raises its hindquarters skyward. These considerable differences correspond to the rising intensity of the greeting, which in turn depends on how much higher in rank the greeted individual is and how close to the greeter. It makes no difference whether the greeting or greeted animal is male or female. Lower-ranking animals, whether male or female, present in front of high-ranking ones, no matter whether they are male or female. Since baboons live in compact bands, one can tell the ranking order of the members among themselves by observing how often each individual presents in front of each other animal.[63] The higher the rank of an individual, the more rarely will it present in front of others and the more often will they present to him.

One can tell the ranking order of a group of *Tropheus* cichlids in exactly the same way. The higher the rank of a fish, the more rarely will it tail-beat in front of the others and the more often will the others tail-beat in front of it. However, this tail-beat of *Tropheus* cichlids derives from

male sexual behavior, while the presentation of baboons
derives from female sexual behavior. But just as a female
Tropheus will very rarely court, a male baboon will very
seldom present before copulation. So, in the sexual context,
these behavior patterns are confined to one sex in each
case, whereas both sexes use them in a general social context.
And just as very young *Tropheus* cichlids already tail-beat,
baboon children who have not yet reached sexual maturity
can be seen presenting. Here too the greeting behavior has
been removed from its sexual context and has become largely
emancipated. When a baboon approaches another, stops in
front of it, turns its hindquarters toward it and lifts its tail,
remaining in this posture for a moment and then sitting
down, this is not an invitation to mating that received no
response, but a greeting to a superior, an acknowledgment
of rank. Directly afterward, the animals will often begin
to delouse each other's fur, which is to say, a social behavior
pattern derived from brood-tending follows directly upon
one derived from the sexual field. But the animals have not
experienced a change of mood in the meantime; they have
simply remained, so to speak, in a social mood.

We find presentation as a social gesture of greeting among
nearly all Old World monkeys, that is to say, baboons,
macaques, who include the rhesus monkey (*Macaca
mulatta*), langurs (*Trachypithecus* and *Presbytis*), and also
chimpanzees. This behavior is always ambivalent. It can be
a female invitation to mating, but usually it is a social
gesture of greeting that is not "meant" sexually.

During the rutting season the females of many species
develop a large red swelling of the naked areas of skin
around the genital orifice. This estrus-swelling reaches such
proportions among some baboons that the animal can
hardly sit down properly. The naïve observer often thinks
that animals in this phase are ill because of their curious
"growth" (see illustration, p. 187). In fact it shows the male
of the same species that the female is ready for mating. Nat-

urally this signal is presented to the male very insistently during the invitation to copulation. If we compare this with conditions among *Tropheus*, who also present a special color signal during courtship, we might ask whether it would not also be in the monkey's interests to use the same color signal for social greeting. Here the female fish imitates the male courtship dress when she uses the male courtship movements as greeting. In terms of their purely functional coincidence, we could deduce a working hypothesis from this for monkeys and expect the males to imitate the female rutting signal when they use the female invitation to copulation as a greeting. And, in fact, so they do.

This is easiest to see with the hamadryas baboon (*Papio hamadryas*) we very often find in zoos. Doguera baboons (*Papio doguera*) have a brownish-gray rump on which the red swelling only shines forth on rutting females. This color signal fades almost entirely as soon as the rutting period is over. The estrus-swelling of the hamadryas baboon, who is more highly specialized on the whole, is larger, and the rump remains red all the time. Among these animals, social presentation plays a very important role—more, it would seem, than with the doguera baboon. And this is why male hamadryas baboons have an equally bright red backside in imitation of the female rutting signal, although they use it not in a sexual connection but merely in a general social context. The females of many macaques, of the mangabey (*Cercocebus*), the gelada baboon, and the chimpanzee, also have striking genital coloring or swellings. But the hamadryas baboon is not the only monkey whose females have an estrus-swelling. And since most Old World monkeys can present as a gesture of greeting, one could expect the males of other species to imitate the female rutting signal too. Or, in simpler terms: If the striking coloring of the rump of male monkeys can be traced back to an imitation of the female rutting signal, then it should occur only among those species where the females have a colored rutting signal in the genital zone. This is indeed so.[124] Cases where only the females of some species of a fairly large related group have an estrus-swelling and where the males of these species, and only these species, have a very similar coloring or even swelling in the anal region, are particularly convincing. Among the many leaf-eating monkeys—guerezas, langurs, dusky langurs (*Semnopithecus*), long-nosed monkeys (*Nasalis*), doucs or variegated langurs (*Pygathrix*)—only a few have a female genital swelling, namely the green and the brown guerezas (*Procolobus verus* and *Colobus badius*). And the males have a swelling of the same shape! Young males, in particular, have such a good "imitation" of the

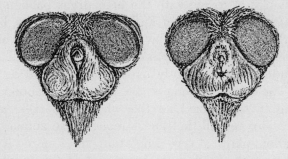

View of the buttocks of a red colobus monkey with genital swelling (left) and imitation of these female genitals on a young male (right).

female genital region that they are not easily recognized as males. Since, moreover, they often display to the adult males of their group,[62] nature seems to have attempted to make them mistakable for females here too, which can mean that young males are tolerated and not harmed in a group of adult males. At any rate there is no doubt that this signal is also borrowed from sexual behavior and put in the service of corporate life.

Plausible as it seems that monkeys should notice such a striking rutting signal with their sharp eyes, it seems equally implausible to many humans if they are told that these monkeys all allow themselves to be misled by an "imitation" of this signal to such a degree that they can take a male for a female. In fact it is due to the "poster" effect. It has been shown that when we buy goods even we humans prefer those car tires or beers that are offered to us on a poster or advertisement with an attractive girl in the background. Naturally we do not take the paper girl for a real girl, but she "pleases us"—the girl-signals she emanates put us in a more kindly, positive mood, which is in the interests of the offered object, that is to say of its manufacturer (for such automatic responses to signals, see pp. 262f.). And this is precisely what is achieved in the animal kingdom by the exploitation of certain signals. It is particularly clear with monkeys how effective this use of "imitation" is when we note that they are specially "manufactured." Since there are enough opportunities for comparison with other species, we know that the aforementioned coincidences between males and females are not by any chance due to the fact that they were never formed differently in the first place. Normally the differences are very much there, and they are only subsequently eliminated among some specialized species. Sometimes the signal is even produced on the male by other means: A red area of color, consisting of naked skin in the case of the female, can be imitated by red hair on the male.

We can observe what responses the signal elicits in the social partner. A baboon, macaque, or other species either does not react visibly at all to the presentation of a conspecific or gives a brief glance, or touches the proffered behind with its fingers, or sniffs it briefly, or cleans it, or stands up and takes it between its thighs, or mounts and makes a few copulatory movements, or actually copulates. This is a series of mating actions of increasing intensity. Which one will occur depends on many contingent circumstances. But it shows that the signal, even if not intended sexually, can still be taken sexually. It is very rarely meant sexually in a monkey society. But the more certain it is to elicit sexual responses, the more surely will it also suppress aggressive tendencies on the part of the receiver of the signal.

It is fairly certain that presentation does not have only the effect of appeasing aggression. If a member of the group is afraid of a higher-ranking member and would like to flee, the same signal can have a calming or even enticing effect because it recalls a female in rut, and it can even override the tendency to flight. Indeed, it can be observed, though more clearly for some species than others, that high-ranking animals sometimes present in front of lower-ranking ones, and that the latter then mount them. It is impossible to list all the possibilities registered so far; many of our investigations are only in the early stages. All we want to show here is that behavior elements and signals from the sexual realm can acquire new meanings in social life. For instance, presentation can appease aggression when addressed to a higher-ranking animal, or help overcome tendencies to flight when directed at a lower-ranking one, and, as a further step in this direction, it can finally become a social invitation to follow, that is, a quite general signal serving the coherence of the group, as when the pasha sets off and entices the others to follow him by motioning with his "female poster." High-ranking hamadryas baboon males do this during their so-called "swing step." They lift their tail and sway their behind from side to side in the rhythm of their big steps, and this can make the entire group suddenly set off after them.[64]

The more such new functions a signal or behavior pattern acquires, the more often will we see it occur. We have already shown this with "delousing" (see p. 209), to which the human observer usually reacts neutrally, simply registering it. Of course, the same applies to functionally changed brood-tending actions; but man usually sees billing and kissing take place with such an obvious social function that it requires some effort to convince him that what he is seeing are in fact derived brood-tending actions that originally had an entirely different function. The reverse is true of functionally changed sexual actions; they are always taken in their original sense, and it takes great effort to explain that they have other functions too. These various attitudes on the part of the naïve beholder are prejudices that can very easily lead to misunderstanding.

25. The Value of Greeting

In very simple terms, a form of behavior has an appeasing effect when it awakens a behavioral tendency irreconcilable with aggression in the aggressor. Here it is enough if the tendency is strong enough to inhibit aggressive behavior. The other, counteracting behavior need not even be visible externally. So the appeasing presentation of the genitals need not elicit sexual behavior on the part of the partner; it is enough if the partner desists from further attack. This is called "change of mood." Fortunately this minimal requirement is very often more than fulfilled, that is to say, it does lead at least to incipient sexual actions or, if we are dealing with appeasement food begging, at least to incipient feeding. So it is easy to determine which behavior has in fact been stimulated in the partner; if nothing was visible from the outside but an absence of attack, it would be more difficult to interpret.

It is not even necessary for all attack to be halted by the appeasing behavior. *For appeasement to acquire a biological social value, it is sufficient for it to make attack less probable.* It is important to realize this, for in the case of baboons one can fairly often see an animal who is presenting violently being bitten by a higher-ranking one in spite of it. This is always a punishment, i.e., an aggressive reaction toward an individual who has behaved counter to the norm. Two examples should suffice to explain what we mean. Male hamadryas baboons keep their harem together by force. If a female roams too far away from the others she is threatened, and if this does not work, she is attacked by the pasha and bitten in the neck; usually not even presentation will help. Moreover, baboons are known to have a fairly firm ranking order when feeding. Now it can happen that visitors try to distract the attention of the pasha for a moment in order to quickly give a lower-ranking animal a tidbit. By doing so they are of course tempting this animal to act against the pasha's prerogative. In any case, the pasha usually notices. There have been cases where the pasha sat in a different section of the cage, from where he could not even see the "culprit" directly, yet he could see its hand, which was stretched out through the bars. This was enough: The pasha rushed up and punished the lower-ranking baboon even though the latter presented very intensely.

But monkeys, as well as less highly developed vertebrates, do not only use appeasement afterward, when the partner has already been provoked to attack, but also beforehand, as introduction to an action that will presumably incite the partner to attack. In the simplest case, a lower-ranking animal will not simply pass close by a high-ranking one and appease it in case it feels irritated by this proximity; instead the lower-ranking animal performs the gesture of appeasement before setting off, as though to "beg pardon" in advance for an action to follow. This anticipatory appeasement has very much of the character of a greeting. We do not yet know whether this behavior is always a matter of instinct or whether it is the result of an intelligent view of the situation and of behavior planned in advance; monkeys, at least, are known to be quite capable of doing this.

But if they are capable of this, one would expect them also to "abuse" this greeting, which protects them against attack; for instance, in order to protect themselves from punishment. As was shown above, however, this does not usually seem to work. It would be amusing to imagine the entire order of a baboon troop breaking up simply because each member could avoid punishment by a humble greeting. At least this kind of functional consideration shows why it would in fact be a disadvantage if presentation were always sure to inhibit aggression. Yet there are fairly common situations in which our human sense of justice does suspect an abuse of the gesture of submission. In technical language this situation is called "protected threat." This can be explained by the following example.

Three monkeys are concerned, of whom one is of very high rank; the other two can be of almost equal rank. For some reason, one of these two violently threatens the other with shrieks, threatening gestures, and all the other movements that belong to aggression. But it places itself in such

The "protected threat" of the hamadryas baboon.

a way as to present its hindquarters to the high-ranking animal at the same time. This achieves two things: The actual threatener who is presenting toward its superior protects itself against attack by the latter. The threatened animal cannot also present toward its superior unless it wants to withdraw, so it cannot secure itself against attack. If it wanted to do so it would also have to present toward its aggressor and thus declare itself its inferior. Added to this, however, is that the high-ranking monkey usually intervenes in quarrels between its inferiors, often simply separating the disputants by passing between them. Often, however, it also threatens one or both and drives them away. But in the case of "protected threat," the disturber of the peace has already presented toward the high-ranking animal "in anticipation," whereupon the latter has to attack and drive off the threatened animal if it wants peace. That happens often enough in this situation to give the impression that by its submissive behavior the disturber is forcing the high-ranking animal to become angry with a third animal who has not in fact given it any cause for anger. In this way even a low-ranking animal can have a fellow member of the group who is superior to it driven away by the highest-ranking animal. We know this behavior from captive and wild rhesus monkeys, from wild doguera baboons from various regions of Africa, and from hamadryas baboons in captivity. Curiously it has never been seen among hamadryas baboons living in the wild in spite of careful observation.[64]

One could perhaps take this as an indication that "protected threat" is not an innate behavior form among any of the animals and that instead they "invent" it and learn to use it from personal experience. In any case, "protected threat" gives the best proof of the strong inhibiting effect presentation has and of how far an originally sexual behavioral element has changed function here. It also shows the danger inherent in this behavior. The animals may rely so heavily on protection by presentation that they exploit it for their own interests, which, as far as we can judge, do not serve the community. An aggressive animal can play out its aggression and alter the responses of the community in such a way as to spark off new aggression in the remainder of the community. This is the first small step on the road to putting self-interest over the interests of the community.

As we showed, the animal at whom presentation is directed can react in different ways, even with mounting and incipient or actual copulation. Then it looks as though the lower-ranking individual were offering the higher-ranking one an opportunity for sexual activity and thus gaining some advantage for itself—whether to evade a threat, temporarily remove a rival, or obtain a tidbit. Occasionally this is described as prostitution. Whether this term is right depends entirely on how we define prostitution. However, we would then have to call the entire appeasing behavior of presentation prostitution too, since the reaction of the partner can range through all possible transitions from the almost invisible inhibition of attack to complete change of mood together with normal copulation. But if prostitution, as we understand it, means wrong behavior, then the term cannot apply to monkeys. For here we are dealing with a behavior pattern that is biologically justified. Nor does it matter that rutting females may perhaps have more success with presentation as a means of appeasement and that they also learn to exploit this because the males like to copulate with them.

26. Hypersexualization?

If we start by making an inventory of the behavior at the disposal of a particular species as the necessary basis for more exact behavior studies, we are proceeding like any naïve observer. First he distinguishes between typical recurrent and recognizable behavior patterns and classifies them according to their biological function. Growling and baring the teeth on the part of a dog belong to aggressive behavior. Prowling on the part of a cat belongs in the functional circle of foraging; the nest-building of the blackbird, rook, finch, and starling belong to brood-tending, and so on. Usually we try to make do with as few functional concepts as possible. This is good scientific strategy. However, we must take care not to put too much trust in these first attempts at classification. In other words, we must be prepared to consider the order we have set up as a provisional one, and alter it as soon as new discoveries require it.

It can easily happen that the observer has already been careless in the naming of the behavior patterns he has recognized; for example, he may have used interpretative names instead of neutral descriptive ones. The first researchers to observe the behavior of the orange chromide began with young animals, who acted out territorial flights and pair-bonding before they reared offspring themselves. One pattern was striking in the behavior of the partners of a pair. One animal would ram its mouth against the flank of its partner. But the ramming was not violent and never led to wounding. Later, among the young who had just learned to swim, the researchers saw a behavior pattern reminiscent of this ramming of adult fish: The little fish also swam up their parents' flank as though to ram it. The form of the movement, added to the consideration that the small fish could not yet fight, led to this behavior on the part of the young animals being entered into scientific literature as "apparent ramming." In fact, the sequence according to which this researcher assembled his observations clearly had an unfavorable effect on his interpretation and naming of the action; for, as we have shown (see p. 150), what the young animals are in fact doing is feeding from their parents; the parent animals continue to use this behavior pattern among themselves in a derived form, and it is this that ought to be called "apparent *feeding*."

So it is only to be expected that the presentation of baboons, the tail-beat of *Tropheus,* and the penis display of the spotted hyena were formerly interpreted uniformly as sexual behavior. This sexual behavior occurred, however, with surprising frequency; more often, at any rate, than among many other species. And it also occurred distinct from direct reproductive behavior, whereas the other species with whom they were compared only behaved sexually in the context of reproduction. So it was more than tempting to speak of hypersexualization here, above all for baboons, who were particularly easy to observe in zoos. Even today many zoo visitors not only find baboons droll but also excited by their strong sexuality. Closer observation and study of typical sequences of behavior will soon show that presentation, penis display, and tail-beating, like the "tail-flirtation" of masked amadines, can all occur in various typical sequences. One of these sequences always leads to mating (or spawning in the case of fish), while the other does not. Continuing from this point, we will soon discover differences in the situations and social constellations that lead to the respective behaviors. Eventually, the word "sexual," in the context of a situation that does not lead to mating, will be left in quotation marks for the sake of caution, and then replaced by another word, which, experience has shown, is "greeting."

At this stage of our research at the latest we will have finally dismissed the thesis of hypersexuality. But could we not retain it? All this would require would be to place a higher value on the form of the behavioral pattern than on the inner drive responsible for its appearance. We might well decide that everything that looks sexual should also be called sexual; in consequence, however, we would then also have to ascribe everything that looked like brood-tending to brood-tending and, accordingly, speak of "hypertrophied brood-tending" for the social grooming actions of the monkeys, the billing of crows, parrots, pigeons etc., which we described in detail earlier. This procedure is generally rejected, because we know that what adults do among themselves is plainly not brood-tending. The case is very clear with those cuckoos who have dropped brood-tending but retained pair-feeding (see p. 133); for brood-tending cannot at the same time disappear and be hypertrophied. The name we give a behavior does not, therefore, depend on the form the behavior takes but on the situation that elicits it, on the inner drive behind it, or on the biological consequence of the behavior. Unfortunately we find no such good arguments for reproductive behavior as in our example of brood-tending, because although a species can abandon brood-tending it can never abandon reproduction. Yet here too, for the sake of the uniformity of the system, we must look at more than the mere form the behavior takes. Then the totally different biological function of this behavior will compel us to find another name for it and to give up the naïve idea of hypersexuality.

I shall deal with the situation among humans in a moment. Here I would merely like to remark how surprisingly often points of view related purely to man, what are called "anthropomorphic" ideas, play a part in descriptions of animal behavior. This can lead to calling the behavior of animals "perverted" whenever it would be called perverted between humans. This is why baboons in particular often seem rather "perverted" to many people. And the impression is even heightened in a zoo situation, where baboons, like men in a large city, are densely crowded and lack the distractions that wild life and their natural habitat could offer them. Yet to proceed from man to animal is just as dangerous as to proceed from animal to man. Even if we can show that the so-called perverted sexual behavior of baboons is seen more often in captivity than in the wild, this could easily be explained by the lack of space in the zoo, which does not permit the animals to keep the prescribed distance from certain other individuals; and if they continually have to fall short of this distance, they are also forced into continual "polite greeting." So what is abnormal is the frequency of the greeting, but not the greeting itself.

Sexual behavioral patterns do not increase in frequency only in the context of social greeting. There is a widespread view that, in the animal kingdom, mating and the foreplay to mating are confined to the times favorable to reproduction. We know that among species who reproduce only at certain times of the year the gonads are set in action by outside signals, for instance by rising temperature or the longer daylight in spring, by rainfall, or such. In this way the reproductive behavior of both sexes is at least roughly synchronized. But among species who can rear offspring throughout the year, like many inhabitants of the tropical zones, there are still times when mating with a female would be of no advantage, namely as long as the female is pregnant or so fully occupied with brood-tending that a new birth during this period might endanger both litters. Indeed, among many animals the female emits signals that show her readiness for mating and upon which the males begin their attempts to mate. There are even indications that the females are not alone in having a cycle of alternate phases of readiness for mating and rejection of mating; male rats, rabbits, cattle (and humans) also have a cycle. Moreover, the length of the cycles of males and females of the same species seem to be adjusted to each other and the males, if they always live together with the same female, eventually become ready for mating at the same time as the females.[53] The sexual behavior of male rhesus monkeys largely coincides with the various phases of the estrous cycle of their females.[80] The frequency of copulation and the corresponding number of ejaculations is greatest in the fertile phase, but sexual behavior does not fade out entirely in the remaining time either. We know that among monkeys and other vertebrates mating also occurs with pregnant females. But it is not even necessary for there to be variations in frequency.

Those species of animal where the males are continually seen courting the females represent an extreme; but the success rate seems to bear no relation to the trouble taken, since the females usually take no notice at all of the males' efforts. A typical representative of these animals is known to every aquarian, namely the guppy (*Lebistes reticulatus*). Other toothed carps behave in the same way, and—from an entirely different group of fish—so do the South American swordtail characins (*Corynopoma riisei*) and related species. In both cases these are fish who fertilize internally, i.e., where the male introduces the sperm into the sexual passage of the female with a copulatory organ. Now one cannot simply say that constant courting is unnatural; rather we must try to find the reasons for it. An exact analysis of the inner and outer causes of this endless courtship and its effects on the female has led to the following conclusions to date.[82]

Most fish eject eggs and sperm at the same time; the water brings them together and it is enough if the readiness to spawn of both sexes gives rise to sexual behavior, and in particular to bringing them as close together as possible. Among fish with internal fertilization, however, either the female keeps the sperm in her body for a fairly long time, or, if we are dealing with fish who bear live young like the guppy, the development of the embryos in the mother's body takes some time. In each case the female must be mated at a time when she is incapable and therefore not even ready to deposit the eggs or the finished young. Now, by nature the female is only inclined to tolerate the approach of a male when she is ready to spawn herself. Outside this time she keeps the males at a distance. But precisely among those species who are fertilized internally this time-lag must be overcome entirely, since direct bodily contact is necessary. The problem is solved here by the male, who so to speak bombards the unwilling female with courtship in order to make her change her mind. Swordtail characins are so eager to mate that not even successful copulation will lead to an interruption in courtship; immediately afterward the male will continue his efforts with the same violence.

While female toothed carps usually try to evade and remain passive, the females of some species of characin become aggressive toward the males. It is interesting to note that these males have developed a form of courtship feeding, in the course of which, incidentally, the females are misled (not to say cheated). None of these species tends or feeds its young, so there is no brood-tending feeding that could be exploited for the introduction to mating. But in spite of this the female is occasionally hungry, and then searches for something edible such as a small *Cyclops* or other small plankton-crustacean. Now the male swordtail characin has a small bony knob on a long stem on the cover of his gills, which looks like a *Cyclops* and in addition is moved like a *Cyclops* when the male spreads his gill cover and parades the *Cyclops* snare in front of the female while executing sporadic courtship movements. When the female snaps for what she supposes is a morsel of food and bites it, she comes close enough for the male to carry out mating in a split second.[125] Such examples do not, of course, mean that hypersexuality does not exist; but they do show how cautiously we must apply the concept.

27. Emancipated Copulation

Where does the procreative process begin?

As we have seen, what is commonly called the foreplay to mating often does not have the aim of creating new life but of binding the partners of a pair more firmly together. An incipient or fully performed act of copulation can still serve this purpose even if ejaculation, the ejection of the sperm into the female sexual passages, is lacking.

To start with, copulation can not only send the sperms on the way to the ova or egg-cells but among some animals it can also send the ova to meet the sperm. Besides those species of animal whose females ovulate spontaneously, and whose egg-cells, when ripe, automatically leave the ovaries, there are some species where the egg-cells are liberated only during the foreplay to mating or during copulation itself, for instance by the stimulus of the contact of the penis with the vagina. Rabbits and cats belong to this category. Repeated copulations often also serve to make the female responsive. With the diamond dove (*Geopelia cuneata*), the male pigeon mounts the female seven or eight times, begins to copulate, then hops down again, courts, mounts, etc., and each time the female opens out the feathers around her cloaca further, until she is finally ready to mate, and the union then takes place.[86] The Indian flying fox (*Pteropus gigantëus*) requires three to seven copulations before he can ejaculate. One only sees a complete copulation sequence during the reproductive period, but individual copulations occur throughout the year, even with pregnant females.[83] It is also known that mice perform a series of copulations before ejaculation. Naturally this is related to the duration of each individual copulation, which is extremely short for mice. Among other animals it can take hours (for instance, the pouched mouse, *Sminthopsis,* takes eleven hours); the male gapeworm (*Syngamus tracheae*), which lives in hens, actually lives in a state of permanent copulation with his female.

Some monkeys, such as rhesus monkeys and baboons, also require a series of copulations, which are separated from one another by an interval of a few seconds to a few minutes, before they can ejaculate. Usually one only sees such a series of copulations on the part of the highest-ranking male, such as the pasha who is the sole owner of all the females in the harem among hamadryas baboons. Yet a group of hamadryas baboons will also include young males. They make friends with one or another female and occasionally copulate with her too. These isolated copulations, to which the female can even incite the male, affirm the bond between the respective individuals, but hardly ever lead to pregnancy since the young males never reach the number of copulations necessary for ejaculation.[63] The isolated copulation has thus become free to acquire a new social function here.

We could perhaps speculate why so many copulations are required before ejaculation. Then it becomes tempting to assume that once again it may have a social significance; for example, the first copulations may not only serve to prepare the partner or make her agree, as we showed earlier, but over and above this also serve to tie the partners together more closely. There have been no studies of animals in this context yet. But we know that in man a union where ejaculation is often postponed for over an hour (*Carezza*) can greatly promote the pair-bond between individuals. The role that orgasm plays here is much disputed.

What is certain is merely that the function of copulation has been extended or even entirely transformed among humans too, so that it is comparable to a ceremonial banquet, which of course does not primarily serve to feed the participants but to strengthen the bond within the community; or it is comparable to the kiss (p. 237), where the feeding function has lapsed entirely.

If a female baboon has mated with a male other than the pasha, one of the two concerned often runs up to the pasha—as though "plagued by a guilty conscience"—and presents to him. The pasha reacts in the same way as to all social presentation, i.e., he may mount briefly and copulate, or at least attempt to do so if the presenting animal is a male. This situation shows the appeasing effect of mounting and copulation, an effect which, as in the presentation of the hindquarters (see p. 207), can be independent of the sex of the participants. The effect becomes clearest when the mounted animal is a male, who naturally obtains no sexual satisfaction from the act but presumably does achieve social satisfaction. But copulation between male and female can have the same social effect. Among rhesus monkeys, if one male mounts another it is occasionally an aggressive threat and demonstration of rank, but sometimes it is also the expression of an acknowledged order, which obviously only serves to strengthen the bond between the individuals. Usually the higher-ranking animal mounts first; afterward he in turn is often mounted by the other.

With langurs, it is known that young males continually mount adult males of their group and often embrace them afterward.[50] The significance of this behavior is not yet known. Its form of movement reminds me more of the spreading of urine on the ground as a mark of ownership (which we see among marmosets) than of copulation. At the Third Congress of the "Deutsche Gesellschaft für Psychotherapie und Tiefenpsychologie" (1960) held in Paris, Roumajon told of extensive observations of gangs of young people in France in which the "chief" played the dominant role. In the course of an initiation rite, and later too, the members of the gang submit to anal coition by their "chief." There are girls too in these gangs, so ordinary sexual contact is quite possible for the members. In any case, it is certainly not rape on the part of the "chief." The youth is merely seeking "support" and affection from his "chief," and he clings to him particularly closely afterward. In the games of classical Greece, the victor among the young competitors is also said to have had the right to placatory anal intercourse with his defeated rival. In a more recent Polish novel there is a reference to shepherd boys raping strangers who intrude into their territory.[60] Similarly, male rhesus monkeys of enemy groups mount if they meet. These examples show two things:

1. That even for man, such "sexual" behavior, which is not tied to reproduction, is not a "degenerate phenomenon."
2. That the copulation of higher animals has by nature a pair-bonding function, and that in this context it can be reduced (mating without ejaculation; mounting without introduction of the penis; etc.).

So even copulation does not have to be the "introduction to a procreative process."

IV

28. Pair-Bonding Behavior Elements in Man

We can sum up the facts that have emerged from this wide range of examples.

1. Just as organs can serve different purposes—for instance, the limbs serve for locomotion and for using tools, the mouth for eating and for speaking—so too can behavior patterns and the signals that accompany them. The same behavior patterns can be an essential part of brood-tending while at the same time serving the synchronization and cohesion of the sexual partners, and, in given cases, also serving to change the mood of aggressive conspecifics and to inhibit their aggressive tendencies.

2. For this it is necessary that these behavior elements with their manifold uses should also be available for a corresponding variety of situations. They must not merely be applicable to one specific situation. But they may very well look the same for different situations. This is even an advantage, since the actions are meant to appeal to a very particular predisposition on the part of the partner who will respond by a very particular behavior, and this is best achieved by an unambiguous, unmistakable signal. This brings with it the risk that the observer will overlook the different natural meanings of the behavior or signals because of their similarity of form.

3. There are three focal points in the corporate life of animals: brood-tending, the relations between the sexual

partners, and the alliance of many conspecifics into fairly large groups. Behavior patterns that have proved themselves in one of these fields can be transferred to others too: Elements from brood-tending and reproductive behavior can be put to use to keep the partners of a pair or a larger society together. This produces freely convertible behavior elements, so that one cannot always tell from which of the three fields an element originally stems.

4. If one cannot always tell the origin of behavior elements, this is usually because they lack something that would make their meaning in this special, derived form comprehensible. We can only understand why a bird holding stems of grass in its beak should woo the female and then throw away the grass if we know that this form of courtship derived from nest-building movements. Because the original meaning of the action, which gave it its form, is now lacking, such behavior patterns are called "rituals"; they come about through "ritualization." (Sometimes the term "symbolic action" is also used; for instance, the form of courtship we have just discussed could be called "symbolic nest-building." But this can easily mislead the reader into assuming that the animal is aware of the symbolic character of its actions.) Ritualization causes a change in the frequency with which a behavior pattern occurs and in the inner drive that impels the animal toward this specific mode of action. The same action can be performed in response to various different moods or, in human terms, it can be "meant" differently. In addition, physical structures can appear that underline the new significance of this action (for instance, the color signals we described for the *Tropheus* cichlid and for baboons).

5. All this applies to vertebrates at very varied stages of development, from fish to the manlike apes, insofar as

they lead a comparable social life. So it must have some-thing to do with corporate, social life. And indeed the close analysis we made earlier shows that the afore-mentioned facts 1–4 are biological adaptations to the conditions of social life—just as the spindle-shaped body with fins that we also find from fish upward to the highest marine mammals is an adaptation to the con-ditions of aquatic life.

We must note, however, that individually this body shape and the accompanying fins can come about in differ-ent ways. Similarly, we must take care to differentiate be-tween the general principles of construction of social life and the specific behavior patterns that play com-parable roles therein. For instance, it is part of the gen-eral principle of construction that brood-tending behavior patterns are built into the pair relationship, yet these brood-tending behavior patterns have a different aspect from species to species.

We were not concerned in this work with explaining the development of the greatest possible number of highly specialized social behavior patterns; rather we wanted to establish clearly that such social behavior patterns did indeed undergo a development and that they always stem from quite definite roots.

6. The more different the animals are who have independ-ently traversed the same paths of development along parallel lines and in whose highly developed social life we can recognize the same structural principle (although each species has its own species-specific behavior reper-tory), the more certain we can be of having found a natural law valid for the group of creatures examined. We shall confine ourselves to the realm of vertebrates here, although this natural law relating to the construc-tion of societies goes beyond the boundary between ver-tebrates and invertebrates—as the examples of insects and

spiders have shown—and although it is legitimate to assume that the same relations between, for instance, brood-tending and pair-bonding behavior will be found again and again among the so-called lower animals too.

7. The laws we have found enable us to predict that any vertebrate that exhibits a firm pair-bond or a complex social life will very probably have taken over behavior patterns and signals that originally served brood-tending or reproduction into the pair-bond and group-bond; as a result these patterns and signals no longer (or not only) serve the production and rearing of offspring now, but (also) serve the cohesion of pairs and larger groups. This is even more probable if the vertebrate in question is closely related to one of the animal species to which the aforementioned laws have already been found to be applicable.

Since man belongs biologically to the vertebrates and exhibits both firm pair-bonds and larger group formations, this natural law should also be applicable to him. We will examine this in the following chapters. And that is why we have given preference to examples that facilitated a comparison with the behavior patterns of man in the preceding section of this work.

29. *Social Feeding and the Kiss*

In order to make clear this comparison between the changes of function of social behavior patterns in the animal kingdom and in man, we shall begin by examining human behavior patterns in the same sequence. We shall, therefore, begin with brood-tending elements.

Mouth-to-mouth feeding is a widespread phenomenon in the "brood-tending" behavior of man too. It is necessary to man for the same reasons as it is to the manlike apes, namely because the children gradually require more solid food. True, they are suckled for a long time; but besides this they are given more and more other food, which must be rendered as soft as possible at first, and then gradually is left increasingly solid. Our own customary use of baby food—which is soft, made of the best foods, and lovingly prepared—is no more than a highly mechanized form of feeding, as accurately attuned as possible to the biological requirements of the child. It goes far beyond what could be produced by purely natural means and is thus a hypernormal adaptation to the needs of the child. In principle, however, it is nothing new. The Greeks fed their children with premasticated food,[5] and even in the past century, in the rural parts of Austria, it was quite usual for the mother to premasticate food and then transfer it directly into the mouth of the infant. In Holstein, Germany, the grandmothers of thirty years ago premasticated butter dumplings for the older infants.[89] I observed the same in a farm in

Münsterland in 1954. The grandmother premasticated dough or milk rusks, took what she had chewed out of her mouth with a small spoon, and fed it to the baby. Characteristically, it was the grandmothers who still practiced this custom. Toward the end of the Second World War, I also saw mothers use this method of feeding during the refugee treks. Mouth-to-mouth feeding was still a normal feature of child-care among various primitive peoples until very recently; it occurred, for instance, in the Carolines, in

Papua mother feeding her child mouth-to-mouth (left),
and Uruku Indian feeding a piglet mouth-to-mouth.

Samoa,[91] among the Naga tribes of Assam,[3] and among the Papua tribes of New Guinea.[103] This method of feeding children was also registered as a normal daily occurrence in Hausa villages on the Niger by Viennese behavior researchers of the biological station of Wilhelminenberg in 1954.

In such cases the premasticated food is transmitted directly from the mouth of the mother to that of the infant.

If the mother approaches her three-month-old infant with her mouth, it purses its lips as soon as she comes close. When the mouth-to-mouth contact has been achieved, the child sticks its tongue out and makes licking movements. Ploog reports that "We repeated this experiment on our own children with the same result."[89] So it is quite certain that the European infant, and probably every infant, is adapted to this method of feeding. It does not have to be forced on the infant, for it already understands it and is probably innately capable of performing its part in it. But infants become adults, and as adults they still retain this ability—and maybe even the need to employ it.

It becomes apparent how firmly anchored mouth-to-mouth feeding is in the brood-tending of some primitive races in cases where other living things take the place of children. Harald Schultz has written about the Uruku Indians from the Amazon area, who often kill sows on their hunts. The Indian women lovingly tend the helpless young piglets who are also brought back from these hunts, chew up food for them, and pass it directly into their mouths.[102] Similarly, missionaries from New Guinea reported that women chewed up vegetables and fruit and transmitted them directly from their own lips into the snouts of piglets.[24, 25] These piglets come from the village pigs and are reared in place of the mother's first born, whom she kills immediately after birth. Since this method of feeding even works with animals, who normally never receive their food in this way, it is not surprising that Brandes managed to feed a young orangutan with premasticated and well-salivated bananas and rusks.[89]

Direct mouth-to-mouth food transmission does not take place only between mother and child, but also between adults, both among primitive races and among the so-called civilized peoples. It is most likely to occur regularly in certain rituals, when it is, accordingly, described as a component of the ritual. The Pygmies of the tropical jungle

Mouth-to-mouth feeding of a dog; three-thousand-year-old clay figure from a grave in Tlatilco, a suburb of Mexico City.

of Central Africa, who still live at the economic level of primitive hunters and food-gatherers, live in residential groups of several blood-related families, seldom numbering more than fifty to a hundred persons. The leader of each group is usually the best hunter. The Pygmies are almost exclusively monogamous. Of the various African groups, the Ituri Pygmies are considered the purest race. They live on the Ituri, more or less where it flows into the Congo. Among others, they occasionally kill elephants in pitfalls with poisoned harpoons. How they do this is shown in a film put together from archive material and prepared for secondary school instruction, which can be rented, from the Institut für den Wissenschaftlichen Film in Göttingen.[108] The film also includes sequences showing the dissection and sharing of the prey. Whoever has set up the trap also has the right of disposal; it is he who parcels out the meat. And here a curious ceremony takes place, whose

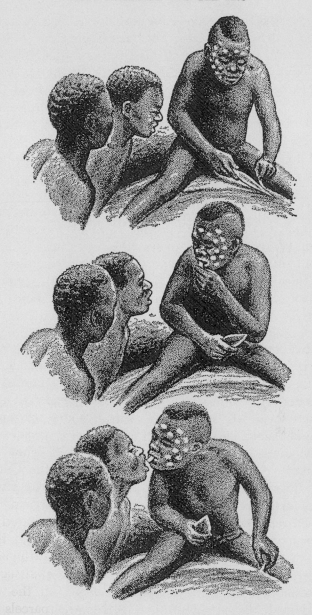

Scene of ritual feeding among Ituri Pygmies.

significance has not yet been understood: A foreman, probably the owner of the trap, cuts pieces of meat from the animals, puts them between his lips, and then transfers them directly, mouth-to-mouth, to a companion. It would, of course, be simpler to pass the piece of meat from hand to hand. The mouth-to-mouth method must surely be a ritual. Unfortunately all we can say at present is that it occurs among adults; from all we know from our comparisons of form and species, it derives from infant feeding.

We can cite another example, from Central Europe this time: In the Ziller valley, the Puster valley, and in Pinzgau, chewed tobacco used to be exchanged as an affirmation of friendship. If a girl accepted the wad of premasticated tobacco, it meant she returned the boy's love. Besides tobacco (and probably the source of the custom, since the use of tobacco only dates from the seventeenth century), they also chewed spruce resin and pitch—at least they still did so in 1912—and these substances were also exchanged after chewing, often during dancing, and in particular between lovers. The young man would let a tip of the piece of pitch show between his closed teeth and invite the girl to grasp it with her teeth—which of course obliged her to press her mouth firmly on that of the young man—and to pull it out. "If the dancer agrees to the invitation of the young man, this is a sign that she feels well-disposed toward him, and often even more," writes Von Hörmann.[43]

Advertising also exploits the motif of mouth-to-mouth feeding, for instance by displaying a friendly man and girl with their faces turned toward each other, and both aiming with open mouth for a tasty morsel lying between them (which the advertisement is extolling), or one of them aiming with open mouth for a tidbit held between the lips of the other.

Bilz defends the rather old interpretation that the human kiss came into being in this way on the basis of ethnological findings.[3] Besides the fact that lovers do indeed feed each other in this way, he also cites a collection of words for "kissing" from different languages that often have the additional meaning of premastication, or a tender gesture. This ethnological interpretation receives strong support from our earlier comparisons with animals. Close bonds between social partners are very generally established and maintained through the medium of transferred brood-tending behavior elements; and brood-tending feeding very often plays a major role in them, although the actual transmission of food can fall away so that a new kind of ritual emerges. This ritual appears most often between the partners of a pair. The same applies to man. The more intimate the relations between two humans, the more easily kissing can turn into feeding-kissing; this transition also goes to show how close the connection between the two is. But quite apart from the "playful" transmission of food, to and fro movements of the tongue can occur that give away the origin of the whole thing.

Primarily, of course, all this applies to kissing on the mouth. Kisses on other parts of the body could have as origin the "tender touching" with the lips that we described for chimpanzees (see p. 169). However, this is also a typical behavior of the mother toward her child and does not, therefore, affect the relation we have established to brood-tending behavior; we can simply say that it did not necessarily derive from feeding here. The kissing that occurs among humans can just as easily turn into nibbling with the teeth, which we find in the primitive grooming of man too. On the other hand, one and the same person can use different types of kiss as greeting, according to the ranking order between him and the person greeted. Herodotus (I, 34) and Strabo (XV, 2, 20) tell of this among the Persians: The Persians greet each other differently according to the rank of each person. If they are of equal rank, they kiss on the mouth; if one is just a little subordinate to the other, they kiss on the cheek; but if one is of much lower birth than the other, he prostrates himself in front of the other. In order to make St. Perpetua recant her faith and to save her from martyrdom, her father kissed her hand, actually threw himself at her feet, and tearfully called her his mistress. When a visitor wanted to kiss the hand of Caliph Hisam (A.D. 724-43), the latter replied that only a coward did this among Arabs. This shows that the kiss can become a fixed social demonstration, in which the presence of a third person can also be of importance. According to Plutarch, Cato the Elder had Pretorius Manilius crossed off the list of senators because he had given his wife a kiss in the presence of his own daughter. It could of course be that the kiss that was originally directed at the mouth was deflected elsewhere because of ranking order. And indeed we know far too little about this extremely common behavior of man, which could be clarified by careful study, to be able to reply to the more specific question about the particular behavior elements within brood-tending from which kissing derives.

The kiss is used for greetings and farewells, for appeasement, and in addition it is one of those actions that occur almost for their own sake and presumably result in strengthening the pair-bond; finally, it is also used in the foreplay to copulation. Furthermore, it plays an important part in religious life. Man worships divine beings by kissing their living representatives (priests), statues, or other holy objects: temple thresholds, altars, the Koran, the Torah, or the Bible. All this is considered part of the veneration, love, or greeting of the godhead; but it can also be used to coax something from it. The Benedictine Father Ohm gives a detailed account, from which most of the examples quoted here were taken, in his modern book on the gestures of prayer.[87]

The kiss can also turn from a greeting into a sign of brothership, of the "union of souls." In the days of the early Christians, the baptist and the assembled Christians would kiss the child to be baptized. Even in Antiquity, the man who was admitted to a council was kissed; and only a few years ago Marlene Dietrich was kissed when she became a Knight of the Legion of Honor in Germany. The *osculum sanctum*, the liturgical kiss of peace, also belongs in this context, and indeed it was not always as pure as the rules would have it. The Church regulations of Hippolytus require that the faithful shall kiss one another; the man shall kiss the man and the woman shall kiss the woman, and the men shall not kiss the women; and the Coptic sources of the Council of Nicea declare: "Thou shalt teach women not to give the kiss of peace to a man except if they are old and if the men are old men, unless they be older women who are very faithful."

We may also note the occurrence among the ancient Indians and Arabs, and in African and other native tribes, of the smelling or sniffing kiss. Presumably this also related to brood-tending; for instance, according to ancient Indian house rules, the father must sniff the head of the newborn child, or of a child returned from a journey, three times.

"Blowing a kiss" very probably also derived from brood-tending feeding. Here one kisses one's own hand and then pretends to throw the kiss to the object of devotion. Indeed, particularly with older children, mouth-to-mouth feeding by the parents is replaced by the transmission of pre-masticated food, which is let fall from the mouth into the chewer's own hand and then given to the child among some native tribes. Since this gesture too is often easily dismissed and not considered worth further attention, these plausible interpretations must remain no more than suggestions for the time being.

What we can maintain here is that the mouth kiss, which has occurred among civilized and primitive peoples from ancient times to today, is a ritualized brood-tending action, and that at least in some of its forms it goes back to the mouth-to-mouth feeding of small children by their mother.

30. The Social Significance of the Female Breast

If we consider the parallels, it becomes clear that it is a necessary consequence of the mother-child situation for the maternal breast to become a place of security for humans too and to acquire secondary meanings in social life very similar to those it acquired among the mammals we mentioned earlier. In the first three days after birth, every newborn baby can be comforted by giving it something teatlike to suck, even if the baby does not receive any nourishment in this way. So even prior to all experience, the maternal breast has a comforting effect. But both animal and human infants also gain corroborating experience of this effect. The following examples will show how great the analogies between men and mammals are here.

Elizabeth M. Thomas described the following scene which she witnessed among the bushmen of the Kalahari:

> When his little son saw what he was doing and realized that his father was preparing to go, he began to cry, saying: "Father, Father," and when Lazy Kwi hesitated a moment, then said he was going anyway, the little boy picked up a handful of stones and threw one at him. This amused Lazy Kwi's wife, who smiled and tried half-heartedly to take the stones away, but it angered Lazy Kwi, who caught his son by the arm and boxed his ears. That made the little boy so furious that he had a tantrum; he screamed and cried and arched

his back to draw away from his mother, who tried to pick him up, both mother and child doing exactly what they had done when the little boy was a baby and no doubt had been doing ever since. His mother always did have a terrible time managing him, and he was still nursing although he was now five or six years old. Before his father left, his mother had managed to mollify him somewhat, and she sat on the ground, letting him sit on her leg to nurse. He drank from one breast and held the other in his hand as he glared over his mother's shoulder at his father, who was already in the Jeep.

Papua woman with her baby at one breast and a piglet at the other.

Another scene:

Hearing me speak of medicine, Little Gashe glared at me balefully. I had treated his eyes before and perhaps he

remembered that the medicine was painful, or perhaps he
was afraid that I would harm his eyes. He scrambled into
his mother's lap to nurse and, facing toward her for safety,
glared at me over her shoulder.[113]

Both these scenes show clearly how the child reacts to an
aggressive, or presumably dangerous, and certainly frightening conspecific, whether father or stranger, how the child
then finds itself in a situation of social repression, and thereupon seeks protection with the mother and takes her
breast.

Many observers of such scenes do not mention whether
the child actually drinks or not. Sorenson and Gajdusek,
who studied natives of various tribes in New Guinea, were
able to record similar scenes on film.[107] Among the Fore
in the eastern mountains, the three-to-four-year-olds were
particularly fearful in the presence of strangers and cried
as soon as they were approached, even if they were close
to their mother. But often they would calm down as soon
as they had cuddled up to her and could grasp her breast
with their mouth, even though they did not drink. In this
position they lost their fear and would even begin to throw
cautious, curious glances at the stranger and his camera.

It was clearly apparent to the researchers that the children did not actually drink in this situation, and yet they
spoke of "nursing." One has to be equally careful about the
details given on the periods of lactation of other tribes,
especially since the respective authors often omit to say
whether they observed constant suckling in these cases or
only occasionally saw children at their mother's breast. I
know from my own experience with Africans that frightened children often took the breast without making drinking motions.

Of course the prerequisite for all this is that the children
should have easy access to the maternal breast. If the
breasts are covered up, children who flee to their mother

still press their face against her breast, but it is no longer quite clear what they are actually seeking there.

In regions where the breasts are still kept free of clothing, mothers usually nurse their children far longer than in places where clothing customs make it more difficult and for this reason alone encourage earlier weaning. Kraho Indians nurse their children for several years,[102] and the Nuna of West Africa (Upper Volta) still nurse them until well past the third year. Bushmen children are still nursed until their fourth year, and in the first eighteen months they live on little else but the maternal milk.[105] Gypsies also nurse until into the fourth year if not longer,[17] as do Eskimos, among whom it even used to be common for the mother to go on nursing the child until her next pregnancy. Freuchen, one of the great experts on the Eskimos in their "primitive state," saw Eskimo mothers from various regions give the breast to fourteen-year-old sons.[33] But the children do not only suck, they also play with the breasts. Eskimo children still do so when they are at least seven years old. This is frequently observed among various native tribes too, although again it is only occasionally mentioned in ethnological accounts. Nursing and playing probably also play a part in the children's fixation on the maternal breast as a place of security. At least it is striking that a short lactation period, covered breasts, and the attribution of an excessively erotic, almost fetishistic significance to the breasts tend to go together, just as the reverse is true: Among primitive peoples we find a long lactation period and uncovered breasts, and the significance attached to them in everyday social life often seems astonishingly normal to Westerners. Naturally many other factors come into play too; but no exact comparative research has been undertaken in this field yet, perhaps because no one has ever thought of formulating the question.

Ford and Beach, when they compared many human groups and peoples, found no direct correlation between the custom of covering up the breasts in daily life and the significance accorded to stimulating the breasts in sexual life.[32] However, direct sexual (fore-) play is not the only possible framework and probably not even the right framework for determining the biological and social value of the breasts as signals. That they have such a signal value between adults is general knowledge. And that this signal value is culturally influenced is equally demonstrable. For while no one objects to the sight of an Indian woman, in almost European dress, calmly nursing her baby in front of a shop entrance in Ecuador, or to an elegant young lady doing the same on a park bench in the smart Corso Vittorio Emmanuele in Naples, many European women scarcely dare to nurse their child at home in the presence even of good friends.

Monkey mothers, who are constantly surrounded by "good friends," cannot afford such reticence. But human mothers can offer their babies feeding bottles as breast substitutes. This can largely if not entirely divest the breast of its original biological function. The extreme care that is lavished on the female breast today relates almost exclusively to its social signal value. The manufacturers of creams, ointments, lotions, tablets, drops, special douches, rotating brushes, and even inflatable or foam rubber "falsies" are all striving to make the breasts into "one of the most attractive attributes of femininity," and "the ideal of feminine perfection." They are not concerned with the baby, but with the most perfect décolleté, with the breast beautiful, whose praises have always been sung by man, as for instance in the Song of Solomon: "Thy breasts are like two young roes that are twins, which feed among the lilies." The scene in Homer where the beautiful Helen conciliates her angry husband by showing him her breasts can be taken as another example of the breasts' value as signals.

This coincides in many ways with the effect the female

breast exerts in the social life of the gelada baboon. However, we must then ask whether perhaps the human female breast underwent a further development in the service of its function as a social signal, as it did with the female gelada baboon.

Now man is the only living mammal in whom the mammary glands are constantly strongly developed and remain noticeable even when they do not produce milk. The difference in size for different women bears no relation to the amount of milk they produce; small breasts can secrete more milk than larger ones, for the form of the breast depends on the development of the stroma, a connective tissue structure into which the milk ducts of the glands sprout during pregnancy. At the end of the period of lactation, when the gland tissue regresses again, the connective tissue increases considerably instead.[2] In addition, the fatty tissue also has a part in the structure of the breast. But fatty and connective tissue can easily accumulate in any part of the body. They are building materials that can be used anywhere, even for building signal structures. For man often uses formal signals where lower primates use color signals. This applies to the infant schema, in which the chubby cheeks that are also built up of fatty and connective tissues play an important role, just as it applies to the female breast, which admittedly has already developed into a social signal among monkeys but which is supplemented by striking colors. Naturally this does not mean that man could not also turn colors to account. Painting and tattooing are evidence of this among peoples who do not wear clothes, as are the sophisticated fashions of our cultural sphere, where clothes are used like an artificial skin and in the bargain aim at the "gelada effect" by similar neck lines—which has led to the jocular christening of the gelada baboon as the "dirndl monkey."

Now that it is becoming less important, since we have artificial baby foods, whether the female breast can in fact fulfill its original function, while at the same time the breast is assuming increasing importance as a signal in the relations between adults, we might well expect its structure and shape to gradually adapt itself more and more to its new function—insofar as this is not easier to do by cosmetic and other technical tricks. There are several examples to show that races with large breasts prefer these, whereas races with small breasts prefer small ones. Whether this means that the form of the organ has adapted itself to the preference, or on the contrary that the latter is adapted to the existing form of the organ, cannot be determined as yet. But it would be possible to examine what role the experience of the baby at the breast plays in the eventual adult's evaluation of the breast by a comparison between adults who were breast fed and others who were brought up on the bottle alone.

However the specific signal effect of the female breast has come about, what is certain is that it plays an important part in the conjugal and general social life of man. This secondary significance is so commonplace today that the breast even counts as a sexual signal, although everyone knows its original significance. This effect is of course enhanced by the fact that the mother does not only take the child to her breast for suckling, but also as a caress or if the child needs comforting and protection. "Cuddling" and clasping to the breast is the emancipated preliminary to nursing. And this reaction is not only addressed to babies and children. In the Song of Solomon, the girl dreaming of her lover wishes: "O that thou wert as my brother, that sucked the breasts of my mother!," and the mystic Mechthild von Magdeburg sighed: "Oh thou god, reposing at my breasts" to her divine husband. No doubt everyone knows further examples from everyday experience.

That sucking at the breast also appeases the woman, i.e., that it can have an effect similar to that occurring with the hunting dog or the Uganda kob, is evident from the example of a Turkish fairytale[8] that we shall quote in part here. A young man is sent on an adventure on some pretext and encounters a dervish on the way. The dervish asks him what his intention is and after being told says: "Oh my son, he who sends you, sends you to your doom. But only go, Allah will help you." The dervish predicts to the young man that although he will meet with huge demons, called Dev, on his way, he will be able to appease them by a specific behavior: "Take these three okka of chewing resin! And now listen well! On the way you will meet a Dev woman. When flies fly into her mouth and come out of her seat she is asleep. When they fly into her seat and come out of her mouth, she is awake. If she is awake, you must immediately put one okka of chewing resin into her mouth and embrace her right nipple. Then she will show you the way; you can ask her." The young man leaves the dervish, and after a while he meets the Dev woman. Since flies are flying into her seat and coming out of her mouth, he immediately throws the chewing resin into her mouth, grasps her nipple, and sucks it. Then she catches sight of him and says: "Oh you human, if you did not grasp my right nipple I would crunch you between my teeth and mix you with my chewing resin. . . . Where are you going?" When he had answered she sent him on to her elder sister, who in turn sent him on to an even older sister. Both times he behaved as the dervish had advised. Thereupon the second sister said: "Oh you human, what shall I do now that you have become my child? Whence do you come and where are you going?" The third sister said: "Oh you boy, if you did not suck my nipple I would crunch you between my teeth and mix you with my chewing resin! Where are you going?"

Naturally man judges the behavior of spirits, demons, and gods according to his own behavior, that is, strictly anthropomorphically. So such fairytales are not descriptions of the behavior of spiritual beings but reflect the behavior and experiences of man. Since we also know that many women experience a feeling of voluptuousness when nursing a baby or when their partner fondles and sucks at their breast during the foreplay to coitus, and sometimes even have an orgasm, this fairytale account is certainly not implausible.

31. The Infant Schema

Twenty-five years ago, Konrad Lorenz coined the term "infant schema" to describe a special perceptual achievement of man that consists of protective responses toward typical infantile characteristics. The generalized attitude that

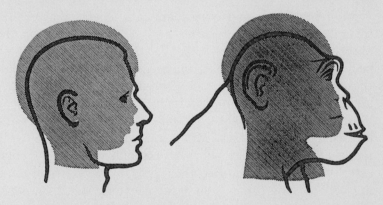

Typical head shape of the human child and adult (left) and the chimpanzee child and adult (right). The eye and ear have been chosen as points of reference, in order to clarify the proportionate sizes of the skull and face.

man adopts toward the still helpless young of his own kind in need of care is characterized on the one hand by certain unmistakable feelings and emotions and connected with a specific experience whose quality is usually conveyed in English by the words "sweet," "cute," and so on. On the other hand it is dependent on surprisingly few character-istics. The characteristics that an object must possess in or-der to elicit the specific experiential quality of "cute" are as follows, according to Lorenz:

1. *A comparatively thick head;*
2. *A prominent cranium with a domed brow out of propor-tion to the face;*
3. *A large correspondingly disproportionate eye situated as low as or below the middle of the entire skull;*
4. *Comparatively short, thick limbs with pudgy hands and feet;*
5. *Rounded body forms in general;*
6. *A very specific, soft, and elastic surface texture;*
7. *Round, prominent, "chubby" cheeks.*

All living things and even inanimate objects that exhibit several of these characteristics have a "cute" effect on the observer. A perfect example is Walt Disney's Bambi. Many pets who, of course, are often treated like babies, exhibit these same characteristics, and Lorenz points out that these are in fact almost dummy infants for childless people.

Naturally man is not the only creature to have these brood-tending responses. Many animals who have a well-marked brood-tending behavior respond to specific char-acteristics that characterize their progeny with brood-tend-ing actions. The turkey hen recognizes her chicks by signs of an acoustic nature; the mother only tends and guards chicks that cheep. Noncheeping chicks are killed, and accordingly a deaf turkey hen who has never heard a chick cheep kills all her progeny.[100] The optical signals that are known include the colored beak flanges and the colorful gapes of many nestling birds, which incite the old bird to feed them. But even among birds we must note that it is certainly not only parents who are in a brood-tending mood who respond to these releasing stimuli; often strange conspecifics who have no offspring of their own, and even juvenile birds, respond in the same way. Herring gulls, who defend food territories outside the breeding season, tolerate and even feed begging young birds in these territories. Although the young birds need not be their own progeny, they still must have the brown plumage of a young bird. Then the adults will at most make incipient moves to drive them away, but they are clearly inhibited in their aggression.[23] Mammals use many olfactory signals that we cannot go into here, most of which have in any case not been sufficiently studied yet. But baby monkeys often have color markings that insure them the protection of the adults.

The fur of the newborn offspring of all African tree monkeys (*Cercopithecus*) has a color that is clearly distinct from that of the adults. At the age of six to eight weeks, the baby color is slowly replaced by the juvenile coat but still remains recognizable until the fourth month. Adult African tree monkeys of both sexes living in the wild react extremely violently if they see a baby-colored young one in danger, for instance if a human holds it in his hand. Large males of the particularly aggressive *Cercopithecus aethiops* species even dare to attack humans in such cases, and utter threatening calls while doing so. It is important that the young animal should move; adults do not react if it is dead. But it does not have to scream, although this tends to heighten the adults' reaction. Adult males and females do not only try to free baby animals in danger; they also take immediate care of an abandoned offspring. When a mother is shot by hunters, unless she dies at once she will push away the baby who is clinging to her, so that it will have to cling to a branch instead, before she falls down. Thereupon it is immediately fetched away by another adult. By contrast, the adults show no reaction at all if a young animal that has already changed color or another adult is captured or wounded.[7] The black-and-white mountain guereza (*Colobus*) responds in the same way to babies who are still colored white all over if they are in danger.

Baboon babies have a black coat for the first six months, while they are still sucking from the mother (adults have brown or gray fur), and so they can play the fool to their heart's content during this period. All the adults, even old males, try to adopt a black-furred baby, groom it, and watch over it. Among hamadryas baboons, the half-grown males in particular are excellent baby-sitters. At first, mother baboons will not normally allow their newborn baby to be touched by others. African tree monkey mothers also guard their baby jealously.

The long-tailed Asian langurs and dusky langurs behave quite differently. Dusky langur babies are almost black, while adults are light gray. Spectacled langurs have a brownish gray to almost blackish-brown fur when adult, but the babies are golden yellow like a teddy bear or almost white. Now, immediately after a langur baby is born, four to ten females from the group, whether adult or still young, seat themselves around the mother, observe the baby attentively, and try to touch and sniff it. Male langurs pay little attention to babies. In the first few hours after birth, the mother tries to turn her back on the other females who are waiting patiently. But once the baby is quite dry she allows the others to touch it carefully, and now it only takes a few minutes before one of the other females has the baby on her arm. Then, as the mother had done before her, she examines the baby carefully, cautiously touches, sniffs, and licks it, in particular on the head, hands, and genitals. As soon as the baby tries to free itself, it is taken over by another female. Many babies are carried in the arms of eight different females on the first day of their life, and sometimes taken up to twenty meters away from the mother. But the mother can take the baby back whenever she likes, especially to suckle it, although the other females also permit the baby to try to drink from them; some females even help it to find the teat and grasp it with its lips. On the other hand, there are also females who are very awkward with their baby and soon hand it over to a neighbor. This interest on the part of all the female members of the band lasts for the first three to five months of the baby's life, as long as it is still characterized by its baby color; then it wanes rapidly. The mother weans it, rather forcefully, in fact, when it is eleven to fifteen months old.[50]

So the langur baby is constantly passed from one female to another during the first three to five months of its life, as though it were common property. But chimpanzee babies constantly remain in direct contact with their mother in the first $3\frac{1}{2}$ to $5\frac{1}{2}$ months, and she forestalls any attempts to take the baby away from her during that time. This builds up a very close mother-child relationship that survives into adulthood, as shown by the fact that the two animals often continue to accompany each other, share food, or come to each other's aid. Chimpanzee babies are not intentionally weaned by the mother; they stop drinking when the milk dries up.

Just when the young chimpanzee occasionally begins to leave its mother and eventually makes more and more distant sorties, it develops a striking color marking, namely the large white tuft of hair that juts out from the dark fur like a little tail. This tuft is small and unobtrusive on the newborn baby and only consists of a few sparse hairs. It is conspicuous by the age of $3\frac{1}{2}$ months, and this is when the young chimpanzee begins to reach out from the mother toward conspecifics. At the age of three years, the white tuft disappears, and from then on the young are repulsed and pushed away more and more roughly by the adults. So the tuft is quite clearly an infant characteristic that becomes most important when the young begin to have dealings with adults, to annoy them, and also to greet them by laying a hand on some part of their body.[72]

These observations on African tree monkeys, guerezas, langurs, and chimpanzees are very valuable because they were all made in the wild, and the animals were therefore living their normal lives. The offspring of all these species grow up in a stable social group, and grow into it. As long as they are still small and need help, they enjoy special protection by the other members of the society. Our comparison shows that this protection is insured by special signals that emanate from the young animal but only appear when it begins to move about freely in the society or when the need for protection by members of the society other than the mother become urgent. We shall now try to examine the infant schema of man in the framework of these findings.

In a fairly wide series of tests of the infant characteristics mentioned at the beginning of this chapter, Nos. 2, 3, and 7 were tried on 330 test subjects aged between six and thirty (male and female children from homes, schoolchildren, and students).[45] They had to choose the cutest, sweetest, or prettiest head from the series of pictures, each of which gave two choices. Most of the drawings were outlines of a child's head, but there were also tests on donkeys' heads with similarly distorted proportions. Our drawing shows a few pictures from various series of tests.

Perhaps it would be advisable for the reader to look at the heads carefully at this point and to try, without much thought, to decide which he himself considers the prettiest, and which, on the contrary, he finds least attractive.

The result of the aforementioned series of tests was as follows:

All adults quite clearly preferred head B2 to head B1; girls already did so at the age of ten to thirteen, boys from about eighteen years old. They never preferred B1.

Adult women also preferred K2 to K1, while male subjects either made no distinction between the two or preferred K1.

Other characteristics were also tested, and this showed that heads with hair were preferred to bald heads (not

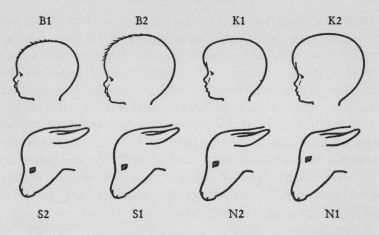

The "infant schema" as shown on children's and donkeys' heads (explanation in text).

shown here), but only if the shape of the head was the same in both cases. Otherwise adult women again preferred a head like B2, but without hair, to the B1 illustrated here.

This is striking because B1 is the proportionally "correct" head of an infant, while B2 is an exaggerated head shape that normally never occurs. Similarly, K1 is the natural head of an eight-to-ten-year-old boy, while K2 is an unnatural exaggeration. The exaggeration always concerns the skull, that is to say, its size in relation to the face and the prominence of the brow. And these exaggerated characteristics are indeed preferred to the natural features, which means that our perception overrates the typical characteristics of an infant and is actually duped by abnormal dummies. The more the dummy seems natural in other respects, the stronger this response becomes. Here we are dealing with simple line drawings. But the doll industry produces much more complicated dummies that play on, and if possible exaggerate, other infant characteristics listed by Lorenz, besides the ones tested here.

This response becomes very clear when the infant charac-

teristics in question are not depicted on a child at all but
on some other object, and nevertheless evoke the same evaluation. The curve of the brow and the height of the upper
skull were also varied on a donkey's head. With the exception of ten-to-thirteen-year-old boys (who pass through
a very realistic and critical phase at this age), all test subjects preferred head S2, where the exaggeration corresponds most closely to the preferred outline in the infant
schema. N1 was liked least. And indeed, N1 corresponds to
an older, N2 to a younger donkey, while S1 and S2 do not
exist in nature. The results of the donkey's head tests are
hardly surprising, for they show how Bambi and similar
figures came into being.

These tests provide several important points of reference
to the social behavior of man. First, it is clear that the
response that was tested is peculiar both to young people
and to adults of either sex. So it is not purely a maternal,
brood-tending response but an important general tendency
to watch over children in our society, as baby-sitters do.
Since this normally only becomes necessary if the child is
outside the immediate vicinity of the mother, it is under-
standable that only the characteristics of the *infant* release
this protective response. For the human infant needs these
signals, which elicit a general protectiveness, just as little
as the chimpanzee baby—indeed, they could even harm it.
If all good acquaintances were to try to caress the newborn
infant and carry it about, as among langurs, this could
seriously affect the development of the intimate mother-
child bond. So biologically speaking it makes sense that the
real infant was not often found sweet or cute in these tests.
The tested response was not meant for it in any case. (This
probably also means that the maternal drive to care for a
child depends on other characteristics.)

The infant characteristics do not have to appear on an
infant. They are as unlikely to fail their effect on an older
child or an adult as on a donkey. This means that we

should expect that even an adult man will be driven into the role of friend and protector at the sight of a pretty face with snub nose and saucer eyes, even if the role is quite out of place. It is not difficult to find examples of this. Experience shows that if there are two applicants for a secretarial job, the prettier girl will have a better chance, even if she has made more mistakes in the dictation test. So although we can argue that secretarial work is not only a question of typing and that the ability to work together as smoothly as possible is equally necessary, we must still remember that simple biological signals can evidently influence the evaluation of a purely technical achievement quite considerably. So there is a danger of social injustice here. It can, of course, be eliminated, but only if one is aware of it and knows its origins. The danger becomes greater if a person deliberately exploits these associations in his own interests. The behavior of a pretty, "scheming woman" is often not so very different from that of the baboons described on p. 216, with their use of "protected threat"; in both cases a biologically important social behavior is being misused, and the user is so successful simply because the response to the signal is an automatic one.

This is certainly not confined to the realm of brood-tending signals. Sugar substances are an important food for man. We recognize them by the fact that they taste sweet. This means that our sense of taste is equipped to recognize the characteristic molecular elements of such foods and evaluates them as "sweet." It is possible to build similar molecular elements into substances without any food value by artificial means. These substances also taste sweet and are used as "sugar substitutes," for instance for diabetics. What is important in this context is that such substitutes, such as saccharin, also taste sweeter to the chemist, who knows their chemical structure and is well aware that they are only substitutes without food value. The fact that he knows it neither alters his sense of taste nor does it stop him from preferring saccharin, i.e., preferring it in his mouth, to quinine, for example. Our response to infant characteristics and many other signals from the brood-tending or sexual field is just as automatic, and "knowing better" makes no difference. If we want to guard against the abuse of these responses, for instance in advertising, we must intervene in the response *after* it has made its primary appeal to us, that is, *not* buy a product although the baby face on the package is very cute, not buy a car simply because truly attractive young ladies in the tiniest of bikinis advertise it, etc. For if we wanted to achieve the effect of preventing the baby face from being considered cute (always assuming this was at all possible), we would by the same count have to destroy our natural response to small children. *The primary response to such biological signals is not an ethical question.*

The preceding example suffices to show how deeply our whole social life is penetrated by brood-tending elements. This is, of course, biologically built in to us and not just there for us to misuse. Our comparisons with similarly structured animal societies suggest that this brood-tending response is directed at children while also playing an important part in the relations between the human sexual partners. Now we have long since known that on a purely external basis, woman looks much more "pedomorphic," i.e., more childlike, than man. On an average, in every race, she is 7 percent smaller than he, has relatively shorter limbs and a rounder face, and her nose and chin are less marked. Whatever the reason for this, one result is that it prevents the man from behaving like a rabid aggressor, and makes it easier to him to fulfill his role of guardian and protector.

As we said, monkeys have evolved from smell-oriented to sight-oriented animals, and accordingly an increasing number of optical social signals were joined to the olfactory signals, beginning with color signals. In the course of further developments, the color markings were accompanied by increasingly well-defined formal signals. Accordingly, the more dangerous color signals (more dangerous because more visible to predators) were gradually replaced by formal signals. This does not mean that smells and colors became insignificant in later development; but it does mean that small gestures and forms have acquired a particular importance in intraspecific communication. (Only at this stage of development do we find, for instance, marked facial expressions. This is most highly developed in man. And it also entails the ability to see the play of features and the development of a complex system of muscular activity that produces the manifold forms of mimicry.) While the infant schema of monkeys largely relies on color signals, formal signals play a major role in the infant schema of man and have been adapted to it: The chubby cheeks of the baby, which elicit particularly strong responses, were evidently developed specifically in the service of the infant schema. At any rate they are not necessary for sucking, as we can see from the thin faces of monkey babies, who suck just as forcefully.

32. Mother-Child Behavior in Society

Like the chimpanzee baby (see p. 186), the human baby is neither a nest-hugger nor a nest-fleer but a "mother-hugger" and should be carried against the mother's body continuously in the early days of its life, as is still the custom among primitive races today. The entire behavior repertory of the newborn baby is adapted for this. For man is not physiologically a premature birth, as is often asserted. Rather, from birth on he possesses all the motor patterns that enable him to live on the mother's body. Accordingly, the baby clings to the mother, especially to her hair, as we all know. The baby only becomes "helpless" in the truest sense of the word when it is separated from its mother. It is not biological for us to place our babies in cribs. Symptomatic of this is that the babies cry out of loneliness with abnormal frequency in our culture, while one scarcely ever finds this among the children of primitive peoples. Equally symptomatic are the "contact dummies" that soothe the baby by deluding it that it is in bodily contact with its mother: namely the dummy and the rocking motion of the cradle or carriage. The way the baby clings to its mother in moments of shock or fear corresponds to the need for close bodily contact with the mother that we have already described in monkeys. And this behavior survives into adulthood: Fright makes an adult want to cling to another and embrace him. The same words are also used in the figurative sense, for we speak of embracing or clinging "mentally" to something or someone, just as one clings to one's hanky in moments of helplessness. Adult male chimpanzees sometimes even embrace little chimpanzees if they are suddenly frightened. Monkeys and humans embrace one another in the same way before going to sleep.

The mutual grooming of humans also derives from mother-child behavior. Describing the Maku Indians from the dense jungle between the Rio Negro and Rio Japura in the Amazon state, Schultz reports: "The reciprocal extraction of unwelcome living things from the hair of the head is a gesture of friendship that can be observed quite frequently among the Indians. If one sees a young man lay his head confidingly in the lap of a young girl, one can almost certainly regard them as an engaged couple. The virtue of giving reciprocal assistance eventually developed into a kind of caress, owing to man's susceptibility to these little animals (i.e., lice). The lice caught after a successful foray are often eaten."[102] The same delousing can also be seen among women who lie comfortably in their hammocks throughout the procedure. These peoples have no effective household remedy of their own for ridding themselves of this age-old pest. So modern chemical preparations are greeted with great joy, for they can very rapidly free the people of their tormentors. Do they also free them from the kind of caressing connected with it? Almost certainly not; for to groom or delouse the body of a partner is a form of behavior very commonly serving as introduction to a sexual relationship. It is found among the Siriono nomads of eastern Bolivia; the Dusun of northern Borneo, who are farmers, fishers, and craftsmen; the Prairie-Cree hunters of Saskatchewan, Alberta, and Montana; the Trobriand islanders of eastern Melanesia[32]; and on our own beaches. While Siriono lovers spend hours searching for lice on each others' heads and ticks on each others' bodies (and eating them), as well as removing worms and thorns from each others' skin, "civilized" Western lovers rub each other with suntan lotion and squeeze each others' blackheads. And almost forty years ago Yerkes wrote: "They [these actions] may very well be basically natural or inherited and only secondarily cultural; but in either event they are biologically important as conditioning comfort and health, highly socialized, strongly motivated, and accompanied by marked positive effects. The student of phylogenesis, with special interest in the evolution of human social service, may very well suspect that cultural developments and transformations of the variously named forms of grooming in infrahuman primates have given origin to tonsorial artistry, nursing, surgery, and other related social services of man."[128] Whether or not this is true, what is certain is that allogrooming also has an important place in the social behavior of man and has enough elements in common with baby care to enable us to recognize its origins in brood-tending behavior fairly easily here too. The tender caress is also addressed to other species: Man strokes his pets, and Javan monkeys delouse a friendly fox in Zürich Zoo. Some primitive races also use their teeth for grooming, and Eibl-Eibesfeldt has recently filmed a scene of greeting among the Waikas on the Orinoco, where intensive nibbling takes the place of kissing the cheek. Like greeting, tender stroking, pinching, and ruffling the other's hair are emancipated, former grooming actions.

Unlike that of many mammals, the ear of the newborn human baby is already fully functional at birth, and the baby can be soothed by certain sounds, ideally by a pitch around 150 cycles per second, i.e., similar to the tender tones of a woman's voice.[4] Adults still respond to this too. Specific sounds from the mother-child relationship also play a role among, for instance, rodents, although here it is the ultrasonic sounds uttered by the young animal that call the mother to it and make her carry it back to the nest. Similar sounds are also emitted during copulation, and in some species they are uttered by an animal if it is defeated in a fight.[104]

We all know that parents lead their small children by the hand. It is equally well-known that this walking hand-in-hand also occurs between lovers and that "to stand together, hand in hand" is a sign of social solidarity. Stroking, caressing, holding hands, and kissing are typical behavior patterns between sexual partners, which derive from the mother-child relationship. We can add to them the sounds uttered between mother and child. And with forms of address such as "little one," or the more modern "oh baby," language goes out of its way to point to the underlying brood-tending mood. We indicated the significance of the infant schema in this context in the previous chapter.

An important, socially cohesive behavior of man is his smile: "Keep smiling." "Smile and the world will smile with you." But here, as with the preening of birds, see p. 145, it is not yet proved whether the behavior was taken over from brood-tending behavior into social life or the reverse. Child psychologists have long since been aware of the importance of the eye-contact between mother and child during nursing. And it was once assumed that smiling developed in this framework. But even babies blind from birth smile when their mother speaks to them; when she smiles they even stop the rolling of the eyes typical of blind babies and turn their eyes to the source of sound instead, although they cannot see it.[28] Accordingly, the form of the smile and the related turning of the eyes for visual contact are just as genetically determined as the situation that elicits the smile, part of this situation being acoustic contact with the mother.[55]

Most people must be familiar with the role that smiling and smiling back, and the exchange of glances between mother and child as well as between the partners of a human couple play. And a little observation of oneself and others will soon show that at the beginning of a friendship, apparently meaningless chatter, holding hands, or laughing have exactly the same effect as the appeasement gestures derived from brood-tending have among other social creatures. They help the partners to overcome their contact shyness and slight fear of each other.

33. The Pseudosexualization of Society

By now I hope the reader will both expect and take a rather cautious view of the constant lament about the sexualization of our society. On the one hand, presumably man too will have put elements of sexual behavior in the service of social life together, and on the other, these elements will presumably have lost their sexual significance and have become just as "emancipated" as the transferred behavior patterns of many animals. Often we cannot tell this from the form of the behavior, since that must remain the same wherever possible. Otherwise it would lose its potency. Such behavior patterns, which have changed function and moved into the social realm, could be expected to appear most conspicuously in very closely settled areas, just as they are most in evidence among social animals under high population density. Indeed, sexualization is as a whole a large city phenomenon. However, a number of so-called sexual actions and signals in our life are not sexual at all by origin but borrowed from brood-tending. This includes the open display of the female breasts on advertisements, "petting" in public places, and many other things.

Here I do not want to discuss such phenomena, which are more or less typical of fairly large societies, for they involve much more than our heritage as vertebrates alone. But it is fairly certain that much of this "sexualization" has more to do with sociability than with sex. The same very probably applies to the fashion for miniskirts and topless dresses, which presumably help to obviate the tensions in our anonymous society by acting as "friendly" social signals that seem equally anonymous—i.e., by means that are biologically built in, such as we saw for the tropical finches discussed on p. 197. We studied the nonsexual social significance of the male genitals in detail earlier (see p. 51); this too is apparent in the history of Western fashion, in the cod-pieces and flaps of knights' armor and lansquenets' trousers in the fifteenth and sixteenth centuries, in the penis decoration of various primitive races, and perhaps also in some modern trouser fashions and advertisements for gentlemen's underwear in our own society, as well as in the various phallic amulets worn as protection from the evil eye, envy, etc., and finally in aggressive turns of phrase, like the Arabic "a phallus in your eye." The image of Priapus with his gigantic reproductive organ, when set up in gardens and at the boundaries of fields, gave protection from thieves and from the effects of envy. Greek and Roman soldiers chose the phallus as escutcheon and for the emblem of their slingshots. The phallic images in ancient cathedrals are also meant to ban evil spirits. They are just as little a sign of sexualization or sexual excess as was the old custom of laying a hand on the genitals of the other when swearing an oath, as Abraham ordered his oldest servant to do (Gen. 24:2).

The figures on ancient castle and city gates, towers, walls, churches, and monasteries, showing the naked posterior, are also designed to ban evil spirits. They are always found on the outer front of the building, that is, they are directed at the enemy, but not in the inner court or on the back of portals. On very stormy nights, the men and women of ancient Germany would stick their bared bottom outside the front door in order to appease Wotan. This was originally the female invitation to mating; then it turned into a gesture of social submission and defense. It is impossible to retrace the gradual changes of meaning in the long development of this gesture. But the female bottom has also become a social signal in another way.

We are fortunate in the existence of the Khoisanide race. These are Bushmen and Hottentots, who still retain many primitive characteristics. The womenfolk have the so-called "Hottentot tablier," a striking enlargement of the small labia that begins with puberty; eventually the labia hang four or five centimeters outside the genital aperture.[117] Richly provided with blood vessels, they change color during sexual excitement, turning from pink to bright red. They are evaluated as a sexual signal by the partner too, for the men are proud of this feature of their women, and play with the labia before copulation.[115] The women of neighboring tribes—the Batetela, Basutos, and some Bantus—try to emulate this natural formation of the Khoisanides by artificial manipulation, in order to become sexually more attractive. We often find actual genital sexual signals among female monkeys, but not among any other human females.

The Khoisanides are further characterized by "steatopygia," i.e., fatty buttocks. This is in part due to the backward curvature of the spine at the sacrum typical of this race, which makes the pelvis rise almost vertically. The seat, which juts out as a result, is further enlarged by a large accumulation of fatty and connective tissue.[69] That this tissue forms signal structures on the human body is clear from our earlier discussion of the female breast and the chubby cheeks of the little child (see p. 251). As far as we know, the fatty buttocks of the Khoisanides are also a signal structure, which, to judge from cave paintings, already existed among the earliest men and can only secondarily, if at all, serve as reserve fat for times of need.[115]

Now it seems that the men of all human races respond strongly to the shape of the female bottom. European fashions have continually tried to exaggerate the female bottom artificially. This probably reached an extreme after 1880

Left: characteristic fatty buttocks of a Bushman woman.
Right: elegant dress dating from 1882.

with the *cul de crin* (called *cul de Paris* outside France),
and naturally it was designed to please man. Like the products of the doll industry discussed in the chapter on the
infant schema, these attempted snares indicate man's susceptibility to certain signals which, although deriving from
the sexual sphere, are certainly not always evaluated sexually; often they simply make a pleasant or agreeable impression.

Besides shape, motion also plays an important role.
Women has by nature a different form of pelvis from man.
This is the cause of her slightly knock-kneed stance, but it
also results in the familiar swaying movements of her hips
when she walks. Since this is easiest to see from the rear,
and since hints of female flight and male pursuit occur quite

regularly in the course of pair-formation, one can assume that the original signal value of these movements lay in the sphere of the foreplay to mating. We also know that today they tend to promote contact but do not necessarily have the effect of a sexual invitation, even when coquettishly exaggerated. High-heeled shoes, which are said to be bad for the health, are unlikely to die out as a fashion, because this unnatural position of the feet forces the woman to assume the "Khoisanide" posture that we like to see too, pushing out the bottom and underlining its motion. Many primitive peoples exaggerate these movements, especially when dancing, and have accentuated the shaking of the bottom and swaying of the hips by means of grass skirts, or colorful tassels or plumes attached above the bottom. This becomes very striking in cases where long dresses covering up these movements are prescribed at the mission and the women then wear a grass skirt on top of the dress for dancing.

Movements that are clearly copulatory also occur in dances, as much in our culture as among primitive peoples. This can look obscene, but is not intended as such by the dancers. In any case these are not exhibition dances by origin. As far as the performer is concerned, many of the motor patterns are emancipated from the sexual realm. But the observer is often unable to tell the difference from the movement alone, as he is unable in the ambiguous social behavior patterns we listed earlier. And if he does not take account of the mood underlying the performer's behavior, he will wrongly conclude that such behavior and corresponding linguistic expressions are evidence of hypersexualization, as he did with baboons. There is in fact an increasing sexualization in our life; this we do not deny. But we must be cautious about lumping together too much under the same heading.

34. Pair-Bonding and Reproduction in Marriage

What we have said of society also applies to the smallest social group, marriage. Man too has borrowed behavior patterns from the mother-child relationship for the foreplay to mating; besides this he has also put them in the service of pair-bonding, together with originally sexual behavior elements. Again, the outside observer can very easily be misled and take this for a sexualization of marriage, in particular if he has had no direct personal experience from which to understand the mood of the protagonists.

By his technical advances man is influencing marriage; for instance, its potential duration can only be realized today, when women very rarely die before men. More children survive too, and thus pair-bonding as opposed to reproduction comes into the foreground in marriage. Everything that serves its interests, without impairing the value and dignity of the individual or his love, can only be good in ethical terms, even if it is an intervention into the biological processes of reproduction that gives free access to the natural methods of pair-bonding discussed here. Inevitably this will also affect pre- and extramarital social life. The various possible types of partner relationships, whose sequence we can follow through history, and our ethical assessment of them as phases in history, can also occur side by side in the plurality of our society.

The following findings seem legitimate and important to me in this context:

1. Natural inclinations do not have to be resisted on principle.

2. Sexual behavior is closely connected with social behavior and ranking order. If a form of behavior acts as a signal, it must remain the same if it is not to lose its signal value. In nature, this general principle always means that signals do, admittedly, extend or alter their function, but retain their form. The receiver of the signal can be misled if he does not distinguish between different situations where the signal has different meanings. This is also the source of misunderstandings about the significance in each case of apparently sexual human behavior. Some species of animal and plant can mislead others in the same manner and even create advantages for themselves at the cost of these others.[125] But the misunderstanding of "sexual" gestures by the general public and the misunderstanding of the nature of the marital act by moral theology are based on a blindness to detail that is the observer's own fault. He receives the signal, but interprets it wrongly, seeing only one aspect of it, because he has forgotten about the reciprocal relationship between sexual and social behavior. This can be seen elsewhere too: The term "moral corruption" is almost exclusively applied to sexual activities now. If the signs of a "decline of the West" appear to be multiplying, sexual licentiousness is held responsible, although these signs are much more likely to be merely one of the many after-effects of a crisis in society than its source. When told about the initiation rites of primitive races, the general public misinterprets them as a display of a predominantly sexual nature, although they are in fact a

lesson in social science that informs us about tribal divinities and the methods of hunting, about behavior toward strangers, enemies, persons of authority within the tribe, and of course about behavior toward the other sex. Carnivals and Mardi Gras celebrations are often seen as an opportunity for sexual license, although economic and political abuses are denounced during the pageants, and the keys of the city hall—i.e., governmental power—are handed to the carnival prince; this is evidence enough that this is a time when general social criteria are usefully re-examined, when, in the framework of merrymaking and high jinks, the basic principles of our rigorous social order are put in question—i.e., subjected to critical appraisal, lest they should rigidify unchecked.

3. In evolution, behavior determines the structure of organs; changes in behavior entail changes in body structure. This is why we cannot deduce binding "purposive norms" for the future use of these organs from the form of organs (see pp. 38 and 185). Conversely, from the standpoint of current usage, we cannot assert that an organ was formerly used "wrongly" either. The same applies to behavior patterns that have changed function. If, therefore, man has the means of obeying the commandment to love his neighbor by emancipating natural behavior patterns (by methods that are, moreover, laid down by nature), we cannot describe this as in principle contrary to nature. The fact that earlier generations did not yet realize this and that other norms were proclaimed as a result does not mean that people erred. Insofar as ethical norms are based on natural laws, they must be able to change with the progress of our knowledge of natural laws.

4. The use of behavior patterns originally derived from brood-tending or mating for pair-bonding in marriage

or in larger societies is a regular occurrence among social beings. The brood-tending organs can have sexual signal functions, and the reproductive organs can have nonsexual signal functions (see p. 51). The dual functions and change of function of organs and behavior patterns originally serving brood-tending or reproduction that we constantly find in the animal kingdom were listed on pp. 233ff.

5. Mating serves to produce genetic variety, reproduction serves to preserve life, and pair-bonding originally served to maintain species-specific characteristics. All three can occur independently (see pp. 87f.). According to the requirements, they can be combined with one another, or they can be functionally dissociated again in nature.

6. Permanent monogamy has measurable advantages in some cases (see p. 105), which increase according to the number of individual variable characteristics that must coincide in the parents. This includes, for instance, the synchronization of physiological processes, the preference for a particular nesting or breeding place, and traditions. Among many animals, knowledge of the prey, of paths, or of the signals needed for intraspecific communication (e.g., the song of many birds), is transmitted. Tradition makes it possible to "pass down" acquired characteristics, to transmit the knowledge an individual has gained. If the offspring have to rely on learning such things from their parents, it can be an advantage for both parents to agree on what is to be transmitted.

7. The specific types of family and marriage (monogamy, polygamy, permanent or seasonal bonds) are adaptations in the biological sense, i.e., they correspond to the typical living requirements at the time of the species

in question. Permanent monogamy can be a transitional stage in the phylogeny of a group of animals, and some species will deviate from it (e.g., tropical finches); but this is neither regression nor degeneration! Moreover, not all individuals of the same species are as similar as we might assume. We say that the graylag goose is permanently monogamous, yet there are some individuals who do not contract a firm bond, in addition to others who have firm bonds with several partners, and yet others who, besides their firm pair-bond, occasionally enter into a sexual and social relationship with different partners (cf. p. 98), as Fischer discovered in our institute. This does not imply that the nonmonogamous graylag geese are failures, "breakdowns," who do not correspond to the type of the species; rather it means that we will have to check whether this difference is not of advantage to the species, just as sickle-cell anemia, as Lorenz explained in the Introduction, also has advantages in some cases and is an adaptation, even though it counts as a disease in our latitudes. It would be equally careless if we were to describe one of the various current forms of marriage among humans as biologically "right" and the others as "wrong" before checking whether the marital form in question is adapted to the over-all life structure of the respective nation or tribe. And probably the question of whether man is monogamous is wrongly put, seeing that individuals are by nature functionally as different among themselves as the graylag geese.

8. In the case of animals, we content ourselves with simply describing their manifestations of life, and therewith also their behavior patterns. But with man, we also evaluate them; *this does not replace description, however, but presupposes it.* Whether it is possible to arrive at an ethical evaluation from a description of nature—

this is the disputed question of the normative value of the real, which cannot be discussed here. But if in some cases a method had demonstrably led to false conclusions, we will have to query all the results arrived at by this method, even if they seem plausible. That man should live in monogamy according to the will of God, because monogamy is the most widespread form of marriage among men, may sound plausible, but it is an inadmissible deduction; for then we would also have to posit lying as God's will, since all men lie.

Man is different from animals. His behavior is that of a thinking being, so it cannot be assessed in terms of biology alone; but neither can it be assessed without biology. Findings on animals cannot be transferred—as findings—either to other species of animal or to man. All that can be transferred are working hypotheses. Their accuracy has to be checked anew in every case. To omit to do this or to fail to transfer working hypotheses is unscientific.

9. Man is an aggressive creature. Presumably primitive mankind was dispersed in groups and, like animals who live in groups, knew two kinds of conspecifics, namely the members of his group and strangers. It was a biological necessity that this should give rise to two different, and in many ways opposed, moral principles: one applying to the behavior toward one's own social group, the other to behavior toward outsiders. In adaptive terms, aggressive animals have aggression-inhibiting behavior patterns (so-called appeasement or submission gestures), performed by the loser in a fight, by which it "admits" its defeat and prevents further attack by the victor. Man can perceive this connection, and as a result he has put himself in a very difficult position. For not only does he improve his weaponry, he also prohibits capitulation to a superior. And another as-

pect of this unbiological attitude is that he does not permit the exploitation of those appeasing behavior patterns with which nature has endowed him and that generally derive from brood-tending or mating behavior. That this is their derivation may comfort those who believed that aggression toward conspecifics is part of an original evil that still has to be combatted by inhibiting mechanisms. The inhibiting mechanisms we use largely derive from reproductive behavior, so their roots are as ancient as those of aggression. It is probably correct that living things could afford intraspecific aggression on top of reproduction, in the interests of extending their territory and colonizing the earth, and that its limits were always fixed by the requirements of reproduction and in given cases by brood-tending—which is why elements from these spheres of behavior are so suitable for inhibiting aggression.

If living things learn much from their parents, or even grow into the parents' group entirely, this promotes the transmission of tradition, but at the same time it increases the risk that the belligerent old males will drive away their own sons as rivals and thus exclude them from the tradition. So it is very important to inhibit the aggression between them, and aggression-inhibiting mechanisms have evolved further and further in the service of social cohesion.

10. Among social animals of less highly developed species, the females are not ready to conceive again during the period of brood-tending; but they become fertile very quickly if brood-tending is cut short owing to an accident. Sexual relations between the parent animals stop during the period when they could disturb the mother-child relationship. But in the case of man, the theologians defend the principle that the mother-child relationship should not affect conjugal relations between

the partners (not more, at any rate, than is inevitable under the circumstances). So man should take active steps to preserve the close conjugal partnership. Many physical intimacies could serve this end besides actual copulation; this is already so in animal societies. There are no indications in biology or ethnology to suggest that the foreplay to mating or even copulation itself are inextricably linked to reproduction—quite the reverse, in fact. Knaus and Ogino have demonstrated that loving union and procreation are not necessarily, by their nature, interconnected for man either. Moral theology even admits of grounds that temporarily or even permanently forbid procreation in a marriage. In such cases, the couple is entitled to desire and request that the natural outcome of marital intercourse should not come about during this period. But the only thing the couple may do besides this is to observe the infertile periods when conception is unlikely, i.e., to avoid conception but not to practice contraception. Circa A.D. 200 the Church father Tertullian forbade women to wear dyed wools, on the grounds that God had not created purple and scarlet sheep. Even in the last century, there was resistance to lighting the streets with artificial gas lights in Cologne, because this infringed the order created by God, according to which the nights are dark. People today are prepared to take deviations from the "natural order" as a matter of course in such cases.

Man must master nature, not become its submissive slave.

Theology has shown itself unable to determine what is natural and what is contrary to nature in love life. It has not proved that the doctrine of salvation is irreconcilable with the following statement—which is not contrary to the nature of man: The morality of the marital act does not depend on the potential fruitfulness of each individual act, but on the requirements of mutual love in all its aspects. The consequence of this statement is that the form of his love life is the responsibility of each individual, that the married couple must decide for itself which methods are acceptable to it, and that these methods can differ from marriage to marriage. Furthermore, each individual must also decide for himself—again given the requirements of reciprocal love in each marriage—what is permissible to him or her in the way of extramarital, so-called "flirtation" as a social bond. In both cases the decision also depends on the consideration of other members of the society who are all more or less affected by it, which makes the question no easier.

BIBLIOGRAPHY

1) *Armstrong, E. A.* (1965): Bird display and behavior. New edition, Dover Publications, Inc., New York

2) *Bargmann, W.* (1959): Histologie und mikroskopische Anatomie des Menschen. Third edition, G. Thieme, Stuttgart

3) *Bilz, R.* (1943): Lebensgesetze der Liebe. Hirzel, Leipzig

4) *Birns, B., M. Blank, W. H. Bridger* and *S. K. Escalona* (1965): Behavioral inhibition in neonates produced by auditory stimuli. Child Development 36, 639–45

5) *Birth, Th.* (1928): Das Kulturleben der Griechen und Römer. Quelle & Meyer, Leipzig

6) *Blüm, V.* (1966): Zur hormonalen Steuerung der Brutpflege einiger Cichliden. Zool. Jb. Physiol. 72, 264–90

7) *Booth, C.* (1962): Some observations on behavior of *Cercopithecus* monkeys. Ann. N. Y. Acad. Sci. 102, 477–87

8) *Boratov, P. N.* (1967): Türkische Volksmärchen, S. 272. Akademie-Verlag, Berlin

9) *Bristowe, W. S.* (1958): The world of spiders. Collins, London

10) *Bruder, R. H.,* and *D. S. Lehrman* (1967): Role of the mate in the elicitation of hormone-induced incubation behavior in the ring dove. J. comp. physiol. Psychol. 63, 382–84

11) *Bubenik, A. B.* (1967): Neues aus dem Leben des Edelwildes. Die Pirsch 19, 322–28

12) *Buechner, H. K.,* and *R. Schloeth* (1965): Ceremonial mating behavior in Uganda Kob (*Adenota kob thomasi* Neumann). Z. Tierpsychol. 22, 209–25

13) *Burckhardt, D.* (1958): Kindliches Verhalten als Ausdrucksbewegung im Fortpflanzungszeremoniell einiger Wiederkäuer, Rev. Suisse Zool. 65, 311–16

14) *Carayon, J.* (1964): Les aberrations sexuelles »normalisées« de certains Hémiptères Cimicoidea. In: Psychiatrie animale (A. Brion and H. Ey eds.). Paris

15) *Cleveland, L. R.* (1949): Hormone-induced sexual cycles of flagellates. I. Gametogenesis, fertilization and meiosis in *Trichonympha.* J. Morphol. 85, 197–296

16) *Coulson, J. C.* (1966): The influence of the pair-bond and age on the breeding biology of the Kittiwake Gull, *Rissa tridactyla.* J. Anim. Ecol. 35, 269–79

17) *Daettwyler, O.,* and *M. Maximoff* (1959): Tsiganes. Büchergilde Gutenberg, Zürich

18) *Darchen, R.* (1968): Ethologie d'*Achaearanea disparata* Denis, araignée sociale du Gabon. Biologia Gabonica 4, 5–25

19) *Davis, D. D.,* and *H. E. Story* (1949): The female external genitalia of the spotted hyena. Fieldiana, Zool. 31, 277–83

20) *Deckert, G.* (1968): Der Feldsperling. A. Ziemsen, Wittenberg-Lutherstadt

21) *Dejung, B.* (1967): Regressionen im Verhalten des Menschen. Juris-Verlag, Zürich

22) *Doms, H.* (1965): Gatteneinheit und Nachkommenschaft. M. Grünewald-Verlag, Mainz

23) *Drury, W. H.,* and *W. J. Smith* (1968): Defense of feeding areas by adult herring gulls and intrusion by young. Evolution 22, 193–201

24) *Dupeyrat, A.* (1960): 21 Jahre bei den Kannibalen. Herold, Wien-München

25) *Dupeyrat, A.* (1963): Papua, Beasts and Men. Macgibbon & Kee, London

26) *Eibl-Eibesfeldt, I.* (1955): Ethologische Studien am Galapagos-Seelöwen, *Zalophus wollebaeki* Sivertsen. Z. Tierpsychol. 12, 286–303

27) *Eibl-Eibesfeldt, I.* (1955): Das Verhalten der Nagetiere. In: Kükenthal, Handb. Zool. 8, Volume 10, 13

28) *Eibl-Eibesfeldt, I.* (1969): Grundriss der vergleichenden Verhaltensforschung. Second edition, R. Piper & Co., München

29) *Eibl-Eibesfeldt, I.* and *E.* (1967): Das Parasitenabwehren der Minima-Arbeiterinnen der Blattschneider-Ameise (*Atta cephalotes*). Z. Tierpsychol. 24, 278–81

30) *Eisenberg, J. F.* (1966): The social organizations of mammals. Handb. Zool. 8, Volume 10 (7), 1–92

31) *Ewer, R. F.* (1963): The behavior of the Meerkat, *Suricata suricatta* (Schreber). Z. Tierpsychol. 20, 570–607

32) *Ford, C. S.,* and *F. A. Beach* (1960): Das Sexualverhalten von Mensch und Tier. Colloquium Verlag, Berlin

33) *Freuchen, P.* (1961): Book of the Eskimos. World Publishing Company, Cleveland, New York

34) *Friedmann, H.* (1960): The parasitic weaverbirds. U. S. Nation. Mus. Bull. 223

35) *Geist, V.* (1968): On the interrelation of external appearance, social behavior and social structure of mountain sheep. Z. Tierpsychol. 25, 199–215

36) *Gwinner, E.* (1964): Untersuchungen über das Ausdrucks- und Sozialverhalten der Kolkraben (*Corvus corax corax* L.). Z. Tierpsychol. 21, 657–748

37) *Haag, H.* (1966): Biblische Schöpfungslehre und kirchliche Erbsündenlehre. Katholisches Bibelwerk, Stuttgart

38) *Haas, G.* (1964): Horst- und Partnerwechsel eines männlichen Weissstorchs innerhalb einer Brutzeit. Jb. Ver. vaterl. Naturkd. Württemberg 118/119, 382–85

39) *Haberland, E.* (1963): Galla Süd-Äthiopiens. W. Kohlhammer, Stuttgart

40) *Harrison, C. J. O.* (1965): Allopreening as agonistic behavior. Behaviour 24, 161–209

41) *Hartmann, M.* (1956): Die Sexualität. Fischer Verlag, Stuttgart

42) *Hassenstein, B.* (1962): Die Spannung zwischen Individuum und Kollektiv im Tierreich. In: Individuum u. Kollektiv. Freiburger Dies Universitatis 9

43) *Hörmann, L. v.* (1912): Genuss- und Reizmittel in den Ostalpen; eine volkskundliche Skizze. Z. Dtsch. Österr. Alpenver. 43, 78–100

44) *Holst, D. v.* (1969): Sozialer Stress bei Tupajas (*Tupaia belangeri*). Z. vergl. Physiol. 63, 1–58

45) *Hückstedt, B.* (1965): Experimentelle Untersuchungen zum »Kindchenschema«. Z. exper. angew. Psychol. 12, 421–50

46) *Hutt, C.,* and *M. J. Vaizey* (1967): Group density and social behavior. In: Neue Ergebnisse der Primatologie (D. Starck, R. Schneider, H.-J. Kuhn eds.), Stuttgart, S. 225–27

47) *Immelmann, K.* (1961): Beiträge zur Biologie und Ethologie australischer Honigfresser (*Meliphagidae*). J. Orn. 102, 164–207

48) *Immelmann, K.* (1962): Beiträge zu einer vergleichenden Biologie australischer Prachtfinken (*Spermestidae*). Zool. Jb. Syst. 90, 1–196

49) *Immelmann, K.* (1966): Beobachtungen an Schwalbenstaren. J. Orn. 107, 37–69

50) *Jay, P.* (1962): Aspects of maternal behavior among langurs. Ann. N. Y. Acad. Sci. 102, 468–76

51) *Jolly, A.* (1966): Lemur behavior. Univ. Chicago Press, Chicago and London

52) *Kaestner, A.* (1960): Lehrbuch der speziellen Zoologie, Volume I. G. Fischer, Stuttgart

53) *Kihlström, J. E.* (1966): A sex cycle in the male. Experientia 22, 630

54) *Klofl, W.* (1959): Versuch einer Analyse der trophobiotischen Beziehungen von Ameisen zu Aphiden. Biol. Zbl. 78, 863–70

55) *Koehler, O.* (1954): Das Lächeln des Säuglings. Umschau 54, 321–24

56) *Koenig, L.* (1951): Beiträge zu einem Aktionssystem des Bienen-fressers (*Merops apiaster* L.). Z. Tierpsychol. 8, 169–210

57) *Koenig, L.* (1960): Das Aktionssystem des Siebenschläfers (*Glis glis* L.). Z. Tierpsychol. 17, 427–505

58) *Koenig, O.* (1961): Das Buch vom Neusiedler See, Wollzeilen-Verlag, Wien

59) *Koenig, O.* (1962): Kif-Kif. Wollzeilen-Verlag, Wien

60) *Kosinski, J.* (1966): The Painted Bird. New York

61) *Kühme, W.* (1965): Freilandstudien zur Soziologie des Hyänen-hundes (*Lycaon pictus lupinus* Thomas 1902). Z. Tierpsychol. 22, 495–541

62) *Kuhn, H.-J.* (1967): Zur Systematik der *Cercopithecidae*. In: Neue Ergebnisse der Primatologie, Stuttgart, 25–46

63) *Kummer, H.* (1968): Social organization of hamadryas baboons. S. Karger, Basel and New York

64) *Kummer, H.,* and *F. Kurt* (1965): A comparison of social be-havior in captive and wild hamadryas baboons. In: The baboon in medical research (H. Vagtborg ed.). Univ. Texas Press

65) *Kunkel, P.* (1962): Bewegungsformen, Sozialverhalten, Balz und Nestbau des Gangesbrillenvogels (*Zosterops palpebrosa*). Z. Tier-psychol. 19, 559–76

66) *Kurt, F.* (1968): Das Sozialverhalten des Rehes. Parey, Hamburg and Berlin

67) *Krämer, A.* (1968): Soziale Organisation und Sozialverhalten einer Gemspopulation (*Rupicapra rupicapra* L.) der Alpen. Dis-sertation, Universität Zürich

68) *Krafft, B.* (1966): Premières recherches de laboratoire sur le comportement d'une araignée sociale nouvelle, *Agelena consociata* Denis. Rev. Comp. Animal No. 1, 25–30

69) *Krut, L. H.,* and *R. Singer* (1963): Steatopygia; the fatty acid composition of subcutaneous adipose tissue in the Hottentot. J. phys. anthropol. n. s. 21, 181–87

70) *Kruuk, H.* (1966): A new view of the hyaena. New Scientist, June, 849–51

71) *Lack, D.* (1946): The life of the robin. Witherby, London

72) *Lawick-Goodall, J. van* (1968): The behavior of free-living chimpanzees in the Gombe Stream Reserve. Animal Behavior Monographs (London) 1 (3), 161–311

73) *Lind, H.* (1963): The reproductive behavior of the gull-billed tern, *Sterna nilotica* Gmelin. Vidensk. Medd. fra Dansk naturh. Foren 125, 407–48

74) *Löhrl, H.* (1968): Das Nesthäkchen als biologisches Problem. J. Orn. 109, 383–95

75) *Lorenz, K.* (1963): Das sogenannte Böse. Dr. G. Borotha-Schoeler, Wien

76) *Makatsch, W.* (1955): Der Brutparasitismus in der Vogelwelt. Neumann-Verlag, Radebeul and Berlin

77) *Martin, R. D.* (1968): Reproduction and ontogeny in tree shrews (*Tupaia belangeri*). Z. Tierpsychol. 25, 409–95 and 505–32

78) *Mayr, E.* (1963): Animal species and evolution. Harvard Univ. Press, Cambridge (Mass.)

79) *McBride, G.,* Mündl. Mitteilung; work in press.

80) *Michael, R. P., J. Herbert* and *J. Welegalla* (1967): Ovarian hormones and the sexual behavior of the male rhesus monkey (*Macaca mulatta*) under laboratory conditions. J. Endocr. 39, 81–89

81) *Mohr, J. W., R. E. Turner* and *M. B. Jerry* (1964): Pedophilia and Exhibitionism. Univ. Toronto Press

82) *Nelson, K.* (1964): The temporal patterning of courtship behavior in the glandulocaudine fishes. Behaviour 24, 90–146

83) *Neuweiler, G.* (1969): Verhaltensbeobachtungen an einer indischen Flughundkolonie (*Pteropus g. giganteus*). Z. Tierpsychol. 26, 166–99

84) *Nicolai, J.* (1956): Zur Biologie und Ethologie des Gimpels (*Pyrrhula pyrrhula* L.). Z. Tierpsychol. 13, 93–132

85) *Nicolai, J.* (1968): Die isolierte Frühmauser der Farbmerkmale des Kopfgefieders. Z. Tierpsychol. 25, 854–61

86) *Nicolai, J.,* Film on *Geopelia*

87) *Ohm, T.* (1948): Die Gebetsgebärden der Völker und das Christentum. E. J. Brill, Leiden

88) *Parkes, A. S.,* and *H. M. Bruce* (1961): Olfactory stimuli in mammalian reproduction. Science 134, 1049–54

89) *Ploog, D.* (1964): Verhaltensforschung und Psychiatrie. In:

Psychiatrie der Gegenwart Bd. I/1B. Springer, Berlin-Göttingen-Heidelberg

90) *Ploog, D. W., J. Blitz* and *F. Ploog* (1963): Studies on the social and sexual behavior of the squirrel monkey (*Saimiri sciureus*). Folia primat. 1, 29–66

91) *Ploss, H.* (1911): Das Kind in Brauch und Sitte der Völker. Th. Grieben, Leipzig

92) *Pocock, R. I.* (1919): On the external characters of existing chevrotains. Proc. Zool. Soc. London, 1–11

93) *Rauh, F.* (1969): Das sittliche Leben des Menschen im Lichte der vergleichenden Verhaltensforschung. Butzon & Bercker, Kevelaer

94) *Reed, R. A.* (1968): Studies of the Diederik Cuckoo, *Chrysococcyx caprius* in the Transvaal. Ibis 110, 321–31

95) *Reynolds, V.* (1965): Some behavioral comparisons between chimpanzee and gorilla in the wild. Amer. Anthropol. 67, 691–706

96) *Sade, D. S.* (1965): Some aspects of parent-offspring and sibling relations in a group of rhesus monkeys with a discussion of grooming. Amer. J. phys. Anthrop. (n. s.) 23, 1–17

97) *Sauer, F.* (1955): Entwicklung und Regression angeborenen Verhaltens bei der Dorngrasmücke (*Sylvia c. communis*). Acta XI Congr. Int. Orn. 1954, 218–26

98) *Schaller, F.* (1962): Die Unterwelt des Tierreiches. Springer-Verlag, Berlin, Göttingen, Heidelberg

99) *Scheven, J.* (1958): Beitrag zur Biologie der Schmarotzerfeldwespen. Insects Sociaux 5, 409–37

100) *Schleidt, W. M.,* and *M. Magg* (1960): Störungen der Mutter-Kind-Beziehung bei Truthühnern durch Gehörverlust. Behaviour 16, 254–60

101) *Schmidt, R.* (1904): Liebe und Ehe in Indien. Berlin

102) *Schultz, H.* (1962): Hombu; Urwaldleben der brasilianischen Indianer. Belser, Stuttgart

103) *Schultze-Westrum, Th.* (1968): Ergebnisse einer zoologisch-völkerkundlichen Expedition zu den Papuas. Umschau 68, 295–300

104) *Sewell, G. D.* (1968): Ultrasound in rodents. Nature 217, 682–83

105) *Silberbauer, G. B.* (1965): Bushman Survey Report. Bechuanaland Press (PTY.) Ltd., Mafeking

106) *Snyder, R. G.* (1961): The sex ratio of offspring of flyers of high performance military aircraft. Human Biology 33, 1–10

107) *Sorenson, E. R.,* and *D. C. Gajdusek* (1966): The study of

child behavior and development in primitive cultures. Pediatrics 37
No. 1, Pt. II, 149–243

108) *Spannaus, G.* (1949): Urwaldzwerge in Zentralafrika. Hoch-
schulfilm C 567 des Instituts für Film und Bild in Wissenschaft
und Unterricht

109) *Sparks, J.* (1967): Allogrooming in Primates: a Review. In:
Primate Ethology (D. Morris ed.), Weidenfeld & Nicolson, London, and Doubleday Anchor Books, Garden City, New York

110) *Spinage, C. A.* (1969): Naturalistic observations on the reproductive and maternal behavior of the Uganda defassa waterbuck
Kobus defassa ugandae Neumann. Z. Tierpsychol. 26, 39–47

111) *Stamm, R. A.* (1962): Aspekte des Paarverhaltens von *Agapornis personata* Reichenow. Behaviour 19, 1–56

112) *Struhsaker, T.* (1967): Behavior of elk (*Cervus canadensis*)
during the rut. Z. Tierpsychol. 24, 80–114

113) *Thomas, E. M.* (1962): Meine Freunde die Buschmänner.
Ullstein, Berlin-Frankfurt-Wien

114) *Tinbergen, N.* (1958): Tiere untereinander. Parey, Berlin

115) *Tobias, P. V.* (1957): Bushmen of the Kalahari. Man 57, 33–40

116) *Tschanz. B.* (1968): Trottellummen. Parey, Berlin and Hamburg

117) *Villiers, H. de* (1964): The tablier and steatopygia in Kalahari
Bushwomen. South Afr. J. Sci. 57, 223–27

118) *Ward, J. A.,* and *G. W. Barlow* (1967): The maturation and
regulation of glancing off the parents by young orange chromides.
Behaviour 29, 1–56

119) *Weller, M. W.* (1968): The breeding biology of the parasitic
black-headed duck. The living bird 7, 169–207

120) *Wickler, W.* (1965): Die Evolution von Mustern der Zeichnung
und des Verhaltens. Naturwiss. 52, 335–41

121) *Wickler, W.* (1966): Über die biologische Bedeutung des Geni-
tal-Anhanges der männlichen *Tilapia macrochir.* Senck. biol. 47,
419–27

122) *Wickler, W.* (1966): Ursprung und biologische Deutung des
Genitalpräsentierens männlicher Primaten. Z. Tierpsychol. 23, 422–
37

123) *Wickler, W.* (1967): Vergleichende Verhaltensforschung und
Phylogenetik. In: Die Evolution der Organismen (G. Heberer
ed.), Fischer, Stuttgart

124) *Wickler, W.* (1967): Socio-sexual signals and their intra-specific
imitation among primates. In: Primate Ethology (D. Morris ed.),
Weidenfeld & Nicolson, London (69–147), and Doubleday Anchor
Books, Garden City, New York

125) *Wickler, W.* (1968): Mimikry; Nachahmung und Täuschung in der Natur. Kindler Verlag, München, and McGraw-Hill, New York

126) *Wickler, W.* (1968): Das Missverständnis der Natur des ehelichen Aktes in der Moraltheologie. Stimmen der Zeit 182, 289–303

127) *Williams, L.* (1968): Der Affe wie ihn keiner kennt. Molden, Wien

128) *Yerkes, R. M.* (1933): Genetic aspects of grooming, a socially important primate behavior pattern. J. Soc. Psychol. 4, 3–25

INDEX

Abilities, comparison of, 17
Acouchy (*Myoprocta*), 51
Adélie penguin (*Pygoscelis adeliae*), 144
African black-backed jackal (*Canis mesomelas*), 164
African didric cuckoo (*Chrysococcyx caprius*), 89, 133–34
African hunting dog (*Lycaon pictus*), 165, 173–74
African tree monkey (*Ceropithecus aethiops*), 257
African tree toad (*Nectophrynoïdes*), 43
Agamy, 93, 94
Albatross, 70, 145
Algae, 23, 25, 35
Allogrooming, 186–88
Allopreening, 142, 145–47, 195
  aggressive behavior and, 146–47
American ringdove (*Streptopelia risoria*), 105
American yellow-billed cuckoo (*Coccyzus americanus*), 133, 134
Ammun Rê (deity), 54
Anal fins, 42
Anteaters (*Manis*), 51

Aristotle, 204
Artificial baby foods, 251
Artificial insemination, 32
Artificial sugar substances, 263–64
Asian marten (*Nyctereutes*), 51
Australian black honey-eater (*Myzomela nigrita*), 114
Australian honey-eater (*Meliphaga* family), 132–33
Autolytus worm, 36
Axillary organ, 179

Bald ibis (*Geronticus*), 132
Bali, island of, 55, 56
Bantu tribe, 273
Basuto tribe, 273
Batetela tribe, 273
Beach, F. A., 249–50
Beak-flirting, 110, 144
Bearded tit (*Panurus biarmicus*), 95–96, 109
Bedbugs (*Cimex*), 37
Bed-wetting, 72
Beetlemite (*Oribatei*), 39
Begging behavior, bird, 141–43
Begging gesture, infant animal, 188–90
Bible, xiii, xxvi–xxvii, xxviii, 6, 244, 272